LONGTIME CALIFORN':
A Documentary Study of an American Chinatown

LONGTIME

A Documentary Study of

by Victor G. and

Pantheon Books

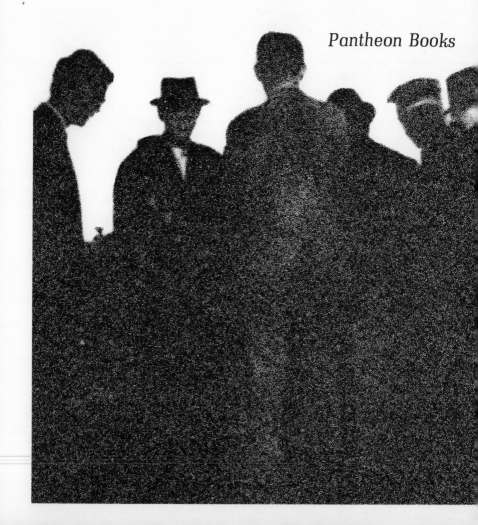

CALIFORN'

an American Chinatown

Brett de Bary Nee

A DIVISION OF RANDOM HOUSE   NEW YORK

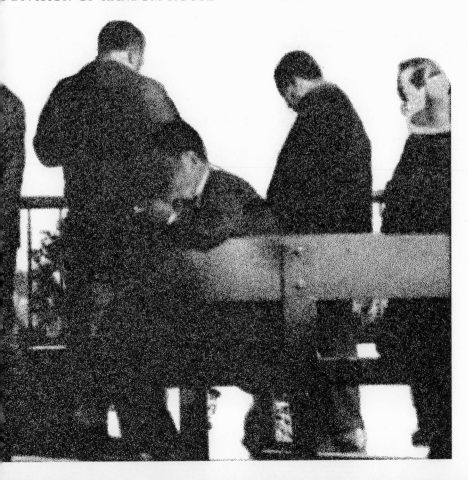

Library of Congress Cataloging in Publication Data
Nee, Victor, 1945–
Longtime Californ'.
1. Chinese in San Francisco.   I. Nee, Brett de
Bary, 1943–   joint author. II. Title.
F869.S3N27   301.45′19′51079461   72–12389
ISBN 0–394–46138-X

Printed and bound by The Book Press, Brattleboro, Vermont

FIRST EDITION

3 5 7 9 8 6 4 2

This book is dedicated to:
Gilbert and Margaret Nee
and Him Mark Lai

Contents

NOTE: See pages 272-277 for charts showing the structure of and relationships among various organizations in San Francisco's Chinatown.

Acknowledgments

A book of this nature could not come into being without the generous contribution of time and effort from all who participated in its making. We owe the deepest thanks to everyone in Chinatown whose memories, insights, and reflections appear in the pages of this book. To the community as a whole, for granting us the privilege of studying its past and its present, we wish to express our appreciation.

Although it would be impossible to mention by name everyone in the community whose effort contributed to our work, there are some for whose assistance we are especially grateful. First, to the writer Frank Chin, Jr., who shared his writing, stories, and vision of Chinese America with us, we extend our thanks. Sam Yuen, of Self-Help for the Elderly, was unstintingly generous in making his office and facilities open for our use, in arranging interviews, and in interpreting. Without the active assistance of Lillian Sing and Frances Lee of the Chinese Newcomers' Service, much of our discussion of the newly arrived immigrants would not have been possible. To Charlie and Russell Leong, whose friendship and uncanny insights into Chinatown life supported us during the entire period of our work, we are grateful. There were many others whose help was invaluable at various stages of our study. We owe thanks to Sue Fawn Cheng and Bill Wu, who made available the programs of the Chinese Cultural Center, and to Dr. Sanford Tom, whose early support opened the Chinatown door to us. Loni Ding, Dr. Rolland and Kathy Lowe, Nelson Wong, Dr. Ted and Anna Lee, Ben Tom, Maurice Chuck, Joe Yuey, Carmen Chow, Linda Zinn, Eileen Dong, Wei Bat Liu, Emile DeGuzman, H. K. Wong, and Stanley Lim also gave kind help.

There are also those outside of Chinatown who contributed to the making of this book. Tom Engelhardt aided us at every stage, reading various drafts of the manuscript, and giving us skillful editorial advice. Jim Peck also read the manuscript carefully and shared his perceptive analytical comments. Claire Seigelbaum, who discussed her experiences working with Oscar Lewis in Cuba with us, gave helpful advice on interviewing techniques. We are especially appreciative of the counsel of Professor Ezra Vogel of Harvard University, who showed his interest in the project from the beginning. Professor Lee Rainwater's seminar at Harvard also gave us many useful hints. We received constant encouragement and support from Professor Paul Lin of McGill University and his wife, Eileen. Professor Herbert Gans generously offered his time for consultation. Thanks also to photographer Ilka Hartmann, and to Bill, Cindy, and Roy Nee for their help.

For technical assistance we would like to thank Gladys Hansen, who gave us her gracious and knowledgeable aid in the Rare Books Room of the San Francisco Public Library; interpreters Rudy Kao, Leland Yee, and Betty Wu, and our unselfish typist, Sheila Lee; Priscilla Mark, who helped in transcription; and Wilma Chen, who not only transcribed many interviews but contributed her sensitive insights on them.

We are, finally, indebted to the editorial staff at Pantheon Books. The book owes its existence to the idea of our editor André Schiffrin, who had the foresight to see the significance of a study of an American Chinatown and whose patience and tireless interest in the book continued throughout.

We wish to acknowledge the financial assistance of the Ford Foundation, which provided a one year fellowship during 1971–1972, and of the late Gilbert C. Nee, who provided funds for typing, interpreting, and transcription.

Introduction

I AIMS, METHOD, AND SCOPE

This book is about a community and a people whose roots extend deep into the American past. Most Americans know of San Francisco's Chinatown, yet few can claim an understanding of this community, the role which its people played in the making of the American West, and the rich tradition and culture which it spawned in its one hundred and twenty year history. In a very real sense Chinatown has been a blind spot of American interest and concern, its people too small in number to pose a serious threat, and the reality of their history in America too painful an experience to remember. This book attempts to bring to the surface the past of Chinatown which has for so long been ignored as well as the present-day life of the people who make up the community. What forces created Chinatown and continue to perpetuate its existence? What has been the source of its exceptional cohesiveness and resilience as an American ethnic community? What is the consciousness of its people? Against the background of the historic process of Chinese immigration as that of the first, free, nonwhite people to America, these are the broadest questions with which this book attempts to deal.

Longtime Californ' is a book which grew in stages. It was initially conceived of simply as a collection of interviews with people who lived in Chinatown. Since we ourselves had read little about Chinatown, American Chinese history, or California history before we began the book, we entered the community in June 1970, with no careful plan for research or hypothesis to prove, just a general interest in talking with people. All the concepts and theories in the book developed gradually after this point—often taking off

xi

from the moment of reflection or the flash of insight of a local resident—and grew directly from our conversations and observations of life in Chinatown. The limitation of written materials on Chinatown published so far in America made it all the more essential for us to rely on oral tradition and physical culture in attempting to understand the community.

Our first two weeks in Chinatown were spent familiarizing ourselves with the community. We had only one contact when we began. While this friend made arrangements for us to meet people, we also walked around starting conversations at random, simply by introducing ourselves to people and explaining that we were writing a book. The striking scene of the darkly-clothed, elderly men in Chinatown, who seemed to spend almost all their daylight hours in elaborate conversations on Portsmouth Square, immediately caught our attention. Our knowledge of Chinatown's history, however, was at that point too limited to guide us into meaningful conversations with these old men, so, while we struck up a few acquaintances, the first attempts to interview them proved frustrating. Otherwise, the most accessible people in the community at this point were the social workers who staffed Chinatown's newly established anti-poverty agencies, church workers, and a few gregarious shopkeepers. Within two weeks, we were able to get some idea of the situation in Chinatown through our talks with these people.

We had two strong impressions of Chinatown during this early period of exposure. The first was a general sense of surprise at the extent of the problems resulting from the low income level of the community. Off the main streets we found that housing was overcrowded and poor, we learned that medical services were limited, and we quickly noticed the presence of conspicuous numbers of unemployed men. The second impression was that Chinatown had been highly politicized. There was an almost visible current of tension running between different groups in the community identified as "the establishment" (the leadership of traditional social institutions, particularly the Chinese Six Companies), the "liberals" (social workers), and the "radicals" (college

students involved in community projects), as well as between smaller, personal cliques which were loosely affiliated
with these central groups. We learned that there were three
major causes for this tension: a bitter struggle which had
taken place since 1965 between establishment leaders and
liberal social workers for control of the Chinatown anti-
poverty program, which had been introduced to cope with
the community's intensified social and economic problems
in the wake of the post 1965 immigration; the development
of youth rebellion and an exploding juvenile crime rate
among Chinatown teenagers; and the recent arrival to the
community of radical students from nearby university campuses who had held public rallies and demonstrations
against the Six Companies. In June 1970, liberal leaders in
Chinatown were attempting to spearhead a campaign
directed toward the city government for greater political
and economic justice toward American Chinese. Emerging
from several years of confrontation with Chinatown's traditional leadership, the liberals were convinced that it lacked
both the financial resources and political know-how to deal
with the community's needs. Buoyed by the rising tide of
minority rights movements among other racial groups,
ethnic consciousness was at a high peak in Chinatown
and references to exploitation and racial discrimination
against American Chinese came up in conversations with
a high degree of frequency.

On the basis of these early weeks of exposure and some
limited background reading we were able to put together a
crude picture of the community's social structure and history and to develop for the first time a systematic plan of
interviewing. Although we later came to perceive differen-
tiations in Chinatown society more clearly, we began map-
ping out a schema of important groups in the community
whom we felt it would be necessary to interview: elderly
people, the "establishment," immigrants, shopkeepers, male
workers, women, and youth. By talking to people from all
the generations present in the community, we also hoped to
be able to trace the process of its historical development
from at least the late nineteenth century on. The garment
industry, which we discovered was the subject of particular

controversy that summer, became a separate and distinct topic to examine through interviews.

We generally relied on personal contacts or references when we set up interviews. In order to constantly expand the circle of subjects, we made it a rule after each interview (particularly if it had been successful) to ask the interviewee for suggestions or introductions to other friends who might be interesting to talk to. Because of the extreme factionalism in Chinatown that summer, maintaining contacts with all the different groups in the community was a persistent problem. We were able to cope with this only through a constant (and often nerve-wracking) effort to minimize the interjection of our own opinions and reactions into conversations, thus maintaining the appearance of "onlookers," since at that time identification with any particular group in Chinatown usually meant automatic rejection by opposing groups. We also, of course, sought to avoid involvement with any single group or nexus of relations in a way that would affect the objectivity of the study.

The method of interviewing we relied on least was formal questionnaires. These we used only when they were asked for in advance and when the interviewee seemed to feel more at ease being able to anticipate questions as they came up. Generally, however, we found the use of questionnaires resulted in a stiff and unilluminating conversation. People tended to respond as if to an exam, in short, functional sentences which involved almost no introspection. For the most part, therefore, we preferred to do interviews informally, rather like open-ended conversations in which the greatest value was placed on letting the individual find and talk freely on the subjects which interested him or her. This second method of interviewing repeatedly seemed to bring richer participation and to involve a full range of responses.

Still, however, we usually found it necessary to guide an interview along certain broad areas of subject matter to ensure that the conversation did not become completely extraneous. Since we were always keenly interested in the defining characteristics and interrelationships of various generations and social groups in Chinatown, we made it a rule before an interview to familiarize ourselves with significant historic events or social processes which may have been part of the experience of the person we were talking to. Whenever possible we met with the person before the interview to help us with this. On the next meeting, we would then begin the interview with very simple questions about the person's life, keeping alert to areas where his own biography tended to intersect with broad historical movements. Usually we would move chronologically, covering experiences common to every life, starting with memories of parents and childhood, education, choice of occupation, and so forth. In most cases we found that after a certain amount of this type of reminiscence, the conversation naturally began to focus on certain events which were seen by the person as pivotal experiences in his own life. Often, a high degree of concentration and clarity developed in the process of this step-by-step reflection on events and resulted in insights of exceptional depth and candor. A second value of covering common life events in the course of an interview was that, once we had collected such information from a fairly broad cross-section of the community, we were able to perceive much more clearly than we had at first the way in which economic position and social background affected and changed people's lives. By including autobiographical questions along with certain questions on distinctive features of Chinatown (participation in its complex institutional life, perception of the non-Chinese society outside, etc.) we tried to build an objective picture of Chinatown society as a whole, based on the way in which different statements reinforced or conflicted with each other. By the end of our research we had conducted four hundred interviews, including informal untaped conversations.

We deeply regretted that our inability to speak Cantonese limited most of our interviewing in Chinatown to conversations we could carry on in English. We discovered quite early that almost all of our meaningful relationships in the community were with people who spoke English. This inability primarily affected our interviews with recent immigrants, and we felt disappointed, in finishing the book, that the depth and intimacy with which we were able to portray this group had been curtailed by our lack. On the other hand, as our interviewing progressed, we found the linguistic problem rather less of an obstacle to understanding life in Chinatown than we had originally anticipated. Contrary to our first impression, with the exception of the recent immigrants a large percentage of people in the different segments of the Chinatown community either spoke or had some facility with English. We therefore developed the practice of doing long and numerous interviews with English-speaking members of each social group, while simultaneously conducting a smaller number of interviews through interpreters, in Cantonese. Although interviewing through interpreters was bulky and somewhat less rich than direct interviews, we were able to use these interviews in Cantonese to check information and attitudes we had discovered in the English interviews. In cases where important experiences emerged which were not duplicated in English interviews, we put a translated Cantonese interview into the text.

We returned to Cambridge at the end of summer 1970, with a large box of taped interviews and notes. That winter, we listened to the tapes again, taking notes on them and checking for correlations and contrasts in what people said. Since, after four months of daily exposure and contact with people in Chinatown, we had gained a fairly comprehensive picture of the structure of the community, its points of crisis and friction, as well as persistent elements of consciousness which seemed to come up in the conversation of almost everyone who lived there, we were now able to define what we thought were critical questions in the study and to check each interview for the ways in which it expressed a response to them. As we sifted through explanations offered by the interviews as to the "whys" of various aspects of Chinatown's existence, a theoretical structure of the book began to emerge. Why had Chinese come to America? How had they sustained themselves economically there? Why did they live in San Francisco's Chinatown? To which society was their bond stronger, American or Chinese? With which people in Chinatown did they carry on their social life? What values defined these relationships? Which institutions and organizations in Chinatown did they feel were important? Why? Who were the leaders of Chinatown? Who were the "rich" and "poor" in Chinatown? Why were wages and prices in Chinatown lower than outside? How was Chinatown regarded by the white society outside? What was their own experience of the society outside? Did they feel there is, or has been, racial discrimination against American Chinese? We put together a first draft of the book composed of selections from interviews which answered these questions, and which we conceived of as a community study presented completely in terms of the words and perceptions of the people who lived there. In structuring the book, we attempted to emphasize a binding theme which struck us as running through all the interviews: that Chinatown (like any other community) does not exist in isolation from the larger society around it; that, in fact, every aspect of its life bears the influence of this relationship with the outside. Thus, while the tie to Chinese society and its cultural forms had been constant throughout Chinatown's history, it had been the demands of the American context which played the dominant role in shaping the community, its distinct subculture emerging, in a sense, as the vector between the two converging forces. Chinatown, then, was not a microcosm of Chinese society on American soil, but a unique American community with a history and language, and institutions of its own, the reality of which reflects life in the growing inner-city ghettos of large American cities.

In May 1971, we returned to Chinatown for a second and longer period of exposure and lived there for eleven more months completing work on this book. Initially, we had come to fill in gaps in the interviews because we felt the evidence they presented raised questions which we were still unable to answer. We wanted to test some of the ideas we had and also compare our first impression of the community with what we found a year later. There was, as it turned out, a striking contrast between the atmosphere of summer 1971 and that of the preceding summer. The continuation of national recession and the failure of federal anti-poverty programs in alleviating long-term problems of the community seemed to have dampened the intensity with which people called for and anticipated changes in the social and economic status of the community. At the same time, the acute sense of racial tension seemed to be subsiding in the wake of the start of improved relations between the United States and China. The mood of Chinatown seemed less agitated than it had been the summer before. But the community as a whole seemed to have changed relatively little. Its pace of life and everyday cycle of activity seemed familiar. The pressing problems which had affected the lives of the people remained unchanged: employment difficulties continued, the housing crisis deepened, the juvenile delinquency rate climbed, depressed wages continued to limit people's options and range of activities. With the change in the political mood of the community, our own focus of observation came to settle more on permanent and long-standing patterns of daily life. When we finished the few interviews which needed completion, we moved into a new stage of work. We terminated taped interviews and began a period of simply watching different facets of life, taking detailed notes on scenes, social situations, and even physical structures, and carrying on long conversations with people during which we attempted to clarify our understanding of various aspects of the community. At this point our idea of the structure of the book also changed, as we began to realize the need for analytical and descriptive writing, in addition to the interviews, to convey the complexity of the background and overall context of the Chinatown community.

The major result of this change in structure was an expansion of the book's treatment of the Chinatown past, going beyond even the memories of its oldest residents. The longer we lived in Chinatown, the more we came to sense that its present configuration grew out of a past which we had not yet clearly grasped. The weight of this past seemed to be an integral part of the consciousness of people in the community and to continue to affect their behavior, so much so that we decided to begin a session of reading in primary sources from nineteenth and early twentieth century history which might illuminate the origins of Chinatown. During this period we read and studied nineteenth century California newspapers, primarily the *Alta Califor-*

nia, congressional records, pamphlets, diaries, and looked
at old photographs all collected in the Rare Books Room of
the San Francisco Public Library. We found these materials
invaluable as documentation of the white response to
Chinese in America and led to a real breakthrough in our
work. For the first time we had a vivid sense of the history
which had so often been referred to by older people in
Chinatown and which we had had difficulty coming to terms
with before. We could now understand the basis for the
harsh or bitter stories of a violent past which we had tended
to discount as exaggerated when we first heard them,
despite the frequency with which the same stories were told
by different people. We realized, in fact, that most of the
experiences we had heard about from men who arrived in
California at the turn of the century did not even extend
back to more intense periods of anti-Chinese violence
between 1870 and 1890. We incorporated much of what we
learned from this research into the second chapter of this
book, "American California."

The investigation of Chinatown's origins also produced
an additional theme for the internal organization of the
book. While maintaining the book's original aim of examin-
ing the present-day community in its totality, we now
attempted to highlight the coexistence in contemporary
Chinatown of three distinct societies, one spawned during
the earliest period of her history and remaining on the
fringes of the two which define the community today. We
identified these three societies as the "bachelor society"
(composed of immigrant male laborers who dominated
Chinatown during the nineteenth century), the small-
business centered "family society" (which grew up with the
increasing presence of women in Chinatown later in the
twentieth century), and an emerging society of working-
class families, composed of new immigrants who have
entered the community in large numbers since 1965. To
clarify the differentiation between the three societies, we
rearranged the interviews in the book to follow a more
"chronological" order, beginning with the oldest generation
of bachelor laborers and their memories. In this way we
hoped to convey what we ourselves had discovered in

Chinatown: that the past is an organic part of the present, that its vestiges are visible in attitudes, physical edifices, and institutions, and that ultimately the causes for much of what is observed in the present lie in the past.

Another development of our second stay in Chinatown was the opportunity to develop friendships with people we had met or spoken to during the first summer. During this second year, almost our entire social life and recreational life centered around Chinatown. We visited friends at their homes, invited them to our apartment, and in many cases, asked for their help in evaluating their interviews (whether they had been superficial or not). We took breaks from writing by going down to movies in the Kearny Street basements, going on long walks through Chinatown taking notes, or sitting in the coffee shops, restaurants, or Portsmouth Square. We began to know a large number of people by name who would give us the latest news when we ran into them on the street, and tease us about walking around with our notebooks and pads. People were always inquiring about the progress of the book and wondering when it would come out. Thus, in contrast to the first summer, when we felt tense and uncertain about our relationship to Chinatown, we now felt relaxed and at home. There were several reasons for this. We became increasingly aware that Chinatown was not at all the "closed" community which it is always portrayed to be by the outside media, but one which had become accustomed to a constant arrival of immigrants and a diverse population. Particularly after the introduction of the anti-poverty programs to the community, many suburban-bred Chinese began to return and involve themselves in Chinatown—Victor was quickly identified as part of this group. We also found that people were generally encouraging and positive about the prospect of a community study done by a fellow American Chinese. They agreed it had been necessary to return to Chinatown for a longer period of work in order to deal responsibly with its complicated society and past. Many expressed a sense that they had been victimized by a long history of misunderstanding, oversimplification, and distortion of the American Chinese community by those who lived outside. They felt there was an urgent need for clear analysis which would dispel destructive stereotypes of Chinatown. Everyone, from the "establishment" to the "radicals," stressed that the book could make its greatest contribution by being objective. We can only hope the final outcome does not fall too short of their hope.

Finally, we were constantly impressed with the deep, humanistic sensitivity of people in Chinatown. Their spontaneous interest in and concern for *society* was exceptional among American communities we have known in the past and was ultimately what made *Longtime Californ'* possible.

II THE SETTING

CHINATOWN

The boundaries of Chinatown are not clearly demarcated. There is the old core area, the newer extended areas, and the outlying suburbs. The old core area has the highest population density and is the center of business, social, political, and cultural life for American Chinese. Along its main street, Grant Avenue, are the sober herbalists' stores, the delicatessens with their strings of cured meat, souvenir stores, import-export houses, and the stylized buildings of the family associations. Just below Grant, on Portsmouth Square, the circles of older men and a smaller number of older women in black velvet *moks*,* whiling away their time with talk, lend an Old World quality to this central part of Chinatown which for decades has seemed to withstand the penetration of urban, industrial culture from outside. A careful look reveals other distinctions of the core area: garment shops, the scattered entrances to the tong rooms, dark signs of age on the tenement buildings which stretch behind the shopping areas, lines of open garbage cans on

---

Note: To protect the identity of those who were interviewed for this book, most of the names attached to quotes and interviews have been changed.

* Simple black caps worn by Cantonese women.

the narrow alleys which branch obscurely off the main streets. Set on an incline, just above the point where San Francisco's land begins to rise steeply into hills, Chinatown's core area commands one of the city's most magnificent views of the bay. Above it, the exclusive Nob Hill residential area forms a border; to the north lies Broadway and the old North Beach Italian Community; to the east and south lie Kearny and Bush Streets and the financial district.

Since the lifting of the restrictive covenant in 1947, Chinatown has grown beyond its old borders and now sprawls through the small valley that lies between Nob and Russian Hills west to Van Ness Street. It has extended its northern borders as far as Beach Street, well into the old Italian community of North Beach. Outlying "satellites" of Chinatown dot San Francisco and can be identified by the presence of Chinese grocery and condiment stores. The largest satellites are out in the avenues, in the middle-class residential districts of Sunset and Richmond.

Census figures for Chinatown have always been inaccurate because of nonreporting by persons with illegal immigration status. According to the 1970 census the Chinese population of the city of San Francisco was 58,696. It is estimated that between 35,000 and 45,000 people live in the core and extended areas of Chinatown, and that the overall Chinese population may be as high as 70,000 to 80,000, roughly ten to twelve percent of the city's population. Over fifty percent of the city's Chinese population is below twenty-one years old. By 1960, after the arrival of thousands of "war brides" and the post-war American Chinese baby boom, the sex ratio became for the first time approximately equal.

The vast majority of those who live and work in the core and extended areas of Chinatown today are working-class families of newly-arrived immigrants and first-generation American Chinese. The second most numerous group are the small shopkeepers and a large number of old "bachelors." The income level of these groups is low: forty-one percent of Chinatown's population falls below poverty level by federal standards. Merchant-businessmen, who form the

Chinatown establishment, and younger professionals and white collar workers form a small but influential minority. Although nearly half of the city's Chinese population lives outside of Chinatown, virtually every Chinese living in San Francisco has something to do with Chinatown. Those who live in the "satellite" areas, even if their work has nothing to do with Chinatown, come in frequently to shop, attend one of Chinatown's numerous Christian churches, entertain friends over a banquet, or to attend one of the annual functions of their family associations. Their ties with Chinatown, however, are far less strong than those of the people who work or live there. A tiny group of well-to-do political refugees from Taiwan and north China maintain no direct ties with Chinatown.

HOUSING

In the 1970s, the core area of Chinatown faces the most severe housing crisis of any ethnic ghetto in San Francisco. The density rate of people living in the core area is 120 to 180 persons per acre, second only to highly crowded areas of Manhattan. Seventy-seven percent of the housing in this area is substandard by city codes. Most of it consists of fifty- or sixty-year-old tenement houses, built after the San Francisco earthquake with 5' by 10' or 9' by 12' rooms for the single bachelors. Only six units out of every hundred has adequate plumbing facilities, as compared to eighty-three units in a hundred for the city as a whole. Communal cooking and communal bathrooms are a way of life in these buildings, where families arrange cooking hours in shifts and where tenants line up with washing items in hand to await the use of bathroom facilities in the morning. The electric wiring systems are antiquated, and many of the windows face into alleys or brick walls so that they are completely deprived of natural light. There is no central heating.

As the population of Chinatown continues to increase, the number of available, low-rent housing units has steadily declined as new outposts of the financial district to the south have eaten away old tenement houses. Thus, although the total population of the Chinatown-North Beach area increased by two thousand people between 1960 and 1970, a high, twenty percent growth rate of the nonwhite population in this period was balanced by the fourteen percent decrease in the white population. There was a net loss of 815 housing units. The quantity of available units either for sale or rent was cut by fifty percent. The quality of available low-rent units decreased even more sharply. Although in 1965, an Economic Opportunity Commission (E.O.C.) survey had estimated that almost 6,000 units of housing available at rents lower than $70 a month were needed to accommodate Chinatown's large, poverty-level population, between 1965 and 1972, the number of units renting for below $100 a month dropped by 160 percent. The number of units available for higher than $100 a month increased by 270 percent. There are 555 units of public housing available in Chinatown to a waiting list of over 5,000 people. The manager of the largest housing project, Ping Yuen, says that a three year wait is "quick" for those registered on this list. Rents for a two to three bedroom apartment in the Ping Yuen housing project run from $300 to $600 a month according to income. The average rent paid by a family of four with an income of $5,700 a year is $475 a month for a two bedroom apartment, with a bathroom, kitchen, and comfortable living room. Some families in the Ping Yuen projects, however, may pay as low as $100 or $50 a month if they have a severely substandard income.

HEALTH

Since working hours are long in Chinatown, and food items such as meat must be economized on, the most frequent complaints of working people is that of constant fatigue. Many of the bachelors, who still have problems with their immigrations status, fear seeking medical assistance from the government health agencies and for years have had absolutely no medical attention. They suffer from general malnutrition, trachoma, tuberculosis, alcoholism, and depression. Until the establishment in 1970 of the Northeast Medical Services, health facilities in Chinatown were extremely limited. For a population of over forty thousand people, there was one hospital with sixty beds. In 1969, it was estimated that there were at least ten thousand people in the community who could not afford medical care. To these ten thousand medically indigent, only one outpatient clinic was available; it included a tuberculosis clinic, baby clinic, dental, immunization, and public health nursing service crowded into twelve hundred feet of converted laundry space in the basement of the southern Ping Yuen projects. In a year, the clinic provided care for an estimated fifteen hundred of the ten thousand people in need. In the area of dental care there were similar shortages, e.g., one dentist per twenty-five hundred residents. In 1969, with only two Chinese-speaking psychiatrists in the entire city of San Francisco, it was estimated that twenty hours of direct psychiatric service was available to the poor and non-English-speaking Chinatown residents. At the present time, Chinatown still has the highest tuberculosis rate and the highest suicide rate in the nation.

EDUCATION

Children in Chinatown attend American public schools during the day. Until the beginning of public school busing in 1971, the majority of Chinatown children attended either the Commodore Stockton, the Jean Parker, or the Spring Valley public grammar schools, which had enrollments which were ninety-five percent Chinese. From four to six, or from five to seven, they study Chinese language in one of the twelve Chinese schools in the community. About thirty-one percent of Chinatown elementary students attend these schools, and a much smaller percent of the high school students. The Chinese elementary schools teach basic writing, speaking, and reading skills. The Chinese Central High School offers its six hundred students courses in Chinese calligraphy, history, literature, and classics. Most children say they go to the Chinese schools only because their parents want them to and drop out by the time they have finished sixth grade.

Recently there has been a serious confrontation between

Chinatown parents and the San Francisco School Board. Liberal leaders of the community have criticized the school board for not being sensitive to the problems of the Chinatown community which affect its school age children. The public school system, they say, has excluded from the curriculum any treatment of American Chinese history and the experience which makes up the daily reality of students living in the ghetto. They are critical of the school board for not hiring more American Chinese teachers and administrators in public schools serving the Chinatown community. At the present time, in predominantly Chinese public schools such as Galileo High School, where over sixty-one percent of the student body is Chinese, ninety-five percent of the teaching staff is white, while only three percent is Chinese. All principals of predominantly Chinese public schools are white. Liberal leaders charge that the school board has been unwilling to make adequate preparations to accommodate the large influx of immigrant youths from Hong Kong, most of whom have serious language difficulties. There is an acute shortage of English language classes for immigrant students and only a very few teachers have bilingual backgrounds and can communicate with immigrant students who have difficulties in adjustment. The unprecedented rise in suspensions and dropouts at Galileo High School, they feel, is evidence of the growing alienation of Chinese students from the public school system. In 1970, Galileo High School, once considered among the best in San Francisco, had the highest number of suspensions among San Francisco's high schools (566 suspensions; the second highest was Wilson, which showed 322).

The widening rift between Chinatown parents and the San Francisco public school system was reflected in the 1971–1972 boycott of integrated school busing in elementary schools led by the Chinese Six Companies. Ironically, parents, while angered at the public school system for its lack of responsiveness to Chinatown's changing educational needs, were led to oppose busing as a solution to the historic segregation of Chinese grammar school students in ghetto schools. During the boycott, the Chinese language schools were used in the day as substitute schools and were staffed and financed by English-speaking parents in the community.

WORSHIP

The most numerous places of worship in Chinatown are the Christian churches. There are eight churches in the community. The Buddhist Church on Washington Street also draws a large congregation. The Jeng Sen Buddhist and Taoist Association is open daily on Waverly Place. Remnants of ancestor worship are visible in many homes where photographs of deceased family members are placed on a table or small altar beside a vase of plastic flowers and a sand-filled container holding burnt-down joss sticks. Occasionally, in a small business, worn stone figures of the household gods stand in a corner on the floor. They are covered with dust and neglected; one new store owner told us he hadn't even noticed the altar when he moved in.

LONGTIME CALIFORN'

Prologue:
Portsmouth Square

The square fills one city block from Kearny Street at its base to Brenham Place. In the city library, old lithographs and photographs record its changes: a dusty, open plaza when the water of Yerba Buena was clear and clipper ships from Boston moored in the cove. A new flagpole went up and a few frame buildings. The lithographs grow more complex. Paths are worn into the square, it is filled with men and carriages, activities vary over its space. Several prints are devoted exclusively to the busy streets along its sides. On Kearny, the great gambling halls of California history face the square: the El Dorado, the Verandah, the Bella Union. Cutting up the hill on the east are young, bustling stores: John Piper's, Lanszwert's Pharmacy, and a gunsmith. Suddenly photographs appear in the pile and the color and quality of the square seems to change. Lightness of open earth becomes the solid black of grass and symmetrically planted trees. Lightness of wooden frame buildings becomes the drab grey of stone and concrete. Where the Jenny Lind Theater stood, heavy columns of a dark building, the San Francisco City Hall, rise up. Where carriages had waited on the sides of the square, trolley tracks lie in asphalt and squat, black taxicabs idle. The square looks run-down. A humorous photograph, labeled *San Francisco Chronicle,* 1922, shows a bum asleep on a bench. In another, a group of Chinese men stand talking in a path. Finally, the black and white becomes clear and recent and presents a glossy plaque resolutely cast to preserve the past of the square: "On this spot the American flag was first raised in San Francisco by Commander John B. Montgomery of the U.S.S. Portsmouth, July 9, 1846. . . . Dramatic and authoritative announcement of gold discovery made by Sam Brannan on

3

May 16, 1848, who displayed glittering samples to crowds on the plaza. . . . First admission day celebration held, October 29, 1850. . . . Robert Louis Stevenson spent many hours here during his visit to the city in 1879–1880."

The square today has neither the hublike activity captured by the early lithographs, nor the run-down abandon of the *Chronicle* photographer's scene, but something in between. The tall symmetrical poplars have been replaced by clumps of younger trees, the paths and some of the grassy squares filled in with concrete. Four years ago, when an underground parking lot was built beneath the square, the gentle slope of its land was cut into two sharp levels, the higher one lined by a railing terminating in the landmark plaque. A small elevator shack, connecting to the parking lot, now stands in the middle of the upper level of the square; sandboxes and a slide form a simple children's play area below. Clearly, the square has declined as the center of activity in San Francisco, but it is still well used. As time passed and the white settlement moved onward, up Nob Hill, Chinatown—which from the earliest days had lain just to the west of the square, on Dupont Street—swelled, pushed forward its boundaries, and encompassed the square. Today, its business life goes on around the plaza, people constantly crossing it in the course of a day, while its oldest men, meeting there daily to wait out time together, have taken possession of the historic square.

The men gather at midmorning when the fog lifts. They stand in groups of two or three on squares of grass and concrete in the central plaza, a few doze alone on the benches in the weak sunlight. As each man enters, he scans the plaza for a knot of friends, nods or lifts his hat in recognition, and walks over. The men greet each other formally, as if they had not met the day before. They seem tall, some of them deeply tanned as the sun moves higher into the center of the sky over the plaza. A few old women enter the square; they skirt the knots of men and take the children down to the lower level to play in the sand. They line the benches there. Throaty gossip drifts back up to the level where the men are standing. Their talk has loosened now, newspapers are brought out, headlines read aloud, the events of the day discussed. The knots of dark figures reflect the style of a single era, the lives of a single generation: the dark overcoats, dark padded suits, vests, stiff collars, and dark felt fedoras were purchased in the late thirties, in the prime of the lives of these men who were seamen, haulers, butchers, frycooks, and laborers in the orchards, the canneries, and the truck farms of California. In the old days, a person standing in the square could look directly out on the bay as the fog lifted. That was long before the time of these men, and they do not remember it. But they remember when ships' freights were carted from the docks right up past the square and they fear the waterfront is dying now. "Used to be every one of those piers down there were progressing. Right now, no more," says Fong. "Even the goddamn pier there is just rotting away and nobody give a damn about it."

At noon the crowd does not thin out. The women reach into bags for steamed dumplings, maybe a piece of fruit, to give to the children. Tourists amble in, officeworkers from Montgomery Street come up with sandwiches, businessmen stroll through on their way to the Ruby Palace Restaurant, perhaps with a visitor from Hong Kong. The old men, however, do not eat in the middle of the day. Their pensions, sometimes as little as $125 a month, provide rent for a single room in $10 a week hotels, the upkeep of their suits, and two cheap meals in the morning and evening. The long daylight hours are patterned only by the elaborate manner, the gestures, the content of these talks on the square or by afternoon games of chess for small stakes. As the sun gets hot, they shade their heads with newspaper or here and there a Panama hat. Stone checker boards have been set up along the railing edge of the upper plaza, but the men do not use the large, red and black squares which have been set into the tabletops. In pencil, they sketch their own boards onto smaller pieces of paper and attach them with masking tape to a sheet of newspaper which is spread over the granite tabletop. Circular wooden pieces marked with characters—for horse, for soldier, for carriage—are moved across the paper. Here too, the men gesticulate, they sing, they harass each oher. The crowd standing around them laughs. Conversation moves from Chinese to English and back to Chinese, then into mock pidgin. "Yes, sullee! Yes, sullee!" How Yu Lan makes the crowd howl whenever he has a good move. Pipes, tobacco pouches, and a black package of Genuine Bull Durham lie beside the paper boards on the table. Baseball games drone from transistors. A few months ago, when the stools at the checkered tables were painted orange, portraits of Mao Tse-tung were stenciled in black paint on the trunks of the seats. The heavy trash can near the tables has crude chalk letters: Off the Pigs.

Everyday, from different parts of the city, a few drunk and crazy men seem to find their way to the square. The gardener at the square says he doesn't know why, maybe the sun in this part of the city is good, but this year, "Why I've even had men from twelve different tribes of Indians come through here." The drunks usually sit on a single bench on the northwest corner of the square just off Washington Street. Those who know the park less well sprawl right on the cement, their backs against the stucco wall of the elevator shack. While the drunks are men of many races, the crazy men are often Chinese, and they rarely sit. They walk alone through the center of the square or stand and speak, moving their hands dramatically. From time to time, the different groups of men turn their attention to the center of the square and, recognizing their own language, comment on what is being said. Usually the speaker has just been released from a state mental hospital where he had been maintained for several years at state expense. He may come from any part of California, but if he has no family and is Chinese, he will be released to San Francisco, and he will come to the square. For a month or so, the other men will see him moving from crowd to crowd behind the checkers tables or speaking from the middle of the square to anyone who listens. Then he will be arrested, perhaps for petty theft or for cashing a false check to buy food or liquor. Most likely, from jail, he will be transferred to a state mental hospital, and in a few years he will appear again in the square.

The chess games last through late afternoon and on into evening. The janitor at the park complains that after he leaves, at four o'clock, the Filipino players begin to drink and tempers flare. A few times, even by late afternoon, he has had to wrest a knife or a bamboo spear from someone's hand. But the men who stand in dignified circles talking move out of the park as the sun begins to fade. Most of the women and children have already left, and the sandbox lies in the shadow of the giant building across the street. Knot by knot, as the whole plaza darkens, the crowd breaks up and the men in felt and straw fedoras begin to walk up Washington Street to Woy Loy Goy, to the New Lun Ting Cafe, to the dark community kitchens along the halls of their own hotels. A few men stay alone on the benches, men who have not talked to anyone all day long. One, in a beige cap and red plaid hunting jacket fastened with safety pins, has his head bent intently as he whittles the cord handle of a fishing rod. The better dressed men take note of him and walk on down the path.

WARREN SUEN, 46

Gardener at Portsmouth Square Park

I was born in 1926. Yeah, served all my time in World War II, and I came back and went and traveled through the South Pacific and the only place I find is right here. That's why I have no desire to go to Hong Kong or Europe or anywhere because there's so much right here to see, really. See, I work for the city for twelve years and the point is there I was serving other people in other parts of the city, while this park for the Chinese people was run down very bad. So I come back to this park and completely prune the trees, and I keep it clean, as you can see, and I work in the bathroom. See, my title is a gardener not a janitor, but I do janitorial, everything. And when they ask me, "Well, are you the janitor around here?" I say, "Yeah." I don't say, "What do you mean calling me a janitor? I'm the gardener." Because what is a title? A title is nothing. You earn respect directly from the people.

Now we have beatniks here, long hairs, short hairs, everything, but whatever they are, if I see 'em, look like they got a little problem, I say, "Everything alright?" And if they

say, "I'm kind of a little hungry," I take 'em over there and
buy 'em breakfast. Now these are all people I associate
with, all sorts regardless of denomination or anything. I
have winos, you stay here a while, you see I have drunks
and bums. I have drug addicts, I have every unmentionable
people here, but there's one thing you will notice, they
respect me and I respect them in turn. And we earn it. Now
the police department comes in, he asks me, "How about
this? How about that?" and I say, "Look, such and such a
guy has a problem, but he's slowly solving it: Let him be."
Why take him to jail? So these are the things that I work
out with people direct, not indirect. And every so often they
get violent and when they do, you got to take violence by
violence, and that's your only thing. But even though I hit
some of these guys, when they sober up, they stop and ask
me what happened, I tell them. And they say, "You alright?"
They don't get mad, because I keep them from landing in
jail, see.

I come in sometime on Monday and on the benches in
front of here will be a big pool of blood. Downstairs will be
a big pool of blood. Because of the fact that you have these
drug addicts. They don't know what they're doing. See,
most of the violence doesn't happen until I'm outta here.
I leave at four o'clock, from there on it seems the violence
comes on, and on the weekends. I have a little control, so
therefore they don't make any trouble. Half of these people
I have here spent time in San Bruno.* One guy this morning
came here, he'll rake the lawn and everything. He'll ask for
nothing. I give him a couple of cans of beer. But, in fact, he
just got out of San Bruno. He beat the daylight out of somebody, somebody beat the daylight out of him. I got guys
here with stitches all down his face. Two of them is in the
nuthouse. You have insane people, Chinese, too. But they'll
stay there for thirty days and then they'll be back again. So
what's the difference?

But I feel that this is a challenge because of the fact that
these are my people, regardless. The very simple thing is
that if you're willing to work hard on a job, people think

---

* A state mental hospital.

you're crazy. The city's not doing anything for the people, but they criticize you. I'm not getting any help, like, for instance, yesterday I cut the lawn here. You know who buy the equipment to cut the lawn? I do, cost me one hundred dollars to buy a mower from Montgomery Ward to cut the city grass. Why? Because the mower they got here is so darn old it wouldn't run. But they say their budget doesn't call for one. So as far as I'm concerned I bring my own.

Like the awning on top of the checker playing. For three years I ask the union, I request and request, and everybody gave you promises about how they're going to try. I said, "Look, put an awning over the top of these tables, so the people, when it rains, they can still sit out there and enjoy the park, play cards, and have a little protection." Sure, sure, they said, they were going to do it. But that's the end of it. Talk is cheap. So there's a lot of things I'm not supposed to do, but I'm forced to do because otherwise this place looks run-down. And when it runs down, the reflection is on the Chinese people as well as on me.

My impression is that basically these old people are a sad bunch of people. For the simple reason that the ones that have a few cents are afraid to spend it because they don't know when the hard time is coming. You know, once a guy got in a fight here, he was lying on the square with his head busted open, and not one person made a move to call a doctor. You know why? Each one didn't want to be the guy that spends that dime on the phone! So that's how tight they are. And the ones that don't have anything don't give a damn. Basically they only eat two meals a day, and that is late breakfast maybe and a late dinner. The rest of the time they hang around the park here. This is their backyard, this is all the yard they have. That's why I work harder, spend so much time to try to give 'em a nice surrounding. Now there's this Holiday Inn going up across the street and they say they're gonna have a Chinese Cultural Center. Supposed to have all these exhibits of art and stuff from China. Well, I'm not going to knock it, now, but there's one thing I'm wondering about. And that is when the rainy season comes, all these people are gonna want to go in there. Now I want to see their policy on that.

So yeah, the old Chinese men are a sad bunch, you know, there's no future and there's no past, so therefore they're stuck. Just like I mentioned many a time, they're just waiting for the box. They cannot go back to China because there is no China, and they do not like the American government because they figure it's not taking care of them enough, so they criticize it. That's why they're open to these Maoists, these radical students.

Not all of them, but some. It throws back to the idea that they are Chinese, they're from the mainland. They are still proud, regardless of whether they're poor or not. They're still proud they're Chinese and not American. Like they say, they put in thirty, forty, fifty years here. They draw welfare, social security, whatever it is, it's always less than two hundred dollars a month, but you come to the park you don't see them in rags. They may have a busted flannel suit, but still they put on a tie or something. And they still try to keep themselves halfway dignified, they don't beg. And that's one thing I give them a lot of credit.

PART *1*

THE BACHELOR SOCIETY

1. Longtime Californ'

We were talking with the men on the square. It was in June, the beginning of the summer, and the square was sunny and crowded. It never seemed as crowded after that. At first we just stood around and looked. There were different kinds of men. Some always stood apart from the groups. There were the very tall men who leaned against the railing of the park, their deep-brimmed hats pushed back on their heads; they were restless, they would shift positions, we would catch their deep eyes and be embarrassed or wonder what they were like. The other loners were small and lithe. They dressed shabbily, like wandering tramps we once saw in Japan, not like American tramps, they wore khaki pants, khaki shirts that hung loosely at the waist, and they were always on the move. They were proud and we sensed their angry pride in being Chinese.

It was easier to talk to the men standing in groups. They were better dressed than the others, but we soon recognized the cut of the vests and the long coats they wore on raw days—their outfits were forty years old. They were proud like the others. They would tell us their names, but not where they lived. They would show us a few carefully folded letters they kept in their pockets, some from relatives in China and sent through someone in Hong Kong. They would speak vaguely of a child or some relative who lives in another city in California, "Yeah, I see him now and again." But if we met or talked with the same man regularly, we would find that the number of folded letters was always the same, there were never reports of visits from the children who supposedly lived not too far away. It was awkward on the night of the fourth of July when we stepped into a bar and found Harry Lee sitting with a drink. "Hey, my son is coming down for the holiday," he hailed us. "He's driving down from Sacramento tonight. I'm just having a drink while I wait." We sit down and talk for a while. Harry looks at the clock behind the bar. He wonders how the traffic is. We talk some more. Harry tells us he rations out his drink money so he can have one shot a night. He looks at the clock again. A lot of accidents on the holidays. We buy Harry another drink and he begins talking about something he remembers from the thirties. We talk until midnight. Harry stops looking at the clock. When we leave, no one says anything about his son. Harry stays on in the bar. We meet him other days in the square, but Harry doesn't talk about his family again.

We wanted to learn from the men who they were. Again, they would reach into their vest pockets as they began, take out a soft plastic folder with the photograph of a young man, black hair combed back, eyes looking straight ahead: an alien registration card. The old men keep these rare pictures of themselves as youths. "Yeah, that's me! 1951. I was sixteen years old when I came in!" They talk of coming off the steamer with a father or an uncle who had already been working here for a long time. "Me longtime Californ'," the oldtimers would say to the immigration officials. But the fifteen- or sixteen-year-old boys didn't get by so easily, this was their first time in. "You had to prove, see, that you were really this man's son," Tom Yuen described his arrival in San Francisco. "Otherwise, if you were just a Chinese workingman, you weren't allowed in." Tom remembered how the men stepped down the gangplank from the steamship and the newcomers were isolated out. "We young ones were separated into a room with no connection with the others. Then, after everyone was off the boat, the newcomers were shipped out to Angel Island." Tom explained that immigration laws were strict for Chinese then: No laborers allowed. You had to prove you were the son of a merchant or a man who was a citizen here before you could get in. "So the lawyers would testify, and then we had to wait on Angel Island while they sent to Washington, D.C., to get the thing cleared up. I was in Angel Island about three months waiting.

"And then, on Angel Island, we were just like prisoners there." Tom Yuen is intimate for the first time. "They had one big room where everybody slept and a dining room. We had to eat our meals there standing up. If someone had to stay a long time—six months, or even a year—they would ask the parents to pay board. And they treated us just like children there. Just no freedom to go anywhere. No freedom to correspond. Whenever you sent mail out, they inspected it, because they were afraid you might be telling your witnesses what to say."

When the boys were allowed to leave the island, they walked in groups up Washington Street; those who came before 1900 rode horse-drawn carriages into Chinatown. Some of them remember being pelted with stones by white boys, boys about their own age, as they came up from the pier. When they got into Chinatown, one of the first things they learned was never to cross the borders of Powell, Broadway, or Kearny alone.

At first we were surprised that when the men began the stories of their lives, they began with their arrival into San Francisco. What about their childhood in China, in the villages in Kwangtung? The men don't talk much about the villages. When they're talking politics, which is most of the time, they go on for hours about China, her wars, the villains and heroes of her history, but talk of the village is spare. The son of a dry goods dealer recalls the rocky mountain behind his village in Toishan. In late summer, he picked fruit there in the forest. In September, during the kite festival, banners were hung on the huge trees. He remembers riding a water buffalo through the rice fields to the pond beside his father's well and letting the buffalo swim out into the water to get the mud off his hide. He used to catch little shrimp in the same pond with a net. He remembers going to the family grave to perform rites to the ancestors. But his family was lucky, he tells us, they had an uncle sending in money from America. Somebody else was farming their land.

Most of the men say less. "Toishan? I remember one thing about Toishan," cracks Paul Wong. He is one of the toughest men on the square. "I remember the dung house. They took shit to make fertilizer out of it." By the time Paul was

thirteen, he had left the village, spent his first night sleeping
in the open air in Portsmouth Square, and gone out to work
the rice fields near Colusa. What is there to say about farming? the other men ask. Get up at seven, work till six. "There
was nothing to do in the village, nothing but farm. Plant
yams, plant taro, gather wood—work all day in the sun just
to get two meals from somebody else." Tom thinks it's about
the same as here. "If you don't work, you don't eat, right?
If you have land or money, you hire other people to work
for you. People like us, we had no money, so we had to
work for others. Maybe they would give us something to
eat." And there was not much money in farming. You work
like a cow or a horse, says Paul, and get enough to eat about
two grains of rice. "You think you can make money that
way?" There were hard times in the village when a harvest
was bad. The whole season's crop would barely fill the
bushels of rice they owed for rent. For some, even that
didn't make much difference. "Whether there was food or
not, it was all the same," Tom remembers. "In the village,
you were always trying to live on nothing. Cut down on
meat, that was the only way we could get by." Then, there
were the bandits in Kwangtung, yes, even after the revolution of Sun Yat-sen. Peasants and landlords alike were their
prey. Sometimes, if too many children had been born, the
parents would have to sell the youngest one to keep the
family going. Usually, it was a girl child, sold as a servant
to a wealthier family or into prostitution. For many peasants, sending a boy to Hong Kong or abroad, wherever there
was a labor market and money to be earned, was the only
way to survive. But above all things, "try to leave the village." Wong Sing Look remembered the letter from his older
brother in Hong Kong. "You can never make a living there."

Actually, in the village all they thought about was leaving.
All they talked about was coming to America. By the time
they were working age, most of the young men in the countryside would leave. In some villages, as many as eighty
percent of the men were overseas, and the whole population
relied on them for income. During the Japanese occupation
in the thirties, the men joke, people in the villages had
nothing to eat. "When the war was over and the men in

America could send in money again, the people in the villages had food on their tables." Wong Sing Look told how the family decided to send him to America. "For a while, my brother was able to do well running a store in Hong Kong. But then he lost money. He came back to the country and got a job helping in a grocery store. Not much income in that. He couldn't support the family. So he decided I should go to America to make a living. I said, 'No, if I go to America what can I do? I can't speak English. What can I do, work for the Chinese? I won't make much that way.' But my brother said, 'Whatever you do there, you can earn more than here, you'll have something to save and send to us. Maybe you stay there thirty years or something, and then you come back.' I said, 'I don't have a family, I'm a single man, if this is what you want, I don't mind.' " Tom explained the pattern: "From one generation to another, everybody tries to send a man overseas. That's the only way you can make things better."

We learned that, although few were born in California, most of the men belonged to the second or third generation of men their families had sent to work in America. Their fathers or uncles were not the first to come to the United States, they say. Those Chinese pioneers came in the 1850s and 1860s when there was gold to be mined and the transcontinental railroad was being built from California; the state's demand for labor was great. They had been peasants, pressed by unendurable poverty to seek work abroad, who borrowed money to pay their passage across the Pacific and spent the first years in California paying off the debt. In ten years, twenty years, a few did well enough to realize their dream; they returned to the village, bought large plots of land, and retired to lives of leisure as landlords. Most never earned enough and continued to depend on wages earned in America to ensure the survival of their families. Too poor to stay in China and not rich enough to leave America, they lived in California for the duration of their working lives. In time, some brought wives; they and their offspring began the slow evolution of a family society in Chinatown. For others, family pressure, lack of funds, and the harsh immigration laws passed after 1882 dictated that they come alone. They returned to China every decade or two, bore sons, and eventually brought them to America where they lived in a male society. These sons were the fathers and uncles of the men who stand on Portsmouth Square today.

Like Paul Wong, most of the men came here as boys in their teens. Their fathers found them work and simple lodging in large rooms in Chinatown which they shared with other men, or in Chinese workcamps on the levees and farms of the Sacramento Delta. For the first few years the youngest ones would work as apprentices or simply help the man who brought them with whatever he was doing. In time, they were able to find their own jobs as cooks, waiters, store clerks, or butchers in Chinatown, or as agricultural workers, laundrymen, or domestic servants outside. Sometimes in five years, usually in ten, the young boy who had come over accumulated the savings and experience to go back to China. There, he was expected to take a wife and procreate a first child. "I saved a little, and then I got a job as a steward on a steamship," Tom Yuen recalled. "So I got back for about a year. Well, my parents had a girl all picked out, so I got married as soon as I got home." Wong Sing Look has been in California for fifty years and back to his village twice. He came at eighteen, went back at thirty to marry, waited for a year, and had a son. He only went back once again, at forty, to have a second child. But the return to the village was often disappointing. They were poor and unchanged, and the men found they missed America. "Same as I told you before," Tom said, when we asked him how it felt to be home. "Never anything to do in the village. It was better working in America, even at fifty dollars a month."

So the men would come back after the birth of the child, and, like their fathers, they returned without their wives. The few who brought wives were exceptions. Wong told us it was too much of a risk to try to get his wife in as a "merchant's wife," besides, he never had the extra six hundred dollars passage. As Tom put it, "In those days, one thing about Chinese men in America was you had to be either a merchant or a big gambler, have a lot of side money, to have a family here. A workingman, an ordinary man, just can't!"

Of course until 1948,* the men remind us, the marriage of a Chinese man to a white woman was prohibited by California law.

With marriage a man's bond to his family and clan in the village was sealed. From then on until he returned to his village to retire he was expected to send regular remittances to support his wife and family. In the first years after marriage these remittances were sent promptly and at regular intervals. The men were keenly aware that the family depended upon them for survival, and when an expected remittance failed to arrive, their mothers could send a reprimand through a relative in San Francisco. While the men were gone, the wives farmed and helped with household work in the family compound. The money they received enabled them at least to live better than villagers who did not have men overseas. Some invested in land.

But the men had not chosen their wives and had spent only a brief time living with them, and as memories of the visit to the village faded, remittances were sent perfunctorily, more out of a deep sense of loyalty than love. For most, after marriage it was possible to go back only once or twice, and over time, the bond to the village was worn down by long years working as single men in America. For some of the men, even their fathers' dream of returning to the village to die began to lose meaning. Tom Yuen felt he did not want to repeat his father's mistake. "He had some crazy idea that his life would be sixty years long. He thought he could work till he was sixty, then go back there and expect to die. But when the time came, he didn't have any money. Well, he had two hundred dollars in bills. That was in 1929. He went back and it lasted exactly one year. I had to send him money myself to keep him going."

Finally, historic events which occurred outside their own lives severed the tie between the men and the village: the harsh years of the Japanese occupation of Kwangtung when many of their families fled to Hong Kong, the partial relaxation of American immigration laws which permitted the

---

* California's anti-miscegenation statute, passed in 1872 to prohibit white-Negro intermarriage, was amended in 1906 to include Mongolians. The law was invalidated in 1948.

entrance of some Chinese women after World War II, and
the Chinese Revolution. In 1950, landowning families up-
rooted by revolutionary land reform took refuge in Hong
Kong and, with the Refugee Act of 1953, were able to join
husbands in America. It was the men who had earned too
little to lift their families out of the peasant class who were
permanently separated from them by the revolution, the
men who spend their days talking to each other on Portsmouth Square and who are talking to us now. We learn that
they are the last survivors of the bachelor societies which
characterized American Chinatowns for nearly one hundred
years.

For the men who spent their working years here, memories of the village have been overpowered by a longer,
deeper experience of California. The stories of their own
working lives, the lives of their fathers before them, richly
mirror the history of California, the growth and development of her land. The men's roots are deep in California.
Their fathers were railroad workers, who came to the West
while networks of tracks still had to be laid in California,
Oregon, Nevada, and Utah. By the 1870s, the blasting of the
Central Pacific through the Sierra Nevadas by the first
Chinese work teams had been completed. But fresh recruits
of labor were needed to extend the networks into southern
California, down through the San Joaquin Valley to Los
Angeles, across the Mohave Desert to San Antonio. When
the railroads were finished, the men moved again, this time
into camps in the swampy tule land of the Sacramento
Delta. After twenty years building the levees, they transformed the valley into fertile land. As farms sprang up in
the valley, and wharves and packing sheds were built along
the Sacramento River, workers from the levee camps drifted
onto the farms or took jobs on the wharves packing fruit
and asparagus, and separating celery and onion seeds for
shipment. A few of the oldest men remember when the last
camps were still working in the delta. Juey Suen Jow remembers going from San Francisco up to a camp on the
levees near Merced, where for the first years of his life in
America, he and his father cooked and served meals to the
men in the camp for two dollars a day, "minus seventy-five

cents for every dish you broke!" On weekdays they went into Stockton or Locke. Juey still talks about the days when crowds of Chinese workers from the farms along the river would jam onto horse-drawn flatbottomed wagons and come in to gamble in the delta towns on Saturday nights. But as with the stories of their entrance into San Francisco, there is an undercurrent of bitterness to these stories of the California past. The men speak matter-of-factly about the Chinese railroad workers, they recall the levees and the reclamation of the delta without pride. During their fathers' lifetimes, they say, the Chinese workcamps that dotted the West faded from sight. The settlements in Wyoming, Montana, and Utah, from California's San Joaquin Valley all the way to the Mother Lode country, died out. The men cannot reconstruct the sequence of events too clearly. What they remember are stories told them by the oldtimers of their own days, knowledge passed on as lessons for survival, and some things, says Tom Yuen, "nobody has to tell you, you just know." The information is fragmented, the dates vague: a feeling in the cities and the countryside already strong by the time their fathers arrived in the 1870s. They remembered nights when bands of white men called out the landowners who employed them, angry exchanges, demands that the Chinese workers leave. Then the boycotts, the burnings of fields, and the shootings. The news of agitation in the city. Riots. Beatings. "The Chinese Must Go!" Then exclusion and the driving-out. The departure.

Their fathers told them that it was after the passage of the Exclusion Act in 1882, which forbade absolutely the entrance of Chinese laborers to America (although merchants and their wives could still legally enter), that the driving-out began. First, not in California, but in other Western states where railroad building was still in process and small settlements of miners remained. They heard that in Rock Springs, Wyoming, twenty-eight Chinese were murdered, hundreds burned out of their homes. It spread to Washington: in Tacoma, men were pushed into boxcars and shipped out of the city. A murder in the hopfields. A murder in the mines. Finally federal troups were sent into Seattle. In Idaho, lynchings. In Oregon, dynamite. And then in California the drivings-out began. Sometimes fire, sometimes threats, sometimes armed crowds, drove the Chinese from the countryside. No, not from every town, sometimes there were white men who defended them. From Tulare and Visalia, from Fresno and Chico, from the Lava Beds, Grass Valley, Oroville, Roseville, Rocklin, Compton, Redlands, their fathers fled. Those who had money departed. Men who could afford it went back to China or to the East Coast, where maybe it would be different. Men who had no money poured into Chinatown, and, surrounded by a hostile city, began the search for new ways to survive.

The men heard that the departures went on for about twenty years. Settlements where there had been thousands of Chinese dwindled to a few hundred. By the turn of the century even San Francisco, to which most Chinese from the rural areas had fled, had had its Chinese population cut nearly in half because of the massive departures for China. It was almost impossible to find work. "About all they could be was laundrymen or vegetable peddlers then," the men remember. "You couldn't work in the cigar factories or the jute or the woolen mills any more—all the Chinese had been driven out." You could shell shrimp if you could live on that. You could be a cook or work as a houseboy in some rich man's house. You could figure out a way, as Wong Sing Look put it, "to work for the Chinese." And if everything failed, you could go back to the countryside again, this time never settling in one town, keeping on the move from season to season, place to place, where Chinese were still accepted as migrant workers to perform the lowest class of labor in the state. "Chinatown was his home base, that was the safest place," Tom says of his father just after 1900. "In the summer he went out to Watsonville and picked fruit. In November he was cutting sardines in Monterey. He went up to Alaska to the salmon canneries in wintertime and then he got back to the valley again in time to harvest the asparagus in the spring."

There were still white employers who used the men for jobs which white workers did not want, and here and there in the countryside, small groups of Chinese who, discharged from the railroads and plantations, had scraped together their savings to rent plots of land as tenant farmers hired the men who came out from Chinatown to harvest. It was at this point, when the Chinese population in America was at its lowest ebb and these bands of Chinese migrant workers were still scattered through the state, that the men in Portsmouth Square entered California. Like their fathers, who could not afford passage back at the time of exclusion and continued to depend on work in America during the dangerous period that followed, the sons had been sent in by poor families in Kwangtung despite all risks and usually on false entry papers. In those days, only the hardiest sons were sent to America, the men say, and they braced themselves for it. Conscious of the defeat of their fathers, aware that with each year the number of Chinese working in the countryside was declining, they joined the last bands of Chinese migrant workers in a life on the move, going in and out of Chinatown, traveling up and down the valleys and the coast looking for work. They were and are the last of their kind.

"In our days, say up until about the Second World War," a friend of Paul's says, "Chinese were just like the Latins are now. You could see them all over the valleys, moving by the season." As a young man, he worked on the tenant farms where Chinese grew fruit: peaches in Oroville, apples from Watsonville to Sebastopol. Since Chinese could not buy land, a group of relatives would rent a fruit-drying plant and operate the kilns at cost. When the fruit was ripe, fifty or sixty men would come out from Chinatown to pit, sulphurate, and dry it. Many of the men would work through a summer, starting with cherry picking, doing a little planting, and ending up with the apple harvest before they went north. Kam Wai started farmwork when he was nineteen. "That was about twenty-eight, twenty-nine, in the summer. For a buck and a half you could ride these little limousines that went out from Chinatown to the farm. In the beginning of the summer, you picked cherries, after that pears, after that you planted tomatoes." Kam Wai was in Courtland, and he remembers how he got out on the farms and mixed with the elderly Chinese, "the old guys who would go from Courtland to Fresno picking grapes, then rest awhile, then come back again." On the farms, the men lived together in crowded bunkhouses where they cooked and slept in bunkbeds that lined the walls. "Maybe ten of us would sleep together. I remember, some of the older ones smoked opium. They used to ask us younger ones did we want to try it, sniff it, but we knew better, we would say no. But it seemed like it was just nothing to them. They didn't get crazy or that kind of thing. I used to watch them every day, you know, and they could climb a tree as well as I could."

The men remember the bleakness of the years on the farms. "For one thing," says Kam, "there's not much life in farmworking. You're traveling from one town to another, and everybody sort of looks down on the farmworkers, you know, the lowest type of people on the totem pole. And then, you don't really have much social outlet as far as I can see. I remember all the men used to talk about was where they were going next. When I finish here, I'm going to so and so, finish there and go to so and so. Saturday night's the only night you go out and do anything, if you do anything at all. Course, if you're married, it's a different thing altogether. Saturday night you might go to a show or something like that. But for the single men like myself, and I saw many men like myself, you can do only two things. I could spend my time in a gambling joint, that's one thing. Or I could go around to the prostitution towns, making all the rounds. So, as I say, at that time, life didn't mean too much to us."

There is one last significance to the era of their working lives which the men do not omit—the passage of the Immigration Act of 1924. The passage of the Exclusion Act had begun the process of the driving-out while their fathers were young. However, the Immigration Act, another act restricting Chinese immigration, brought the final death of the Chinese settlements in the countryside while these men were in their primes. Even in the difficult decades at the beginning of the century, the men remember, about 150 Chinese women a year would manage to get in. They had come legally as the wives of merchants, who were exempt from the exclusion law, or on forged papers purchased at high sums by the "big gamblers" Tom talked of. Very rarely,

late in life, a Chinese laborer was able to save enough to
bring his wife in on false papers. But with the Immigration
Act of 1924 all these possibilities were gone. The entrance of
any Chinese woman immigrant to the United States was prohibited. In the five years that followed not a single Chinese
female entered California to live, and in the next decade, for
the first time since the years just after exclusion, the number
of Chinese men who returned to China permanently was
larger than the number coming in to look for work. Although
many younger men, perhaps more realistic about conditions
in the villages, decided to stay, the older men were completely disillusioned. "The way the older ones saw it," one
of the men thought back to how the men spoke on the farms,
"they had been holding on here a long, long time, but they
could see America didn't have any place for them. A few
of them brought over wives and there were starting to be
families at that time. And then it was as if the Americans
noticed it, we were beginning to repopulate a little now, so
they passed this law to make us die out altogether." Especially in 1929, with the onset of the Depression, the older
men decided to leave. "First, they can't bring their wives
over now, no matter how much money they make, can't live
like family men. We can't marry white women either. And
then when the Depression hit, everybody went broke." It
was during the Depression years that men like Tom's father
went back to China after a lifetime of work in California,
sometimes with just a few hundred dollars in their pockets.
The others worked on as single men, farming in the valleys,
until they died.

"When my father was young, that was the time for the
heroes for the Chinese in America. It was the hardest times,
because of what they've been through, but they were the
greatest ones. In our times, it was just dying out." Perhaps
of all the men we talked with, Johnny Ginn expressed the
feeling of his era most poignantly. Johnny is a wiry man, he
looks past us when he talks, veins on his arms beneath
short sleeves. He is one of a dying breed of Chinese
migrant workers. "Since 1934," he introduces himself, "I was
traveling from one end of the United States, matter of fact,
down the whole Pacific coast. I was working up in Oregon,

Washington, in the great farm country, mostly in apples. I
came down to San Francisco around the time of the '34
strikes and I puttered around the waterfront for a while,
saw the conditions there with the troops shooting and all
that, and I thought that was no place for me so I got out
fast. Since that time, I worked in City Lights, Fresno,
Dianoba, Reedley, Porterville, any of those farm towns. I
picked grapes, I picked oranges, I picked lemons, I picked
pomegranates and whatever there is. And I worked down in
Watsonville, too, on the apples, and then I worked all up and
down the Salinas Valley, King City, and a few other places
I don't recall, mainly on lettuce and carrots and not much on
beets, and so I worked on up to '42. And the way I traveled,
see, is mainly by boxcar from one destination to another."
Johnny's life as a migrant worker grew out of the failure of
his father's dream.

Johnny's father, Ginn Wall, came to America in the 1870s
to build the Union Pacific. At the age of sixty-three, he spent
his life's savings to bring his wife across the Pacific, thus
becoming one of the rare Chinese laborers to live with a
family in America. It was on the apple orchard where his
father was a tenant farmer outside Sebastopol, California,
that Johnny became aware of the effects of a history he had
not seen. "There were about three hundred Chinese farmworkers up there, and they were all old men. I asked my
dad about it and he told me they had come over here about
the same time he did and they were working on the railroad.
Then he began to talk a little about the railroad, something
happened after they were done building it, but I didn't listen
to him carefully enough then. I just knew that after the
railroad was over, these guys worked on a lumber mill for
a while doing shingle work, and then when the lumber mill
shut down, they went from there to farming. Naturally,
they've been doing this type of stuff most of their lives
anyway." Johnny helped his father on the farm, gathering
wood, cooking for the crew, picking in the field with them,
and came to understand the lives of the men. As he grew
into his twenties, he realized that the farm settlement in
Sebastopol was dying. "Well, there they were, with three
hundred Chinese workers, and except for my mother, not a

single woman. That was the whole Chinese settlement in Sebastopol. All those old guys thought about was how they wanted to go back to China. But there's only about six months work in the year on apples, so they never saved a thing. And the only other thing besides work was gambling. Gambling was the social life, and gambling was the pastime. Everybody hoped to make a few bucks so they could go home in the easy way. The others lost their money and got stuck from year to year. And the reason there's no Chinese in Sebastopol today is that eventually they all died off because there was no reproduction."

In 1929, the only Chinese woman in Sebastopol died. In the years that followed, for the first time, Johnny's father unfolded the story of his past. "In March 1929, my mother took sick and she died in May. With the Depression, my father already lost all his money on the farm, so when she passed away he was heartbroken. He began to get sick, too, and never got better after that. That was when my dad began talking like the other men, always wanting to go back to China. He kept saying, 'Let's just fold up here. You come with me and we'll go back home.' And I think in those years, if he told me once he told me five hundred times, 'This is a white man's country. You go back to China when you make your money, that is where you belong. If you stay here, the white man will kill you.' At first, when he told me that, I used to get very angry. I felt he must have been very badly treated sometimes in the United States, and I didn't want him to talk about it then. But in 1934, we finally saved up the six hundred dollars to send him home. He didn't want to go at that time, because he wanted me to go with him. I think he felt if I married in China, I'm more apt to tie with my home country than with the United States. Now, it wasn't that I didn't want to get married in those days, but I didn't see any future in going back. I would only have to come back here to work, and I knew darn well that I would never in my life be able to sponsor my wife and family over here. Then, there's no use kidding myself I can have the money to go back there and visit any time I want to, either. So I convinced him that he should go back there alone, he has a sister there, he has the tie.

"Well, he did decide to go back in the end, even though he went back broke and sick. We were still up in Sebastopol before he left. And I never used to listen to him before, when he talked about the old days, but this time the story came out. He told me that he was working the Union Pacific, laying the tracks from California to Utah, and he worked there right up till the railroad was done. And when the railroad was done, there was this chasing of Chinese. Chasing from one end of Utah to the other, all over Utah state. The Chinese were stranded out there, he said, didn't know where to go. And the ones that got beaten and the ones that got killed have never been stated, to this day, I don't think the United States government has ever made reparation to our people for the ones that lost their lives because of brutality. Well, at least the railroad did one good thing for our people. They rounded up as many as they could find and brought them back to San Francisco. Then the railroad people took them to an army stockade, by the wharves, and then the city people could come down from Nob Hill and Pacific Heights to pick up the Chinese they need. You know, this guy as a farmer, this guy as a cook, this guy as a laundryman, and so forth. So that was what happened to the railroad workers. But my father remembered a lot of men committing suicide then. Ran out and threw themselves in the bay.

"That was how my dad got up to Duncan's Mill. There was a lumber company up in Sebastopol and they sent two men down to the stockade, John and Robert Dollar, and they saw my dad. I guess he was bigger than most of the Chinese, he's part Mongolian, so they picked him up to be foreman of the lumber mill at Duncan's Mill, working on the shingles. Then when the war started in 1919, they closed the lumber camp down and they gave my father a certain amount of money to pay him off. That was when he started the farm, him and most of the other Chinese in the camp.

"After my dad went back, I couldn't make a dime. And I felt I no longer had any tie to Sebastopol, I had no property, no relationship, no nothing there. So that was when I began to travel from job to job on the farms. Actually, I wanted to find something steady, then. I know farmwork is never steady except when you own your own farm. Working as a migrant worker, that's only seasonal. Three months here, two months there, and in between you're lucky if you don't get caught in the rainy season. But at that time, back in Sebastopol, I guess I didn't know what I wanted. I was the sort of person that didn't have much of an interest in anything because, to begin with, my family was gone, and when your family is gone you have no place to go. You have no one to turn to. So what are you going to do? The only way I knew how to survive was by doing the work I did before. So therefore I had to travel a lot of different routes."

2. American California

The response of white Americans to the fathers and grandfathers of the men who stand on Portsmouth Square today
had decisively shaped the American Chinese society they
entered at the turn of the century. The arrival of these
Chinese pioneers to the shores of California signaled the
beginning of the first large-scale migration of a free, nonwhite people to the North American continent and with it
California became the final battleground for the borders of
the European New World. The struggle that followed
unleashed on members of the Chinese race the same
fury and violence with which large regions of the continent
had already been won from the American Indians. The
struggle left on the North American continent an infinites-
imal minority of a people whose settlements had once
spanned the Far West from the Rocky Mountains and the
Sierra Nevadas to the swamplands of California valleys
and the deserts of the Southwest. "We remember distinctly
the complacency with which the people in this city thirty
years ago looked on the comparatively few Chinese who
had at that time become dwellers here," a San Francisco
newspaper editor reflected at the height of the anti-Chinese
struggle in 1880. "No one here at that time took any offense
at the event. No one felt that the locusts had come to eat up
the honey of the white man. The Chinese invasion then made
no more ripple on the surface of this city than did their junks
create a dangerous wave on the waters of this harbor."[1]
Two years later, through the defeat of Chinese migration
by the passage of the Chinese Exclusion Act and the forceful
expulsion of thousands of Chinese from the Far Western
states, the entire North American continent had been
secured as an extension of Western Europe and a preserve

for the migration and regeneration of the European race. The assumption that the New World would spawn a new people, born of the amalgamation of European national groups, underlay the early definition of California society. In 1848, simultaneous to the arrival of the first Chinese in San Francisco, California's newly written constitution defined the state as a white California. Naturalization, it was assumed, would be conferred only to members of the white race and suffrage was granted to "white, male citizens of the United States and Mexico."[2] Two years later Section 14 of the Criminal Act excluded nonwhite persons not only from participation as citizens in California's political life, but from the exercise of its justice as well. "No black or mulatto person, or Indian shall be allowed to give evidence in favor of or against a white man."[3] The high idealism of Californians for building a "Free State" unsullied by the system of slavery was posited on the assumption that the state's members would be white. "We left the slave states because we did not like to bring up a family in a miserable condition . . . surrounded by slavery," the San Francisco *Californian* had announced the year before California entered the Union, and concluded: "We desire only a white population in California."[4]

A critical element in the meeting of white and yellow races in California was the confrontation of two societies at different phases of their historical development. With the entrance of Chinese to California, the representatives of an expanding, industrializing capitalist democracy confronted peasants and merchants from a disintegrating agrarian society, China. China, in 1850, was emerging from a decade of defeat. The shattering British victory in the Opium War (1840–1842) and the First Unequal Treaties had thrown the ruling Manchu dynasty into crisis, humiliated it, revealed the incompetence and corruption of its leaders, and opened China to the penetration of Western imperialist powers. Opium, imported by the British, had incapacitated the Mandarin officialdom and weakened the Manchu army. Peasant rebellions against landlords and the ruling dynasty, extreme population pressures, incessant clan feuds, the attacks of roving bandits, and periodic floods, famines, and droughts, all further ruptured the fabric of Kwangtung society during the first decade of migration. Under pressure from these forces, which often made it impossible to sustain a living, peasants and small merchants from Kwangtung came to search for gold in California, where they confronted American pioneers. The Americans came from the Eastern manufacturing cities, the slaveholding South, and the farm-land of the Midwest. Swept toward the Pacific by Manifest Destiny, the exalted vision of their own expansion, they had carried the banners of a triumphant Western civilization to the farthest reaches of the New World. Emerging from a holy war of conquest of the Indians, they then wrested the new territory of California, with its immense wealth, from the Mexicans and California Indians. The vision of the society they would build there combined their sweeping democratic idealism with a firm belief in Anglo-Saxon superiority. Their confrontation with the Kwangtung peas-ants rapidly burst into the thirty year conflict which culmi-nated with the passage of the Chinese Exclusion Act of 1882.

Because of the tremendous differences between Chinese and American society at this point in history, certain his-torians have attempted to interpret the conflict between the two peoples as rooted exclusively in the clash of their cul-ture and institutions.[5] While it is true that the cultural and institutional gulf between Chinese and American Califor-nians was great, it is euphemistic to ignore the persistent definition of Chinese as a nonwhite race. Almost as soon as the Chinese in California became subjects of legislation, they were defined as nonwhite people. In the first such deci-sion in 1854, "Mongolians" were categorized as "Indians" and therefore subject to the prohibition from testifying in court. "Chinese, and all other people not white, are included in the prohibition from being witnesses against whites."[6] In 1859, California's superintendent of education asked that state funds be withheld from public schools which enrolled Chinese. "Had it been intended by the framers of the edu-cation law that the children of inferior races should be educated side by side with the whites, it is manifest the census would have included children of all colors. If this attempt to force Africans, Chinese, and Diggers into one school is persisted in it must result in the ruin of our schools."[7] The devastating assumption, and later ruling,* that Chinese were ineligible for naturalized citizenship, and therefore "aliens" no matter how permanently they settled in this country, remained in force for almost a century in America, until the Second World War. Careful examination of the events and legislation, the newspaper accounts and popular attitudes toward Chinese during the period of decisive confrontation reveal, as we shall see, that, far more than clashes of values and ideas, it was repeated clashes of economic interest that brought to the surface the wave of racial hostility toward Chinese in California.

THE FIRST OUTBREAK

During the initial three years of emigration, Chinese were tolerated, even welcomed into San Francisco, where they settled freely in every part of the city. In the labor-short boomtown, they were readily accepted to perform basic services such as cooking and laundering, desperately needed by men who left wives and families to seek a quick fortune in the gold fields. The editor of San Francisco's *Alta California* in 1850 wrote warmly of Chinese as "very useful, quiet, good citizens . . . deserving the respect of all."[8] It was not during this early period of settlement in the city, but in 1852 when Chinese miners joined the search for gold and found themselves for the first time in activities which were competitive with, rather than complementary to, those of white miners, that expression of anti-Chinese hostility began to erupt.

The first whites to engage in a major struggle with the Chinese were the enterprising, individualistic, anarchistic soldiers of fortune seeking gold in the mines. The clash manifested itself not only in physical violence but in verbal debate, and thus may be treated as a serious attempt of Californians to determine the shape of their future society.

---

* The Burlingame Treaty of 1868, while recognizing the right of Chinese to emigrate to America, expressly withheld the right of naturalization to Chinese. The Exclusion Act of 1882 incorporated a reiteration of the denial of this right.

The debate centered on the issues of free man versus slave and small producer versus monopolist and was sparked by the presence of slaveholding Southerners, Europeans, Spanish Mexicans, and Australians who brought teams of Indian and Asian servants in the mines. It was also true that as early as 1848–1849, there had been some talk among California's nascent capitalist class of bringing large numbers of Chinese laborers into the country.[9] In this sense, the early movement in the mines can be seen as part of a nativist, populist tradition which harked back to the ideals of Jeffersonian democracy. Miners gave speeches stressing the threat to men of small means like themselves from monopolists who hired teams of "serfs." "How can the evils of slavery be tolerated in the mines by the thousands of white men to whom the habits and education of their whole lives have imparted a hatred of the institution?"[10] an editor of the *Alta* expressed the spirit of the miners. On July 7, 1849, a mass meeting of miners on the Mokelumne River and its tributaries ordered "foreign taskmasters" and all colored men, who were assumed to be their servants, to leave the mines. To American miners, many of whom were adventurers or men who had left small farms to come to the mines, a democratic system of free competition offered the greatest advantage.

That greed, rather than political idealism, lay at the heart of the conflict in the mines became more obvious when, after the successful ejection of slaveowners and "foreign taskmasters," the struggle increased in ferocity and became directed against all foreigners, pure and simple. "If the foreigners come, let them till the soil and make roads or do any other work that may suit them, and they may be prosperous," a writer for the *Panama Star* inveighed, "but the gold mines were preserved by nature for Americans only, who possess noble hearts and are willing to share with their fellow men more than any other race of men on earth, but still, they do not wish to give all. We will share our interest in gold mines with none but American citizens."[11] In reading early California newspapers, with their reports of almost daily shootings, murders, lynchings, and duels between Americans and French, Mexican, Chilean, and other "foreign" miners, it is impossible to avoid the impression of greed gone wild. "Doubtless many of our good friends at home read with horror the accounts of the executions of summary justice which are continually occurring in mining regions of California," the *Alta* tried to allay the fears of Eastern readers when California legalized lynching, "but it must be remembered that in the wild mountainous golden region of California, seats of justice are often few and far between."[12] In 1850, American miners convinced the state legislature to pass a bill requiring the purchase of a license at an exorbitant monthly fee by all persons not native-born citizens of the United States. There was some initial armed resistance to this tax, but it quickly resulted in the departure of almost all foreign miners and a drastic depopulation of the mining camps.

By 1852, there was virtually no Mexican or Chileno population left in the southern mines, and many American miners had started to drift northward to newly discovered placers. Simultaneously, in 1852, there was a drastic jump in the number of Chinese entries to the state; twenty thousand in that year alone. Although a small number of independent Chinese had worked the placers inconspicuously during the first years of the gold rush, they were far too few to be seen as serious competitors and had been affected only incidentally by the anti-foreign movement. Now, however, as companies of Chinese miners appeared in the gold fields, Americans began to take note. Their changing feeling toward the Chinese miners is reported in the miners' journals and newspapers of the time. "Three years ago it was a matter of no little curiosity to the American miner, to see a real live representative of the Celestial Empire, with his wooden shoes, his prodigious hat of fantastical proportions, his shaven head, his long black queue dangling at his feet. . . . But the time has now arrived when the Chinaman begins to be regarded with other feelings than those of mere idle curiosity," wrote "Zack" of the *Shasta Courier* in 1853. Zack notes that "we occasionally hear the deep toned murmuring of discontent and even threats of violence" toward the new "race of foreigners." In his interpretation of the growing hostility, Zack articulates the

idealized vision of the American pioneer and sense of
Anglo-Saxon superiority characteristic of American miners:

After the American miner with the spirit of courageous
enterprise so peculiarly his own, at the cost of the thousands
of dollars, has explored the wild mountainous and savage
regions where a Chinaman dare not set foot . . . after he has
encountered and overcome numberless difficulties and dangers, in the shape of Indian pillage and Indian barbarity . . .
after he has settled down to work with a partial feeling of
security, in the hope of realizing at last some reward for his
years of suffering and privation—what must be his feelings
to find himself suddenly surrounded and hemmed in on every
side, by a motley swarm of semi-barbarians, eager to grasp
the spoils. . . .

Is our golden State to be peopled, through all future time,
by two separate and distinct races, having no more affinity
for each other than oil and water, and occupying the relative position of master and servant? . . . or . . . if the Chinese
are to live amongst us as our equals, exercising the same
political rights as American citizens, it may be well for us to
pause and consider whether we are willing that they should
enact our laws, fill our judicial tribunals, testify in our courts
of justice, to the jeopardy of our lives, our fortunes, and our
liberties. And finally, are we willing that they should marry
with our sons and daughters, and people our country with
a motley race of half-breeds, resembling more the native
Digger than the Anglo American?[13]

The reaction to Chinese in the mines rapidly followed the
pattern of the earlier anti-foreign movement. By winter
1852, a miners' delegation in Sacramento pressed for a renewed Foreign Miners' Tax, directed specifically against
Chinese. When the legislature failed to respond quickly
enough miners in the Columbia Mining District called a
mass meeting of citizens to "take things in their own hands"
and "apply such exigencies as the case demands." The
Marysville *Herald* reported that the miners resolved that
"no Asiatic or South Sea Islander shall be permitted to
mine" and proceeded to send representatives into the different mining areas to announce the decision.[14] A wave of
expulsions, accompanied by the burning, beating, and shooting of Chinese who occupied camps desired by whites,

swept through the southern mining regions. Within a few weeks of the mass meeting, miners in El Dorado County turned back all stages carrying Chinese passengers and freight; the tents and mining equipment of many Chinese working in the district were burned. The anti-Chinese agitation of the miners in that year was followed by a sharp decline in Chinese arrivals in the following year. From an entrance of twenty thousand in 1852, the number dropped to 4,470 entries in 1853.[15] Expulsions occurred sporadically through the late 1850s. In some areas, signs were posted threatening Chinese miners unless they abandoned their campsites. One, posted in the Agua Fria Creek District, proclaimed:

Notice is hereby given to all Chinese on the Agua Fria and its tributaries to leave within 10 days from this date, and any failure to comply shall be subjected to 39 lashes and moved by force of arms.[16]

In fact, those Chinese in the district who did not respond to the sign found their cabins on fire when the ten day deadline was up and, when they ran from the burning cabin, were beaten by the miners who awaited them. Expulsions took place in the Marysville district, along the North Fork of the American River, at Horseshoe River, and climaxed in 1859 with the mass kidnapping of Chinese by armed white miners in an incident known as the War in Shasta County.[17]

"The amount paid into the Treasuries of the mining counties in state license by the Chinese was so large that we were surprised at the vote to exclude them," a journalist for the Sacramento *Union* commented in 1858. "The money received for foreign miners' licenses enabled the mining counties to pay their expenses without levying much of a property tax."[18] Despite the physical expulsion of many Chinese miners by jealous whites, a renewal of the Foreign Miners' Tax created a counter pressure for tolerance, on the part of the county governments, which derived the principal part of their revenue from this source. With the departure of increasing numbers of white miners for new areas in the North, the presence of groups of Chinese who worked abandoned placers was by and large accepted. Because of the prohibition against their testifying in court, however, Chinese, who financially supported the governments of California's mining counties, did not receive their protection. As competition for the mines decreased, the Chinese miners became vulnerable victims for a new predator, the Foreign Miners' Tax collector. "I was sorry to have to stab the poor creature; but the law makes it necessary to collect the tax; and that's where I get my profit," one tax collector's diary recorded.[19] Physical brutality toward Chinese was apparently accepted as a matter of course by the tax collectors, as it was among many other miners. A California folk story describes a man who ran out of funds in the mining district and "sat on the roadside waiting for a Chinaman to come along" so he could rob him. "He thought no more of it than knocking over a jackrabbit to satisfy his hunger."[20] It was not until the 1860s, however, that the state legislature appointed a committee to investigate crimes against Chinese in the mines. In 1862, the investigators reported:

Your Committee has been furnished with a list of eighty-eight Chinamen who are known to have been murdered by white people. The above number of Chinese who have been robbed and murdered compose probably a very small proportion of those who have been robbed and murdered, but they are all which the records of the different societies or companies in this city show. It is a well-known fact that there has been a wholesale system of wrong and outrage practiced against the Chinese population of this state, one that would disgrace the most barbarous nation on earth.[21]

WORKING ON THE RAILROAD

While the Chinese were the objects of bitter hostility in the every-man-for-himself struggle in the mines, California's nascent business class and political leaders wrestled with the problem of finding adequate labor to develop the rich resources of the state. They were distressed at the overflow of adventuristic miners who came to California without wives and family and with no desire to settle permanently in the state. When, in 1852, Congress announced that vast areas of swampland in California would be turned over to the state on condition the state reclaimed them, it was murmured that this was not a very generous gift since so much would be required to reclaim them. Soon after, a bill was proposed in the California legislature providing for the sale of swamplands in sixty-acre lots "to those who will be settlers only." The *Alta,* reporting the bill, lamented that it was evident "that one of the greatest obstacles in the way of agriculture is the high price of labor. That high price of labor must continue for a long time to come."[22]

Developers of California were quick to notice, as a correspondent for the *Californian* put it as early as 1848, that "the Chinese work faithfully for low wages," and might be used to substitute for white labor should it prove too costly.[23] In March 1852, the first attempt was made to legalize the importation of Chinese contract labor. Senator George B. Tingley, who introduced the bill, called it a "measure of great importance" which would "place within the control of the people of this state a certain class of labor that now enters into competition with our own citizens."[24] The bill proposed that contracts made by Chinese laborers to work for employers who paid their passage to America be made binding by state law. Supporters of the bill argued that admission of Chinese laborers to California through the contract system would "give us the advantage experienced in its application by the English, Spanish, and Dutch colonies."[25]

There was wide popular opposition to the Tingley Bill by those who feared it would "overturn" the democratic relationship between labor and capital in California and produce the situation of "many countries," where "the capitalist is the real tyrant who fattens and thrives upon the necessities of those whom a conventional and unjust social system has made his slaves."[26] It was also opposed by those who, like California's Governor John Bigler himself or State Senator Philip Roach, opposed further entrance of Chinese into the country on racial grounds. The idea of utilizing Chinese laborers, however, did not fade in the imaginations of ambitious agriculturalists and developers in California.

Finally, in the mid-1860s, when terrorism and a dwindling
income in the mines left many Chinese seeking employment
elsewhere, Charles Crocker of the Central Pacific Railroad
became the first American capitalist to take the controversial step of employing large numbers of Chinese.

Desperation over the scarcity of men who were willing to
endure long periods of exhausting and dangerous physical
labor in railroad construction drove Charles Crocker to experiment with the use of Chinese labor in 1865. Faced with
the task of cutting through the granite mountain ridges of the
Sierra Nevadas in the race to meet the Union Pacific coming
from the east, Crocker at first relied on the young Irishmen
who were coming into San Francisco by the shipload to
escape severe depression in Ireland. Two years after starting construction, only fifty miles of track had been completed and skeptics in Washington challenged Crocker to
reach even the eastern border of his own state before he
was met by the Union Pacific coming from the east. As
Crocker drove deeper into the forbidding terrain of the
Sierra Nevadas, however, it became more and more difficult to attract the force of laborers sufficient to carry on the
work. The rate of attrition among young Irish laborers was
high. In 1865, extensive advertising for a force of five thousand laborers failed to rally even a thousand, and it was at
this point that Crocker directed his construction superintendent, John H. Strobridge, to experiment with the hiring
of fifty Chinese from the mining districts.

In February 1865, the first Chinese hired on an experi-
mental basis by the Central Pacific were given the simple
work of filling dump trucks. They did this so well they were
"tried" with picks, working on the softer excavations.
Again, they were highly successful. By autumn of that year,
there were three thousand Chinese on the payroll, and
schooner wagons sent out by the Central Pacific scoured the
California valleys recruiting Chinese. Eventually, Crocker
got permission to advertise in Canton for workers. Although
it has never been determined exactly how many Chinese
came directly from overseas and how many were ex-miners,
Lewis Clement, a member of the Central Pacific's engineering department, later testified to the Pacific Railway Com-

mission: "We had a good deal of difficulty getting labor. . . . The labor was not in the country and had to be imported."[27] Whatever, at the height of Central Pacific construction, nine out of ten workers were Chinese.

During the three year period when the Central Pacific was pushed through the Sierra Nevadas, Chinese laborers performed the most difficult and arduous work, and loss of life was high. In 1865, the path of the tracks had to be cut across the face of Cape Horn, a nearly perpendicular cliff one thousand four feet above the American river. Wicker baskets were lowered from the cliff with Chinese workmen inside, who would drill holes, insert gunpowder in the rocks, and quickly hoist themselves up the line before the explosion. A year later, in the winter of 1866, Chinese began blasting the tunnel through the Donner Summit. Rare photographs from the time show their camps literally buried to the rooftops in snow, and narrow, steep paths cut through the snow to the work sites. It is said that some of the Chinese shacks were buried in snow so deeply that they had to dig chimneys and airshafts, and burn lanterns even by daylight. They worked long shifts in underground tunnels, and blizzards and snowslides took a heavy toll in lives. "The snowslides carried away our camps and we lost a good many men in these slides; many of them we did not find until the next season when the snow melted,"[28] Strobridge admitted to a federal investigating committee many years later. Consistently throughout the construction period, Chinese worked from sunrise to sunset, several hours longer than the working day for white workers. Initially their pay was lower than white workers', and even when it was raised to the level of the white workers (thirty-five dollars a month), Chinese had to pay for their own food supplies which were given to white workers as part of the contract. Only once, in June 1867, did two thousand Chinese workers in the High Sierras go on strike. They demanded a raise in pay, the reduction of a work day in the open to ten hours, and in the tunnels to eight hours. "Eight hours a day good for white men, all the same good for Chinamen," a spokesman for the Chinese workers is reported to have said.[29] But Charles Crocker felt he could handle the strike easily. "This

strike of the Chinese was just like Sunday all along the
works. The men stayed in their camps . . . no violence was
perpetrated along the whole line. I stopped the provisions
on them, stopped the butchers from butchering, and used
such coercive measures."[30] The strike failed because it
lacked support from other workers, although alarmed railroad directors did wire east for several thousand Negro
replacements.[31] Thereafter one of the highest recommendations for Chinese workers was their reputation for not
striking.

In 1869, when the hammering of the golden spike finally
joined the Central Pacific with the Union Pacific at Promontory Point, Utah, there was jubilant celebration at the construction site and in Sacramento. At none of the festivities
were the Chinese workers present or mentioned, and the
railroad was toasted as the greatest new achievement of the
nation. Judge Nathaniel Bennett, an orator in San Francisco,
reflected popular feeling of pride in the accomplishment:

In the veins of our people flows the commingled blood of the
four greatest nationalities of modern days. The impetuous
daring and dash of the French, the philosophical spirit of the
German, the unflinching solidity of the English, and the light-
hearted impetuousity of the Irish, have all contributed each
of its appropriate share.[32]

In 1869, thousands of Chinese released by the Central
Pacific drifted once again through California looking for
work. Throughout the 1870s, these men were used to build
extensive railroad networks up and down California, Oregon, Washington, Nevada, and Utah, and to extend the
Southern Pacific Railroad through the Mojave Desert, where
again many lost their lives in the intense heat. When this
construction was finished and there was once more a surplus of Chinese labor looking for employment, the men
were recruited into the long-planned task of reclaiming
California's tule land (the swampy areas along the Sacramento River), back-breaking work which had been shunned
by white labor. Chinese were also employed in large numbers as farms grew up in the reclaimed Sacramento Delta.

"The availability of cheap Chinese laborers gave the fruit growers hope," a delta newspaper observed.[33] In the 1880s, just prior to the passage of the Exclusion Act, it was estimated that seventy-five percent of seasonal farmworkers in California were Chinese.[34]

In 1868, the passage of the Burlingame Treaty, which attempted to establish the principle of reciprocity between the United States and China, facilitated the use of Chinese labor by men like Crocker and those who followed his example. The treaty recognized the "inalienable right of man to change his home and allegiance" and "the mutual advantage of the free migration and emigration" of the citizens of the United States and China. The carefully worded treaty however excepted Chinese in America from the right of naturalization.

WORKINGMEN VS. CAPITALISTS: "THE CHINESE MUST GO!"

The hammering of the golden spike at Promontory Point was followed by the rapid integration of California with the industrializing Northeast. As a new, massive wave of immigrants from Europe entered crowded Eastern cities which were wracked by strikes and the economic depression of the 1870s, an overflow of men who took to the rails seeking opportunity in the West brought the birth of California's urban working class. When these men looked for jobs in San Francisco, or occasionally for small plots of farmland in the countryside, they found the Chinese in their way.

The completion of the Transcontinental Railroad in 1869 did not result in the anticipated economic boom in California. Land values did not rise, as had been expected. The opening of the railway caused severe unemployment among steamship workers. The phasing out of railroad work teams brought the discharge of an additional ten thousand Chinese and white laborers in to the California market just prior to the new influx of immigrants from the East. As thousands of men entered San Francisco in search of work, the racial conflict which had been briefly subdued in California by the absorption of all available labor into railroad construction was exacerbated afresh. Faced with stiff competition from manufacturing firms in the East, San Francisco's new industrialists discovered in Chinese workers the same qualities which had so impressed Charles Crocker. By the seventies, when the Chinese male population (58,633) in California was fourteen percent of the total work force,[35] the massive employment of this efficient and economical labor supply had begun in earnest.

The increased conspicuousness of Chinese in San Francisco after the mining period had already made them the butt of violent pranks by rowdy young toughs. Sporadic incidents of brutality against Chinese by bands of hoodlums were the subject of frequent brief news reports in the 1860s. The San Francisco *Times* of July 30, 1868, after reporting the discovery of a Chinese crab catcher who had been dragged beneath a wharf, beaten with a hickory club, robbed, branded with a hot iron, and left with split ears and tongue, observed, "There was apparently no other motive for this atrocity than the brutal instincts of the young ruffians who perpetrated it. Such boys are constantly hanging about our wharves, eager to glut their cruelty on any Chinaman who must pass."[36]

With the gathering of crowds of discharged white laborers in San Francisco in the early 1870s, the restless and discontented unemployed began to join the city's hoodlums in their persecution of Chinese. Hatred arose when these men found that Chinese workers were being used to take their place in the city's industrial force and to break the back of their nascent attempts to organize for higher wages and better working conditions. Thus in 1869, simultaneous to the completion of the Transcontinental Railroad, the first Chinese workers were introduced into San Francisco's boot and shoe industry to break a strike by white workers.[37] Four years later, at least half of the boots and shoes made in California were made by Chinese. By the late 1860s, Chinese workers dominated cigar-making in San Francisco. ". . . it is safe to say that if it had not been for the Chinese industry, the trade would still be in the hands of the eastern men," a cigar manufacturer explained to a group of anti-Chinese laborers.

"The Chinamen do not receive any pay for nearly a year or until after they have learned their trade, which they acquire before seeking employment from white factories. . . . It is an impossibility to take green hands (untrained whites) and pay them to spoil our material. . . . There are not more than 150 white cigar makers in the city, and if we discharge our Chinamen we must close our trade."[38] Chinese were also extensively used in the manufacture of slippers and woolens, and in the sewing trades. "To our white help we have to pay wages far in advance of what is paid in similar institutions in the eastern states," the president of the San José woolen mills testified in 1876. "To Chinamen, on an average, we pay less. . . . If the Chinamen were taken from us, we should close up tomorrow."[39] At this same hearing, the proprietor of a nautical cords factory testified that he had to pay white male laborers $2.25 to $5 a day, white child laborers $1 a day, and "young Chinamen .90¢ a day." He rarely found white boys "as steady and reliable as the Chinamen."[40] As panic and unemployment among white workers intensified in response to this, there was a growing public outcry against large corporations and monopolies, particularly the railroads, and the underpaid Chinese workers who were seen as their pawns. The physical attacks against Chinese in San Francisco became grave enough by 1871 that they were mentioned by Governor Booth in his inaugural speech: "Mob violence is the most dangerous form in which law can be violated . . . and when . . . banded ruffianism selects for its victims a race notoriously defenseless, when pillage are its exploits, the race from which such wretches are recruited, the community which suffers such deeds to be enacted, the officials who stand supinely by without an effort to prevent the crime, are sharers in a common disgrace. . . ."[41]

The rapid expansion of the population of laborers in San Francisco, however, made it a critical force in the politics of the city and the state. As workingmen increasingly banded together as a unit, winning the labor vote became critical to winning a majority and to political success. When the panic of 1873 sent a new, large influx of immigrants from the East, who confronted severe competition from

Chinese laborers in San Francisco and found themselves unable to buy land for small farms in California because it was held in huge parcels by men who were developing it with teams of Chinese workers, the outcry of workingmen against the Chinese became incessant. From that time until the passage of the federal exclusion laws in 1882, an anti-Chinese platform became crucial to a politician who wanted advancement. And in time, politicians who had initially yielded to the demands of workingmen in adopting anti-Chinese positions came to rely on the practice of stirring up popular feeling against Chinese in the pursuit of their own political ambitions.

It was the coincidence of just this brand of political opportunism with a crash in California's economy which led to the period of most severe anti-Chinese agitation in San Francisco. A brief, tranquilizing spell of prosperity in California during 1875 was rapidly broken by the events of 1876. A severe drought during the winter, the death of thousands of cattle, and the decline by one-third of the output of the mines, now added unemployed farmhands and bankrupt miners to the mass of drifting workers in the city. As the tide of discontent swelled, the Democratic Party, anxious for reelection, sought to capitalize on the antagonisms toward Chinese. In April 1876, it announced the formation of a committee of the California Senate to investigate the problem of Chinese immigration; the "evidence" gathered by this committee, stressing sensational claims of vice and immorality among Chinese, was distributed freely in pamphlets all over the city. The mayor of San Francisco appointed a twelve-man committee to spearhead a concerted movement against Chinese throughout the state. On April 6, 1876, when the city was still crowded with thousands of unemployed who had come during the winter, the Democratic Party held a mass meeting to inveigh against the dangers of "coolie immigration." The danger of riot at this point in the city was so great that extra guards were stationed at the Pioneer and Mission Woolen Mills where Chinese were employed, one hundred extra police officers were enrolled for the meeting, and the militia was called to stand by. Although a crowd of twenty-five thousand attended the meeting and listened to the incendiary speeches by politicians peacefully, tension in the city was high during the summer and into the fall as the campaign reached its climax. The cases of assault of individual Chinese on the street grew so frequent that the Chinese Six Companies petitioned the chief of police for greater protection. That summer, the level of panic and agitation in San Francisco became high enough that even the business class, which had consistently been in favor of Chinese immigration, began to consider exclusion as the only way of regaining domestic order. On July 31, Governor Irwin, of the traditionally pro-Chinese, procapitalist Republican Party, analyzed the situation thus: "It is appalling to think what he (the workingman) may attempt in his despair. In his desperation he may, like blind Samson, lay hold of the pillars of the temple and seek relief in one common, indiscriminate destruction. To be plain, the discontent of the workingmen on the Chinese question is a constant menace. The danger from this source can only be removed by removing its cause."[42]

In January 1877, a drastic drop in the output of the Comstock-Lode mining region sent stock values in San Francisco plummeting. Men who had left lifetime professions to accumulate California gold speculated wildly and were left paupers; since gambling and speculation prevailed among all classes of people in the ore-rich state, even small-time merchants and clerks saw their life savings disappear overnight with the crash of the stocks. The unemployed, transient population of the city grew to even greater proportions, one-half of it consisting of foreign-born immigrants. That spring, activities of the workers were stepped up. Boycotts, fires, and personal intimidation were directed at businessmen who persisted in hiring Chinese. Following the pattern set by the anti-coolyite meetings held by the Democratic Party in the preceding spring, workingmen now began to gather in vacant lots and deliver violent harangues against their twin enemies, the huge California corporations and the Chinese they employed.

As rage and frustration among workers grew, the line between frustrated laborers and lawless hoodlums became

almost indistinguishable in regard to their treatment of
Chinese. The excitement and discontent carried into the
summer and climaxed on the night of July 24, 1877, with the
riot of several hundred men who rampaged the city attacking any Chinese in sight. Several laundry houses were
wrecked and one, on the corner of Turk and Leavenworth,
set afire and burnt to the ground. Chinese men wandering
on the street were beaten and Chinese prostitutes hauled
from their houses and abused by large gangs of men. By
morning the National Guard had been called in and reinforced by a voluntary militia of two hundred men formed
to put down the riot. Still, six more Chinese stores and
laundries were vandalized on the morning of July 25, and
in the afternoon a crowd of five hundred men gathered at
the wharves to set fire to the decks of the Pacific Mail
Steamship Company, which transported Chinese to the
West Coast. After a shooting battle that lasted several
hours, the mob was driven back from the docks. Full order
was not restored to the city for three days.

Two months later, the Workingmen's Party was formally
organized in San Francisco. It began with a series of open
air rallies and harangues denouncing the "millionaire gang"
(the volunteer militia) which quelled the summer riot in
order to maintain the presence of Chinese in the city and
"make serfs of the working man."[43] That winter, as the city
again filled up with crowds of men, the leader of the party,
Dennis Kearny, headed a march to city hall demanding work
from the mayor. In the rallies that followed, he inveighed
against "thieving millionaires and scoundrel officials,"
threatened to lynch railway magnates, burn the Pacific Mail
docks, and drop balloons filled with dynamite into Chinatown. Two arrests and charges for conspiracy and riot
briefly put Kearny out of commission during this period,
but he was released after explaining away some of the more
violent slogans. In 1878, as the leadership of Kearny and
the influence of the Workingmen's Party grew in San Francisco, the focus of vehemence gradually shifted to the
weaker of the two enemies. "Down with the Bloated Monopolists" and "String up the Bloody Cormorants" were
replaced by a new rallying cry, "The Chinese Must Go."

TESTIMONY IN FAVOR OF CHINESE IMMIGRATION

By the early 1870s repeated declarations of the unconstitutionality of California's anti-Chinese laws by United States circuit courts convinced California politicians to seek such legislation from the federal government. Attempts to enact laws restricting immigration consistently failed to win support, however, because they involved abrogation of the United States' Burlingame Treaty agreements with China. By 1876, the only federal response to California's demands was the appointment of a congressional committee to hold hearings on the question of Chinese immigration in San Francisco and Sacramento. The hearings provided ample record of the fiery anti-Chinese invective which had become standard fare among laborers and politicians. The sole testimony in support of Chinese immigration came from international diplomats, clergymen who had lived in China or worked with Chinese, and from California capitalists.

It is as a rare record of the attitudes of the last pro-Chinese group—the manufacturers, railroad men, and foreign traders whose public statements on the Chinese question had been as infrequent over the preceding two decades as those of miners, workingmen, and politicians had been prolific—that the documents of the congressional committee have their greatest value. The speeches of such men as Charles Crocker, who employed nine thousand Chinese on the Central Pacific in the 1860s, or agriculturist George Roberts, whose Chinese workers reclaimed thousands of acres of tule land, pay a moving tribute to the tremendous Chinese contribution to the economic development of the state of California. At the same time, their support for Chinese immigration reveals a mixture of economic self-interest and racial chauvinism strikingly similar to that of their opponents. Agriculturalists, railroad men, and manufacturers alike reveal a clear and conscious vision of Chinese, noncitizen laborers as the backbone of a working force which would build the prosperity of white California.

**Excerpts from Report of Joint Special Committee
to Investigate Chinese Immigration:**

ALFRED WHEELER

*Identifies himself as "a landowner to a large extent in the
vicinity of this city."*

If I did not think Chinese immigration beneficial to white
labor I should feel much more inclined to consider that it
ought not be encouraged, because it is not from any humanitarian point of view or friendliness for the Chinese that I
think we ought, by any means, to encourage their immigration. . . . It has opened avenues to white labor which never
would have existed without it. That can be demonstrated in
a dozen matters.[44]

CHARLES CROCKER

Question: How long have you been in the state?

Answer: I have been here twenty-six years.

Question: What has been your business?

Answer: For the last fifteen or sixteen years I have been
building railroads. . . .

Question: State what, in your judgment, is the effect upon
white labor, whether they (the Chinese) have the effect to
deprive white men of employment, or have had that effect
at any time?

Answer: I think they afford white men labor. I think that
their presence here affords to white men a more elevated
class of labor. As I said before, if you should drive these
75,000 Chinamen off you would take 75,000 white men from
an elevated class of work and put them down to doing a low
class of labor that the Chinamen are now doing, and instead
of elevating you would degrade white labor to that extent.
For any man to ride through California, from one end of
this State to the other, and see the miles upon miles of
uncultivated land, and in the mountains millions of acres of
timber, and the foothills waiting for someone to go and
cultivate them, and then talk about there being too much
labor here in the country is simply nonsense in my estima-
tion.

Question: You think, then, that there is no conflict between the interest of the white and the Chinese laborer?

Answer: No sir! I think if the white laborer understood and realized his true interest he would be in favor of the present portion of Chinese labor in this state.[45]

GEORGE D. ROBERTS
President of the Tideland Reclamation Company whose Chinese laborers have reclaimed 30,000–40,000 acres of tule land.

Question: Do you believe that the tendency of the Chinese laboring classes of this country is detrimental to white labor?

Answer: Possibly, to a certain class of white labor; but, to the general prosperity of the country, I think they are a great advantage. I think they fill the places that white labor would fill very reluctantly, and it would be a long time before we could get white labor to do it. I think the wealth they produce stimulates prosperity to such an extent that it gives white men higher positions. I do not think the presence of Chinese here affects the price of intelligent labor. It is possible there maybe a class of labor that is affected by it, but to sustain that class of labor alone, we would have to hold back the enterprise of the country.

Question: What do you mean by the reclamation of these lands? What kind of work is it?

Answer: . . . Building dikes, gates, and ditches, preventing the overflow.

Question: . . . They (the Chinese) have added materially, then, to the wealth of California, in your opinion?

Answer: In my opinion, the aggregate product of the wealth produced by Chinamen in this state is equal to the mines, including the mines of Nevada and Dakota. Probably they produce sixty, eighty or ninety millions a year in wealth.[46]

The hearings of the congressional committee had no immediate result on the level of national politics. A report

was published which carefully screened out pro-Chinese
evidence, although it admitted that California had gained by
the presence of Chinese, "at least this was true of the capitalist classes," and that there was "a considerable and
respectable class in California"[47] which did not share the
anti-Chinese views of the majority. This report was extensively circulated by California congressmen as evidence of
the need for a federal exclusion law.

THE DRIVING OUT

Violence of workingmen against Chinese and their
employers flared up again in the late 1870s among farmworkers in the rural areas where Chinese, expelled from
railroad work, had come to compose seventy-five percent of
the labor force. Following the pattern of the city Workingmen's Party, white farmworkers held mass meetings where
they demanded the discharge of Chinese labor, and used
physical means of coercion such as threatening letters and
occasionally setting fire to the barns and fields of those who
employed Chinese. In Grass Valley, Colusa, and the Lava
Beds, Chinese quarters were burned down. In Chico, five
Chinese tenant farmers were shot to death and their cabins
and bodies burned.[48] When, from 1878 to 1879, a State
Assembly convened to rewrite California's constitution,
radical political caucuses representing the interests of rural
and city workers pressed for and won the passage of the
strongly anti-Chinese Article 9. This forbade the employment of Chinese by corporations, penalized corporations
who were found importing "coolie labor," and endowed the
state legislature with the (unconstitutional) power to regulate the immigration of aliens "dangerous or detrimental to
the state." Simultaneous to the constitutional convention,
California's Senator Booth proposed the first anti-Chinese
immigration bill to win the approval of Congress. It was
vetoed by President Hayes in 1880 because of the Burlingame Treaty.

While California politicians continued to fight for a
national exclusion bill, the Workingmen's Party and other
labor groups in San Francisco took the responsibility for

expelling "Chinese competition" into their own hands. The newspapers of 1879 and 1880 contain almost daily reports of marches of unemployed workers against establishments demanding the discharge of Chinese workers. After marching, workers would gather in the sandlots to report the successes of the day and to give further incendiary speeches. Under pressure, many employers agreed to discharge Chinese, although for some, such as the Pacific Woolen Mills, this necessitated the closing of the entire plant. In February 1880, labor pressure forced the passage of a still more sweeping bill against the employment of Chinese. It stipulated that no "Chinese or Mongolian" could be employed in any manner or capacity as "officer, director, manager, member, stockholder, clerk, agent, servant, attorney, employee, assignee, or contractor to any corporations now existing, or hereafter formed under the laws of this state."[49] Workers in San Francisco welcomed the passage of the bill triumphantly. On February 19, a sandlot rally speaker challenged the federal government to test its constitutionality. He warned that there was a revolution sweeping the country for the interests of the workingman. Several days later, labor leaders called on men to "take up arms and enforce the law of the state."[50] The following day, the Workingmen's Club of the Ninth Ward passed a resolution to "form a military company, which might be required for a week." "They call us a mob," said Mrs. Ana Smith, chairman of the Workingmen's Committee. "It was a mob that fought the battle of Lexington, and a mob threw the tea overboard in Boston harbor, but they backed their principles . . . and you should do the same. I want to see every Chinaman—white or yellow—thrown out of this state."[51]

The corporation law quickly went the way of past anti-Chinese laws and was declared unconstitutional by a circuit court. But businessmen and conservatives now joined the Democratic Party in pressing for an end to Chinese immigration, which they saw as the only way to bring industrial peace to the city. After Garfield's assassination, the exclusion bill was again offered to Congress by California senators who warned that social order would never be restored to California without an end to the immigration of Chinese.

Senator Miller went so far as to assert that thousands of white citizens had left California because of the Chinese problem. The bill won the national support of the Democratic Party with its strong commitment to organized labor, the support of Southern congressmen who empathized with a racial problem which seemed similar to their own and which was confirmed by the negative image of the decaying Chinese Empire prevalent in America even before the start of Chinese emigration,[52] and the unanimous support of the bloc of congressmen from the Far West added credibility to the racist propaganda of Californians. In 1882 the bill was passed over the opposition of a small minority of New England Republicans, and was signed into law by President Arthur.

The depth of racial hatred of Californians for Chinese had its most stark and tragic manifestations only after the passage of the exclusion law. The simple cessation of any new influx of Chinese to their shores failed to satisfy Californians who now turned on Chinese wherever they lived and worked in an effort to rid the state entirely of their presence. Particularly in rural areas where, as one grower claimed, "Chinese are the mainstays of the orchards,"[53] and few employers were willing to lose them in exchange for more expensive, less disciplined white labor, the violence which had begun in the late 1870s intensified after the exclusion laws had been passed. There were more mass meetings and burnings. In 1886, the barn and soap factories of the wealthy Bidwell family in Chico were burned in protest of their employment of Chinese.[54]

After 1885, reports of a massacre of twenty-eight Chinese strike-breakers in Rock Springs, Wyoming, fanned the flames of working-class agitation in neighboring states. Chinese were driven bodily out of Tacoma, Washington, and most were driven out of Seattle. Violence spread to San Francisco, which was already turbulent with the conflict between labor unions and employers over the hiring of Chinese. By the mid-1880s, Chinese workers in the once thriving white-owned cigar industry had virtually disappeared. Employment of Chinese by shoe and boot factories had ceased.

Competition of Eastern mills and pressure to fire Chinese
workers eventually led to the end of the woolen industry
in San Francisco. In 1893, another panic and high unemployment in California brought a crisis to rural California
and a condition "approximating civil war"[55] to the Sacramento Valley. Rioting spread through the area and Chinese
were driven from the fields and forced to find employment
in Chinatowns. In the San Joaquin Valley, armed mobs in
Tulare, Visalia, and Fresno intimidated Chinese with blows
and pistol shots and drove them to the railroad station,
where they were loaded onto departing trains. The rioting
then spread to Ukiah and Vacaville. In September 1893,
raiders swept into Redlands Chinatown, broke into houses,
set fire to buildings, and looted Chinese stores.[56] This terrorism and violence resulted, between 1890 and 1900, in the
first real drop in the Chinese male population in California.
Those who could afford it returned to China, many others
departed for the East Coast. Still others sought refuge in
the crowded Chinese settlements of the large cities from
which it had become unsafe to venture without fear of
being beaten as late as the 1920s, within the lifetime of old
men alive in Chinatown today. Here, they were limited to
the same marginal work as houseboys, laundrymen, vegetable peddlers, and cooks in which they had originally been
welcomed to California.

THE EXCLUSION

*"They call it exclusion; but it is not exclusion, it is
extermination."* —Chang Kiu Sing, 1904[57]

Anti-Chinese legislation enacted by the United States
after the passage of the first Exclusion Act in 1882, provided not only for the exclusion of incoming Chinese
laborers, but for a slow termination of the Chinese population living in the United States. In 1884, a federal court
ruling clarified the provisions of the 1882 act to ensure that
the wives of Chinese laborers would also be forbidden
entrance to the United States. Anti-miscegenation acts in
all states which had Chinese populations prevented the

intermarriage of Chinese men with white women. The anti-
miscegenation law in California remained in force and
was not repealed until 1947, after the Second World War.
Thus, male Chinese laborers who remained in this country
after the Exclusion Act had to remain single, which largely
explains the overwhelming preponderance of men over
women in America's Chinese population, a characteristic
that is still visible in the elderly, bachelor society of Chinatowns today.

In 1898, the secretary of the treasury refined the Exclusion Act which suspended the entrance of "Chinese
laborers" to include as many categories of work as possible.
Salesmen, clerks, buyers, bookkeepers, accountants, managers, storekeepers, apprentices, agents, cashiers, physi-
cians, proprietors of restaurants, ministers, preachers,
missionaries, tailors, cooks, boarding housekeepers, laundrymen, and peddlers all became "laborer" under these new
stipulations.[58] Those Chinese exempted from the Exclusion
Act—merchants and their wives and minor children, diplomats and their staff and families, students, travelers, and
American-born Chinese and their children—were often
humiliated at the port of entry.[59] They were detained for
weeks and even months, at the crowded and unsanitary
detention center called "The Shed," a run-down two-story
building at the end of the Pacific Mail Steamship wharf,
until their immigration status was clarified. It was the policy
of immigration officials to presume all Chinese entrants
"guilty" of illegal immigration until proved otherwise. "No
one need be surprised at these abuses," observed John P.
Irish, Naval Officer of Customs in San Francisco. "So completely are these safeguards of human liberty withdrawn
that if you, sir, landed in San Francisco on a Pacific liner
and had an enemy sufficiently virulent and of sufficient
influence with some inspector, you could be deported as a
Chinese and would find yourself utterly powerless to protect yourself or to make proof to the contrary."[60]

NOTES:

1. *Alta California,* March 26, 1880.
2. Constitution of the State of California.
3. *People* v. *George W. Hall,* 4 Cal. 399 (1854).
4. San Francisco *Californian,* March 15, 1848.
5. The major proponent of this interpretation is Gunther Barth, who wrote *Bitter Strength: A History of the Chinese in the United States 1850–1870* (Cambridge, Mass.: Harvard University Press, 1964). His book is, in effect, the most sophisticated apology for the anti-Chinese movement of the nineteenth century. An unabashed acceptance of Manifest Destiny underlies his analysis of Chinese immigration: "A series of obstacles blocked the road to the true American state. The Indians and Mexicans on the scene were the earliest impediments. Their way of life thwarted the Californian dream." (p. 135) Then came "the regimented Chinese miners" who slavelike "posed an obstacle to the building of the true American state. They endangered Californians' hope for the realization of their dream about the future." (p. 131) Barth has skillfully transposed the framework of the anti-Semite onto Chinese American history. For Barth, anti-Chinese hatred is reduceable to the fact that Chinese, who came as sojourners, refused to acculturate into American culture and society, and thus posed a threat to the realization of the "true American state." "The goals of Californians and the Chinese differed. The former attempted to extend the blessings of American culture to all Chinese as an answer to the challenge of their humanitarian concepts. The latter ignored the overtures. . . ." (p. 157) "The sojourners' goal influenced the American reaction. Their world raised up specters that challenged American values. The work camps which regimented anonymous hordes of laborers resembled gangs of Negro slaves. The control system extended debt bondage and despotism to the United States. Chinatown, which harbored indentured emigrants in dilapidated structures, suggested filth and immorality as the sojourners' second nature. These images impressed themselves firmly on Americans and determined the reaction toward the Chinese even after the sojourners had abandoned their traditional goal for the promise of life defined no longer in terms of mere survival, but of liberty." (p. 213) A deliberate obfuscation of the nature of the American response to nineteenth century Chinese immigration makes Barth's book racist history.
6. *People* v. *George W. Hall.*
7. William Warren Ferrier, *Ninety Years of Education in California, 1846–1936* (Berkeley: Sather Gate Book Shop, 1937), p. 98. Cited in Stanford Lyman, *Asian in the West* (Reno: Desert Research Institute, 1970), p. 23.
8. *Alta California,* March 8, 1850.
9. Thomas O. Larkin, *The Larkin Papers,* George P. Hammond, ed. (Berkeley: University of California Press, 1964), p. 167.

10. *Alta California,* May 4, 1850.
11. From the *Panama Star,* February 24, 1849, as quoted by Ruth E. McKee, "California and Her Less Favored Minorities," cited in Paul Jacobs and Saul Landau, eds., *To Service the Devil* (New York: Vintage Books, 1971), p. 79.
12. *Alta California,* February 9, 1851.
13. Shasta *Courier,* "What is to be done with the Chinaman?" December 3, 1853.
14. Marysville *Herald,* May 4, 1852.
15. Mary Roberts Coolidge, *Chinese Immigration* (New York: Henry Holt and Co., 1909), p. 34.
16. Cited in Charles Caudwell Dobie, *San Francisco Chinatown* (New York: D. Appleton-Century Co., 1936), p. 51.
17. *Ibid.,* p. 53.
18. Sacramento *Union,* June 15, 1858.
19. Reverend William Speer, *An Humble Plea Addressed to the Legislature of California in Behalf of the Immigrants of the Empire of China* (San Francisco, 1856), p. 35.
20. Dobie, *San Francisco Chinatown,* p. 50.
21. Stephen Williams, *The Chinese in the California Mines 1848–1860* (unpublished M.A. thesis, Stanford University, 1930), pp. 92–96. Cited in Thomas Chinn, H. Mark Lai, Philip P. Choy, eds., *A History of the Chinese in California: A Syllabus* (San Francisco: Chinese Historical Society of America, 1969), p. 32.
22. *Alta California,* February 4, 1852.
23. *Californian,* November 4, 1848, cited in Barth, *Bitter Strength,* p. 136.
24. *Alta California,* March 6, 1852.
25. *Ibid.*
26. *Alta California,* March 10, 1852.
27. *Pacific Railway Commission* VI 3224
28. Cited in Chinn, *et al., History of the Chinese,* p. 47.
29. *Ibid.,* p. 46.
30. From Crocker's Report to the Special Committee, p. 669. Cited in Ping Chiu, *Chinese Labor in California* (Madison, 1967), p. 46.
31. San Francisco *Commercial Herald and Market Review,* July 11, 1867.
32. From San Francisco *Bulletin,* May 8, 1869, cited in Alexander Saxton, "The Army of Canton in the High Sierras," *Pacific Historical Review,* Volume 35, 1966, p. 152.
33. Cited in Cary McWilliams, *Factories in the Field* (Hamden, Conn.: Shoe String Press, 1969), p. 67.
34. Chinn, *et al., History of the Chinese,* p. 157.
35. Coolidge, *Chinese Immigration,* p. 358.
36. From San Francisco *Times,* July 30, 1868, as cited in Herbert Asbury, *The Barbary Coast* (New York: Alfred Knopf, 1933), p. 155.
37. San Francisco *Bulletin,* May 29, 1870.
38. *Alta California,* February 15, 1880.

39. *Report of the Joint Special Committee to Investigate Chinese Immigration* (44th Congress, 22nd Session, 1876–1877, Senate Report 689), p. 553–558.

40. From Senate Report 689, cited in Augustus Layres, *Evidence of Public Opinion on the Pacific Coast in Favor of Chinese Immigration* (San Francisco, 1879), p. 35.

41. *California Senate Journal*, 1871–1872, pp. 115–116.

42. Senate Report 689.

43. Dobie, *San Francisco Chinatown*, p. 108.

44. Senate Report 689, p. 512.

45. *Ibid.*, p. 66.

46. *Ibid.*, p. 649.

47. *Ibid.*, p. iii.

48. Joseph McGowan, *History of the Sacramento Valley*, Vol. I (New York: Lewis Historical Publishing Co., 1961), pp. 324–325.

49. *Alta California*, February 18, 1880.

50. *Ibid.*, February 25, 1880.

51. *Ibid.*, February 27, 1880.

52. Stuart Creighton Miller, *The Unwelcome Immigrant: The American Image of the Chinese 1785–1882* (Berkeley: University of California Press, 1969).

53. *Pacific Rural Press*, September 10, 1893.

54. McGowan, *History of the Sacramento Valley*, p. 325.

55. McWilliams, *Factories in the Field*, p. 67.

56. *Ibid.*, pp. 75–76.

57. Cited in Coolidge, *Chinese Immigration*, p. 302.

58. *Ibid.*, pp. 278–301.

59. Only merchants with established businesses in America were permitted to reside in America beyond a temporary basis. According to the McCreary Act, November 3, 1893 (8 Stat p. 7), a merchant was "a person engaged in buying and selling merchandise in his name, and who during the time he claims to be engaged as a merchant, does not engage in the performances of any manual labor except such as is necessary to the conduct of his business as such merchant." The act went on to state, "he shall establish his credentials as a merchant by the testimony of two credible witnesses other than Chinese the fact that he conducted such business . . . and that during such year he was not engaged in the performance of any manual labor, except such as was necessary in the conduct of his business" (quoted from Coolidge, *Chinese Immigration*, p. 293). Scholars, students, and travelers were limited to short stays.

60. *Ibid.*, p. 278.

3. Oldtimers' Tales

After 1870, as anti-Chinese agitation drove Chinese from their settlements in rural California, the Chinese community in San Francisco grew in numbers and significance as the center of American Chinese life. However, the turn of the century, which marks the limit of the memories of today's oldtimers, was a period of decline even in Chinatown. Between 1890 and 1900, the force of the exclusion laws, the refusal of readmission to 20,000 Chinese laborers temporarily visiting in Kwangtung, and the decision of thousands of discouraged Chinese to return to China, led for the first time since 1850 to a decline in the total population of Chinese in the United States. The decade witnessed a drastic drop in the male population from 103,620 to 85,341. This had its effect on Chinatown, too, and perhaps never was Chinatown's isolation from American society so great as during the two decades at the end of the nineteenth and the beginning of the twentieth century.

The sense of being physically sealed within the boundaries of Chinatown was impressed on the few immigrants coming into the settlement by frequent stonings which occurred as they came up Washington or Clay Street from the piers. It was perpetuated by attacks of white toughs in the adjacent North Beach area and downtown around Union Square, who amused themselves by beating Chinese who came into these areas. "In those days, the boundaries were from Kearny to Powell, and from California to Broadway. If you ever passed them and went out there, the white kids would throw stones at you," Wei Bat Liu told us. "One time I remember going out and one boy started running after me, then a whole gang of others rushed out, too. We were afraid of them, and there were more of them than of us, so we would come right back. Angry? Well, maybe in those days when we were young, we were not so angry. Just tired of it." Naturally, it was impossible for Chinese to find living accommodations outside the seven block area whose boundaries they were afraid to cross. Mr. Liu remembers looking for a house on Powell Street, just one block above Chinatown. "I had trouble finding a good place in Chinatown. It was so crowded, everyone was sleeping in double-decker beds and all that. So I went up just one block to Powell Street and asked in three places there. They all told me no, no one had ever heard of Chinese living on Powell Street before. So we went back down to Chinatown, where all my cousins lived in one room. No bathroom, no kitchen, just like the apartments down there now." By being excluded from white public schools, Chinese were denied access to the very skills which could have helped them transcend this isolation. In 1885 a public school for Chinese, Japanese, and Koreans was established in Chinatown and known as the Oriental School. *De facto* segregation of Chinese children into this school continued through the early 1900s. Finally, the expulsion of Chinese from all the industries in which they had been competitive with white labor before exclusion severely limited the available means of making a living at that time. As a child, carpenter Jack Wong witnessed the final phasing of Chinese out of the industries they had once relied upon:

Maybe because I began talking to some oldtimers or maybe because I was a little more observant than the others, I began to see it, slowly but surely—the phasing out of many industries in Chinatown. It was a crime actually, because of the human factors, but I could see it was inevitable.

When I first came in, there were three broom manufacturing companies in Chinatown, and they were producing the majority of brooms in the Bay Area. But the industry was deteriorating because the price of making a broom by hand was so high. You see, in Chinatown we lacked the capital to install the new machinery they were getting in the mechanized factories, and we lacked the knowledge of industrial techniques. So, unfortunately, the broom factories ceased to exist and as a result I saw the men in Chinatown lose about 100 or 150 jobs.

Now another thing was the cigar makers. There use to be about fifteen or twenty cigar making places in Chinatown. They had their own leaves and fiber fillers, and there were hundreds of people working here in cigar factories run by Chinese, even after they had been driven out of the white-owned factories. But when cigars started being produced on a mass production basis, these died out, too.

Thirdly, there were the shoe manufacturers. When I got to Chinatown in 1913, there were only five or six shoe manu-facturers left in Chinatown. Of course, the most successful Chinese shoe manufacturer was Little Pete, the tong man, back in the nineties. He was wise enough to put a Caucasian brand name on his shoes and use Caucasian salesmen. And he was very successful until it was found out that he was a Chinese manufacturer, and once that was found out, that was it! But again, because of the labor unions and discrim-ination, and because they weren't competitive after a while, the shoe factories were phased out, too.

Well, at that time, people weren't as open-minded as now and they preferred to patronize their own. So I guess the Chinese kept existing because they were still used as domestic labor, because they were able to make a living among them-selves, and also by selling art objects and relics. That was the only way you could exist. We did seem to isolate ourselves, I guess, and I suppose we did feel more at ease among our own, but at the time it was for protection.

At the turn of the century, a small number of native-born women, wives of merchants and imported prostitutes com-posed the tiny female element in Chinatown's overwhelm-ingly male population. Men in Chinatown had three possible origins: native American Chinese who were born in China-town, native American Chinese who came into Chinatown from the rural settlements, and immigrants. Some of these immigrants entered the country legally under the provisions of the exclusion laws because they were merchants or members of a merchant's family. But many were members of the poor peasant families which had originally sent men as laborers to California. Dependent for their income on the employment of their men in America, these families sent men in with falsified birth certificates identifying them as sons of merchants or sons of native-born American Chinese (and therefore citizens according to federal law). Since there were many merchants who, for a small fee, willingly assumed "fatherhood" of these "paper sons," during the periods of strictest exclusion, the practice thrived. Frequent stories told by today's oldtimers describe how San Francisco's historic earthquake of 1906 provided thousands of men with the opportunity of becoming "paper citizens." Hay Ming Lee recalled:

In the beginning my father came in as a laborer. But the 1906 earthquake came along and destroyed all those immigration things. So that was a big chance for a lot of Chinese. They forged themselves certificates saying that they were born in this country, and then when the time came, they could go back to China and bring back four or five sons, just like that! They might make a little money off it, not much, but the main thing was to bring a son or a nephew or a cousin in.

Now my father thought he was even smarter than that. When he came in the second time he didn't use that native-born certificate he had. He got a certificate saying he was a student. But that didn't make sense at all. He thought he was so smart being a student, but then, if you come in as a student, how could you bring a son into this country? If he had used his birth certificate, I could have come in as a native son. Instead, we had to go back to the same old thing, "paper son." They had to send me over not as my own father's son, but as the son of another cousin from our village.

Excluded from participation in American political, social, and economic life, and offered minimal social welfare services only by a handful of Christian missions, Chinatown by the turn of the century had developed within itself a complicated organizational network to answer the vital needs of its population and to some extent to substitute for their lack of authentic family life. Molded partly by traditional social patterns carried over from Kwangtung and partly by the specific demands of the American situation, the richness of the organizational life thus evolved has been Chinatown's distinction among ethnic communities in America. On the one hand, because of constant competition between rival groups seeking to dominate the community by their control of various bodies, Chinatown's organizations have been the focus of almost incessant cleavage and conflict within the community. In the face of the most powerful threats from outside, however, they have proved capable of unifying and mobilizing Chinatown in the critical struggle for survival as a whole. By reinforcing its cohesiveness within and buffering it from hostile forces outside, they, have been an important source of the exceptional resilience and continuity of the community over its century of history.

A three-tiered institutional structure, in which the basic unit was the clan association,* encompassed the Chinatown remembered by oldtimers. It was on this level that the influence of Kwangtung custom was most conspicuous, for a striking characteristic of South China society was the predominance of kinship relations. Whole villages were made up of families whose male members claimed direct descent from a common ancestor thirty or more generations back, venerated in ancestral halls to perpetuate a sense of family continuity and unity. In Kwangtung villages no aspect of an individual's life took place outside of kinship relations, and men who left the villages to come to California set up institutions which resembled the clan associations in their native Kwangtung. Unlike clans in their villages, which were based on direct lineage, clans in America, because of the small size of the Chinatown population, were broadened to include all those who shared the same last name and, therefore, a mythical, common ancestor. The Wong, Lee, and Chin families were the largest and most powerful clans in Chinatown. Basic everyday needs were dealt with within the framework of the clan unit in which a sense of shared collective responsibility and mutual loyalty were central values. Thus, the most common form of housing in early Chinatown was the room shared by men with the same family name. The men slept and cooked here, all expenses were added and shared at the end of the year. Wei Bat Liu described the living arrangement during his first years in San Francisco.

In 1913, all the cousins from the Liu family in my village had one big room so all the members could fit in it, and we slept in that room, cooked in that room, one room. Anybody who

---

* Popularly known as Family Association.

had a job had to sleep outside the room, because he could afford to rent space and get a bed for himself. Anybody who couldn't find work slept in the beds in this room. At the end of the year, all the members would get together and figure out all the expenses. The ones that slept in the room most were willing to pay a little more. But even the ones who didn't sleep there were willing to pay something for the upkeep of the room.

In larger halls, which were set up as headquarters for the whole clan association, general councils were held, ritual obligations to the clan ancestor were carried out, and communication with village lineages was maintained through a secretary who wrote and read letters for the illiterate men. (And sometimes had to remind them to send remittances home!)

On the level above the clans, men were organized into larger groups according to their districts of origin in Kwangtung Province. In Chinatown at the turn of the century, almost all the population traced its derivation to the densely populated Pearl River Delta in Kwangtung. The Sze Yup or "Four Districts" (Sunwui, Toishan, Hoiping, Yanping) of Kwangtung were located southwest of the provincial capital, Canton. They were impoverished rural districts which had experienced nearly a century of disintegration and social upheaval. Most emigrants from these districts were poor peasants who became laborers, domestic servants, and, in fewer cases, labor contractors who negotiated the work of their countrymen for Americans. Seven out of ten Chinese in California are reported to derive their origin from the "Four Districts," four of the seven from Toishan alone. The Sam Yup or "Three Districts" (Namhoi, Punyu, Shuntak) were northern and adjacent to the city of Canton. The early emigrants from Sam Yup were small merchants and skilled craftsmen. Those who originated in Sam Yup, the wealthiest area in Kwangtung, spoke a more refined city dialect and regarded themselves as superior to the illiterate peasants from Sze Yup whose coarse village dialects were practically unintelligible to the men from Sam Yup. From the heartland of the Pearl River Delta, south of Canton, came Chungshan peasants who formed the second largest group next to the

Sze Yup. These peasants from the Chungshan district came to control the fish markets, the ladies' garment factories, and the chrysanthemum and aster farms along the California coast. Lastly the Hakkas, a traditionally despised minority which migrated to Kwangtung from northeastern China during the thirteenth century, formed their own district association and remained marginal to the society of early Chinatown. Linguistic differences reinforced the loyalty of these districts of origin.

Since the district associations were larger than the clan associations, they were more powerful in Chinatown. In the early period of the Chinese emigration, the district association welcomed incoming Chinese at the pier, provided employment, gave lodging and board, if necessary, until employment was found, provided medical attention for the sick, helped the infirm return to China, and arbitrated certain disputes of individuals within the district associations. Subdistrict groups known as the *sin tongs* or "fellow villagers' clubs" sent the bodies of the dead for burial in native villages. Because the larger clans were quickly dominated by the numerically strong Sze Yup members, men from Sam Yup and Chungshan districts withdrew and made "pseudo" family associations out of their *sin tong*, composed of men from neighboring villages.

At the pinnacle of the three-tiered structure, to resolve the almost constant feuds and disputes between clans and district associations, an arbitrating board, empowered with supreme jurisdiction within the community, had been organized from representatives of six district associations within the first decade of Chinatown's history. In 1880 this early arbitration board was consolidated on the advice of the Chinese consul in San Francisco to enhance its prestige in the fight against anti-Chinese legislation and was given the official title Chinese Consolidated Benevolent Association of America. At the turn of the century, however, it was popularly known, as it is now, as the Chinese Six Companies.

Merchants easily assumed a position of dominance on the three levels of clan association, district association, and Six Companies in the absence of China's upper classes of

gentry and scholar officials in Chinatown. In the early days
of immigration, their power had emanated out of their positions as brokers and contractors who extended credit and
negotiated employment for impoverished peasants seeking
passage to America. A substantial part of an immigrant's
time in America was spent working off this debt, contracted
at high interest rates to a merchant in Hong Kong who then
transferred the credit to another merchant in San Francisco.
This merchant, typically a member of the laborer's own
district association, negotiated the credit into a contract
with the laborer to work for an allotted period of time. In
addition to providing employment, merchant contractors in
the district associations were also the source of provisions,
imported rice and so forth, for the laborers and as elders
within the associations they controlled all decision-making
which affected the group as a whole. As the American
Chinese population grew, merchants, with their superior
wealth and education, received additional status by assuming positions as spokesmen who represented the community
to the outside. Thus while the leaders of family and district
associations offered certain benevolent services to the community, they were also in a position to exercise despotic
control through these institutions for the purpose of maintaining their own dominance. Every Chinese laborer who
left America to return to China was checked by an official
of his district association at the pier to make sure all of his
debts were paid and his financial obligations fulfilled. Even
if the man was completely clear, the district associations
required the payment of a special exit tax before he received
the exit license permitting him to leave. These taxes went to
support the activities of the district associations and later
the Chinese Six Companies.

Resentment against merchant domination of early Chinatown society found expression in the growth of a parallel
network of tongs which offered protection and security on
a more egalitarian basis. The tongs were patterned after
secret societies which flourished in eighteenth century
China and attracted unsuccessful scholars and merchants,
members of the lumpen-proletariat, and other discontented
elements of society. In time of economic and social crisis in

China, these societies often rose in rebellion against the established dynastic order. One of the most powerful of the secret societies in Kwangtung, the Triad Society, took part in the devastating and unsuccessful Taiping Rebellion (1851–1864). Although the Taiping armies did not operate in Kwangtung Province, members of the Triad Society led a series of rebellions known as the "Red Turbin Uprisings" in the Pearl River Delta between 1854 and 1864. After the suppression of the Taiping rebels, Triad members became involved in illegal activities such as piracy and smuggling. Some fled to America, where they established branches of the Triad Society known as the Chee Kung Tong. There are scattered reports of Chee Kung Tong extortion attempts in the early 1850s and of feuds between rival branches of the secret society for spheres of influence. Along with its illegal activities, however, the Chee Kung Tong remained dedicated to its political goal of the overthrow of the Manchus (Ch'ing Dynasty, 1644–1911) and the restoration of the Ming Dynasty, and continued to function as an international revolutionary network. At the end of the nineteenth century it was successfully harnessed by Dr. Sun Yat-sen's revolutionary movement which sought to topple the Manchu government and establish a new republic of China. The Triad Society welcomed Sun in overseas Chinese communities around the world and provided him with its own centers as a basis of operation.

American tongs combined both the anti-establishment and illegal tendencies of the Chinese secret societies. They drew their membership largely from discontented elements in society, particularly from men who lacked the family or geographic background to find a place in the institutional structure of Chinatown, or whose family associations were small and weak. Indigenous American tongs, however, while they were patterned after the Triad Society, did not share its international political perspective. In most cases, they were formed to deal with some local situation of oppression. In the 1880s, for instance, the Suey Sing Tong was set up as a fighting organization to overcome the domination of the Wong family. An even more central conflict motivating the formation of tongs was that between Sze Yup laborers and the wealthy Sam Yup merchant minority. In the late 1880s, twelve tongs banded together to do battle with the Sam Yup district association, and a fierce struggle for control took place throughout the 1890s until it terminated in a Sze Yup victory in 1896. During this entire period, as the prestige of the Six Companies fell to a low ebb because of its unsuccessful efforts to win a reversal in the exclusion laws, the tongs dominated Chinatown. While Chinese suffered restriction to marginal jobs as domestic servants, laundrymen, and vegetable peddlers, underworld activities flourished in Chinatown. Tong leaders, acting in complicity with city hall czars like Abe Ruef and "blind" officers of the police department, made huge profits from gambling and prostitution rackets, and "tong wars" for control of the rackets were numerous. It was only after the 1906 earthquake that the Six Companies with the help of Protestant missionaries and a small squad of police officers brought an end to this period of underworld control of Chinatown. After this time there was a tendency for merchants to enter tongs to seek protection for their businesses, attain leadership, and thus co-opt them. Tong wars, however, continued sporadically until the early thirties and sensational descriptions of them by white journalists sold like hotcakes on the newspaper stands. But for the majority of workingmen in Chinatown life consisted primarily of hard work. "Lot of people never belonged to a tong," a Chinese Christian told us. "Only mainly the gamblers. Of course, if you form a tong, you can all get together and fight back, it's stronger. That's why we had about twelve tongs in Chinatown then. But in the whole history of the tong wars there weren't that many people killed." It has been estimated that at their height of activity the number of professional fighting men in the tongs was no more than three thousand in the entire United States.

For the laborer in Chinatown, the main concern was simply to survive. The men remember the difficult search for employment, long hours of work, the small, crowded rooms where they lived with their cousins, two or three beds nailed one above another, like shelves, onto the walls. They remember periods when the room was so crowded that even those beds had to be used in shifts by the men going back and forth to work. They remember hauling crates from the streets of Chinatown up to the rooms to use as tables and cabinets, and, where there was no gas or electricity for heating and cooking, the crates were used as firewood. "You know, they never used those big crates again after they took the merchandise out," Hay Ming Lee said. "Just throw it out on the street. So we never had to buy firewood, we'd look around and bring some of that stuff up to burn in the stove."

At the end of the year, men living in the room would gather together to total their expenses and divide them. Some of the funds were used to keep a bed open in the room constantly for those who had no work. Another allotment was spent to keep a sack of rice in the room for the unemployed men. But it was never that difficult to find food in Chinatown. "We got by on what you'd call soul food," Johnny Wong joked. "You could walk down to the butcher shops near Italian town and with a purchase of 2½¢ worth of beef, they'd throw in the parsley and green onions free. I guess that's something the world will never see again— 2½¢ worth of pork and 2½¢ worth of beef." Johnny remembers the Chinese farmers near Colma and on the peninsula, who eked out a living by driving their wagons into the city every day, selling onions and parsley for a pittance to the thriving butcher shops. Hay Ming Lee still marvels at the price for a noontime meal. "At lunch hour, we could come out and go to any restaurant and two of us could get lunch for a nickel. A pot of coffee, two biscuits, and we'd bring it out and eat it. Just five cents!"

For entertainment, the men remember long nights visiting each other's rooms. They played mahjong and storytelling was a highly respected art. Almost any subject provided an opportunity to display one's skill as a debater. "Everything, anything that comes along to our minds we made a story out of it, and chat," Fong said.

Any subject that comes along. For instance, one time I had an argument with one guy about taxicabs. I came back to him with some news, I said, "You know, the taxicab used to go by the meter, but now you can go across town, the whole thing all the way through San Francisco for a dollar.

And it doesn't matter how many people there are, that's what they claim." So this guy here, he got hot head and he argued with me, said, "You're crazy. No such thing!" And he argued with me. He said, "You mean to tell me you gonna carry coupla bars of gold up a hill, would you be willing to carry one bar or would you be willing to carry five? Like five passengers in a car." I said, "Now look, this is going a little too damn far! You're talking about carrying gold and I'm talking about taxicab!" See, he's absolutely a thickhead. See, I mean we talked about everything.

On free days when it was still light and the weather was good, they would stroll around Chinatown or maybe gather in Portsmouth Square. In the evenings there was opium smoking or the theater on Kearny Street. "Kearny Street used to have a regular show. It wasn't a burlesque, but they did have dancing girls and all that, and next door was the regular movie house, for five cents. We'd go there all the time."

We discovered in Chinatown's oldtimers a deep resentment of the curious and exotic picture of their lives which prevailed in white society at the turn of the century. We were surprised, early in our first summer, when we eagerly questioned Gim Chang, a retired rice merchant, about old books and newspaper accounts of Chinatown we had found in the library. Did he remember sword dancers who performed in the streets? we asked him. "No." The actor Ah Chic? "No." There were repeated negatives as we went through the geography we had studied from the old books. Finally we got to the notorious network of underground tunnels, filled with opium dens and gambling joints. Gim exploded:

You read about underground tunnels in old Chinatown? I know nothing about them. I'm quite sure they didn't exist at all. When I was a boy, you know, I used to follow the older boys everywhere and I knew all the dirty, secret places. When white people come to Chinatown looking for curiosities I used to tag along behind the Chinese they took as guides, but I never saw an underground tunnel. Just mahjong rooms in the basements. I know there was a man on Jackson Street who lived in a dirty house with sand and mud floors and never took a bath in all his life. "The dirtier the better" was his motto for making money with the tourists. And there were a lot of people who visited Chinese ladies, to look at their small feet. I myself rarely left Chinatown, only when I had to buy American things downtown. The area around Union Square was a dangerous place for us, you see, especially at nighttime before the quake. Chinese were often attacked by thugs there and all of us had to have a police whistle with us all the time. I was attacked there once on a Sunday night, I think it was about eight P.M. A big thug about six feet tall knocked me down. I remember, I didn't know what to do to defend myself, because usually the policeman didn't notice when we blew the whistle. But once we were inside Chinatown, the thugs didn't bother us.

Isolation and resentment developed a strong orientation to China, a pride in being Chinese, which is marked in all the old men of this generation. For many oldtimers, the visit of Dr. Sun Yat-sen to San Francisco in 1910 is still a proud memory. Inspired by Sun's speeches in large auditoriums and in the basement rooms of the Chee Kung Tong, many of them joined his revolutionary party, the Tung Meng Hui, and devoted themselves heart and soul to his movement. It was laboring men and members of the Chee Kung Tong who gave Sun his broadest support in Chinatown as opposed to the Six Companies, which already had strong ties with the established government of China. These men joined the underground party, although a death penalty was set by the Manchus for any member, or his relatives if the member were in America. They raised funds, set up newspapers, and even returned to Canton during certain periods of the struggle. Yet at the same time their memories of Sun and the inspiration he gave them reveal the depth of isolation and frustration which existed in their own lives here in America. It is as if, excluded, rejected, and even physically beaten by the white society around them, they transposed the sense of oppression which permeated their everyday lives into the context of Chinese society of which they still could claim to be a part. John Jeong, recalling his sense of inspiration when he first heard Sun speak, seemed unconsciously to be describing his position in America. "As Doctor Sun spoke, everything he said seemed to be true. We had no rights, no freedom, we were not proud of ourselves. He gave us the courage and hope to overthrow the men who oppressed us."

JOHN JEONG, 84

A retired dry goods clerk, he still keeps the medal he won for recruiting new members to Sun Yat-sen's revolutionary party, the Tung Meng Hui.

In 1900 the Immigration Office was not on Angel's Island, it was upstairs on the pier. So when I arrived in this country I had to stay in the place on the pier about two weeks, because they were investigating my case. There was a big room there, for everyone to sleep in, and then a big eating hall with long tables. I remember we ate our meals standing up and we weren't allowed to write letters there. Finally they said I and a few others were alright. They put us in a horse carriage and we drove into Chinatown. It was an open carriage with standing room only. Halfway there some white boys came up and started throwing rocks at us. The driver was a white man, too, but he stopped the carriage and chased them away. I was thirteen at the time.

My brother had me start second grade at the Oriental School. I went there for two years. Then I wanted to change over to the American school on Geary Street, but after I was there a week someone told me it was not for Chinese. We were only supposed to go to the Oriental School. So after that I just studied at home and worked in my brother's store.

Everyday our friends would come in and visit with us while we were working in the store. Oh, they talked about business, and as I got older I got interested in politics. One day in 1909 our friend Mr. Wu brought Dr. Sun Yat-sen into the store. Of course I recognized him because I had seen his face in pictures. I knew he was fighting against the Manchus and he had already lost a few battles in Kwangtung Province.

Yes, I admired Dr. Sun even before I met him. There were so many people in Chinatown who agreed with him! At that time, you see, we Chinese seemed to be without a country.

We were just the servants of the Manchus, just like slaves, doing what we were told. If we didn't obey, they cut off our heads. But Dr. Sun spoke to us about China and told us not to be afraid. He said we could defeat the Manchus even without any arms. If we were patient and strong, he said, his organization could take positions in the government quietly, and seize their arms. Then Chinese people could become free again.

I went to some speeches and listened to all of Dr. Sun's ideas. Some friends and I decided to join his party, so we invited him to talk with us and have dinner with us at the Kam Wah Restaurant. When dinner was over we went up to his room and he gave us each a paper to sign so we could become members of the party. I was just twenty-one years old then, you know! In order to join, I had to have someone to introduce me, so Brother Choy was my sponsor. Then after we signed they told us about the party. Did you ever hear about the signs we had to use? We learned that when you meet a stranger, you should check to see if he is a member of the party or not. First shake his hand and scratch the inside of his palm a little. Second, if he is a member, he will ask you, "What's the matter today?" And you say, "The world's affairs." Third, he asks you, "What kind of person are you?" And you answer, "I am a citizen of the Republic of China." Just as I was joining the party, the newspaper the *Young China Daily* was started, and I became very busy working there. I used to do setting and printing and sometimes even on Sunday I worked until one o'clock at night.

In March 1910, there was a big uprising in Canton. It failed and many of our members were killed. In July and August 1910, I decided to go back to help the cause. I was ready to do anything they asked. If I had been told to fight, I was ready to die for our revolution. But I didn't learn how to fight when I was in America. Our China was very poor then and Dr. Sun had told us that our main job in America was to raise funds. So I was not trained to fight, and when I went back to China, the best thing I could do was work on a newspaper again. I joined the *China Press* in Hong Kong. I didn't see much change when I was back in China in 1910. The only difference was that many people sympathized with the cause, and there were many magazines and books and songs about our party. But all in all, I had the impression there was no progress in China and the Manchu government was still losing in its dealings with the foreigners. I stayed about one year in China. In 1911 I came back to the States.

LELAND CHIN, 73

When we meet him, he is bending over an open drawer and stacks of paper are on his desk. He is preparing to retire from the staff of the Young China Daily, *founded by Sun Yat-sen when Leland Chin was a student. A bank clerk, he was active during the 1930s and 1940s in the Cathay Post of the American Legion, which pressed for the right of naturalization for Chinese. He was also a member of the Chinese-American Citizens Alliance, a civil rights group for native-born Chinese.*

My father came over here in 1877, and when he first came in he worked in a hemp factory. You know, in those days it was slave labor, and besides, it was hard to get a job. And my father went around and peddled vegetables. In those days they carried two baskets over their shoulders, so he peddled vegetables for a while and then, later on, he learned to be a tailor, and he ran around and peddled ladies' wear. In those days, there were a lot of, you know what I mean, they had red lights and all that district, and my father was making all this ladies' wear to sell down around the red light district. Then later on he and a few cousins organized a little shop, and then from that shop, they kept growing, and grew until the business was destroyed by the earthquake. My father never had much education, but he picked up English pretty well. So in those days, if you could speak English it meant a lot to the community, to the individual, it's quite a qualification. Also, when you knew how to speak English, the community always asked you to be an interpreter, and then you had a chance to contact a lot of Caucasian friends. So that's how my father started business, and he would go down to the wholesalers and suppliers, and he did quite well at it. He made quite a little fortune.

And then the earthquake came and everything was destroyed. It was in April 1906. And it was around five o'clock in the morning. We were all in bed. In those days we only had a gas light, didn't have electricity in the house. But you could still have hot water, because people used to have a little hook, you see, get a little wire, and get a pot, and let the jet, the flame of the gas light heat the water. So when you get up in the morning, there's the hot water! (Laughs) So the day of the earthquake, it happened, my, where I slept, it happened they had the pot there, and it struck out the gas light, and it shake and the water spilt, see. And the water dripped on my head, I feel a little hot, I wake up, and here everything is shaking. And then, it shook quite a while, and of course I was only a child, but, then, here went everything tumbling down! And then I went out to the door, and looked out way down California Street. I used to live on California Street, where the Dr. Sun Yat-sen statue is, we used to have a lot of wooden buildings on the block, and the first thing you know there's a big crack there. And the street had a big hole there. And then later on the sparks, the fire, the blaze began to start down around Montgomery Street, along the financial district. At that time only the Merchants' Exchange Building was there, that's about the highest building they have, and just about all, all the whole building was enveloped with flame.

At six o'clock the flames began to spread and they got around about to Kearny Street. And then our family went down to Taylor Street. My father had a shop down on Taylor Street. And from there the whole family, and our employees and neighbors in our building, began to move. And some of these ladies had small feet. Like my mother was a villager, she had small feet, do you see what a hardship it was on these women walking that way? Finally we got up to the park at Washington and Steiner and we rested up there. In the morning the army came in and noticed a big group of Chinese all in the park there without any shelter or any food, so they got the army truck and took us to stay in the Praesidio. Then when communications were restored, the ferry boat took us over to Oakland.

In the meantime, during this running, this escape, some of the children got lost, and of course you know how mothers worry about the old people, might be lost in the fire. So some of them stayed in Oakland to wait for the lost ones and some of them went up to Richmond.

Now Richmond in those days was nothin' but shrimp camps. There was a lot of shrimp in the bay, and at least thirty shrimp camps in Richmond. Sure, all Chinese! Everything was Chinese in those days. They started everything, you know. Oh, a lot of things in agriculture, in farming. When they started fishing shrimp, you know, they got all their nets from China. The Americans said, "Those Chinese are really able to do a lot of things we never thought of!" And then, Chinese were the first ones to get the abalone. In those days the Americans didn't even know what abalone was. They said, "Is *that* something to eat?" "It's so dirty!" But the Chinese people got the abalone. And the crab. Then later on, they knew how to get all the seaweed and dry it and make nice soup! Oh, there's so many things that the Chinese started! Asparagus, too! And they were laughing at the Chinese, "Why do you eat grass? That grass is for the horses!" But the Chinese knew that where that grass was coming up there was a little sprout coming up, and they thought, "That must be good!" you know, the green part, so they plucked it up in the middle and got it out, and it actually turned out to be asparagus!

Now we left Oakland and went up the Sacramento River and settled around there. My father went down and opened a store in Isleton to begin with. Not a ladies' wear because there's no such customer down there (laughs), but he opened a store to cater to the farmers. You know, candy for the children or whatever they needed. And then he had the foresight to say, "Well, if I pay three and a half for a dozen shirts, if I buy gross, it only costs us two and a half." And he said, "Well, why don't I spread out?" and then he opened a store in Walnut Grove. And then later on he opened another one in Locke. You know these old gentlemen were pretty wise (laughs), those days they had no schooling, but still, they figured on the cost.

Well, in 1910, my parents sent me back to San Francisco because Orientals weren't allowed in the schools down there. I was going to Lowell High School, and there I met some young Chinese students. They were really disheartened by the way China had been surrendering her rights, you know, giving up each territory and making all these unequal treaties, giving extraterritorial rights. So they said we had to find some way to get rid of the Manchurian dynasty, and that was to revolt. And they were talking about how Dr. Sun Yat-sen was the man who started this revolution, and we got together, and then Dr. Sun came over that year. Of course, he wanted a lot of young men to join his revolutionary movement. So these three or four schoolmates and I joined him. The Tung Meng Hui had already been started, so we began to bring in new members. At the same time, these people needed a mouthpiece, so we started the newspaper.

Then my father got interested in it, too. He joined, and gave some money, so Dr. Sun naturally went up to Locke and spoke about his movement there. Pretty soon about thirty or forty percent of the people joined. Later on they set up Kuo Ming Tang (Chinese Nationalist Party) branches in Cortland, Walnut Grove, and Isleton. In Cortland there were the most members, because all the farmers were concentrated up there in the fruit orchards. You see, Dr. Sun Yat-sen was from Chungshan,* and the farmers were mostly from Chungshan. So they were all in favor of a man from their own district. Of course, some of them didn't even understand what the movement was, because they had no learning, just came here as laborers. A lot of these people formerly worked on the railroad. Then they drifted around, drifted around, and finally they settled down in the valley because they had a cousin or someone who was already there. So pretty near the whole area was Chungshan people.

* A small rural district south of Canton.

And that's one reason why so many people around that area belonged to Dr. Sun's movement.

Another reason was, even before he came, we heard so much about Dr. Sun, about his escape, about how he went to Japan and London, the news spread around pretty fast. And people began to understand Dr. Sun Yat-sen because at the same time, they knew they've been discriminated against, and pushed around so much, I mean our people in this country had been pushed around so much they wanted some way to, sort of revenge, to get themselves a better way to survive. Survive all these different discriminations and kick around, you know. You can't even go into a restaurant and sit down and enjoy a meal. You're afraid to go in the barbershop and get yourself a haircut. Things like that.

In 1915 we moved up to Locke again. And then in 1917 I was the first Chinese to be drafted. When the United States entered the World War, when they sank the Lusitania, we were forced to join. I heard in the paper they were going to draft men and I got a hunch I would be the first one to go. So then I read the paper and then the next thing I knew it's me, and I figured, "Oh, by God, I get a chance to see the world in the United States Army!" (laughs). Anyway, so I got my little card, beanie, and so forth, and I went up to Sacramento and those men gave me an examination. OK, all set, first thing I know I was shipped up to Camp Lewis, then to Camp Muir, and the next thing we knew we were over in France. Spent Christmas in the transport.

Well, nothing brilliant or conspicuous about myself in the army. After a couple of weeks I got appendicitis. When I got out of the hospital I didn't go back to the front again. I was working as a houseboy in the Officers' Training School.

In Europe, I found a lot of coolie labor there. The French people brought, oh, I figure about ten thousand, maybe not exactly coolies, but laborers over to work on the railroad, do all the storage work and move heavy equipment. I didn't talk to them because they were mostly Mandarins, from the North. But they were big, husky fellows, because they were selected to really work. They wore that cotton clothing, you

know, they all wore blue uniforms. And after work they'd
go into a stockade, they had no freedom, they just went into
a stockade. And oh, the way it looked to me, why is a man
working if after he finishes work he goes in a stockade? I
don't know, it just kinda hurt . . . the way you feel. Everything is so, you know. They're human beings, they like to
have a little fun, but when they finish working, bang, you
go in the stockade and you're locked up till the next morning, sort of like a bunch of cattle or a bunch of horses. And
probably when their contract's finished they'll load them on
the freight boats and ship them back, just like the way we
went overseas. Like the colored people, they were nothing
but scavengers, they were doing scavenger work, they
shipped them over there to do cleanup work. They put them
in the bottom of the boat, and then they couldn't go past a
certain part, and then they warned all the soldiers not to go
down there. It, it hurts your feelings, you know. Or maybe
it's just people like me, in the minority group, that feel it.
The other boys, they don't feel it. In my company out of
about two hundred twenty-five, two hundred fifty people,
I was the only Chinese boy. Only one Japanese and myself.
But even in the army you can feel this thing.

LEW WAH GET, 84
An officer of the Suey Sing Tong

*A quiet and soberly dressed man, he, too, likes to spend
time chatting in the square.*

*He tells us the tongs are slowly dying out in Chinatown
today. Here and there on the streets and alleys, you can
still see the unpainted doors of small rooms owned by the
tongs, but they are shabby places, secondhand couches and
spittoons inside, mahjong tables, a heater, someplace to
prepare food in the back. You can get a meal in a tong room
for 25¢, if you're a member; you can warm up and chat with
friends when the weather is cold. But the same men are
there all the time, says Lew Wah Get, and there are only a
few of them. "In the old days, when there was mostly men
living in Chinatown, there was a place for the tongs.*

Women, gambling . . . well, those were part of a single man's life, and we needed to protect each other, too. But today our Suey Sing Tong doesn't have a purpose any longer."

When we asked what the tongs still do, he told us that since the crackdown on prostitution and gambling concessions at the end of the thirties, income has been severely limited. Leaders of big tongs like the Suey Sing and Bing Kang are still influential men in the community, but this is largely because they hold important positions in other organizations as well. The tongs do provide a few services for the retired laborers, many of whom are quite poor, that make up their constituency. If a member becomes ill, the tong sends someone to arrange for medical attention and will cover bills if the member himself cannot. If a member dies destitute, the tong will pay for his funeral. At New Year's, ten days of free meals are offered by the tong.

I first heard about the Suey Sing Tong in 1917. All the gambling houses were prospering around that time. I decided that if I went to work in one, I might make a better living than by working as a cook. I knew that in Stockton, especially, there were lots of gambling houses. People used to say that the Chinatown there was just one street long, with the businesses on one side of the street, and nothing but gambling houses on the other. I learned that all these houses were owned by the Suey Sing Tong. So when I went to Stockton and became involved in one of the houses as a dealer, I also became a member of the tong.

If you wanted to join a tong, you had to have a friend who was already a member sponsor you. He had to swear to your good character, and even then the tong would investigate your name for one month before they let you in. This was the rule for everybody. You could be a cook, a waiter, work in a gambling house or do any kind of work, but you had to have a friend to sponsor you. And once you were a member, you were on your honor to follow all the rules. If you did, then the tong would protect you. If anyone threatened you, or interfered with your business, the tong would help you out. Or if you couldn't find a job, the tong would send you someplace, or introduce you to someone who could give you work. This was why so many people wanted to join.

After you were in the tong for one year, you were eligible to become an officer. Only officers could participate in the business meetings, while the other members had no say. I became friendly with many different members and learned quite a bit about the affairs of the tong. So I was chosen to be a liaison officer, and held that post for over ten years. My job was to handle business between our tong and other tongs. If another tong wanted to have some transaction with us, I would discuss the matter with them, listen to their proposals, and then report back to our tong so a decision could be made. Fighting was a very frequent issue. If members of our tong had been threatened or their businesses tampered with, naturally we had to take steps to protect them. Or suppose another party owed us money and refused to pay, we might decide to bear a grudge and force retribution. Sometimes, when the other party kept refusing to pay, that's how trouble started.

I was an officer during the last big fight in 1921. Our tong paid to bring a woman over here, but then the Hop Sing Tong took her and refused to pay us back for the expense. Not only that, while they were doing business with us, they shot and killed one of our members. Society at that time was very dangerous, you know. It's not like today where there are so many laws to regulate what you do. We decided to take revenge and fight back. That fight lasted ten months and we had to have a committee from outside to settle it. I don't remember how much money we got in the end.

Well, after the Sino-Japanese war our people were not so old-fashioned any more. During the war, many people began to say, "The Japanese are attacking us, why are we fighting among ourselves?" The Chinese people here realized we were one people and we saw no purpose in fighting each other. We cooperated in different projects to save China, such as raising funds. We all worked together. Chiang Kai-shek was our hero then. Later, when he was handling affairs, we were very disappointed. Chiang Kai-shek wanted to make the nation strong, but he did not work for the whole of China.

The new China? Yes, I know about it. I read about it in the papers. Whenever there's a new movie down at Kearny Street, I go, along with the other old people who want to pay their respects to their country. With Mao Tse-tung China is different. He works for the whole people. Whether the nation is strong or not is not the question. The point is that he has given machines and highways to the people. In the movies I saw a bridge being built across the Yangtze River. Friends who have left China have told me that the rice paddies now are bigger than any I have ever seen. I'm Chinese and this makes me feel proud. The white man can't look down on us any more.

You know, when I first came over here as a teenager to work on the levees, we were stoned when we got off the ship. We weren't allowed to leave Angel's Island because they said our feces had worms in them. They fed us like pigs because they thought we were filthy. Finally a group of old men came and led us into Chinatown. But on the way, people shouted, "Chink! Chink! Chink!" and threw stones at us again. After I went to Merced, working as a cook and a waiter, I made five dollars a week minus seventy-five cents for every dish I broke. I had no money to go to school. No wonder I can't speak English! But as a Chinese, I know what China was like before and now. Before, we used to lower our eyes before the white man. Now we can look straight at them without being afraid.

LILAC CHEN, 84

She was "rescued" as a young girl by Donaldina Cameron and worked as an interpreter for many years at the Presbyterian Mission House in Chinatown.

She opens the door of her small room at the Conifer, a home for retired missionaries, with a cane. She is wearing a dress of brilliant blue and her hair, still dark and thick, is pulled back into a full braid. The room is immaculate. Sun beats through gleaming glass onto the potted plant on the

*windowsill. There are careful rows of photographs, paint-
ings, tiny shelves of Chinese knick-knacks attached to the
wall. She asks if we would like a sweet drink, and seems
disappointed when we decline. But she says, "Of course,
we should get busy with our work right away." She sits
down, bows her head, and says a short prayer asking God to
bless our undertaking.*

*Across the room is an old-fashioned desk and a cabinet
built over the writing surface with glass doors. Three photographs in circular frames stand on the top shelf. "There's
Miss Cameron, she always used to have a piece of hair
falling in her face. She was the baby of the family, you
know." She points to the picture in the middle. "This one,
on the right, is my dear, beloved benefactor, Mr. Coleman.
And this other one is my sister and I, back in China, all
dolled up. They must have put fancy clothes on us just for
the pictures because I never remember wearing anything
like that."*

I was six when I came to this country in 1893. My worthless
father gambled every cent away, and so, left us poor. I
think my mother's family was well-to-do, because our
grandmother used to dress in silk and satin and always
brought us lots of things. And the day my father took me,
he fibbed and said he was taking me to see my grandmother,
that I was very fond of, you know, and I got on the ferry
boat with him, and Mother was crying, and I couldn't understand why she should cry if I go to see Grandma. She gave
me a new toothbrush and a new washrag in a blue bag when
I left her. When I saw her cry I said, "Don't cry, Mother, I'm
just going to see Grandma and be right back." And that
worthless father, my own father, imagine, had every inclina-
tion to sell me, and he sold me on the ferry boat. Locked me
in the cabin while he was negotiating my sale. And I kicked
and screamed and screamed and they wouldn't open the
door till after some time, you see, I suppose he had made
his bargain and had left the steamer. Then they opened
the door and let me out and I went up and down, up and
down, here and there, couldn't find him. And he had left
me, you see, with a strange woman. That woman, it was

suppertime, took me to Ningpo, China, to eat, and I refused to eat, I wanted to go home, and then she took me after dinner to Shanghai and left me with another woman. That woman never asked me to work, and was very kind to me, and I was there I don't know for how long. Then a woman from San Francisco came, and picked me up and brought me over.

Oh, God has just been wonderful. Just think, I was in such close waters for damnation myself! This woman, who brought me to San Francisco, was called Mrs. Lee, and she kept the biggest dive in San Francisco Chinatown. Oh, she had a lot of girls, slave girls, you know. And every night, seven o'clock, all these girls were dressed in silk and satin, and sat in front of a big window, and the men would look in and choose their girls who they'd want for the night. Of course, I didn't know anything, never heard about such things, you know. And whenever police or white people came, they always hid me under the bed and pushed a trunk in front of me and then after the police had left they let me come out again. And I saw these girls all dressed in silk and satin, and they were waiting for their business, see. But I didn't know anything.

When this woman needed money, she had to sell me to another party. Everywhere I had been they were very kind to me, except this last place she sent me. Oh, this woman was so awful! They say she was a domestic servant before and was cruelly treated. She used to make me carry a big fat baby on my back and make me to wash his diapers. And you know, to wash you have to stoop over, and then he pulls you back, and cry and cry. Oh, I got desperate, I didn't care what happened to me, I just pinched his cheek, his seat you know, just gave it to him. Then of course I got it back. She, his mother, went and burned a red hot iron tong and burnt me on the arm. Then someone reported me to the home. But they described me much bigger than I was so when they came they didn't recognize me. And then the woman who had reported to the mission said, "Why didn't you take her? She's the girl." They said, "She looked too small," and then they came back again. But even then, they weren't sure that I was the one, so they undressed me and

examined my body and found where the woman had beaten
me black and blue all over. And then they took me to the
home. Oh, it was in the pouring rain! I was scared to death.
You know, change from change, and all strangers, and I
didn't know where I was going. Away from my own people
and in the pouring rain. And they took me, a fat policeman
carried me all the way from Jackson Street, where I was
staying, to Sacramento Street to the mission, Cameron
House. So I got my freedom there.

After I helped Miss Cameron I had five dollars a month
and I saved and saved and then went to China and thought
I could find my village. I couldn't find my family, you know,
never got there. But I felt I must come back to help Cameron
House because they had helped to rear me—well, I tell you,
all I've been through! And yet when I look back I'm so glad
I heard about Jesus and know all about Him, and He took
care of me. Just think of the narrow chance! So many girls
were sold to be prostitutes, you know. And why should I
be exempt? It is only the mercy of God.

The work I did with Miss Cameron was called rescue
work. We would find the Chinese girls who were sold to
work in the dives, or as domestic servants, and bring them
to Cameron House so they could be free. Sometimes people
reported to us or sometimes the slave girls themselves
would slip a note under our front door and we would find
it, and go to the place where the girl wanted to be rescued.
Usually we had to go to the dives. When we went on the
raid we always took several of our own girls with us to help.
Generally I would follow Miss Cameron as interpreter and
she and I would go into the house through a door or a window. Sometimes the slave girls got scared and ran out, so
the other girls from the home had to wait outside and grab
them when they tried to run away. Then when they caught
the girl they would blow the police whistle, so we knew.
After we got the girl, sometimes we had to go to court over
thirty times to free her from her owner. They always get
the best attorney and they're so smart, you know, these
slaveowners. They had lots of money to spend and they
always found out where the girls were. I remember the first
time I went to interpret before Judge Coffee, how he teased

me! When I was young I had very rosy cheeks and a round face, they say. When people came to visit the mission they saw me and, see, Chinese never had rosy cheeks. So one American woman actually wet her handkerchief and rubbed my cheeks to see if the color would come off. And then, she finally decided it was natural (laughs).

Oh dear, there were certainly hard times. One time we went back to Marysville, we had rescued a young slave girl and two little children in a brothel, and we had to go back to Marysville for the hearing. Oh my, we went and on the way we had to stop at a little country town. Oh, it was black and just a tiny kerosene oil lamp, you know, at the window there. We didn't have a searchlight or anything so Miss Cameron would have to go to each room and feel the bed to see if anybody was there. And when she found a body, she would go to another room. Finally she found a room, and, oh my, you should see the black! Bedsheets filthy and Miss Cameron had to take it off and turn it inside out, and just lie on it. Just black and pillowslips, black, you know. But that's all the place we had to sleep, because in the morning we had to be in Marysville to go to court with this girl.

All sorts of things, it's a wonder we never got all diseases. Poor Miss Cameron, she never knew about these dives when she was growing up, you know. Scottish people, especially the refined, never discussed these things, they never heard of it, you know. So nobody told her, she was so innocent. These slave girls used to have terrific sores, and she had to dress the sores, you know. She never wore gloves, you see, and really, it's just the providence of God kept her from these diseases.

But also, the police always had raids, you see. That is why the dives had thick doors to protect themselves. I think some of the white officers took bribes, but still they made one big raid every year. They didn't seem to arrest the owners until years later, but they would get the girls, you see, and send these girls to our mission home. When they got there, oh my, you ought to see them! They didn't want to stay, and they spit on the chairs they were sitting on and tried to be as cussed as possible. Oh, we just dreaded to

have them come! And when we had new girls we always
have to hide them between the folding doors, you know.
That's because they're small, you see. And then another
place under the shelf was this gas meter, we used to hide
them there. Because the slaveowners would get writ of
habeas corpus, to try to get them back. And they would
search the whole house, even dig into our rice bins to see
if we put any there!

Sometimes highbinders would come for the family to try
to rescue them. One time they came for a girl, oh, there was
an empty house next door and we had to hide her, so we
pulled a rotten board out of the floor and let her into the
empty house so she could escape from there. The whole
school was surrounded by these highbinders, watching out.

But after the girls were with us for over a year, we could
scarcely find any employment for them. And they just
couldn't do without money, you see. In that other life, they
have men friends who take them out, lavish money on them,
and they're used to good food, and silk and satin clothes.
The mission, of course, gave them just the plainest clothing.
So most of them didn't want to stay. Well, it was hard sometimes, living at the home. We had no toys whatever because
the mission board was stricter then, you see. We all had to
make our own toys. I remember, oh, I was dying to learn to
jump rope, and we couldn't get a rope. I picked up lots of
ends in the backyard, just short ones and tied them together.
The basement ceiling was low, so another thing I tried to do
was make the rope into a swing and kick up to the ceiling.
I thought I was kicking very high, but of course the ceiling
was low, you know. And I really had fun that way.

Then one time, you see, the big girls never let us into the
kitchen because we got in the way, but there was a lattice
in the basement where you could look in. I saw somebody
throw rotten potato seeds down there once and I kept thinking, if they had sprouted there must be potatoes inside. But
nobody dared go in and see for fear of the ghost. So finally,
I was anxious to get those potatoes to eat, so I said, "Now
I'll be your captain," and we took a tin oil can this big and
that wide and a stick, and I was the leader going into this
basement under the ground. And I bang, bang, bang to chase

the spirits away so we could get to the other end where the potatoes were and we dug the potatoes. Then after the girls were through for the night and nobody was in the kitchen we went in and washed the potatoes and put them in the oven.

Sometimes I also used to try to remember what I had to play with in China. Suddenly I thought of the boat people. They wear something like Japanese shoes, you know, wooden. And I would get two bricks from under the basement and tie one on each foot. During the rain I'd get a big pole and then pretended I was a boatwoman and called out my wares. "Gee Gou Ma Tai Le!" Those are the things they sell, you know. And then one time, we found a little bird that died and we decided to give him a pagan burial! Like the Chinese ones we always saw, you know. So we went out to the backyard. And mourning is all white for the Chinese, so we got bedsheets, and draped ourselves. The chief mourner, Yahoo was her name, knew all kinds of incantations. So she was the chief Buddhist. And she said all these things and we just ducked down one on each side of her with the white bedsheet, and we were the deep mourners. And she would cry out all the sad tones, "Aiya! Aiya!" You know, it just sounds like a cry.

I went East to school, just a year before the earthquake and fire. I told Mr. Coleman, my benefactor, "I need more schooling, because I have to go to court to interpret" because I didn't understand all the English, and, you know, the American attorneys like to use technical terms. Especially when they see a helpless, inexperienced girl, they choose harder words, you know. I remember the first case I went before Judge Coffee and when they just started the case, Judge Coffee said, "Wait a minute, I have something to say." Then he turned around, and he said, "What made you throw those eyes at me?" I had very rosy cheeks, round face, and fat, you know. And then, I went on a court case before Judge Graham, he was another one. The case had been started, it was in the midst of hearing, and, oh, that day it just poured cats and dogs. And of course, you wear your old hat. I wore my old slouch cap and raincoat. And as soon as he started the case, he said, "I would like to

know who's going to pay the Mission Home interpreter."
Then he started in and asked some questions, but then he
stopped again and said, "But I wanted to know who is going
to pay the interpreter's fee, for she needs a new hat."
(Laughs) Aren't they crazy, for a judge on the stand! They
just loved to tease me, for I looked innocent, you know,
and rosy cheeks, and I guess they thought they were having
lots of jokes with me.

BIG PETE, 72
A gambler

*Big Pete has been a member of the Suey Sing Tong for
over forty years. He came to San Francisco from Kwangtung
in 1905.*

*His chivalrous manner and slightly drawling English
reveal the influence of Texans with whom he served in the
36th Division, World War II. We find him sitting alone in
the Buddha Bar, a handsome man with a portly mustache
and a tweed suit. He is absorbed in his thoughts, melan-
choly, but when we introduce ourselves he responds with
expansive gestures and a droll smile. "Call me Big Pete.
That's how everyone knows me." We ask Big Pete if he
has lived in Chinatown a long time. "Oh, sure, I'm a famous
man around here, you know!"*

Well, it's the same like any other gambling, same as anywhere. You go to one, you go to every one. But then in those
days it's more like cat eat dog, you know. There's one place
run by one certain tong, another place run by another tong,
and whenever there's a beef there's always shooting and
everything else, but you don't see that any more. Now all
the tongs have a share in one gambling house, two houses,
whatever they allow for Chinatown. That's the only way
they can open up.

Well, you don't know about this and if I was you I'd stay
out. But all Chinese people know, especially gamblers, they
go to one place all the time. They don't move around like
they used to when, well, it was before your time, but do

you remember Sergeant Mannion? He was an inspector and there was another inspector, Sergeant Dyer, and they were rough men. When they raided a place, anybody behind the table, if you don't get off that stool they'll bang the table against you. I went through that a lot of times. I mean they were cruel, they just didn't want anybody to gamble. And they have a point there, but all Chinese people, regardless wherever you go, gambling is their life. Now, the police are more relaxed because they're getting paid, and they don't allow so many places to open up. But years ago when it was wide open there was a lot of places, and these old big-timers, they used to bring girls from the old country to work in the gambling houses.

Well, I don't have to tell you exactly what they do, but they were called what they call "call girls." And I mean, you have to be somebody before they even go out with you! Even for dinner they won't go out with you. Because the one that brought them over here tells them what to do and where to go and what time to bring the money home and all that. It's different nowadays, it's whatever you can pick up, the girls are on their own. But in those days you don't go out and solicitate, you work in the house and you live in the house. There's no such thing as living by yourself. Nowadays they're running around in the streets doin' what they want for themselves, or maybe supporting a boyfriend, but in those days there was a madam to take care of those girls, and what she says goes. You don't listen to anything and back to the old country you go, see.

I mean, they were not exactly slaves, but the madam always got the money. The money has to be in her hand before she let the girls go. She said, "Be sure you bring them back by a certain time." And those madams, they belong to all these tongs here, so if they make a squawk, you better get your fanny out of Chinatown! If you don't bring in the girls like you promised, at a certain time, the hatchetmen will go after you, see. They're out looking for you already. And you can't get through these people because they all know the ropes. They'll probably throw you out in the river someplace, or in the desert, and nobody can catch them.

Now, you want to know how a lot of tong wars started? Say, I own a girl and somebody tries to take her away from me and he succeeds. If he happens to belong to a different tong or a different family, that's it. He pays the damage. Like, if it cost five thousand dollars to get her into the United States, he can have her, but he gotta pay that five thousand dollars or he'll never see those lights again! (Laughs) That's exactly the way it was! Sure a lot of people's crazy to fall in love with somebody, but that somebody don't happen to belong to you. It cost a man money to bring that girl over here. She's makin' money for him, because she have to pay that money back. So it's worse than bein' a slave to be what they call a "call girl." You go out and slave, you make that money.

A lot of the time I used to work in a restaurant. Even when I was a kid I worked in my uncle's restaurant in Oakland. Then, in the thirties, in the Depression, I was workin' in a restaurant here for a while. Oh, I'll tell you, the Depression was nothin' much. I was doin' better than I did before, in fact. Got a new suit every couple of weeks. Only thing is, there was too many picket lines, you know. And it's hard to buy food. But being a Chinese, and working in a Chinese restaurant, you can buy all your Chinese food there. Of course it's not one of these big restaurants where they have banquets and all that. We had a few booths, a balcony, and we had two cooks, one dishwasher, I was the waiter. But I made more money than the chief cook.

Yeah. I'd say between two o'clock and closing time was when all these, well, people that's in the money come in. You'd take care of one table, four of them, they'd eat about ten dollars, fifteen dollars worth. Now, you know, during the Depression time that's a lot of money. But they were makin' it. They always come in between three and six in the morning, all American couples, you know. What kinda business they were in I never questioned. One and one together, I know what they were doin' at that time of night. And when they can dish out fifty-dollar bills, mind you, maybe give me three to four dollars tip, they must be in some kind of business. And mostly monkey business!

Then, there were a lot madams who had something to do

with Chinatown then. Have you ever heard of Sally Stanford? I'll tell you one thing, Sally Stanford was a very shrewd woman. She owns more property, and never pay a penny income tax, because she knew people. And she gets away with murder because she has more say down in city hall than any madam that I ever knew in all the years I been here. In fact, she has been known as the madam of the West Coast. No matter what you ask for, she can supply it. You see, she and I were good friends, we were drinking partners. She used to tell me, "Pete, one of these days I'm gonna bring you up there and I'm gonna show you something. Believe it or not, anytime you feel like it, when I have those customers in, I'll call you and show you something that you've never seen in your life!" I said, "You mean to tell me there's something I haven't seen in my life? Sally, you've known me for years!" But she says, "This is something you've never seen before." So sure enough one day she sent somebody down to pick me up. I went up there and she had these French windows, you know, where you can see from one side and they can't see you from the other side. Mirrors. And she said, "Pretty soon somebody's gonna walk through that door." She point to the middle of the room, very dim lights, and there was a coffin with a nude girl in the coffin. She said, "You wait another five minutes and you'll find somebody walkin' through the door." And sure enough, here comes a elderly man. He was naked. I says, "Now what's he gonna do?" She said, "You just keep quiet, don't talk so loud." So I watch and watch.

This man, he may be in his fifties, grey hair and everything else, all he'd do was walk, walk around the coffin. Never even touch the girl, the same way as though she was dead. He walked around then finally he'd kneel down and say something, get up again, put his arms around the girl, start kissing her and all that. But I mean, you oughta see that man, he was just out of his mind what he was doing! He stayed there for one hour without even touching her sexually. Just admiring her beauty and figure and all that, but just all he ever done was kiss her. I said, "Sally, how much you charge for that?"

"Five hundred dollars."

"Five hundred dollars? For what he's doin'?"

"You come back to my office and I'll show you. When he walks in he'll give me five hundred-dollar bills. And that's not including the money he gives the girl." Just for fifteen, twenty minutes, maybe half an hour! She said, "There's many of those who come in." I said, "He must be a rich man."

She made millions and millions. Not only in San Francisco, all over the west coast. And all that time, the police force, the police commissioner, everybody had a cut. Nobody's blind, see? They were getting their cut outta what she was making. And Sally never failed, every year at Christmastime she spent maybe ten, fifteen thousand dollars just for gifts. What the heck? She makes it back in two or three weeks!

Now, I met Sally through the MacDonald Bail Brothers. They used to have a bail bond office right down here at the edge of Chinatown, and those brothers had more power than the police commissioner ever had. Naturally Sally was friends with them. They were very good friends of mine, too, because they knew I was a gambler and they wanted to, well, make approaches. But I'm not that type, you know, that's dirty money to me. Even if I starve I never get that kinda money, that's the honest truth. So help me. But I was approached every time those two brothers ever met me down at Cookie's Bar. Used to be next to the city hall. Well, those times are something fantastic. If people don't never see or hear about it, they wouldn't believe it. A lot of these oldtimers that comes around here, they went through it, seen a lot.

Oh, yeah! If there were no gambling, no girls, you know, it's not Chinatown. And no dope, opium dens, always a lot of opium. But one thing, you didn't already know the people, you better keep outta their business. Otherwise you'll find yourself someplace where you wish you hadn't say one word.

Yeah, there was a lot of madams. Josephine Andressi, she was a powerful woman here in Chinatown itself. And Sally Stanford is outside of Chinatown, although she knows everyone here. But the one thing about Josephine, she was

a lot different from Sally Stanford. She was what they call a
friend of the Chinese people. She had three places down on
Kearny Street and she made a lot money offa Chinatown.
Now Sally Stanford was strictly a business woman, but
Josephine was not. She always maintained, and she told her
husband, "I made my money in Chinatown, I'm gonna spend
my money here in Chinatown." And that's what she did.
She'd go into Chinatown bars, no matter who it is, black,
yellow, or white, she'd sit down beside them and order a
drink. And the bartender every time they see her coming in
with a coupla girls, they know they're gonna get a good tip.
And I'll tell you one other thing about that woman, she
never refused anybody that went up to one of her places
and he was down and out, said to her, "Jo, gee, you know,
I don't have any money to eat." I bet to this day, if she ever
get all those money back, she'd be a wealthy woman. Sally
was all for herself, that's all, but she was a lot different
from Josephine.

At that time, just before the Depression, a lot of the
gambling places were closed, except over in Oakland. She
had one place in the Fillmore district and us boys, when
we'd get out of the gambling house in Oakland, two or three
in the morning, we'd come over here for chow because the
restaurants in Oakland were lousy. And we always go out
to see Josephine, walk in there, there was a big parlor
reserved for the boys from Oakland. We used to stop first
in Chinatown, buy grub, buy everything, and take it to
Josephine's, it was just like a banquet. I'm the one she trust
with the key to her liquor parlor. When we walk in there,
"Well, what do you want to drink today?" We'd say, "Oh,
anything!" But she always stocked good booze there, good
scotch, good bourbon. We used to drink Johnny Walker
Black Label. I'd take two bottles out for the boys who were
gambling, give her back the key, she'd say, "No, keep it,
keep it! I know damn well you're gonna drink some more."
She don't care because it was all bootleg whisky that she
get cheap, you know. Sometimes it woud be ten in the
morning when we'd leave. And a lot of times, when the
house closes, she'd say to me, "Now you're a gambler, you
count the money." So I'd sort it and count it, the way they

count it in gambling houses, and then the girls come in with their receipts for the day, I'd pay 'em. Well, I think Josephine is dead now. If she isn't dead she must be around ninety. A good old lady. She was especially nice to the Chinese. She said, "If all my money comes from Chinese people, why shouldn't I love Chinese people?"

They pulled in more money from gambling than they pull in now. The main difference is the protection they're getting now. They pay five hundred dollars a day for police protection, you know. And they raid you even so. Before if they collected the money from you at least usually they never touch you. But now some of those big wheels up on top, in city hall, they're getting their cut, and they put two and two together, the protection money's already in their pocket, so what's to prevent them from making it hot every once in a while to get a little more? So you can never tell when they're gonna close you up, see. In one pinch, if they take fifteen, twenty people out, that means five thousand dollars more. Because a lot of these Chinese people, they have no passport, the gambling house has got to bail them out before they get sent back to the old country. So from the number of places open in Chinatown, you just figure out how much those guys are taking in. And who's losing? It's the gamblers, the ones that run the places. If they squawk, it don't mean a thing.

FRANK LEE, 66
Carpenter

He entered California in his teens as a "paper son" and was apprenticed at his stepfather's carpenter shop. "Hard work and frugality," he remembers being taught by Chinatown's oldtimers, were the essential ingredients for survival in the difficult life of American Chinese.

My stepfather was so frugal he refused to hire a truck to take the lumber up to Stockton Street from our shop, which was located on Sacramento Street. He used us, and gave us a hand truck that would take two or three hundred feet of lumber by manpower up from the shop. But because the hill between Sacramento and Stockton was so steep, we had to take a detour all the way down to the other end of Grant, out on Broadway, and all the way back down Stockton to Sacramento Street. Because this was a lesser grade. That was cheap labor. We earned $1.50 a day and it would have cost him three dollars to hire a truck. Well, at any rate we suffered this for many years until he finally saw the light and hired a truck to carry the lumber up there. Well, it was a hard life, but we were taught that hard work was beneficial to us. It doesn't kill you. In fact, most parents demanded that their sons and daughters worked after school. So this so-called hard work and frugality went together. Hard work and frugality. That was drummed into our heads so often it wasn't funny. I guess everything has a termination point. And we got saturated with it in such a way that we actually resented those words—"hard work" and "frugality."

Of course, the old idea is not to spend money, whether it's for equipment or anything else, but proving that to a Chinese person of the old school is a waste of time. If you can finally manage to prove it to them, it's always given a blessing to go ahead. But trying to prove it is something else.

Since my stepparents practiced frugality, I was denied a lot of things that should have been mine. In fact, I was told not to go to school after I finished grammar school. Fortunately, there was the compulsory education law in California. You have to go to school until you're sixteen, and parttime until you're eighteen. But when my teacher asked me what high school I wanted to go to, what was my choice, I told them, " I'm not going." She said why, and I said, "My father told me not to go to school. So the next day she came to our house with the principal and started dressing my father up and down. So very reluctantly he let me go to high school. I had a heck of a time going to school as far as allowance is concerned. At fifty cents a week, twenty-six cents for carfare, I don't know what I ate for lunch. I remember everytime I went to school I lost some weight.

FONG, 67
A laborer

Wherever he is, he's the loudest one. His angry voice dominates the others in Portsmouth Square. One night when a
free movie had been cut in the Kearny Street basement, he
yelled, "What is this stinking swindle?" all the way through
the second half. He didn't tell us where he lived or his name,
"Call me Fong." But he told us he didn't come to the park
too much in the winter, the cold made his bones ache.

   In the summer, Fong was in the park every day. He was
a big man. He wore a windbreaker and an old woolen
sailor's cap, navy blue. We taped him a lot of times. "I'll tell
you what," he said, "they talk about brainwashing, well,
anybody who's lived through this part of a life, like I did,
and learned something, gradually you begin to understand.
You start asking yourself questions after questions, and
gradually in due time the thing begins to come out by itself.
Nobody gonna brainwash me, that's one thing for sure. I
don't care how good of a talker he is. No, I got no schooling.
Do you know how many years I went to school? About four,
that's all I got. I didn't even went to the fifth grade. But I'll
tell you what, nobody's gonna talk me into anything. Because I got it all layed out, all the damned thing what's going
on. I keep thinking about things, and gradually it comes out,
I know why they turned out the way they did. Which means
a lot, you see what I mean?" Fong keeps a pipe in his mouth,
and he turns his jaw up so he can catch the warmth from
the sun while he talks.

Clay Street, when I first come over here in 1917, it was cold.
Everywhere it's so damn cold you have to have an overcoat
on. Before, there's no such thing as jackets and things like
that, see. You gotta have a suit of clothes everywhere. It's
foggy and there's two things definite: they've got fleas all
over, everywhere you go it's full of fleas, and it was so cold.
Every day they used to have that fog horn out there, blowing, Boooooooo booooooo, you know, all day long, all night
long. During the daytime it probably stop somewhere in the

afternoon, but sometimes it continues all along through the evening, it never stop. Why? Because it's always foggy, see, and once in a while you see the sun shine somewhere around half past three up to half past four and that's all, one day, finish. It used to be like that all the time, but now the weather change.

When I first come over here Clay Street is supposed to be the most flourishing street of all. They have a lot of wagons and this is the main street that they come up with the stuff into Chinatown from the warehouse and the wharf. Rice, food, Chinese things, and all that. And you take, like one guy who sits here in the square, I could get him to tell you how he made a living hauling up the street and all that, but he broke down and anyway, it's too big a story. As I said, I'm tryin' to keep what I tell you in one line, but I can't, because the damn thing always jumpin' or something. Now this street here, Washington, it is so goddamn wet, it used to be cobblestone and full of telephone poles. And it's so wet that the lines between the cobblestones were all molded because of the horse manure, people spit on it, the wets from the horses, and plus the fog, daily fog. The street was never, never dry, never.

Now another thing, weird as it seems, as the years goes along it moves, the kingpin street of Chinatown, one street right after another from Washington to Jackson and then into Pacific. Pacific is a special place, used to be nobody there, nobody even walk there. Right now you see the Ping Yuen project there, but before's nothing but a garage and a coupla funeral parlors. And smooth as it is yet weird as it seems, very few people walk there. That's because Ping Yuen is one place, there's two or three places in Chinatown's got the jinx. One is a theater on Grant Avenue, upstairs, the other is the Ping Yuen project, that's the worst, and the place near the Chinese Hospital, it got so famous with ghosts people just don't want to live there. Even though the rent was so damn cheap. There's always a ghost who walks around there at nighttime and things like that, awfully scary. But anyway, to get back to the main line, then Pacific Street got to be more or less a main drag of San Francisco. There used to be the Barbary Coast there.

Now the Barbary Coast, I got nothing to do with it, I don't know nothing about it. All I know is what's left of it, the survival of the Barbary Coast, because it was there on Pacific Street. All along on the doorways you could see carving, dancing girls and all that all along down to the International Hotel. After they change it, what's left of the Barbary Coast is so decayed, nevertheless the doorways and the panels, you know, are just like all those Broadway dancing halls now. All carved, great big carving of dance girls with the ribbons waving and all that, with unicorns blowing flutes, and all that thing goes all the way from the International back up to the housing project, Ping Yuen.

It was during the Depression, right after that, was the change in Chinatown. You guys were born nowadays and you think it was always like that, but this is not so. You see, before in Chinatown, they only had the curio shops down the other end, and in here on this end, around Clay Street, was all grocery stores and things like that. Then during the occupation, when the Japanese was in power in China, the Japanese almost took over the whole Chinatown, right down to here. But then when the World War came the Americans took the Japanese into the concentration camp and locked them up, so it came back to the Chinese again. Although the Chinese did not have such good things to sell, but then it's just one of those things, how life is. I don't know, the whole thing gets so complicated, every time I begin to talk on one subject it jumps into another. And I try to keep it in one line, but I can't.

Now I had been living out in the country for a while, but I came back around 1932 and the Depression changed a lot of things. You have guys going around from building to building selling meat. They sell pork for twenty-five cents, thirty-five cents a pound, cheaper than the butcher shop, and you don't have to walk around, they come to you. Now during the Depression I was so broke, quite often I was with no money in my pocket. The most I ever had is maybe one or two dollars, the least was, well, normally I got ten, fifteen cents. You wonder how I lived? That's a different question. We got a room, there's five or six of us and some-times we pay rent, sometimes we don't. We got a sack of rice for a coupla dollars and we all cook every day and we eat there. Sometime one night you see forty or fifty guys come in and out, the old guys go to each other's place, sit down, talk all night long before they go to sleep the next day.

But as I said, you eat Chinese food, it's very cheap. At that restaurant that's famous for rice porridge, Sam Wo's, they used to cook pig's stomach called the *ji tu*, where they take the crunchy part from the middle and then sell all the leftover parts of *ji tu* right outside Sam Wo's; it's just only a nickel. The American doesn't know how to eat it. You can see how bad it is, but those days, we used to buy a lot. And every few days one guy would go up to Sam Wo's and come back with all those *ji tu's* in an old fashion rice sack made out of mat, like, that's come from China, fifty pounds of rice sack. And he brings those *ji tu's* back, and I clean 'em, get a great big pot, and we stew it up, oh, hell, we eat for a whole goddamned half a week all we want to eat! So we got our food one way or the other, lots of vegetables real cheap at the time, and that's how I passed by.

Then Roosevelt come out and he created the word NRA, gave work to people, a lotta guys, but later on it got so sour. Like they got jobs, for instance I went in on one of them, a railroad job inside Elko. They paid seventy-two dollars, I think, and they give you jobs like that so you can make a living, and I worked there a few months. It was awfully hot, hot like everything! In fact you could see the blaze in the afternoon, when the sun shines so blazing you can actually see the atmosphere of it, just, the blaze movin' around hotly. And people come back workin' in the railroad, they come back for dinner they practically stink because their clothing been in that sunlight so damn long. And that's the way it is, I lived out there. You don't go nowhere, it's right out in the middle of the desert, see, that's the way it is. There's quite a few jobs similar like that that Roosevelt put out later on.

I was, well, just only a helper at the time. I would say I did almost any kind of work, I'm acquainted with a few of them, but nevertheless at the time I was nothin' but a helper, a waiter, dishwasher, and all that. See. The whole thing regardless, like you asked me about discrimination, it's all, all long. They're always trying to push you down to these jobs, no matter how much or how good you are. Like that NRA was like all the other things, at first you don't realize, but nevertheless, in due time and in the long run, you find out it will never have any advantage toward the Chinese. The thing is that they do it in such a close way, undercover way, that you barely notice it. So, as I said, that NRA, "Never Rebuffed American," pretty soon the thing went sour all around and people began to sneer at it. I mean by saying this: "Nice Round Ass." About the girls, you know, all these B-girls and whores and everything, swinging around in the street and everything, because they're beginning to make money. So that's what it meant: "Nice Round Ass." Through the grapevine people talk about it, you know. Stink out the whole country.

While I'm at it, I'll tell you a story how a guy sneered at me. There's a guy who came out of the country when I was living in that room, and he probably had a little money, couple of hundred dollars in his pocket, but, as I say, in those days his money looked like something. He probably knew I didn't have any money then, which is only natural, a lotta guys didn't have any, not only me. But one day he came up to me when nobody was around. And he said, "Come on, let's go to the show." Now usually I'm kind of a humble one, I don't like to horn in and chisel anybody unless I really know him. So I said, "No, thank you." But he said, "C'mon, come on, let's go." And he kept asking me until I said, "Alright, let's go, I'll meet you at seven o'clock tonight after dinner." That was the habit of everybody, go to the theater right down here on Kearny Street, it only cost a dime and there's all kinds of things you get, movies, comics, they even got girls dancing there, all that strip-dancing, that was those days. And though the police station, the court house was right there, doesn't mean a thing because they pay black money, but anyway, that's the way it goes. So that night I came in, seven o'clock, and he said, "Let's go!" So I said, "Alright, you got me into it. Alright, let's go." Then right before we go out he stop. "I change my mind," he said. And he sneered at me, "No, I don't think you better go. You ain't got no money."

But I'm gonna show you a different side. Around that same time, there's another guy, I used to play mahjong with him. He got a terrible temper, talks, slanders, and weird as it seems, we very seldom have meals together. But still he always seems to like me a lot, he's about fifteen years older than I am. I am around twenty-two during the Depression. And one night we played mahjong. You know people, some of them is awfully stingy and some of them fight over a few points. And yet with all the extra points and all that he got left over, he gave them to me. So even though he's got a terrible temper, doesn't talk too much, he's very friendly to me in a way and we joke at each other once in a while. I called him "Godfather" and he called me "My godson," his adopted son. Well, during the Depression, one time not long from the other story, the same thing happened and I was really down to nothing. And he came out one night when we were playing mahjong in the store, and he said, "How is it?" I said, "Hello there, pop!" He says, "How is it, son?" I said, "Well, so so." And then another old man, he was considerate to me also, said, "Oh, things real bad for him." See. So my godfather say, "What's the matter?" And I just say, "Ah, you know how it is. Depression and all that. Just down, that's all." And right after he heard that he threw somethin' like forty dollars on the table. Now, you know, I'm just one of these guys that isn't like any other guy, if somebody lends you money you're happy. Well, sometime I worry more than I'm happy. So when he put that money down I said, "I didn't ask you to lend me money anyhow. You just threw it on the table." He said, "Pick it up." So I said, "Now look, it's nice, that money there." (Which is true! It will set me up a long time, see, especially during the Depression.) "But the thing is," I said, "damn it, there's no jobs, no nothin', I don't know when the hell I'm gonna pay you back." He said, "Pick it up. Shut up. Don't talk so damn much, just pick it up and shut up."

Well, later on I paid him back, when I found a job. You know, nowadays everybody makin' half a hundred dollars a week, even dishwashers, but you don't find people that loyal to you. You couldn't even go out and borrow a quarter or something, it's pretty hard. Before, people make only a few dollars a day, and yet you can go out to friends and you can borrow even forty dollars very easy. Now everybody is cutthroat, no more of that business exist. It's just one of those things. Anyway in about 1935 or something he passed away, and he had been in China for a while so I didn't see him much. But that shows you there are two ways. Some guys would come out, you don't know a damn thing about it, and he would throw mud at your face when you're down. And yet some guys, if you're just joking along and he has enough, he helps you. And that really meant something to me, sentimentally you see. Like all these years, I don't go out every year, but whenever I do go out I take joss sticks or something and I burn it on his grave. And I always could memorize it, the day he pass away, just one of those things.

As I said, during the Depression, a lot of changes is going on gradually, unnoticely. Slowly, some buildings and some stores is beginning to get more fancy and bigger. I used to come out at nighttime, after dinner, and stroll around on Grant Avenue, slowly, with a couple of friends. Well, in the beginning of the Depression it used to be that down there on Grant Avenue where the Federal Savings and Loan is now is so beat up, it's dead. And maybe that's one reason I like to walk on it, nighttime, it's level and nobody bother you, because it isn't like right now, no tourists and even Chinese is very few. You can practically have the whole sidewalk to yourself. And all along there the places was so beat up, so old, the man either owned the store himself or the rent was cheap, probably he wouldn't have the money to rent a higher place. And they used to have all the chickens, and sell fish, and all that. Used to be awfully cheap. You go in there, the store is still in the old fashion way and who cares, see, whether they do business or not. They're makin' out just as well, pass the day, not like right now when they all look like gangsters, racketeers, and like everything in the store cost a thousand dollars. And their windows sometimes were broken by accident, or maybe somebody went to drive them out, but they don't care, it wasn't as violent as nowadays. All they do was to take a piece of cardboard from their things and cover it up. Cover the window up, nobody break in, and that's all there is to it. Well, these were stores that used to sell things only to Chinese people. Laundries, aprons, cook's hats, shoes, old good shoes, but old fashion. And you know the merchandise is always hanging from the ceiling, you go in there and they got it on a string and wrapped up. They wrap it up because they afraid they get dirty and get browned up, so they wrap it up with a paper and hang it on the ceiling. And if you go in there and ask him for something, he'll think a minute or so and then he'll reach up there and unloose the loop and bring it down and show it to you. That's the way it is. He doesn't do very much business, but that's the way it is, just stays there for tens and tens of years, I don' know, God knows, he probably been there all his life and they can't go back to China, or maybe later on they did, I don't know, or die. They were old, but not too feeble, and they still stuck on to their business, that's the way it is.

But then around the middle of the Depression the change come along and everything goes zoom! The whole place begins to look different because they start building it up. Now the first thing they change is they change the names. Before that, not that there wasn't any bars in Chinatown, but they weren't noticeable nowhere. They were just down, beatup places, the bars for low-down people and drunks and all that. But during the Depression a bar changed names to some kind of a club, and then all those fancy names comes. Then the same thing happens with the restaurants. Used to be only Chinese people comes in there and eat, very few foreigners comes around. I mean, people did come in one of them. Hang Ah, the most famous one on Clay Street. But the little restaurants in Chinatown they used to look down as very low, nothin'. But then the change came and these new restaurants sprang up, too. In fact, maybe Chinatown is the place that start everything rumbling during the Depression. Such as like these dance halls, the bars, and all that.

But the last thing I gotta explain to you, during the Depression there's three walks of life. Daytime there's the business, throughout Grant Avenue you see people movin' around with their products and open up for business. After dinner there's another walk of life and that's our kind, who bums around the street doin' nothin', just to pass the time away because there's no work nowhere. The students don't got no work because they don't know how to do dishes or hard work or anything, they'd rather hire our kind for that, but even us, we don't get no work. Everything was so dead there was hardly anything goin' on. So in the evening we come out and walk around the street and pass, it was nice summertimes, you know, and we seemed to enjoy it very much. After eight or nine o'clock we'd go back, as I said, and then we got all kinds of visitors comes around, talk all night long. Everything, anything that comes to our mind we make a story out of it, and chat.

But anyway after dinner my kind walks on the streets and go down the theater on Kearny Street. Then after ten o'clock a third kind comes along, the Americans. All those rich guys, they start coming more and more to Chinatown. Why? Because as I said before there's no bar except some bum place those rich guys doesn't like to go. But then, in Chinatown, all of a sudden in a year or two it pops up eight or nine bars. Little compact one and they try to modernize it, see, and that's when the bars begin to flourish in Chinatown. So these guys, from ten o'clock they hanging around, and then for a couple of years it been going on like that, they come more and more, and they made their hours longer and longer until four o'clock, until the next morning, until seven o'clock, before they go home. And the funny part of it is this. I mean, that's a third round of people, class of people, that moves around in Chinatown. They used to got those long gowns, dancing gowns, white, beautiful gowns, rich. And believe it or not, they really swept the sidewalks. They really swept Chinatown sidewalks, every night, they just drag those gowns throughout Chinatown, in and out. No, they don't make too much of a commotion, but they do, you do have this class of people from the outside comes into Chinatown and enjoys themselves, throughout the night,

just goes like that. And it ran until next morning, seven
o'clock or half past seven or eight o'clock in the morning
before they'd go home, that's the way it is.

CHING WAH LEE, 79
Art collector with a museum in Old Chinatown Lane

One factor which bound the Chinese together in the early
days was a certain loneliness. They felt that the people here
were not too interested in them, except as curiosities, and
then when the gold mines petered out and there was competition for jobs, there was actual antagonism toward the
Chinese, especially among the laboring class. There were
frequent anti-Chinese agitations and one leader known as
"Sandlot Kearney" was famous for his speeches on street
corners and sandlots saying that the Chinese must go. So
in a negative way, this fear was a cementing factor, too.
Because of the agitation, a lot of Chinese leaders, the cream
of the crop, eventually did go back to China. The ones who
remained felt almost deserted, and that was another factor
which brought them together.

After this time Chinese began organizing their own societies for mutual protection. There were many hoodlums
who would attack Chinese for no reason whatsoever, and
that caused them to look back to China. Before the revolution of 1911, or at least before the turn of the century, the
Chinese here still had great faith in the "mandarin system."
They thought if only they could petition the mandarin or
viceroy to petition the emperor for them, problems could be
settled. But early in the 1900s, after the fire, they realized
that the Manchu government was tottering and they were
completely disillusioned with it. Then they began to look
to the Chinese revolutionaries. The province we come from,
Kwangtung Province, is rich with revolutionaries. One,
Kang Yu Wei, was able to influence the emperor to start a
series of reforms in education, modernization, and national
defense, and so forth. By 1900, however, the new hero was
Dr. Sun Yat-sen. The Chinese here raised a tremendous sum
of money to help him, and there were street corner rallies in

the evenings which would draw hundreds of people who contributed money generously. Towards the end, people were a bit disillusioned in Sun Yat-sen, too, because he failed to create a stabilized government.

Now this was all on the political side. On the religious side it was very interesting, because the early Chinese leaned toward gods which would protect them. One of the most popular was Kwang Kung, the god of literature and war. Bak Ti, the god of the north, was known in Chinese religious lore for doing away with ten thousand demons who were organized to fight him. Perhaps, since Chinese call many Caucasians "foreign devils," this played some part in the significance of Bak Ti. The third thing, strange to say, was the cult of Hou Yin, the monkey god. This was a small cult which grew out of the novel about a monk traveling to India with a pig and a monkey. The pig represented the greedy qualities of man, and the monkey, who was somewhat of a magical creature, represented his mischievous qualities. I think in this cult he was worshipped for the ability to cope with all kinds of unusual situations.

In the day to day life of the early Chinese-Americans there were many festivals and ritual observations which have disappeared today. The best remembered by anyone who is still alive now is probably the funeral procession. A substantial part of Chinatown's economy was even involved in this. There were two stores on Jackson Street, for instance, which dealt with funeral items. One, the Tai Yuen, is still there. It sold candles, incense, paper money to throw at demons during the funeral procession, and gold and silver paper bullion in the shape of ingots. They also sold colored paper garments to be burned at the cemetery and as offerings to the deceased. Selling these things supported one whole store. Then diagonally across the street, at 741 Jackson, was a store which produced figures which were used in the procession to accompany the deceased as servants. These were made of paper and rattan work, about a yard high, in the form of a jade girl and a golden boy.

Funerals in Chinatown would be most elaborate if a man was wealthy or well-known. First there would be a sort of preliminary wake. On the day of the funeral a platform or shed would be built, with a framework of white banners, and usually one tall vertical banner would give the name of the man who had died and some of his deeds and his relations. Food and wine would be offered to the deceased for the journey. There were deep-fried noodles, dyed red, yellow, and green, which couldn't be eaten, actually. Fruit, wine, and imitation foods of other kinds would be offered, too. While the coffin was at rest there, there would be the wailing of all the children and relatives of the deceased.

When it was time to go to the cemetery a horse-drawn hearse and a horse-drawn carriage carrying a portrait were used. The mourning relatives of the deceased would all wear hemp cloth, buff in color, and walk behind the hearse through the length of Grant Avenue. At the outskirts of Chinatown they got into the carriage and rode to the cemetery. Usually there would also be a horse-drawn truck filled with flowers. A member of the family who was not in mourning, that is, once removed from the immediate family, would sit with the driver of the hearse and throw out "devil's money" to keep demons from molesting the spirit as it went to the cemetery. When they reached the cemetery there was more crying and wailing.

Usually the funeral would begin quite early, if my memory serves me correctly. I would say about eleven o'clock. Because the horse-drawn carriage took quite a lot of time to reach the cemetery and then they would have to be back before it is dark. The cemetery was near Colma, adjacent to San Francisco proper, and it's still there. Once there was another cemetery as well, in Lincoln Park right next to the present Legion of Honor Museum. That was mostly for Chinese seamen, who had their own burial society and their own cemetery. They chose the spot, which at that time was completely desolate, by having a specialist study the *shan-shui* or "wind and water" configuration, to determine a place which would please the deceased and be auspicious for the relatives. Actually, I think the site was chosen with the idea of peace and tranquility. So that was the best-chosen cemetery. It's on a little hill looking out over the Pacific Ocean.

For years the Chinese couldn't be buried in, say, Masonic

cemeteries or Jewish cemeteries, so they had their own. Anyway, before World War II it was the general custom for at least three-fourths of the Chinese to have their bones exhumed later and packed in tin cans, and sent back to their ancestral cemetery in China. It was purely sentimental, of course, like many Americans I know who write in their will that they want to be buried in Iowa or Nebraska or wherever they come from and it's something of the same situation, you see, because the early Chinese looked on the country here as rather hostile to them. They felt more comfortable if they knew their bones would be sent back to China.

JOHNNY KAN, 57

Above the street level storefronts, two signs identify the square, four-story, brick building which dominates the corner of Grant and Sacramento. A red and green sign, hanging at the level of rows of nylon-curtained windows on the upper stories describes the building as the Republic Hotel, opened for business in 1915. On the second-story level, amid a series of red banners and arched French doors behind a grillwork balcony, a red and white square sign with gold-etched edges marks the location of Kan's Chinese Restaurant. It's noon. We follow a large corridor into the restaurant and wait with the crowd in the lobby beside photographs of Danny Kaye, Kim Novak, Eva Gabor.

We have come to talk with Johnny Kan, a pioneer in the rise of luxury restaurants in Chinatown in the late thirties. The maître d' tells us Johnny has been expecting us; we are surprised at how tall he is when he walks into the room. In a dark formal suit, Johnny seats us and orders drinks for everyone. Although we know he is fifty-seven years old, in dress, manner, and speech he is completely different from the old men with whom we have spent the last few weeks learning about the history of Chinatown. Johnny tells us he did not live in San Francisco until he was nine years old. "We had a very difficult time growing up. At one time there had been over two thousand Chinese living in Grass Valley and working in the gold mines. But by the time we got up there it had dwindled down to a few hundred. A lot of the men had fallen back on vegetable peddling. I remember when we were very young, after school my sister and I would go from house to house peddling strawberries for something like a nickel a basket. I guess people bought them from us whether they wanted them or not because they were sympathetic with the way we looked, and we probably looked pretty hungry. My mother was a good baker, and she would send us down to Chinatown on Sunday mornings with covered baskets to sell cha shew bau* to a few Chinese who would come down from the hill, the gold mines, or wherever they were living. I remember a particular character whose name was Duck Egg, he walked with a stoop. He was getting old and living a little bit off charity. You know, whenever you walked into a Chinese store or laundry, or any kind of business, if you were Chinese you would receive hospitality, food, and whatever help they can give you. Duck Egg was one of those. Later on, I would say fifteen or twenty years later, there was a group of businessmen here in San Francisco, I would say, whose consciences probably bothered them because they had stoned Duck Egg. You know, it was a rough bunch of characters who came to California to the Mother Lode, and they would treat Chinese as inferior and stone them because we looked different and acted different. So they used to stone the vegetable peddlers, they would stone Duck Egg, and they used to throw stones at us on the way home. Oh, they would wrap rocks in snowballs and throw them at us. Of course, children we must forgive, because they were innocent, but at that time it was a very confusing thing for me." Johnny's family came down from the Mother Lode in the early 1920s. When he finished grammar school, they could not afford to send him on to junior high school, so he began training in a grocery store at 1040 Grant Ave. "I had a lot to learn when I first began working there. There were so many customs I felt awkward with. I guess I never realized till then that I had practically grown up in a non-Chinese district."

---

* A steamed Chinese meat dumpling.

This was when I was nineteen and I was working at a grocery called Sam Hing and Company at 1040 Grant Avenue. I remember we had an old sign on the window and it wasn't attractive. I wanted to create a better image with a better designed sign and matching stationery and business cards to indicate what we had for sale. So as a partner and assistant manager of the store, as well as the *Choot Fonn*—the English secretary—I took it upon myself to have the sign changed. Now my oldtimer partners in this store had been picking on me a lot, saying we American-born were lazy, we weren't fluent enough in Chinese, *"Tow-gee jai mo no,"* you know, "the American-born have no brains." I knew it would be useless to try to discuss my ideas about the sign with them, so I just went ahead and had it done. At the time, nobody said a thing. They barely seemed to notice the change. But at the end of the year, when they were ready to pay out our small dividends, I got hauled in on the sign.

They said, "Now you're taking too much for granted. You're making expenditures without the approval of the rest of the partners." I told them I had thought it was just in the line of duty to repair that sign, to improve the business, and to make progress. I told them, "We can't operate as if this were the horse and buggy days, we've got to make time!" But they said, "No, everybody should be consulted. In China, the older the sign, the more venerable and reputable the business is. You have destroyed and taken away the old frayed sign which was our symbol of being long-established." And I said, "Well, this is not China, this is America. And all over the world business people are changing their ideas and their trademarks."

The old sign had said something like this: "SAM HING & CO., Groceries and Peanuts." I had changed it to a better script, and underneath the top line, "SAM HING & CO., Grocers," I put another line "Wholesalers in Peanuts." I thought this was important because this way it made it clear that our peanut business was in the wholesale class, it wasn't just a store that sold bags of peanuts. Fortunately, something happened to prove me right. A few weeks later my brother, who was between jobs, came to the store to help out and catch some meals. He asked me, "Why don't you advertise in something like *Variety Magazine,* or *Show Business Magazine?*" I said, "What good will that do?" He said, "You dumb cluck, the circus people read it, too!" So I went and bought a small ad in *Variety.* (My brother Sam later became the United States Treasury Department's first Chinese narcotic agent.)

Months later a man walked into Sam Hing's and said, "Let me try some of your peanuts." We brought him samples of Virginia peanuts and Chinese peanuts, quoted a price, and finally he chose a brand. He said, "Can you deliver two tons by tomorrow morning?" Two tons! That was practically our whole stock! It turned out this man was a buyer from Ringling Brothers and Barnum and Bailey. I was about to tell him it was impossible when my brother started shouting in my ear, "Take it! Everybody roasts peanuts all night long!" So we worked all night and we got the order out. In the morning we drove it, ten sacks at a time, to the circus grounds in our little truck. We shoveled all the peanuts into the big circus trucks and they sold so well they asked us to come back every day. At the end of the year, when my partners had made such a fuss about that sign, I told them to deduct forty dollars from my salary. But after this order came in, I got my forty dollars back pretty fast.

After working at Sam Hing's for eight years, I still didn't see eye to eye with my partners on progress. I thought we should convert the grocery department into a self-service operation, they kept holding back, so finally I left and went to L.A. for a while. When I came back, things were not good in San Francisco in the thirties, and I had to do all kinds of things, janitorial work, dishwashing, cooking, anything to get started again. Then my future brother-in-law introduced me to a man who was not many years from China. This man and his partner had been doing routine baking for Foster's Cafeteria, and it wasn't long before they decided, since they were working the night shift downtown, there was no reason why they couldn't have a little shop in Chinatown, too. They could do some baking after they got off work, then go back to Foster's—the trouble was, who would they get to keep the store open during the day? I became a candidate. They called me in and said, "Now after work, we're

gonna bake all night here, then we'll go to work at Foster's,
come back, take a little nap, and take over the place when
you leave." Well, it turned out things went great. After two
or three years, business became so good they quit Foster's
and spent full time there. So one day I said, "You know,
fellows, now that you have a little reputation, it might be a
good idea to expand, and set up a bakery-fountain right on
Grant Avenue."

We started the Fong-Fong Bakery-Fountain in 1935. We
had a beautiful, long counter, the latest equipment, stainless
steel, nice-looking bakery cases full of fancy, decorated
cakes and flaky French pastries, and it was the first place,
you know, that had uniforms in Chinatown, regular soda
fountain uniforms, all white. I told my partners my policy.
"Now we're going to cater to the younger generation and
turn this into a gathering place for all of the young
American-born Chinese in San Francisco." And we did. On
weekends, students from Berkeley and Stanford would
come in droves. On Sunday morning, people waited in line
to get in. And we really fractured those hack-sawed oldtimers with goodies Chinatown had never seen before—
Napoleon pastries, wedding cakes, bon voyage baskets,
nobody had ever seen a banana split made in Chinatown
before, nobody ever saw a parfait decorated nicely. At the
same time, I had enrolled in the University of California's
Davis Farm Dairy School, and as I became a little more
adept at ice cream making I had an idea: ever since we
opened, tourists in Chinatown would keep coming into
Fong-Fong's and after staring at the twenty-flavor ice cream
listings they'd say, "Cheeze, don't yuh have any *Chinese*
ice cream?" That's when I started to invent Lichee ice cream,
Ginger ice cream, Chinese fruit ice cream, and finally we
even invented Chinese Sundaes, which were unheard of
before. I wanted to see the company expand, possibly into
nationwide distribution of Chinese ice creams and cookies,
but again, I ran into difficulty with my partners, so no gain
there.

Well, by the thirties Chinatown was already becoming a
neon-sign salesman's dream with every shop competing for
space and gaudiness. I began talking with some friends and

joined a little project to restore "Old Chinatown." Our aim was to bring back the old jewelry, slipper, and lantern manufacturing shops, to make it look like Chinatown before the earthquake and fire, no neon signs, no jazzy commercial appearance. Unfortunately, due to mismanagement, the project flopped. But then I began thinking about something else. I thought back on the success of the Chinese restaurateurs in New York and Chicago in the roaring twenties. They were operating huge-size places along the Eastern seaboard, and they were packing in four to five hundred customers at one seating on Saturday nights. These were the restaurants where many big names in the band business started out, long before the famous "Big Band Era"—people like Paul Whiteman, Kay Kyser, Paul Tremaine. You know, Chinese from San Francisco would willingly go to New York or Chicago just to work as waiters in these places. The crowds were so large and the tips so good, they wouldn't even ask for salaries!

Also, I had studied the old Mandarin Restaurant here on Bush Street and figured out why it had failed. First, for lack of professional restaurant experience, and second, because it had too many partners—a lethal combination! And finally I realized that the reason there were no first-class restaurants in Chinatown was because no one ever bothered to study, and to teach their employees, how to run a really fine place. And nobody had tried to educate Caucasians to an appreciation of Chinese food. There were over fifty restaurants in Chinatown—papa-mama, medium-sized, juke and soup joints, tenderloin joints, and others—where the waiters just slammed the dishes on the table and cared less about the customer or what he wanted to eat. So we decided to launch the first efficiently operated and most elaborate Chinese restaurant since the collapse of the old Mandarin. Our concept was to have a Ming or Tang dynasty theme for decor, a fine crew of master chefs, and a well-organized dining room crew headed by a courteous maître d', host, hostesses, and so on. And we topped it all off with a glass-enclosed kitchen. This would serve many purposes. The customers could actually see Chinese food being prepared, and it would encourage everybody to keep the kitchen

clean. Also, in those hectic pioneering times, in a party of
six or eight persons, there would always be one who dis-
liked Chinese food. No matter what the captain or waiters
may say to him, his answer is, "I hate Chinese food, bring
me a steak!" Then what?

Well, with our glass-enclosed kitchen, we could say to
the difficult guest, "Will you please do us a favor? Come
and watch us prepare fresh food and see our *woks*." It
usually took me about fifteen minutes to educate a disliker
when I could have him smell the aroma of fresh, barbecued
pork coming out of the oven, or sizzling filet of chicken
breasts in a *wok* with beautiful, fresh vegetables around,
snow peas or chard toss-cooked for just a few seconds.
Usually a man like this will end up being a real enthusiast.
Why? Because he never knew how real Chinese food was
prepared. Now he was no longer a chop suey believer. And
of course, in the years since that initial education period,
we've introduced our friends to Peking Duck and many
other complex dishes enjoyed by Cantonese people on the
mainland, in Hong Kong, and here in San Francisco.

I guess I'd say what kept me going in this business, even
when there were all the setbacks, was the sense that there
was such great potential in it if people are properly trained.
I think the restaurant business is something like show
business. Now back stage, the chefs may be sweating and
arguing with the waiters, and the waiters are arguing with
the busboys, and everything is clanging away. But when
they come out to the dining room everyone smiles. The
maître d' greets you, the waiter bows, the cocktail girls are
very gracious. It's what they call being a trooper, you see.
And I've been backstage in theaters and seen the same
thing. The lights aren't working, the sound is wrong, everything is wrong and Danny Kaye is saying, "How the hell can
we put on this show." But when somebody gives the announcement, "And *here* comes Danny Kaye!", he comes
right out and he's all smiles. As if nothing had happened. I
guess I came to realize that anything you do in life will be
like that—movie production, stage production, restaurant
production—it won't show all the effort you went through
to produce it.

GRANT AVENUE

It took us months walking through Chinatown to see what Fong talked about in the streets. Eras, hats, buildings, shoes, faces, Chinatown's generations are on Grant Avenue, but first we walked too quickly, minds concentrated on going to see. We knew the sun in the middle of the day and the crowds, we knew objects randomly behind plate glass windows, crates on the sidewalk, smells. You can't walk straight on Grant Avenue. We were always stepping around things, boxes of vegetables, garbage cans, women with shopping bags, we stepped out on squashed paper cups and gum wrappers in the gutter. It was only after a long time that we began to look at things. We learned how Fong walked the streets, how he became familiar enough with them to know their infinite diversity and to feel the air change block by block. For the first time, we understood the kingpin of Grant, that two blocks within the monotonous thickness of the crowds that is the energy vortex of Chinatown. The kingpin is not where people come to eat restaurant food, to purchase dolls and teacups, lanterns and souvenir ashtrays made in Japan, but to buy what they need. And we began to see in the avenue the record of the two Chinatowns Fong demarcated before and after "the change": the market generated by the needs of people living within and the tourist center directed to the tastes and minds of people living outside.

We came down in the morning. We came down when it was dark and no one knew how early the farmers had come in trucks from Fremont and Union City and unloaded the produce crates on the sidewalk. Grant Avenue was empty. The stacked crates stood at intervals along the length of the street, they stood under tin awnings that look grey with no sunlight on them, white stalks of *bok choy* bunching out between the planks into the air. Crates of snow peas. Tight yellow blossoms of *choy sum*. The first men come onto the avenue. They are old men, they look smaller than the men who stand in the Square. They are the storeworkers. At seven o'clock they turn keys, open the wooden doors of the shops, put on faded tan and blue smocks, and drag the vegetable crates from the sidewalk.

We recognize stores from before "the change" easily by the worn-down wood of the doors and the window frames, the shape of the gold letters spotting away on the glass, the dampness that comes from the floors when we walk in. Mirrors, shining flatly, of plate metal. Metal scales hanging from the ceiling. Ancient, heavy cash registers on dark wooden counters with high, glass-paned cabinets above them. Long, carved benches lined with cup-shaped spittoons. The very oldest stores are the stores that Fong talked about, they "sell things only to the Chinese people." They are the herbal stores, with glass jars and plates of dried root, tiny red and gold disks of *ENG AUN TONG* in the window. They are the sausage factories, flanks of barbecued pork, bunched sausages on even lengths of red twine in the window. They are the poultry stores, white feathered live chickens in crates behind the window. They are the Chinese vegetable markets, the fish markets, the bean curd factories, the noodle factories, the pastry shops.

They're unpacking the vegetable crates at Mow Fung. Mow Fung Company established 1912 is a little below Grant Avenue, on Washington Street, a little above Portsmouth Square. We go in, the floor is cold, men in blue smocks are weighing crates on a huge, black Toledo scale. Others rip open crates, take out vegetables, sort them, pile them on open crates, the color, quality, boundaries of crates and smell of wood, bitter melon, purple yams, white radishes, fuzzy squash, taro roots, green leaves of *bok choy, choy sum,* Napa cabbage, scallions, garlic, ginger root, brownish, elliptical, jointed tubes of lotus root. The floor is damp, the ceiling spacious, above the leafy and tubular vegetables in crates, the emptiness of the tall wooden shelves is striking. Lines of shelves up to the ceiling hold only a few giant winter melons, leaning heavily on the boards, their green skins dusted with white powder. How long since the shelves have been empty? We perceive forms on the wall between the shelves. Bodies of Hong Kong movie stars recline in silk robes, pasted on the green paint. The dried, curling paper edges of the contours of their figures, their hairdos, and their smiles, like those of American movie stars, date them. The pinups must be two decades old. As we go out of the

store through a second storeroom filled with empty and
collapsed crates, we see the blond hair, red-lipped smile of
Marilyn Monroe, pasted onto the grey wall in a bevy of
black-haired calendar girls.

A slab of meat, one stiff leg in the air, goes in the door of
a store. It's seven-thirty, and the butcher trucks, the Italian
fish trucks, are making deliveries. "Yeah, Joe. This is Chinatown. They keep the damn water running over the fish all
day in there." The men on the sidewalk take a break
between deliveries as we go up to Grant. We follow the
leg of meat into Sang Wo. Sang Wo opened in 1860 and
string still hangs from the ceiling here, as Fong said it
used to, brown paper bags hang from a hook beside the
string, scales at both ends of the bar. We see one counter
with heavy wooden drawers, a small glass window in each
drawer reveals its contents: soybeans, peanuts, salted
plums, preserved dates. Across the store, from hooks in the
ceiling, pork sausages, thick slabs of smoked bacon, trian-
gular salted liver sausages with fatty meat stuffed in pur-
plish skins, hang over the counter. We look into the room
at the very back of the store, a tall man in a beige smock
cuts into the new stiff leg with a thin knife. An old man in
sagging pants, brown hat pushed back on his head, a pipe in
his mouth, shuffles up with the trimmed pieces of meat and
vegetables to the front counter. We guess he is a relative
of someone in the store, an old man who earns breakfast
by working for an hour or two in the morning.

When it's after eight on Grant, the vegetables and fish and
meat have all been unloaded, taken into the stores and
sorted and the sun gets into the street a little more. There's
a feeling of relief, the avenue begins to change, the first cold
effort of the day is over. The men who have been working
in the stores filter out in their smocks, to have coffee. Men
who work in real estate offices, insurance offices, travel
agencies in Chinatown and are coming in to begin the day
have coffee. The men who have been standing in the street
since early morning, taking what work they can get unload-
ing the trucks, have coffee. We walk along Grant and
between the dark windows and closed doors of the souvenir
shops and the bigger, better restaurants in Chinatown, the

narrow windows of the coffeehouses are lighted, their long counters filled with men in smocks and suits and heavy jackets, having coffee. Newspaper stands, still in the chilly shadows of buildings, open up.

On the north end of the avenue, from Broadway to Clay, the older stores have been sprinkled among the newer supermarkets, where plastic laundry baskets are set on the sidewalk with cellophane packages of instant noodles and soup, canned fish, and canned vegetables. There are the new bakeries, with stainless steel cases, a few new hardware stores, clothing stores, stationery stores, but within these boundaries, all of the stores serve daily needs. The kingpin comes at the end of this northern zone, between Washington and Clay, and it is after the kingpin that the market stores fade out, the souvenir shops begin. Just after Washington crosses Grant, close enough to share the color and noise of the kingpin, two self-service souvenir stores stand. This is the shading-off zone, and after you cross Sacramento and Grant, there are no more market stores on the street. As when Fong walked, the energy and motion of the street changes as you walk from one end of the avenue to the other.

We pass the window of the City of Shanghai. On the carpet with the elegantly displayed lacquer-ware there is a photograph of Mae West, her shoulders wrapped in white fur. "Thank you for the lovely robes," she wrote, her name signed with a flourished M and W. We remember Fong's image of white, silk skirts sweeping the Chinatown streets. A little beyond, the balcony of the Shanghai Low Restaurant hangs over the sidewalk, with the same white neon sign we had seen in a photograph of the restaurant taken in the thirties. Today, only the smaller, neon-lettered sign DANCING and black sedans with floorboards that had been parked in a rainy street are missing from the old scene. Beyond, more balconies, awnings of mustard, gold, green, and red, slope down the hill to the gate that officially ends Chinatown at Grant and Bush. Only here on this last block of Chinatown, after the blocks of crates and gaudy windows, do potted laurel trees line the sidewalk at regular intervals, as they do on the more prosperous streetfronts downtown.

At the beginning of the last block, a pagodalike tower rising from a tan brick building catches our eyes. A slab of black marble identifies the building as the Peking Bazaar Company. It epitomizes the fading, elaborate elegance of this street. Thin, fragile squares of old glass set in wood bear gold letters: Importers of Fine Chinese Arts. Red tiles form a curving roof at the top of the tower and one empty flagpole juts up at the top of the turret. Outside the door of the store, a sculptured wooden pillar branches out of the sidewalk into sprays of leaves, peacocks, dragons, forming an archway over the door. There is a faint gilt on the winding dragon tail, and the patterns of clouds and streams, women bearing baskets of fruit, and robed men carrying pieces of ivory on the pillar. Someone is sweeping the floor behind the door.

We had not yet looked carefully at the displays in the windows. We see them now, walking through the door, the windows are lined with dusty, crowded shelves. On the top of the front shelf, an artificial pine branch is laden with green plastic cord, with unlit electric lights in the shape of miniature lanterns, with artificial birds. Set below are a line of Japanese *kokeshi* dolls, pairs of Chinese-robed figures balanced against each other's lips in a kiss, tiny plastic boxes of green frogs and black and red spiders. The other window is full of plastic flowers, glass vases, animal figurines, a long line of beige plastic, elflife figures, titles on their stands I WUV YOU, QUITCHURBITCHIN, WE NEED EACH OTHER. As in the last store, the room is dark and at first we can't see anyone. Finally we locate the cash register in the corner, the man who had been sweeping the floor sits next to it beside a thin woman in a dark green smock. We want to talk to him. "Sure, go ahead!" he interrupts us with a smile and waves us back out to the pillar; perhaps he thinks we want permission to make sketches of it. We explain we want to ask him something about the design. He speaks slowly. He tells us the men in the robes are officials, they are carrying something that, he fishes for the word and finds it, represents their position. They're symbols, he says. But we tell him we don't recognize the shapes of the symbols, some look like ivory tusks, some

have a curling, fan shape but look too thick to be fans. He's
tired, though. "I don't know what they are." The young
woman shakes her head, she doesn't know what they are,
either. He gets out a ballpoint pen and writes a character
on paper, we can look it up in the dictionary, that's what
they're carrying. We ask him a few last questions about
the buildings on the street. Yes, he says, they were built in
the twenties and thirties, but a lot went up right after the
earthquake, that's how old they are. Chinatown must have
been an elegant place in those days, we say. "Yes, it was,
then. You know, then, people thought of Chinatown as very,
very high. Because we had all these things from China
then." He tells us how the avenue looked in the thirties,
filled with visitors and lit up at night. "There used to be
strings of lights all over these buildings. Lights around the
showcase windows and lights all over the tower here. The
place was beautiful at night. I guess about five or six years
ago we turned our lights out. Business got so bad, nobody
wanted to pay for them any more." He tells us he worked
in the store as a clerk for forty-five years. By the time he
got to be owner, there were only a few good years of business left. But he tells us he never minds talking to people
who come in. Even if they don't buy, it helps to pass time.
We say we'll come again some time, go out to the street, and
decide to walk back toward the other, livelier, end of Grant.
We go under the carved arch, look at the pillar once more,
and notice the bare pipes of an awning frame hanging out
over the plate glass window. A heavy electric cord is
wrapped around the pipes, and unused blue, red, yellow,
green light bulbs dangle in their sockets over the street.

PART 2

THE REFUGEES

4. Returned Students

GINARN LAO, 77

He does not live in Chinatown, but in the Avenues, and we notice a small courtyard garden behind the garage as we ring the bell. He welcomes us, leads us upstairs, he is wearing a suit and freshly pressed shirt, his Lions' Club pin on his lapel. The room seems a little bit dark when he brings us in. First he points to the scroll painted by his father, hanging on the wall. The character for his family name, he explains, is quite rare. He shows us a picture of his father dressed in a swallowtail suit, a photograph of his uncle in a high-collared jacket and round official's cap. He tells us his uncle passed the highest literary examination in the old Ch'ing system, received the han-lin degree, and became a high official in Canton. He walks over and kneels down beside a bookcase at the end of the couch. It's full of photograph albums, maybe there are thirty. "I brought these all the way over with me on the boat. All the times we moved, during the Japanese invasion and the Second World War, I carried them everywhere I went. My children were always laughing at me and saying, 'Daddy, why do you carry all those junks around?' " In a second, tears come to his eyes. "But now I can use them while I tell you the stories. I've saved everything."

We sit down and look through the books. There's a small book of childhood pictures, the leaves are almost falling out. The second book is larger, rectangular, he opens it and we see a sea of faces, tables, at the Plaza Hotel. At the central table there's a slight figure in a high-collared shirt, swallowtail suit, a title on the picture: Ginarn Lao, guest of honor, American Bankers' Association. He tells us he was twenty-six years old then. Photographs of the Grand Canyon, he's standing with Sara there, she later became his wife.

A Christmas card he sent Sara when he was back in New York, after they had become engaged. Wedding pictures. Pictures of China again. The Majestic Theater in Shanghai. The Lakeview Hotel in Hankow. Mao Tse-tung now has his winter retreat in Hankow, he laughs. When he owned the hotel, Dr. and Madame Sun Fo, Mr. T. V. Soong, and Mr. Chang Gar-au honored him with their visits. "When Generalissimo Chiang Kai-shek was out of politics and resting in the Ching-lo Villa in Hankow, he used to spend many afternoons in my pavilion on top of a hill, watching the sunset." Pictures of Hong Kong just before the Second World War. His Cafe de Chine. His amusement park, the Ritz. Hong Kong after the war. Pictures of large banquets. He is standing with the international manager of Universal Films. He is president of the Lions' Club and he is standing with the governor of Hong Kong. He is entertaining American movie stars like Grace Kelly and Henry Fonda, lots of pictures of Cary Grant, thank you notes, he must have saved every one. An autograph book, pages inscribed, "To the Man with a Thousand Friends." A very thick address book, "This is for the English addresses," and a slimmer one, "This is for Chinese." Photographs and newspaper clippings recording his retirement in 1963 as manager of Universal Pictures of Hong Kong.

Ginarn Lao is one of a smaller group of "oldtimers" in Chinatown. He did not spend the major part of his adult life here, but settled recently after becoming a political refugee in the wake of China's recent Great Proletarian Cultural Revolution. While men like Lew Wah Get were leaving villages in Toishan to find work as laborers in California, a privileged group of Chinese, men like Ginarn Lao, and a smaller number of women, came to America to study in elite universities on the East Coast. For immigration purposes, this privileged group was not considered "laborers or merchants," but students. Accordingly, American Chinatowns, in their eyes, were settlements of Chinese of a lower class than themselves, places which they bypassed during years spent living in university dormitories or with American families.

Unlike the laborers and merchants who entered the

country and settled in Chinatowns, traveling back to Canton on the few occasions when they had money to pay passage, Chinese students who came to American universities on their own funds or on scholarships provided out of the Boxer Rebellion indemnity sought training in Western scientific and business methods with which they could return to become the leaders of a modernized China. After graduating from Lehigh, Mr. Lao gained a year of practical experience in American business by working at the Irving Trust Bank and with Roger Brown and Company, an import-export firm. He then returned to Hong Kong and after one year at the Bank of Canton was sent back to New York to open the first Chinese branch bank in America at Number 1 Wall Street. This was the period when the Plaza Hotel photo was taken, and Mr. Lao warmly remembers relationships established then. "I was able to borrow an experienced American from the International Bank to assist me. We handled most of the Chinese remittances to Hong Kong and also the commercial bills for the American manufacturers and exporters, whom we told of the great prospect for American capital in China, then, one hundred to two hundred percent profit easily. I had a good opportunity not only to build up a trade but also to strengthen the relationship of good will between the two republics. This I have been doing ever since. For whatever I have done, I have felt a desire to develop better relationships between the two people." When Mr. Lao met us to check the interview transcript we were using for the book, he reminded us, "The one thing I hope you mentioned was that all my life I have wanted America and China to be closer together."

During the period of the Chinese civil war, in the 1940s, many of China's "returned students" found themselves forced, like Chinatown's laborers, to come back to America to settle permanently. As the leadership of modern China was captured from these sons of large landlords, compradores, and bureaucrat capitalists by Communist revolutionaries, they became political refugees seeking asylum in Taiwan, Hong Kong, and in the late 1940s a steady flow of these refugees settled in San Francisco. Many have maintained the traditional sense of class dis-

tinction in relation to the Chinatown population, and have settled with their considerable wealth in exclusive parts of the city or its suburbs. A few, sensing solidarity with and responsibility toward the new American Chinese population they found themselves part of, chose to involve themselves with Chinatown. Despite the late arrival of this group, we considered it an integral part of Chinatown and included representative interviews.

After giving up his hotel in Hankow in 1946, Ginarn Lao assumed the position of manager of Universal Films in Hong Kong and held it for twenty-one years. It was not until he was seventy-two years old, when rioting and turbulence spread through Hong Kong in response to the Great Proletarian Cultural Revolution in China, that Mr. Lao decided to retire from his position and join a daughter and son living in San Francisco, "because the disturbance in May 1967 gave them a great deal of worry and anxiety over our safety." Although he was invited to join an insurance company and to organize a Chinese restaurant with a friend, "I politely refused these offers. Since I had already pioneered many of these projects, I now preferred to help the poor rather than the rich." Several months later he took a position in Self-Help for the Elderly, a senior citizens' service center in Chinatown. Now, entering his seventy-sixth year, he is a fulltime worker there. In the final part of his autobiography he wrote, "I enjoy this work because I can serve the senior citizens, particularly the old Chinese. As a Lion, I used to plan big projects for underprivileged people, but now, in San Francisco, I am in direct contact with the poor old Chinese. We have a Chinese saying, 'If one does not go into the lion's den, how can one get the lion's cub?' "

My father used to come in a carriage to visit me. I remember the first time he visited the school, not knowing he was coming, I was hard at work in my room. My father came up the stairs, through the door, and stood behind me, watching me. I was greatly surprised. Yes, I was the youngest student in the school at the time. This was St. John's, one of the American missionary schools in Shanghai, and it was quite far away from my home. But it was the best school

at that time, and many of my schoolmates became prominent men. T. V. Soong was one of them, he used to stand
ahead of me in my military company. Oh, he was very tall
and thin, then! And one thing, often he had his left boot on
his right foot, and the right on the left. I don't mean to criticize, but I could never understand this, you know. It seemed
to me most comical!

Oh, it wasn't my father who wanted me to go to an
American school. I made my choice. Because somehow I
always had a feeling that China and America should be
together. I don't even know how I got that idea, because my
father was working in a British firm, he was the compradore
at Reiss Brothers. But somehow, as a boy, I already had that
feeling. Maybe it was the Boxer Rebellion, you know. Of all
the countries, only America turned back the indemnity to
China in the form of scholarships to Chinese students. So I
knew they were not for themselves alone. America and
China should get closer and closer. But before I could do
anything, I had to learn. So I determined to enter St. John's.

Two years later I transferred to Nanyang College and got
my degree there. In 1914 I wanted to go to America to fur-
ther my higher education. Still my father was uncertain.
"There's a world war," he told me. "You better not go to
America." But I said, "Dad, the war is in Europe, not in
America. I'll be safe." So I left. I still remember how he
wrote to me again in 1917. "Now what about America?
America has joined the war." I said, "The war is still in
Europe. Don't worry, I want to finish my education before
I come back." And I did go back to China right after I
graduated. My father sent me to our coal mine in Wuchi,
Hunan Province. But there was civil war there at the time,
and bandits. Being the son of the proprietor of a coal mine,
there was a rumor that they wanted to kidnap me. For ran-
som, of course, not for political purposes. So I told my
father I didn't want to stay there and risk my life. I wanted
to leave, I wanted to work, see. Then I went back to America. I learned banking from Irving Trust and import-export
from Roger Brown and Company.

Of course, when we first landed in San Francisco, in 1914,
everything seemed to be on such a big scale, you know. The

buildings were high and tall, and the construction was substantial. After graduation, when I went to Europe, I was
greatly surprised. When I landed in Southampton, the
railroad cars were so small in comparison with America!
The station in Southampton could not even compare with
the station in Shanghai. And I hate to tell you this, but
really, the sanitation there was terrible. So . . . everything in
America gave me the most wonderful impression. It was the
biggest democratic country at that time. And the most
modern, you see? And also, being born under a monarchy,
I noticed the freedom here.

Being governed by the Manchus, naturally we had wanted
to be free, you see. And we wanted to know how to get
freedom. Of course, we had the revolution of 1911. But that
was not quite settled yet. We still wanted to get real freedom from the point of democracy. The feeling in my
younger days was that as a country we were so backward
in science, in everything. And we suffered from several
wars, you see. The Sino-Japanese war, then the Russo-
Japanese war. The Japanese fought on our behalf, of course,
but just because they wanted to grab a part of China. They
took it away from Russia, but it was all Chinese property!
So we wanted to see how China could be free. Under the
Manchus we had suffered too much. That's why, when we
first came, we at once felt the freedom.

My father kept urging me to return to work in the Bank
of Canton and finally I agreed under one condition. I wrote
to my father, "If I prove myself capable and honest, I want
them to send me back to New York to open up the first
branch of the Bank of Canton on Wall Street." Well, that
was exactly what I did.

We wanted to develop the business relations between the
two countries, you see, through banking. You know, in our
country, we had resources, untouched resources, plenty.
But we didn't have the capital, and furthermore we didn't
have the men. Manpower, yes, but men with brains . . . that
was important, too. So I urged the Americans to invest in
China. It was difficult for us returned students alone to do
the work. We needed their capital, and we needed their
brains, to help us out. I often suggested that. And even what

I said fifty years ago is still true! Even now, in Hong Kong, people make two hundred, three hundred percent very easily! My nephew, for instance, is operating three sweater factories. Not for domestic consumption, but for export to America. And he's making a big fortune. My wife's brother is operating a glove factory . . . All those things I proposed before, after fifty years, are still good.

When I was young, even just a young kid in Shanghai, I always wanted to do something new. When I was working in New York, I thought, we have import-export already, but we haven't got a Chinese bank in New York. I never thought of opening a chop suey restaurant, you see, because they already had that. Later, when I went back to China, I did the same thing. The first time, I told my father I had been greatly impressed by the American nickelodeon. It would be a wonderful business to get into. He said, "Son, no nickelodeon. Stay in the bank and learn to be a banker." I stayed in the bank and saved some money, and after a while, I was able to get some friends my own age to go in with me. We built a very modern theater, just like the American nickelodeon in those days. Admission was thirty cents and in the first year we paid a dividend of sixty percent, sixty percent the second year, and in the third year thirty percent. People were amazed we did such a good business. My father said, "Why didn't you tell me in the first place?" I said, "You would not believe me. You said no nickelodeon. You thought banking was the only business." He said, "When you start the next one, let me know."

When I went into the hotel business it was the same. He said, "You know, hotels are operated by rough people. Not people from our class." I said, "Dad, no. We have to improve. If I don't go into that business myself, how can you expect the profession to improve?" So I'm always for something different. That's how we improve.

Certainly most Chinese students, educated like myself in America, were anxious to go back and put new ideas into practice. Unfortunately, we met many obstacles. The political situation was unsettled. The laboring class hadn't much education. We wanted to open up our land, but we had no machinery. In the country, there was no way to get from place to place, you had to walk miles and miles. Railroads were few. So how far could you get, see? How much time did you have? We learned modern ideas, modern ways from America. Then we got back to a country which was still a hundred—I can easily say even a thousand—years backward.

In my case, for instance, ten years after my graduation I decided to build a hotel in Hankow, on the other side of my father's summer home. But at that time there was no water system in Hankow. How can you build a modern hotel without a water supply? Finally I decided to bore an artesian well on our land. It was the first engineering job I ever did. We drilled four hundred feet deep and found enough water to supply our every need. Everybody was happy, especially my American guests. In fact, my first guests were Americans who had been invited to teach at the Chinese Aviation School in Hankow. Their dormitory was not finished on time, and they begged me to rush construction, which I gladly did for them, because I will never forget what I have learned in America. We felt very much at home with one another, being trained in America, you see. We could understand one another thoroughly.

In fact, at that time, permit me to say, that I felt much closer to the Americans than to the Chinese. Because we had the same training, same education, see. We can understand one another much better. You must have something in common before you can understand each other, you see. Back in China, at that time, over fifty years ago, so many of these old Chinese haven't learned or heard anything about modern business or modern science. You cannot convince them, you see. So I can really talk to the Americans much better, much easier, more friendly. It's not that people in China were stubborn, see. But they didn't have the training. They didn't know about these things. Education was not for everybody, you know. Only for the rich people, they could afford to go to school. So we returned students were very few. We wanted democracy. We knew it would take a long, long time. But someone had to start, even if it was difficult. We knew we had to educate the people. We understood it would take time. But if we didn't start, nobody

would. It would always be the same. Especially in the
countryside, we had to educate the people in many ways.
We had to show them, tell them what could be done. Now
the Chinese peasants, of course, as a whole, they were very
nice, very honest. But it was not easy to convince them. As
we have a saying, you cannot train an old dog to learn new
tricks. And the people in the country have no confidence in
you, you see. When I opened up my hotel in Hankow, there
was a family which ran another hotel, before I came, which
also catered to our European and American friends. They
had nothing, you see, they used water from a well, they had
no comforts, no sanitation. But it was only after I put up
my hotel that they came to learn from me. They came to see
why I got all the business from them! When they saw all my
rooms equipped with Simmons beds, Beautyrest mattresses,
finally they bought ten. Ten for their whole hotel! So you
see, they liked to learn, but very slowly.

REV. MAVIS SHAO-LING LEE, 66

Minister of the First Chinese Baptist Church
She came to the United States in the late 1940s to further
her ministerial training at the Harvard Divinity School.
Unable to return to China after 1949, she lives and works in
Chinatown.

There was one thing I always noticed. I noticed that my own
school, all the mission schools, many Chinese schools at
that time were set up by England or America. All the people
sent to be teachers were white people. So I said, "Why? I
can be a missionary, too." So I made up my mind when I
was in high school, "I must be a missionary so that I can
teach to my own people, instead of always having white
people preach to our Chinese." And I won't forget that,
because at that time it was always on my mind that any
country in a good situation always sent white people to be
the heads of departments, the principals, the teachers in
schools in China. When I was young, of course, I didn't
understand the different types of boards, but we knew the
school was supported by the mission board, that that was

how everything was paid, so they had all the authority in the school. And there was no Chinese to be principal.

Then when the first movement of Communists entered Canton, they disturbed all the mission schools. They gave lectures and they said, "You Chinese should have your own principals." And all the college students, and the seniors, and the high school students said, "Yes, why don't we have a Chinese principal?" That was how they stirred things up at the time. That's the reason I was in the student movement, too. No, I wouldn't say the anti-Western feeling was too strong at this time, but when we heard these people from the outside give lectures, saying the Chinese should have Chinese leaders, a Chinese principal, we said, "That's quite right."

Then when the student movement started, all the students in different schools united together, and we went to our schools, and told the trustees and the board we needed a Chinese principal. "Needed," we said. We were very polite, you know. We didn't say, "We don't want white people," because they supported the school, after all. Well, at first the board was very surprised. They kept saying that we must be influenced by the Communists, everything was "the Communists." And the board said, "Your Chinese leaders are not well-qualified. They do not have overseas study, advanced study, master's degrees or doctor's degrees." And we said, "You can send some of us to go there and study." And then at last some people on the mission board were very good. Some paid no attention, but at that time the principal of our high school was Miss Mary Sanders, she was American and she was very good to the Chinese. She said, "We should hand it over to the Chinese. Though I am the principal, I resign and let a Chinese be the principal." Then the mission board decided to train some of the Chinese to be their own leaders. Of course, a missionary was still the advisor. They still wanted to have someone there, but they changed the name to advisor (laughs).

Then I came here for advanced study. When I was studying here, war broke out, and the Communists took over China. The immigration officers called me and I said, "If I can, I want to return to China to work in our own schools."

But now I was a missionary educated in America and I was told I would be unable to return. The Communists might have beheaded me if I had gone back, you know. Since I'm a running dog of imperialism (laughs). Of course, I'm still homesick for our own land, because my first motive in coming here was to study, and to help our own country. But now I can't. And yet staying here I often feel Americans can do their own work, you know. So I've tried to dedicate myself to helping Chinese people here.

MRS. M. J. FUNG, 44

She and her husband own the Gate of Shanghai, a silk and art goods store on Grant Avenue. They, too, found themselves in the position of "stranded students" after 1949.

Oh, I never think about how much business I do each year. As long as I'm happy, my customers are happy, and we get along peacefully, my children behave well, I'm counting my blessings. My children are in college, they don't have any bad habits, I'm really more than grateful.

You know, many of the art goods in this store, in the old days we used to see them day after day and we never appreciated them. My grandfather was one of the tutors to the Ch'ing emperor, the young emperor near the last part of the dynasty. He was lucky, because he not only collected many treasures himself, but many pieces were given him by the emperor. Since he was a very fine scholar, he appreciated them.

Now in China, they never make a big thing of who these pieces are passed on to. When you have a large household and so many treasures as we did, all you care about is keeping them within the family. My relatives felt, if we wanted something they could give, fine. They sent it over.

We had several homes in Shanghai and also some in the country. The ones in the country especially were very beautiful, we had huge gardens that were almost like parks, and we would have visitors come just to see the gardens. Of course, these were all destroyed in the Japanese war. In the country, our family owned the whole town where the

estate was. We used to go there during the summertime—
oh, those were the really happy days! You know, we would
get all the cousins together and it was almost like a fairy
tale.

I always think that my childhood in China was almost
like a fairy tale. Almost like a princess, it was beautiful. We
had such a large family, naturally we lived with my grand-
parents and it was very harmonious. You never heard about
fights between mother-in-law and daughter-in-law. They
never happened, and we respected the old folks. We had
our family celebrations, and I remember one time it was my
grandfather's birthday. I think that celebration lasted a
whole week. Relatives came from far away, they all made
a special point of coming. And then they all stayed at our
place, oh, it was fabulous, a great feast. We had every kind
of dishes, roast chicken, all types of fish, geese, duck, anything you can think, we had it. We had afternoon snacks,
dinner, midnight snacks, it was just fantastic. And I think
we had games, but they were not too strenuous. Then we
each had our nursemaid, so it was a tremendous combination from all different angles. You always felt that you were
loved. And we had so many uncles and aunties, when
Chinese New Year comes along, you really can get rich just
by collecting red paper.

So in things like that, if you compare America and China
together, they are like two different worlds. You know, in
America everybody is busy, they don't have time just to
entertain in the grand way, the traditional Chinese way.
And they don't have the energy, either, because everybody
works. After you work, put in eight hours, you go home and
still have to keep your own house going. So you don't have
time to entertain friends splendidly. But in China it was
different. We didn't have to keep up with the housework
because there were always house servants. We had enough
energy to entertain, so naturally we could talk more, appreciate things together or admire each other's possessions,
whatever you want to do. But here everybody has a rigid
schedule, a time to leave for the bus, a time to be in the
office, a time to have lunch . . . it's an entirely different life.

I can't even correspond with my family any more. They

didn't want to leave their property unattended and just run away, so most of them did not flee from China. But then they were no longer able to collect rent. And in the meantime, they still had to pay taxes. That was the joke. I don't know what they are doing now, because we don't keep contact. They said, well, they would figure it out and manage things themselves.

I had no great awareness of the revolution building up in China when I was there. I didn't think the peasants were resentful. Of course, maybe I'm prejudiced because I come from a well-to-do family, but they did not suffer. For instance, we had servants, and when they worked for us, naturally our family became like parents to them. We would take care of all their family, their wives, their children, their own parents. Many times we married their children off for them, found them a good job and helped them to get started. And if the weather was too dry or too wet, if the harvest wasn't good, we never pressed them. If they wanted to give us a little rice as payment for the land, fine. But if they felt that year they couldn't afford it, we never pressed them. If they got sick we always helped out. So I don't think the peasants would ever really feel resentful. That was more or less propaganda from the Communists, or maybe some other part of China.

PART 3

THE FAMILY SOCIETY

5. Pacific Street Laundry

"Maybe when my old man stops working we can sell these to a museum." Don shows how the black bar twists steadily under the ceiling of the cellar, the hot rubber pulleys extend down to the rollers, the wooden vats, the mottled iron spinners with bronze plaques which read Troy, New York. "Maybe someone could come down and take a photograph of these machines, they're about a hundred years old." The cellar is close and we can feel steam and dampness when we breathe in. There's a narrow channel in the cement behind the machines with a dirty crust of minerals and soap in it. Don says the channel is supposed to drain the water out when the machines overflow but it's too shallow, so the water always washes back to the center of the room. We're standing on slippery planks that have been put down in the pools of water around the greasy black bases of the machines. There are a lot of dirty rags on the planks, it's as if the air is damp with their rotting. "I think some law in the Department of Health or something says they have to be higher than the floor. Not just flat like this." Don says oh, well, his old man wouldn't be operating the business anyway, but there's nothing else to do. There's a heavy wooden dolly near one of the vats, nothing in it. A galvanized pail with a stick, soaking clothes in it. Then all over the planks and all around the mouths of the machines there are pails, damp net sacks, laundry bags, socks, shirts, towels, and undershirts in wicker baskets. The wooden handles of two brooms have been bound tightly with red yarn and strips of green cotton so their brushes form a double thickness, a double width of sweeping surface. "This is to get the water off the floor." Don glances at the broom. "He's kind of backward, you know."

Light bulbs hang from the iron bar beside net cages that cover the pulleys of the machines, casting a glare on the grease. There is a table behind the planks we're standing on and a heavy layer of dust on a plastic tablecloth, but we can hardly see what's piled on top: old paint cans and oil cans, brushes sticky with paint, the stiff forms of empty white plastic Clorox containers. Somebody from the presses calls Don. A wooden washer has to be stopped. We go back to the machines, Don bends over the pulleys and cogs of the vat. He says a few years ago the latch that stopped the washer broke, since then the only way they can keep the cylinder of the machine still is to jam it shut themselves. We watch him stick his hand under the cylinder, thrust a piece of scrap lumber, a two by four, under the moving log, it catches one of the teeth, the cylinder holds still. "Most of his stuff is broken down here and he just makes up something to keep it going."

Don takes us to the other end of the cellar. It's dark here, too, but one electric light bulb over the presses illuminates steam rising off the rollers, the figures of his mother, his older sister, her husband, and a cousin, working at the four corners of the machine. His sister's baby girl, in sneakers and pink pajamas, runs again and again the lengths of sheet stretched between her mother and her grandmother, they laugh and keep feeding the material steadily into the press. Don's mother is wearing a dark blue *cheong sam** and tiny jade earrings. She seems about fifty-five. His sister wears a plaid wool jumper, white blouse, her hair in long braids. Don tells us the whole family grew up here in the laundry. Three years ago, when his older brother got a job as a computer analyst for General Foods, he bought a house in Redwood City and five of them moved out there. Now only his sister lives here with her husband and child. We ask Don if his brother-in-law is taking over the business. "No, he's a waiter. He only works here on his day off." Don says his father keeps the laundry open seven days a week. The work takes from nine in the morning until eight or nine at night and anybody in the family who's around helps out. "You

---

* A high-collared Chinese dress.

earn something here?" we ask. "Are you kidding? It's all free down here." Don tries to get his mother to talk to us. She's been talking and laughing with her daughter and the child, but she doesn't want to stop work for a conversation. She's brusque. She says are we sure we want to write about a family in a laundry? After World War II, when she came over here, a lot of families were still running laundries in Chinatown. But you don't see the laundries doing a good business any more. Maybe we should go up the street to the housing project and talk with a family there.

Don says, "You have to understand this is a nonprofit organization. They're just making it here." He doesn't think the laundry has had a new customer for five years. All those men we saw sitting around upstairs are steady customers, they've been coming here for twenty years. He says even the low-income housing projects in Chinatown have washing machines in the basement now, so who wants to pay to have their laundry done? Only the men in the old buildings, the tenement houses, and the one-room hotels. They like to hang around in the store and visit when they drop off their wash. He thinks most of his father's customers are over fifty. "So you'd never see any new customers coming in here. Never see any white people coming in here." Then how much does the business bring in a month? He stops a minute. He doesn't think his father keeps records, "he just takes it as it comes." He guesses the laundry bills bring in about five hundred dollars a month. Then the rent is $350 a month on this place. Running the machines, buying the bleach and the soap, that costs about one hundred dollars a month. Probably there's about a hundred dollars left, that's what he clears as profit. Oh, yeah, that's enough for them. As long as he can remember they never needed to buy new clothes. Food, they always ate the same thing—rice, bean curd, and salted fish. "I guess you're wondering why he operates a business like this. But you know Chinese. What else is he gonna do?" Suddenly Don's eye catches the baby running back and forth along the sheet in her pink pajamas. He turns to his sister, he's angry, says something in Cantonese. She shrugs him off. He looks at the baby again. "Every day I have to keep telling her mom not to dress her

that way," he says. "So old-fashioned." Don's mother tells
him to stop loafing around and get back to work. He tells
us the next thing we should do is go upstairs and see where
they lived as kids. How was it growing up there? "Oh. Hot.
No shower." He's still angry at his sister. He says when we
go upstairs we only have to look at the kitchen. The loft is
too old and beat up, ceiling's cracked, leaks in the rain, the
only things up there are beds and suitcases. "Anyway, my
sister might chew me out if she sees me take you up there.
She's so private, it's creepy. That loft used to be so dark
up there I got scared when I was a kid, and you know what
she does when her husband moves in? Board up the only
two windows in the place. Put boards over them so no one
can see in." He begins to go back up the stairs. The little
girl sees us and runs after us.

At the top of the stairs there's a vestibule that forms the
passageway from the front of the laundry to the living quarters in back. It's a very small room, shelves on all the walls
stacked with brown paper packages of laundry. The room
is quite warm. A red upholstered sofa with stuffing bursting
from its arms is sunk under the shelves on one wall, covered
with a piece of fringed, pink cotton. Hangers with freshly
pressed shirts balance on the arms and back of the couch.
A few feet across from it, a counter has been built beneath
the shelves on the opposite wall. There is an abacus and
scattered slips of pink paper on its green linoleum top. The
little girl climbs up onto the counter and speaks to us for
the first time. "Who picture?" She touches a metal photograph frame, three tiny American flags stuck in the top,
the frame leans back against the packages in its stand. Four
or five family snapshots have been fitted unevenly against
each other behind the glass. On the top, there's a wedding
picture, then a snapshot of people on an outing; it looks like
Golden Gate Park. Near the bottom there's a picture of a
young man in fatigues and army cap, someplace hot with
palm trees, bigger men with their shirts off stand around
him, one GI kneels in front strumming on a guitar. The
central, biggest photograph in the frame is of this same
young man. It's a portrait of his face, fatigues and cap
replaced by full dress uniform, buttons of his epaulettes,

dark khaki collar, shiny visor of his hat pulled over his brow. "Who picture?" the little girl asks again. We say, "Grandfather," but she doesn't respond. There's a slim campaign leaflet pressed over the top of the last two snapshots. LYNDON JOHNSON-HUBERT HUMPHREY tilts at a slight angle behind the glass.

We aren't prepared for the smell of the room in the back. It seems to come from the hot, damp air, the damp floor, the sticky plastic tablecloth on the table in the center of the room, the garbage pail, and the garbage in plastic boxes along the wall. We hear the rumble of the boiler. Across the room, through the door frame next to the sink, we can see flames beneath the boiler, sooty earth at its base, heavy wooden planks of the circumference of the tank protrude in and fill an entire corner of the room. The planks rise like a gigantic wooden wall from the floor almost to the ceiling. Beside the tank, the only window in the room is screened over and grease and soot block the netting so no light comes in at all. Don says this is why it was so hot living here. "And the funny thing is, there isn't one drop of hot water in this room. It all goes downstairs to the machines." We notice the sink, just inside the door, has only one faucet. The wall next to it is covered with tinfoil. Don says again that his old man is very backward, this is how he keeps the water from leaking through the wall. Well, they had to live with this until his brother bought the house in Redwood City. "And I'm telling you he never had nothing in this house. No nothing. No TV, no radio, no oven, no shower, the toilet's broken so you have to get water from the sink to flush it. I don't even want to think about it." Don sits down on one of the folding chairs beside the table. The little girl comes in, sees us standing by the sink, she runs over to a corner of the room underneath the stairway to the loft. Four crates have been stacked in the corner, the tops covered with napkins, paper cups, boxes, huge mayonnaise jars filled with pickles, toothpicks, cough drops, and cheap candy. She pulls a facecloth out of the pile, comes over to the sink, fills a shallow pan with water from the faucet, and washes her face. She goes back to the crates again, pulls out a paper cup with a toothbrush in it and brushes her teeth.

We look around the room. A chipped cabinet of dishes is dwarfed by the boiler next to it. There's a series of four gas burners with black skillets and pots hanging above it on the wall. The only other furniture is the table, the folding chairs around it, and a fantastic series of splotched cardboard and wooden boxes, containing household supplies, which fills an entire wall. At the end of the boxes, near the stairs, several crates have been hammered together into a surface for preparing food. There's a bowl of fresh chard leaves standing on the counter and a deep earthenware bowl, covered with an empty egg carton, containing leaves of cabbage pickling in vinegar. Don's talking again, he's thinking about some girl from Singapore who tells fortunes. "She's one person in Chinatown you really oughtta meet. I couldn't believe it, but the first time she ever saw me she told me the whole story of my life. 'You had a big change when you were seven, in second grade . . . your parents had hard times . . . such and such a year . . . don't like to talk about it,' no kidding. She's probably still around if you want to look her up." The little girl is playing with the plastic canisters underneath the stairs now. She opens one, a cellophane bag tumbles onto the floor, and salted plums spill out. She picks them up painstakingly, carries them to the garbage can beside the boiler tank, lifts the cover, and throws them in. She begins to run up and down the steps to the loft, beckoning us to come. Don says go ahead with her, he doesn't care to see that place again, he'll wait out in the store.

It's dim up here. We hear the ticking of a windup clock. We make out the shape of beds on the floor of the loft, one crib, a pile of suitcases. There's another series of cardboard cartons up here, hammered into shelves. They are filled with thin paperback books written in Chinese. There's one bureau beside the bed closest to the stairs. On top of it there is a pressed white lace doily and a wedding photograph in a stand—we recognize the couple downstairs. There's not much else in the loft. The little girl has gotten up onto one of the chairs beside the beds and she talks again for the second and last time that day. We can't understand. She throws her arms up in the air and says, "No cha."

Throws them up again, "No," calls out, "No," waves them in the dark room, "No, no, no . . . . . match!" Her voice raises at the end. We don't know what she meant. Don calls up from downstairs and says why don't we come down and meet his dad. We go back through the kitchen, the vestibule with the packages, out to the front room of the store. A lot of men are sitting and standing around out there, at first we don't know who his father might be. A grey-haired man is lifting a shirt off the press by the window, that's not him. Two men talking to each other beside the door—he's not there. We notice a small wooden counter coming out from the wall a little past the middle of the room, a slight man with his back turned is sitting at it, he has an army fatigue cap on his head. Don taps him on the shoulder and he turns around, smiles at us through his glasses, extends his hand.

6. Growing Up

The same immigration laws which gave rise to a society of male laborers in Chinatown slowed the growth of families among American Chinese. During the long years when village custom and American law had compelled men to marry in Kwangtung and commute back and forth to visit their wives, the presence of families in Chinatown was rare. "The greatest impression I have of my childhood in those days was that at that time there were very few families in Chinatown," a "paper son" who arrived in 1913 recalls. "Babies were looked on with a kind of wonder." It was not until the 1920s, seventy years after the beginning of Chinese life in California, that the reproduction of a visible second generation began. These few families grew up in the midst of a declining bachelor society where children, like women, were prized.

Men in Chinatown tore down the walls of tiny rooms in the old bachelors' quarters in Chinatown to make room for their families. "Our room was designed for the old bachelors who used to come over here," a middle-aged man who grew up over a store told us. "All my father did was break down some of the walls and we lived there over the store." With few exceptions, the men who began Chinatown's early families were the owners of small businesses, often former laborers who after many years had saved enough money to begin a modest enterprise. Since once they had registered as merchants, they and their wives could be exempted from the exclusion acts, these former laborers would return to China in their new status as owners of import-export firms, groceries, or hard goods stores, choose a woman for marriage, and bring her back on the long ocean journey. In California (except during the six years while the Immigration Act of 1924 was in effect*) these women could then settle permanently, although, like their husbands, they were ineligible for citizenship. Occasionally the owners of laundries, restaurants, or even hired laborers (all of whom were subject to exclusion) also managed to bring in wives by bribing wealthier Chinatown merchants to list their names as partners in business. Finally, a slow increase in the population of native-born Chinese women also contributed to the gradual proliferation of families in Chinatown. These families literally filled the spaces left by elderly bachelors whose numbers were declining through death and retirement to China.

As the number of families grew, the center of gravity of Chinatown life gradually shifted from the bachelor society to the families of small businessmen and the nexus of social relations and concerns which accompanied their existence. Bachelor laborers and small business families continued to live side by side in Chinatown, but increasingly family life came to dominate the focus of community attention and to define the external image of Chinatown to American society. As the more successful families prospered, they were in time capable of hiring workers who were often younger relatives from villages in Kwangtung. Men from these prosperous families entered the institutional life of the community and reinvigorated the merchant leadership of family associations, district associations, and the Chinese Six Companies. Their participation enhanced the strength and prestige of these institutions and brought them more fully in line with the needs and interests of small business and the family society, the emergence of which marked the real decline of the Chinatown tongs and the eventual eclipse of the once colorful life which revolved around the lives of the single male laborers.

Memories of a secure childhood and family-centered life

* No Chinese women were admitted to the United States from 1924 to 1930, including wives of American-born Chinese. However, in 1930, the harsh act of 1924 was revised to allow for the admission of Chinese wives of American citizens who were married prior to May 26, 1924. Between 1906 and 1924, an average of 150 Chinese women per year entered the United States. From 1931 to 1940, an average of sixty Chinese women entered each year.

in small shops are common to offspring of the family society. In the stores, family life was integrated to business so that there was little boundary between the two. Mother and father worked together while they raised the children in the stores, and from an early age the children helped with small tasks involving the business or with household chores. "I began by helping my parents fold towels and handkerchiefs, very simple things," one professional described his childhood in a laundry. "When I got to be eight or nine they showed me how to work the presses and I went from T-shirts and handkerchiefs to complicated things like shirts. After I got into high school, I used to put in an hour a day watching the counter and putting laundry in the machines. Then, since I could read English, I began helping my father with forms and some of his business work." Because long hours of work by father and mother were a necessity to keep the family business going, maturity, contribution to the common effort, and the assumption of mutual responsibility for each other were highly valued qualities in the children of these small business families. Most remember caring for or being looked after by other brothers and sisters, fixing simple meals for themselves, and being constantly reminded by their parents that the purpose of the business and all their own hard work was to provide for them. Only in the evenings, when relatives or friends dropped by for long chats and games of mahjong, did the business oriented effort of the family relax. Occasionally, when special visitors arrived, the children were permitted to stay up late, playing with their cousins downstairs or outside the store in the street.

In accordance with the Confucian family tradition they had known as children in Kwangtung, parents in Chinatown taught their children to subordinate their individual interests to the welfare of the family, which was the basic unit of society. The Chinese family, with the father as patriarch and center of authority and its Confucian-defined hierarchy of duties and obligations, was the familiar model which these parents attempted to fulfill. Although the ideal was approximated with only varying degrees of success, the presence of a strict father and somewhat more lenient mother, both of whom insisted on obedience and respect, is remembered by most offspring of the family society. "Our parents told us to stand and we stood," as one woman put it. "They told us to sit down, and we sat down." This same woman pointed out that another tenacious influence of the Chinese patriarchal tradition on Chinatown family life was the tendency to consider girl children less important than boys because boys carried on the family name.

Although Chinatown children spent their grammar school years at the local Commodore Stockton public school amid a student body which was almost entirely Chinese, entrance to junior high school brought exposure for the first time to a white world which they constantly compared to what they had known at home. In most cases, parents carefully prepared their children, particularly the males, to "take advantage of the opportunity" of so many years of free education in America. Still sensitive to the low position assigned to merchants and the high status and influence of scholars in Chinese society, they urged their children to prepare themselves for mental or professional occupations (except in the case of those whose pessimism about employment discrimination against Chinese made them feel this was impractical). Adages like, "You can make a million dollars, but a good education is better than a million dollars" and "You can lose everything but a good education" are familiar phrases to those who grew up in the family society and reflect the commonly held priority of values. Beneath their enthusiasm for education and advancement, however, Chinatown parents could not repress a sense of anxiety about their children's entrance into outside society and the possible erosion of values which prevailed at home. While they supervised homework required in public school and conscientiously followed their children's progress there, they also insisted that they attend classes in "Chinese school" after public schools were over. Here, for two hours daily, they studied primarily Chinese language and, as the classes became more advanced, the classics and history. Although attendance became increasingly irregular as experience of social life and activities in the public schools deepened, parents were insistent that children grow up with some awareness of "their thousands of years of Chinese civilization," and memories of late afternoons in a Chinese school are invariably among the memories of anyone who spent a childhood in Chinatown.

Nevertheless, in the course of their years in junior high school and high school, it was the influence of American social practices and patterns which proved the decisive influence on second-generation American Chinese. A slow fading of the virulent anti-Chinese prejudice of the nineteenth century, combined with the greater security of their own, stable family lives, made the sense of discrimination less sharp in this generation than it had been in lives of the oldtimers—indeed, a tolerant attitude toward discrimination has been one of its distinctions. "It didn't anger me," a middle-aged man reflected, when he described how he had occasionally been called "chink" by other boys in his school. "I just thought, well, there are people in this world who are ignorant, so why get into a fight? If they are that ignorant, what's the use?" Although Chinatown children in each class tended to group together and carry on social life with each other, they attempted to re-create among themselves the same activities and patterns they saw in their classmates. Sports, dating, sharp-dressing, cars, and popular music maintained the same central importance in the lives of Chinatown's teenagers as they did in adolescent life outside. "By the time I was in high school, the big thing, if you had money, was to have a car," the son of a grocery store owner told us. "Then a girl. You would have to dress fairly well, not in dress-up clothing but in sports clothing. My father wouldn't give us any money for working in the store, but we did get an allowance, and I'd use that to try to get the right clothes. Of course, athletics was very important. I guess you could just call us all-American types."

These children felt uneasy with the old world social conventions which their parents still sought to impose on them. Women, for example, attempted to break out of the confinement of home life, and the subordinate position which they held in their families. Because they proved to be more easily "accepted" by white society than men of their generation, they were able to find white collar jobs as secretaries and clerks in downtown insurance offices and banks which provided them with a measure of independence. For both men and women of the American-born generation, the conception of courtship and marriage also differed significantly from that of their parents. As in American culture, romantic love, together with practical considerations such as family background, education, and career potential, were seen by them as the basis for choosing a partner in marriage. They conceived of marriage as a union between two individuals rather than a matter which the family decides, and thus rejected their parents' efforts to arrange marriages for them. Although many parents strongly encouraged their children to follow the village custom of marrying somebody outside of the family name whose parents came from a nearby village, such practices declined among the American-born generation. Instead the preference was for American weddings in one of the Chinatown Christian churches followed by a Chinese ceremony in a higher-class Chinese restaurant. After their wedding, the newly-weds established their own household distinct from that of their parents. Although relationship with parents and in-laws would continue to be intimate and often included a certain amount of economic cooperation, the new couple oriented themselves to moving outward into American society and to acquiring the comforts of middle-class life. The parents, on the other hand, remained in Chinatown where they lived out their lives within a Chinese-speaking world tending to the family business.

Stable home life, a measure of economic security, and the emphasis placed by their parents on hard work and high educational achievement, prepared a surprisingly high proportion of children from Chinatown's small businesses to go on for college degrees. Parents wanted their children to do better than themselves by "entering one of the professions." By the 1930s, their children were able to enter City College, San Francisco State, University of California, Berkeley, and occasionally private colleges like Mills and Stanford without much difficulty. They undertook their higher education, however, with an awareness that occupational opportunities for Chinese were still severely limited. A housewife recalls a conversation with a registrar at San Francisco State College: "In fact, when I entered and registered, they told me very definitely that I could take the courses, 'but after the course don't expect to be placed, because you are Chinese.' They were very frank. The registrar said, 'I want you to understand this because I don't want you to go through four years and find yourself disappointed.' I told them, 'actually, I wasn't planning to teach in the United States, I was planning to teach in China in a missionary school.' And she said, 'Oh, well, that's alright.' Because there would be no demand to place me in schools. Because of the war, of course, I was unable to go." Particularly during the Depression years of the thirties, the first Chinese graduates from colleges and professional schools did indeed discover that jobs in their fields were almost impossible to find. Many turned back to enter their parents' businesses or to open their own small businesses in Chinatown. Not infrequently, a young man with ambition and talent considered "returning" to China where he imagined becoming a successful professional or even leader of a nation keenly in need of men and women with modern education and training. Though few actually did leave for careers in China, many middle-aged American Chinese remember attending conferences as young men where they weighed the pros and cons of finding jobs in China. By the forties, however, war and revolution in China had strongly discouraged this alternative.

It was not until the Second World War that the rapid expansion of the American economy and a new prestige which accrued to American Chinese from America's alliance with Nationalist China brought the first major entrance of the American-born generation into white and blue collar occupations. As journalist Charlie Leong put it, "To men of my generation, World War II was the most important historic event of our times. For the first time we felt we could make it in American society." Charlie explained how the war had taken men out of the ghetto, put them in American uniforms, and sent them overseas, where they felt "they were part of the great patriotic United States war machine

out to do battle with the enemy." Many men from Chinatown joined a special American Chinese infantry division
formed at the suggestion of Madame Chiang Kai-shek and
sent to fight in China. This first contact with China had the
surprising effect of making the men realize how American
they were. Charlie told us that in the thirties there were still
"a lot of people you heard about who wanted to go back
and rebuild China. I had one friend who was a movie actor
and amateur flyer, and he did go back just before the war to
work with the Chinese Air Force. But he found out he didn't
like it very much. Although it was Chinese, you know, the
social structure there was so rigid that he was, in essence,
an American. He couldn't quite penetrate. And in fact when
I got over to China during the war, the same thing made me
turn down a job with the Central News Agency." He and his
friends returned from China with a new sense of confidence
and a determination to enter every field of American life.
In 1947, the lifting of the restrictive covenant which had
prohibited Chinese from buying homes outside of Chinatown made it possible for the newly successful generation
to move to the lower-middle-class Sunset and Richmond
districts of San Francisco where they established a new
"suburb" of Chinatown. A striking indication of the difference between the careers of these offspring of the early
American Chinese family society and those of the older
bachelors was revealed in California's 1960 Census figures,
which attributed to American Chinese both the highest percentage of college educated and the highest percentage of
near-illiterate population of any ethnic group in the state.
Professional and white collar offspring of the family
society, however, point to lingering racial discrimination
which affects them. "We get steady positions as professional workers," an engineer said, "with a steady, middle-
class income. We'll get a slight promotion, but after that the
subtle discrimination comes in." They find that while American Chinese are hired in large numbers for work such as
accounting, engineering, and computer programming which
requires a high level of competence and accuracy, they are
usually kept from going one step further to the level where
decisions are made.

As members of American Chinese families found themselves drawn more and more deeply into the process of
becoming successful in America, the gulf between the family society and the bachelor society widened. Occasionally,
an old uncle or a grandfather would be brought into the
family, and would add his own effort to the family's quest.
Engineer James Low had fond memories of the years when
his granduncle lived in the same building with his family.
"My granduncle was a funny old fellow, he used to buy
canaries and he must have had about a hundred canaries in
cages in his room. But when we were growing up, he did
everything he could to help us. For a while, he had a job
peeling potatoes down at the wharf. So he used to bring
potatoes home all the time to supplement our food. Then
when he had a little extra money to spend, I remember he
used to buy us Chinese books, things like the *Romance of
the Three Kingdoms*, to read." Other children knew the old
men distantly but held them in respect. Many were taught,
however, that success in America hinged on the rejection of
the past, and the old men who embodied it. "I remember to
this very day the old men on the streets who were considered bums," a lawyer told us in his Sunset district home.
"They used to go through garbage cans for their existence
and slept in the park, they slept out in Portsmouth Square
in the evenings. I just wondered at that time what they did
with their lives. They were the ones who we would keep
away from. Our parents would say, 'Don't associate, don't
get close to them.' We used to call them 'flea men,' I forget
what the Chinese word is now, but they were supposed to
have a lot of fleas on them, and we were not supposed to get
close to them at all. You would just kind of shun, and keep
away from these people. You got to know them after a
while, and then when you saw them coming down, you
would walk on the other side of the street. I remember that
very vividly."

FRANK ENG, 33

*He works for the City Department of Parks and Recreation.
Frank's father keeps the truck parked beside the sidewalk, he*

*walks out and brings crates of pears into the store on and off
during the day. In the back of the store, we can see the loft
that he built below the ceiling, it's completely covered by
a red cloth.*

*About eight winter melons are piled on top of each other
in a huge stack next to the cash register. There doesn't seem
to be any order to the arrangement of goods on the shelves.
Boxes of sugar and Betty Crocker cake mix stand next to
cans of chicken broth, bottles of soy sauce, and peanut oil.
There's a plastic clock radio on the middle of the shelf above
the counter. Beside a scale, a galvanized tub is full of rotting
pears. His disordered tray of candies is set on a counter next
to the soda cooler. Underneath bags of salted peanuts, we
find the cloudy cellophane packages of shrunken persimmons, red dates, and translucent pieces of water chestnut
and coconut, all coated in white crystalized sugar. The labels
on the bags are made of inexpensive pulpy, off-white paper,
purple letters from a rubber stamp give the name of the
store, no price. Frank's father says he only makes the candy
at Christmas now.*

Well, my father makes Chinese candy, coconut candy and
melon candy, and there's a lot of work in preparing that, so
we ended up doing a lot of little things to help. We would
help with the coconut, you have to boil it, cut it in half, peel
it, then take the meat out of the shell and cut it in little
strips. That's all tedious work that has to be done by hand.
There was no machinery, my father just used to saw
the coconut in half, and then we used something like a
potato peeler to peel the skins. In fact, he still does all this
by hand, but now some of his relatives and other people
come in, it's like a meeting place for them. You know how
Chinese people are, the clan always had a place to get
together. I think my dad's store is like that, so many of his
old friends who are still around come over when they have
nothing to do and help. Afterwards they have a couple of
drinks. They don't get paid or anything but it's part of their
life.

We lived in the store. I guess, looking at it now, you'd say
it was one of these old mom-and-pop stores. Nobody really

makes money but they're happy with it and they get by with
it. He's never owned the property, you have to realize this.
It's owned by somebody else. For all these years he's rented
the place and it's very old. Never had hot running water, we
had to boil the water to wash, so I guess they would say the
health conditions were pretty poor. We lived in one big
room when we were young, all ten of us, and then during
the war when three of my brothers were in the military
service we only had seven or eight. What they did, you see,
was divide the whole room. There was a high ceiling and
they just built another floor between the ceiling and the regular floor, and we lived on top. As I said, there were usually
a lot of other people around, too, and I remember that they
had mahjong tables, people used to come in and play mahjong and have a great time. I remember hearing them late at
night, but I guess we got used to the mahjong rattling because it didn't seem to bother us, even when they played till
early in the morning while we were sleeping upstairs.

My father was never very structured as far as business
was concerned. I think he could have done better, could
have made a little more money if he had more guidelines.
He's in the fruit business, for instance, so he sells a lot of
perishable items. There are some things he can buy, say he
buys a crate of persimmons, they don't go, and after a week
he has to throw them out. But then the next week he'll go
and buy persimmons again, they still won't go, and he'll
throw them out again. So he's losing money on all these
items, but he continues to buy them.

He had the store before I was born. I guess there just
wasn't anything else he could get into. He came from a farm
in China and I think my mother was a laborer, picking
fruits. There wasn't any other opportunity open to them.
Probably opening a store was one of the few things that he
could do other than opening a laundry. It had an advantage
because it was a living quarters, too.

My father was always a disciplinarian. He always worked
very hard. That has been his life, and I think the one other
important thing to him was the family association. We belong to a very small one, but he's always been proud to be
part of that, and he's served as local president several times.

But primarily his life has been spent on the job . . . including Christmas and New Year's. For instance, Chinese New Year is a big holiday and most people are closed. He is closed as far as the sidewalk part is concerned, but the door is open. Anybody that wants to come in and buy anything, he's still sitting in the store waiting for them.

I'd say he puts in more than twelve hours a day and in the past he even worked longer than that. He would get up or leave the house about six in the morning and not close the store until almost nine at night. So what's that? Fifteen hours? Now it's a little less, because he's older. He gets up about six in the morning and he closes about six at night He's about seventy-three now.

One of the things he does is he has this truck and he makes a lot of deliveries. He handles winter melon, the big squash-type vegetables Chinese use for soup, they're about twenty or thirty pounds apiece. When somebody phones to order, say, five winter melons, he takes them over. But it's physical work because he has to keep running up and down those stairs from the basement, you know, one trip for each melon. I've never seen anyone work as hard as he does for that long a period and not be tense. I guess he is, but he doesn't show it.

Then when he's not delivering he handles the selling. He sits in the back and maybe somebody walks in every fifteen minutes and buys something, or sometimes nobody comes in for half an hour or so. So it's not a booming business, and I think most of what he can make is from wholesaling. Winter melon throughout the year, fruits during the summer. Again, with the fruit it's hard work, because he picks up about a hundred boxes at a time from the farm. If no one helps him, he has to unload these hundred boxes by himself. And then the rice he sells at the store comes in 150-pound bags. He does all that lifting at his age. But, well, actually I think he's so used to physical labor that if he didn't do it it would be a big void in his life. It wouldn't be a complete day for him. He likes to drink, too, like most Chinese, like any Chinese, but I've never seen him unable to do a day's work. It just doesn't stop him.

One thing I've noticed is that he has lost a lot of weight

in the last few years. And he has bad eyesight. That's been a problem for a long time and it's getting worse. I remember a few years back he needed glasses, so he just went to the five-and-ten and picked out the glasses that are on display there. I remember him buying glasses like that when I was young. I think that's what ruined his eyesight. But he has still never been in a hospital.

I wouldn't say we were "close" to my parents the way Americans use the word. I guess Chinese parents, well, my parents, don't like to show you their affection as such. They loved us, but they never really wanted to show it, you know. That was the way they lived. And I never had any qualms, I never wanted to change things, because that was just their way of expression. Maybe my mother was a little more sentimental, but even she always had to try to be very fair, you know, with ten kids in the family.

For instance, when we were younger, we all had a night to mind the store. We kind of worked it out together, one person would take Monday, then Tuesday, and so on, so we all wouldn't have to stay around every night. It got to be sort of a hang-out for some of my friends, too, because the door was always open and they didn't have to worry about no one being home. We used to play cards in the back. But I remember my dad used to be stern about any of my friends coming. He used to tell us, "Don't fool around out front. This is still a store. If you want to do something, go to the back room and do it. This is a business establishment." Sometimes my friends and I used to stand around in the store and there would be boxes to unpack, tissues or napkins to stuff into containers. He would putter around for a while and then say, "Oh, well, I guess I might as well ask you boys for a hand." I think he would pick the nights when we were all together! Or he would have a package to deliver and he would come over to me and whisper, "Why don't you ask your friends?" But he's very cordial to them now they've all grown up. I don't think anybody has any gripes about how he was treated by my father.

I would say all my friends were Chinese kids who lived in the immediate two block area around here. I can't tell you a lot of fantastic stories about what we did, because our lives were pretty quiet. My friends and I were all in one club, at the Chinatown Y, and we would have basketball games, volleyball, soccer. We hung out at the Y a lot.

I guess when I look at Chinatown now, I think there is more change now as far as people are concerned than when I was young. I always felt that things were changing in Chinatown, buildings were being changed, but the friends and the people were all the same. But when I look at China-town now, I see strangers. Well, when I was a kid China-town wasn't the attraction that it is now. I felt most of the stores and restaurants then were really catering to the Chinese people. But now, take the parade at Chinese New Year, for instance. I don't believe it is really catering to the Chinese people. You know, my parents used to take us down and they would be very happy, now, to go down with my kid, but they can't even get close enough to watch. You have to fight people off even to get near the parade, and then you have to pay for the seats. We used to have these parades, everyone remembers them from the forties, where they'd carry a huge flag of China down Grant Avenue. The flag was about a quarter of a block long, with the red and white stars on the blue, and people would throw money in for relief funds for China. We used to bring out wooden boxes and go down with the family or friends to watch. We didn't have to fight off the crowds that we fight now, we didn't think outside people would be interested. And it seems as if Chinatown had an operation or something. It's just like, I still know everything like the back of my hand, you see. But it's like having your hand, having it operated on, it's so much different now as far as the past is concerned.

LISA MAH, 36

Lisa was brought up in a herbalist's family which had moved outside of Chinatown. In 1968, she left the Berkeley faculty to work fulltime in the Chinatown Neighborhood Arts Pro-gram. Of her return to Chinatown, Lisa says: "I feel more at home in Chinatown than anywhere else. Chinatown always felt like a community to me. Of course, I have to recognize that this is based on my own vision and my own very selec-

tive way of seeing and feeling the world. A lot of times I realize I'm actually lonely here. But it's as if people here just live their lives, and it's a life that has reality to me. Not that it's a rich life, maybe it is rich, I don't know how to describe it, but life feels real here in Chinatown."

When I was three and a half my family moved out of Chinatown to the Mission District. We still had a herb store right on Grant Avenue and I would come in with my mother every day until I was ready for school. I remember I would always sit in front, right next to the engine man, they used those electrical and hydraulic brakes, and I used to watch the guy stop and start the car. I was very conscious that Chinatown was a long way from the Mission District and I was coming from another world. I was aware of that experience. Then when I would get to Chinatown I would stand in front of this big glass door which faced out on Stockton Street and look at people walk by. I remember noticing things like how much of an ice cream cone they would throw away. You know, would they eat the whole cone or just eat a tiny bit of the cone and throw it away. Because if they did throw the cone away, I wanted to go out and get it. But I noticed that in Chinatown very few people threw any part of the cone away. Whereas out in the Mission District where I lived they threw quite a bit of the cone away and sometimes part of the ice cream. But anyway, the ice cream cone was too gooey and I didn't want to eat it, I just wanted to eat the crisp cone.

So I had two years of just looking through the window. There was a building across the street, it was the Chinese-American Citizens Alliance building, and I used to look at that building for hours every day, but I never knew what CACA stood for. I knew it was some kind of Chinese building, but it didn't look Chinese to me. And it is typical that I never knew certain things like that that you would think I should know, because my parents would never explain enough to me. All the feeling I had about Chinatown was just what I picked up on my own standing behind that door. I remember another thing I used to watch very carefully was the way mothers related to their children, and that was very important to me. I would go to a playground right behind my mother's place, and one image I have, I think this is my most basic image of what mother love means, was one day when I saw an old village woman there. She spoke really bad Sze Yup language, you know, the only way I could have thought of her was just as a woman from some country village in Kwangtung. She had short, straight hair, very crudely combed, no curve in it, just straight hair pushed across her head with a little barrette holding it. She carried a baby on her back in one of those criss-cross holders. And you know how you sort of sense classes in people? I sensed it then. That she was not of our class. My parents had made us very aware of class, not in terms of money or power, but in terms of those who knew the world and could move in it and those people who were uneducated, primitive, easily taken advantage of. I immediately knew that this was a woman who had been pushed around. Well, there was a small child with the woman, as well as the one which was on her back. The other kid was sucking a lollipop, and suddenly he dropped it in the sand. I was watching this very carefully. Dropped his lollipop in the sand, and of course he started screaming, and I felt it too, I was thinking, "Dropped it in the sand. That's the end of the lollipop." I don't know why food was such a thing I seemed to notice! But anyway the mother picked up the lollipop and licked it all off, both sides, very thoroughly. Then she spat out the sand and gave the lollipop back to the kid. That's what I remember.

After I started to go to the school and I'd come back and play at home, I had the feeling that my own mother was gone a lot of the time. My father would run the herb shop in our house, on Mission Street, and mother would go in to the one in Chinatown and stay the whole day until about eight o'clock at night. But even though it was my older sisters who really did a lot of the housework, I always felt that it was my mother who gave it whatever shape or order or character it had. My father was a little inept around the house, but my mother was a very strong person, she had a very definite character to her. For instance, I felt her presence in the garden. She loved flowers so she planted gladiolas and sweet peas and roses. It was a big garden and there were beds of them that she would tend to with whatever time she had.

And then she would sew me dresses. I would lie awake at night waiting for her to come home, and she would have maybe two or three little dresses she had made that day in the store. It was always the same kind of dress, a little rectangular dress with a slot for the arms, a slot for the neck, and some piping around the neck with a tie string on it. It had no waist, no darts, no shape to it. She always made them out of very interesting material, but I remember feeling ambivalent about those dresses because they were square, they didn't have puffed sleeves, they didn't have lace. I was aware that they were not quite like other little girls' dresses. But anyway I was thrilled with these dresses when she came home. And the way I felt about my mother was that she had a very hard life, yet she did all these things. I guess, in a way, what you feel about being Chinese depends on your parents, because your parents are not only your parents, your parents are Chinese, and I felt that the things my mother did, the way she worked with her hardship was a very Chinese thing. You know what I mean? It's as if I thought all whites had it easy. Not had it easy, but they didn't have the same kind of hardship and they did not even deal with it in the same way, they didn't overcome it in the same way as Chinese.

What my parents told me about being Chinese, and the outside world, was a very mixed thing. Even in the Mission District, I always had the feeling I was seeing things through the window because my parents didn't want me to go out there, they said it was a bad place. It was an area where, if I went out to play with another little girl in her home, her mother was probably a laundry woman who came home quite late, and her father was a drunk. I used to notice things like, in my friends' families they ate margarine, but we ate real butter, I was fascinated by that. I used to think that the margarine was more fun, because you could squeeze the color around in it, but the butter was more real, a better quality, more expensive. My parents never tried to save money on food and books. We had seven kids in the house, and they would buy crates of eggs and gallons of milk. I had a sense of the largeness of everything, that my family was on a large venture, we were a large household eating up large amounts of food. I would go home to lots of people, lots of things going on. And that was in some ways stronger than what I saw outside, kids with broken families who played in their houses alone.

I think the people we knew were poorer than we were, and yet I felt we were poor. In the sense that all the money we had would be put into business investments, the business part of the house. My father's office was down on the ground floor, and every inch of that room—the floor, the wall, the furniture—was covered. Not only would there be a plush sofa, but little velvet squares on top of the sofa arms, and silk fringe hanging down from the little squares. There was a gilt clock with a pirouetting ballet dancer, and next to that were these altar-piece types of paper—gold, buddha-shaped, flame-shaped decorations which I used to study by the hour because they were so beautiful. Now that was a place we could use as a living room when the customers were not there. But basically we all knew that that was the presentation we made to the outside world. It was the way you dealt with the larger white world, it was the way you made a living. I was aware that our very best, aside from what went into food and clothing, went into meeting that world. It was the main floor that had everything, that was comfortable and plush, while upstairs, where we actually lived, had bare floors, unpainted walls, no refrigerator. We used to jell our jello by setting it outside on the window, which reminds me of how cold and drafty the house was, all the warmth was downstairs.

When my parents would talk about the outside being a bad place, they would refer sort of generally to "the whites out there," they always called them *sai yen*. To me, of course, that meant the whites right around us. It meant the bar downstairs where there was an Irish tavern, Cavanaugh's, that we could hear coming up through the floor every night. We'd hear this crashing, singing, people being thrown around down there, they would have brawls and they would pee on our doorstep. Every other day we would go down there with a bucket to wash it off. But at the same time my parents kept reminding us that "the whites out there," the same people who would vomit and pee on our doorstep, were the people who had the power to take our home away from us. We had to do a little placating of them. Every Easter, every Christmas, every American holiday, I would be sent on a little tour of all the local businesses. I would go to the bakery across the street, the barbershop down the street, the realty company, and the bar. I would deliver a little cake to each one. We wanted to be known as that nice Chinese family upstairs or down the street, you know, whom you wouldn't ever want to hurt in any way. My family was very aware that they were embattled Chinese in a white district, that they had spent many years finding that place to live, and that at any moment they could be asked to leave. And somehow a quality I sensed out of all this, about being Chinese, was a vulnerability. At any moment you could be thrown out. So you had to watch your step and you had to be very clever, you had to placate, you had to maneuver. And no matter what happened you did not get openly angry, because if you did, you would have lost your dignity. No matter what they did you had to be stronger than they, you had to outlast them.

But there were other things my family would tell me. Like when my mother got locked out of the house, she would go down to the bar and one of these men would go around back, climb up some steps, crawl across a ledge and in through the window to open the door for her. And my mother would tell me. "You know, only a *sai yen* would do that for you." She made it very clear to me that there was a certain openness and generosity that *sai yen* had that *t'ang yen* did not have. In Chinatown a relative would do it for you, but you wouldn't ask a stranger to do that.

So I was always lining these things up in my mind, trying to make sense of it, and I would always get a mixed picture. When I started to go back to Chinatown to Chinese school, I was very curious about how the kids there lived. I wanted to get into homes very badly. There was one girl in my class named Cynthia. As I remember it now, the reason I really admired her was that she seemed very much like a *sai yen*. She was athletic and, what I thought was like a *sai yen*, she

was kind of loose-limbed and very willowy. And she was a
great basketball player. I used to love anybody who was
good in that sport, and she was a natural. I was always
working at it, practicing, but she would just sort of bounce
in, dance all over the court, and I used to think, "You know,
she's got something I don't have." But when I finally went to
Cynthia's house, the only way I can remember feeling about
it was that she lived like a *sai yen* did, she did not live like a
Chinese. I remember feeling strange in her house as a result
of it. She had a piano, for instance. We had a piano in our
house, too, but hers was all nicely waxed, when the cover
was down and you lifted it up all the keys were clean. Yet I
didn't feel I would want to put my fingers on it. The one at
home was beaten up, but somehow I would rather play on
that. It was interesting, you know, I had been dying to see
the inside of Cynthia's home, but when I finally got to see it
I just thought, "So? I wouldn't want it." (Laughs)

I don't know how right I was about what *sai yen* were
like, but I know I kept track of these contrasts in my mind,
these two worlds that I was comparing and picking from. I
had my idols in regular school, too, and they were all white
girls. One of them was a girl named Dale, who was freckled
and wore her hair all curled up into little Shirley Temple
sausages. What I admired about her was that her mother
obviously lavished a lot of attention on her. She was a
homely girl, yet her parents made this enormous effort to
make her look good. The other thing was that Dale had a
pair of stilts. It was the first time I was introduced to walking
on stilts and suddenly I thought, "Gee, I wonder what else
they have at home that I don't know anything about!" And I
know that later in my life, things like this would come up in
my dreams, I would dream about somebody who had some
secret that I didn't have and when I woke up I thought, "Oh,
that's how she does it!" Like when I went to college it was
those other girls whose shoes were always whiter than
mine. I kept wondering, "What do they do that I don't do
right?"

I still feel, even now, that there's a kind of naïveness in
myself which I can't get rid of and which comes from being
Chinese, too. Which comes from the protected life, unrelated

to the world, that my family lived. . . . We were embattled and they kept us in. And they told us, "Don't associate with *sai yen*," but there were no Chinese to associate with where we lived at that time. I feel my life was in some ways quite distorted by not having lived in Chinatown. In the sense that if I lived in Chinatown I might have had a better understanding of what evil was, and the mix of it. Because in Chinatown I could have lived a fuller life, I could have gotten to know, really, what people were like. Even today I feel as if sometimes I know what a situation is like and what people are like. I'm very confident. Yet at other times I get the feeling that I see things very differently from people around me.

MARK WONG, 47

When we were kids we found that six or seven people could not easily occupy two rooms. So, we felt like being outdoors a lot (laughs). When the cable car came up and down Sacramento Street we'd race right behind it. Those were the happy days. But I became very conscious, even as a youngster, of working. We'd help shelling shrimp, wrapping them. Just general things. And I think that working hard has formed a habit with me that has never been completely dissolved. I don't really know how to enjoy, and you know, even on my days off, I feel like I have to work. Otherwise, something is wrong.

Well, the food was pretty meager and even in my teens we only had fish and meat to sort of go along with the rice. You know, you'd get a piece of *cha shew** and divide it by the half-pound, you had twenty pieces and if you had ten people in the family everyone would get two pieces.

During the Depression, I'd see these people taking canned goods from school. And my dad refused. He told me simply, "You're not going to bring back any canned goods back here, period." I think the pride of the Chinese is very strong, we're not going to accept food from anybody, even to feed ourselves, even when we're eating less. But I remember I

---

* Barbecued pork.

was a bit jealous because my classmates were grabbing things. I remember they used to tell us about the peaches, but we never ate peaches, because we never had canned goods during those days. And I remember we went down stealing. At that time the Golden Gateway was an old wholesale market. So we'd go down and steal a couple of things here and there. It wasn't necessary for survival, but we just had the feeling that we had a right to some of that food that was lying around. So we started off with bananas, then we went to onions, and then we went to apples. We didn't go far enough. I don't see how stealing for people who are undernourished is wrong, there's no ethics involved.

JAMES LOW, 45

An engineer
He remembers being a bookish child, who spent hours reading the Chinese novels brought to him by an old uncle.

My father used to tell me, "Look at your boss, he was going to be an engineer, look what happened to him! What are you studying engineering for?" At the time I was working for a man who had trained to be a mining engineer, but had ended up running a sewing factory. This was one of the reasons my father really disapproved of my going to school. Also, the shipyards were beginning to hire Chinese at that time (in the late 1930s), and they were paying more than my father was making as a garment worker. So he kept on giving me hell for going to school and I just ignored it and went on and on. I had some crazy idea about going back to China: I'd get back there, somehow everything would be alright, I'd say, "OK, here I am, use me," and they would welcome me with open arms. Just the dream of a young guy, I guess.

I went through the whole gamut of public schools for Chinese . . . Commodore Stockton, Francisco, Galileo, but I think, politically, it was certainly the Chinese schools that influenced me the most. In the school I went to the principal for quite a few years was the nephew of K'ang Yu-wei, and he was always attacking Chiang Kai-shek for not fighting the Japanese and so forth. The teachers in the Chinese

schools were pretty conservative really, very strong Confu-
cianists. But then during my younger days the whole thing
was the national salvation. Ever since I was small the Japanese had been committing aggression in China. I was born
in 1925, and already by the time I was old enough to understand, there was the Mukden Incident in 1931. Then practically every other month in the Chinese school the principal
made a speech about how Chiang Kai-shek wasn't fighting
the Japanese. There was a whole string of National Humiliation Days . . . the day when Japan forced the Twenty-one
Demands on Yuan Shih-kai, that was May 9, then September
28, the Mukden Incident, January 28, the Shanghai Incident;
they were all sloganized so you could memorize them by
heart. There were a lot of demonstrations and parades, also;
you know the kind of atmosphere. And speeches on the
playground, half the time I had no idea what they were talking about, but still, you kind of got the feeling.

And if you were Chinese-American you certainly felt the
fate of China was important. In fact we followed Washington politics very little! I remember the teachers would always complain, "China is weak, and look at the treatment
we get here." Because what chance really was there for an
old Chinaman here? When we got all the business about
reconstructing China and all that, lots of us felt this as a
mission. Quite a few of the older Chinese-Americans went
back as aviators for the army.

I guess it sounds as if we were pretty pessimistic about
Chinese "making it" in America. Well, this was during the
Depression. And there were people like the man I was working for, who got a degree in mining engineering and ended
up running a sewing factory, so, I mean, naturally . . . But
then, I didn't really have much contact with white society.
We just took it for granted they would be prejudiced against
Chinese, I guess. Of course, the parents didn't say much
about those things. But in the Chinese school they were
always talking about imperialism and prejudice, how imperialism was the cause of China's downfall, how the British forced opium on the Chinese, *et cetera, et cetera,* and
that the Chinese don't have a chance here. It wasn't really
specific but then you didn't need specific examples in those

days because you would go anywhere and you would find out very easily. Or maybe you didn't even have to find out, you just tried to avoid it, because you know very well from other people talking. You know, certain places would not rent to Chinese, alright, so you would stay away from them. Of course, we couldn't afford those places anyway.

But the thing was, when you come out you find people aren't really that bad, after all. I found Berkeley quite, fairly open, you know, it wasn't like they said. I wasn't socially oriented, of course, always introverted, because even if . . . well, I thought maybe it was good I didn't have the urge to socialize because there might have been a conflict there, and I wouldn't know how to resolve it. And I did have to work very hard. But in those days it's true, I was still very uneasy and uncomfortable. I guess I was expecting prejudice from these people, so I had that kind of uneasiness, I was always unsure what they thought about me. I still feel that's the thing I hate most about racial prejudice. It's just corrosive, it warps the mind of the one who's doing it and also the one who's receiving it. I see it happen at work, guys who think they are not being treated fairly, because they are getting lower pay than the other people. You know, it's very corrosive, very bad.

MAY LOW, 38

She was raised by her mother in a village near Canton while her father worked in San Francisco. The partial relaxation of immigration restrictions after World War II made it possible for her to join him.

She is married to James Low. A quiet woman, when she told the story of her life, she spoke passionately.

My mother use to doll me up. She picked my eyebrows, washed my hair, cut my nails, put makeup on me and all that. She was just trying to dress me up and keep me clean, trying to make me look pretty or something, you know. I resent that. I guess it's not because I didn't want to look pretty, it was just too much bother for me. And then, I'm the sensitive type of person, it actually hurt me, you know, taking all those hairs away from me. It was like a torture to me rather than making me look pretty. Then, when my father came back to Hong Kong, when he went out with me, he used to say, "Look how ugly that woman is, with all her makeup," you know, so I liked his ideas very much.

It was only small things, of course, I had enough to eat, enough to wear, I was better off than most kids, in fact, but it was just that she was always emphasizing my brother. Let's say we were eating dinner. My brother would have all he wanted first, before I got my share. If he didn't like a particular dish, he didn't have to eat it. If I didn't like it, I had to. My mother thought of the boy as everything, the girl as nothing. Well, the whole village, probably the whole of China was like that then. And my mother was an old-fashioned woman. So I was raised under that kind of family.

After I had my education here, I realized it really wasn't my mother's fault. She was taught that way. But for a long time, during my childhood, I actually hated her. There were two other girls in our house, my mother had bought them with her money from America. It was a hard time in China then, you know, and people were selling their children in order for them to eat. So my mother had money, and she had those two girls with me to help, more or less as slaves I guess. But to me, I didn't see it that way. I thought they were kind of in the same situation that I was in. They were being discriminated against because they were slaves, and I was being discriminated against because I was a girl. So whenever my mother and brother were pairing up against me, I used to cry with them. And I used to spend most of my time with them. We would go out to the garden to pick flowers, out to the mountains to gather dry wood for the cooking. Or we used to go down to the sea to gather clams and oysters for the meal. I used to love to do that better than going to school. And, do you know, my mother didn't even mind! For one thing, she said, girls don't have to know anything. They end up getting married and raising children, And then, on the other hand, if I went out with the others, so whatever they learn from school doesn't do a bit of good. I could gather more wood, more oysters for the house. So for those two reasons she didn't mind, and I was never sent to school until I was nine years old.

But one thing I really give my mother credit for, she was a good woman for her family. So many fathers didn't tell their wives what kind of hard time they were having in America, but my father had been writing to my mother all along and she kept telling us, "Your father did not earn this money easily. That's why I don't want to spend anything the wrong way." She was pretty smart. My father had a house built, and we had no rent to pay. Then she saved what he sent back every month, enough to buy about thirty acres of rice field, so we would always have food. Of course, a lot of people in the village were jealous of us. And since we had a different family name from them—we were the Cheungs, and the rest of the village were the Tongs and Leongs—a lot of people picked on my brother and I at school. But I really give her credit for that, because I saw other families starve during the Japanese war and World War II. The mothers had used all the money for gambling, for jewelry, for eating.

Until I was twelve years old, I never saw my father. I just knew the pictures he had been sending all along. In 1945, when I was twelve, we left the village and went to Hong Kong. Then all of a sudden one day my mother told us we were going down to the pier to pick up our father. She just said, "This is your father," and we welcomed him, took him home, and I offered him tea and sort of officially greeted him and called him "Father."

I remember he was like a stranger at first. But a nice stranger that I had met, he seemed to be a very nice man. Then, when he began to tell us his ideas, I liked him right away. Because he had been educated, he had seen the world. And he had tasted so much discrimination himself that he didn't want to discriminate against anybody. So, anytime the slave girl did a service, my mother just took it for granted, but when she did anything for my father, he thanked her. And when he asked for a service, he always said "Please." Before, in America, he had been a family cook, you see.

So, I decided my father was a nice man, I liked to learn

things from him. Then when he said he was going to bring us over to America, I think that was the best news I had ever heard since I was born. I hadn't done much schooling, but for the next three years I really studied. I was so pleased I could leave my mother!

When I got here, it was October 1949, and I was sixteen years old. I was so glad to be free, but then I had the roughest three and a half years in my whole life! All I knew was "Good morning," "good food," and a few loose words like that. I couldn't carry on a conversation in English at all. My father sent me to school, and on top of that, my father was anxious to start us working. And so was I, because I didn't want to continue spending his money. He was just earning enough to rent a two room apartment for my brother and myself, but he lived at work most of the time. The problem was, what could I do? The only thing was to help clean house. So I got my first job.

It happened this woman had a three-story house. Maybe she had had a big family, but nobody lived on the third floor then. She wanted me to live up there. Now I had only been in the United States six months, and I didn't know about the foghorn. Also, at home, I had been afraid of the dark and that girl used to take a kerosene lamp and go upstairs with me, cover me up before she took the light away. I was very spoiled in my way, you know. So, I wasn't used to living alone, I was afraid of the dark, and I was up on the third floor all by myself on one room. Then I heard the foghorn, and I didn't know what it was. I ran to the phone and called my brother. I told him I was so scared, I told him I didn't understand the woman, what she wanted me to do, how she wanted me to do it, I didn't know how to do anything, and maybe when she was teaching me I didn't even understand the instructions. And I started crying, and I was partly talking to myself, that I lived there like a slave girl, you know, like the girl that used to live in our house, and I asked why do I have to be so, why am I all of a sudden downgraded? I used to live without doing anything, and now I'm working for other people and I have to live by myself, get scared, and all that. Well, there were extensions all over the place, and just by accident the woman picked one up and heard me crying. So she came to me and said, "I think you better go home." And she paid me five dollars. She was very nice to me, of course. She felt sorry for me. So she said, "I think you better go home," and I went.

My English was bad, I had to start out in the third grade. After a few months, I was transferred to high school. When I was already twenty years old, I decided to finish all my requirements in a half year. That was the worst time of all! Bookkeeping 3 and 4, and United States history, which I knew nothing of. But that year was when I met James. He was a history bug, you see, so he would help me with United States history, and walk me home every night. He lived on Jackson and we were on Montgomery, so it wasn't far. We got to know each other in the regular American way, I think. The day after I graduated we went to the city hall and got married.

Oh, I forgot to say that my mother had come here three years after me. She was here before I got married. At first I had to educate her, you know. Point things out to her. I told her girls were as good as boys, that they should have education and jobs just like boys. They can be on their own feet. She and my father knew James because he used to take me home. They were against me marrying him. They said it was because I was from Chungshan district, and his parents were from Namhoi. So in Chinese geography it was far away. They said, "Why are you marrying someone so far away?" And I said, "He is not far away. He's on Jackson and we're on Montgomery, you know." Then my father said, "Why don't you go to college? After you graduate you can choose from all kinds of boys." So evidently my parents didn't think James was good enough. Too far away, for one thing. So they thought, gee, he wasn't worth marrying, you know. But I told my parents, "Well, my mind is all made up. Whether it's now or two years later, I'm going to marry him. I have decided." And I said, "If I get married now, I can go to school, and instead of walking me home every night, he can help me with my homework. We'll be right there. It will save all that traveling time." I was being practical. After I got back from my honeymoon, someone offered me a job. Later I went into key punch training, and I've been working ever since.

It's a funny thing, you know, but when people say, gee, they wish they could be young again, I always say, "Not me." In fact, when I talk about the old days, sometimes I still feel like crying, you know. It was just a big cruel world then! Of course, after I got here, I understood it better. I knew my mother hadn't meant to hurt me. Everybody in China was doing what she did. She just followed the crowd. And I was not educated to understand it, you see. I was just a girl, played outside or went to school, and went home to dinner. I didn't understand much about the whole situation.

I did know people in the village were not happy in those days. Some of the bad things I myself didn't see or experience, but what I did see, I didn't like. My mother, for example, wasn't the worst landlord in the village, but still I didn't like her attitude. She leased rice fields out to farmers and they had some kind of agreement, each year, how many barrels of rice they would give back to the landlord. Or if they raised sweet potatoes, how many they should return. Well, to me, it seemed they lived less for themselves than for us. I mean, they brought us more. And sometime, when they had a bad storm or a flood or a drought or something, and they had to maintain their quota, they ended up giving us practically everything. I would hear them, you know, beg my mother not to take so much, so they could have something for their children.

That was one thing I never did like. I remember I once heard my mother say that it wasn't that she didn't have feelings for others, but that she didn't want to sacrifice herself for anybody else. If someone farmed her land, they should give her whatever they promised. If they didn't have enough to eat, maybe they could delay for one year, but that was the most she could do. She wouldn't sacrifice the rice completely, even though she had enough. She'd rather get more, get money or something else, you know, instead of helping the family. Relatives were different, but as far as the village was concerned, she had no relation with it. She didn't care. Of course, I was too young to do anything or to really feel for them myself, except the girl who lived with me I don't know, maybe I was in a different situation from the other people you talked to. Maybe their parents were different. But being that my mother was partial to her son, and I was treated more or less in the class with the slaves, when I saw these other families, not having enough to eat, not even going to school because they had to help grow rice or sweet potatoes as soon as they were old enough to do anything . . . I wondered about it. I wondered why China was like that. Why did we have to live that way, you know.

LAMBERT CHOY, 29

He is a leader of the newly organized Chinese for Affirmative Action, a young liberal group which has been active in fighting employment discrimination against Chinese in San Francisco.

Before he died, my father was always doing things with my brother and me. I guess because he was a bookmaker, unofficially, my father just knew a lot of people and I used to go around with him, as a child, when he saw his friends. We had many uncles who used to run different gambling establishments. Not blood uncles, you understand, but uncles by default or because they happened to be around. Whenever we went to their places they would be full of men, in densely smoke-filled rooms, we'd walk in and find everybody playing mahjong. There was always a back room and I could never figure out what was going on in there. But when I tried to follow my father in he would tell me to wait outside. So I began to wonder what was happening in these back rooms (laughs). Well, I think it was in places like this that I picked up the sense of humor I have about the community. A lot of my friends and people I grew up with have a very anxious feeling, especially when they talk about it today. But for myself when I look back on it I just kind of laugh about it, thinking about things like those back rooms.

Chinatown has changed. I remember when I was a kid this was a very close community. Groups of people used to get together, you don't find that happening today. If we get together it's only because some crisis has come up, or we're trying to avoid a crisis and that brings people together.

I remember the coffee shops of old Chinatown. Even after my father died, many of these old men who were presumably my uncles would take me around to the coffee shops. Actually they were tearooms rather than coffee shops, but they were places where you could go in and within a half an hour you would find five or six people around you. You would wonder where they all came from, but they were there, and they could sit around. There wasn't the rush you have in the coffee shops today. The conversations that went on were usually about Chinatown. I remember one that was about the need for better transportation. A group of men (I don't remember ever seeing women in those places) were debating about how to get trolley cars to run through Chinatown. All the trolley stops were outside of Chinatown and it took too long to get to them when you wanted to go anywhere. They talked about who to see, where to go to get it done, and so on. And I get the feeling, when I look back on it, that maybe this was the beginning of social awareness for me. Those conversations where the men were really concerned about the same type of problems that we're concerned about, and sat around tables talking. They never seemed to get any resolutions, but they wouldn't be anxious about that.

When I was eleven or twelve there was one uncle, I guess he wanted to play a father to me, who used to take me out to the coffee shops quite regularly. He always headed for a particular place first. When I asked him why he said, "Well, it's a ritual. We have to do things in a certain way." He told me that whenever he got up on the days he went out, he would come over and get me, that was the first thing he did. Then the second thing was to go down and get his morning coffee in this particular place. I said, "Why always the same place?" He said, "There is no other place." (Laughs) I told him there were coffee shops all over Chinatown. But he said, "No, as a child you don't understand this, but when you become a man, you will understand." Of course, I still haven't found out. In fact in the past few years I've tried to get together with a lot of these men and talk to them about what life was like when my father was around, when I was a child. But I found that many of them don't want to talk about it. And in digging into it the only reason I've found so far is that it wasn't a good past. Then I begin to tell them some of my memories, and how I felt that as a child in Chinatown it was a happy thing to be going through. They just say, "Well, you were a child then. But it was really difficult for us." One of them used to tell me, and I never would believe him, how Broadway used to be the border of Chinatown and if you crossed it you were risking your life. He told me stories of how he had crossed the border, sometimes, and had literally run back to Chinatown. They chased him back because he was a Chinaman and he had a queue. Now it took me time to believe these stories, but when someone close to you tells them to you, even when you haven't experienced it yourself, you begin to feel for him. And when I think of myself now, working in the Chinese for Affirmative Action, I wonder whether unconsciously these were some of the things that influenced me to be doing the kinds of things that I'm doing today.

PRISCILLA FONG, 34
Hairdresser

If you're not exposed to anything that's wild, you wouldn't think just living is dull. You don't know what it's like to be wild. Growing up around Chinatown in the forties and fifties was very enjoyable because we respected our parents. You know, they told us to sit, we'd sit, they told us to stand, we'd stand. I used to play across the street in that park on Portsmouth Square. I'd play there all day long, in fact, I slept there all night long. You think I would worry about raping? There's no such thing! We would all sleep in the park under a big tree when it was nice weather. We didn't even have to camp, we'd just sleep in our clothes. On weekends we'd go eat *wonton* and drink orange freeze at the soda fountain. We walked everybody home by four P.M. in the evening. Nobody's going to do anything to you and besides there's lots of people you know around.

We'd go with our parents to see the Chinese opera and the Chinese movies, everyone just played around more then. We'd visit one another more. We didn't have cares in those days. And if your parents had a business definitely you're going to stay around to help. You don't even demand to be paid because it's your duty to do so. Yes, it was a duty.

I come from a family of nine children. We always had a lot of fun among ourselves. I'm the youngest of nine. My parents were really old-fashioned and I still think of myself as being that way, too. We always waited for holidays like the August Moon Festival and Chinese New Year. We would sit for days and days to prepare the flowers. We'd spend a lot of time kneading dough. Oh, we spent a good three days preparing for Chinese New Year. Of course, you know how everyone goes through cleaning house and getting new clothes. My parents would take us to all the stores and we would meet people. So you can see, even though it was a little bit harder economically in those days, there was a lot more harmony than there is today.

Of course, there were things that weren't good in Chinatown. We used to see the public operators going right through the park. A lot of them worked with the restaurants and the different associations. You know, when the men were gambling and they had a lot of money, they would keep all these women around and the men would just go off with them and spend the night. I remember very clearly when the farmers, the ones that sell chrysanthemums and different flowers, would come in around Chinese New Year. They would come out of the country with five or six thou-sand dollars in their pocket, they never kept anything in the bank, and they would eat, and drink, and spend, and I would watch those gals running back and forth, you know.

But I guess if you live in Chinatown all your life you see all kinds. You knew which ones were friendly and which ones were the hustlers. So it didn't bother me, I had seen it ever since I was a kid. It didn't seem like anything unusual and I could always say that the bad parts of it didn't involve me, so I didn't care. Besides, if you think back twenty or thirty years ago, none of these men could bring their wives over, and they couldn't afford living with another woman because they had to send the money home. So the only way for them to have their kicks was to have a woman once in a while. Besides, it was so inexpensive. We used to see one old woman who had been a prostitute from way back. She was a pretty little lady before but she had lost her hair and all her teeth and everything. In the beginning she had all these men down in the park and she would bring them home with her. But then we saw her getting older and older. Finally the old men were just giving her money to help out. A quarter or something like that.

7. Clans and Elders

With their French windows, balconies, and elaborate façades, the elegant presence on Grant Avenue of buildings owned by the wealthier "families" in Chinatown gives testimony to the central role of the clan associations in the history of the community. On the visible surface of life in Chinatown today, however, the significance of the buildings is difficult to detect. On weekdays and during business hours, they stand vacant, their doors locked, not a sign of activity. On weekend afternoons we discovered it was possible to go inside, and became familiar with the pattern of family association halls: at one end wide windows and a balcony overlooking the street, at the other a portrait of the clan's ancestor with an altar beneath, in the center one long conference table and rows of ornately carved wooden chairs. In the large buildings of the wealthy clans, we found three or four floors might be maintained for clan activities and the upper altar room decorated with valuable antiques. Smaller clans held their activities in a single room, furnished functionally with formica tables and inexpensive chairs. In all the buildings a coffee pot, newspapers, magazines, and mahjong sets had been set out on the conference table as if in a gesture of hospitality to visitors. Yet even on these weekend afternoons the buildings were deserted. A solitary elderly caretaker would sit dozing beside stacks of untouched magazines while incense burned on the altar.

It was only by chance that we discovered the one period of regular activity in the clan association halls: weekend nights. It was Saturday, sometime after nine, and as we passed the Lee Family Association building on Grant Avenue we noticed cracks of light between the curtains which had been drawn over its window. A roar of mahjong pieces flooded the stairwell when we opened the door. We followed an acrid smell of smoke up three floors, entered a door marked "Men's Recreation Room," and found twenty-five or thirty men gathered in small clusters around mahjong games that were being played at scattered tables. A few men from Portsmouth Square were there: Ed Lee, the tall waiter from the Sun Wah Kue Cafe, a shoe repairman from Kearny Street. The men looked uncomfortable when they noticed us in the room and we left quickly. Otherwise, an occasional poster advertising a banquet or picnic, a few summer conventions in larger halls, were the only conspicuous signs of the activity of the family associations (as clan associations are commonly known). Eventually we learned that, with a few exceptions, only three formal functions are carried on by most family associations in Chinatown today: the maintenance of the clan hall as a meeting place and informal recreation center for members, the maintenance of the altar to the family ancestors, and the sponsoring of one annual banquet open free of charge to all members of the clan.

What is the continuing social significance of clan associations in Chinatown? To what extent does the community support and benefit from their existence? A cross section of comments and opinions reveal that prestige, accumulated resources, and continuing appeal to significant segments of the community have managed to sustain the influence of the clans as basic units in Chinatown's traditional institutional structure, while sharp changes in the nature of the American Chinese population in recent years are slowly eroding their base.

The surprisingly persistent loyalty of American Chinese to their family associations, making them still the most comprehensive social organization in Chinatown today was brought home to us by the fact that almost every American-born Chinese we spoke with had had some contact or experience with his clan. At a banquet, we talked to children who had fled the crowded dining room to toss paper cups around on the roof. Most of them didn't know what the words "family association" meant, but downstairs their mothers, many of them suburban housewives, said this was the one Chinatown event they brought their children to every year, "just to keep them in touch with the old traditions." A librarian, whose family's three generations were all present at the banquet, had insisted her daughter write an essay for the event: "How Youth Can Help Our Family Association." Another woman, who had just finished describing how she used to take her son and daughter to a downtown restaurant every week "so they could be at ease in the world of Caucasian manners," said that there were only two points she absolutely required of her children: that they register their names with the family association and that they attend the yearly banquet. "It just makes me feel better to know that no matter what big city they're in, they can always go to their own family association if they need help," she said. Men were more taciturn, but we learned from many of the store clerks, butchers, and restaurant waiters in Chinatown, men who lived in Ping Yuen housing projects or on Stockton Street, that perfunctory attendance at the family association banquet was their sole outside-the-family social activity of the year.

Despite this vague sense of attachment to clan in so many American Chinese, however, a high level of criticism for the family associations in Chinatown today symbolizes their undeniable decline. The process began in the early fifties. First, the sweeping social transformation that followed the Chinese revolution removed a primary reason for the existence of American clan associations, which had hinged on the continued existence of true lineage clans in China. In the revolutionary land reform of the early 1950s properties owned by clan associations in China had been expropriated, ancestral halls claimed as schools and meeting places for newly established peasant cooperatives, and the control of clan elders over villages eliminated. The resulting death of lineage clans, combined with the severing of physical ties to Kwangtung in the wake of the American containment and isolation of China, marked the first stage in the slow weakening of Chinatown clans. The process was accelerated as American society became more open to American Chinese after World War II, reducing dependency on institutions in Chinatown and therefore the authority of clans and elders. The movement outside of Chinatown to lower-middle-class suburbs by a large proportion of offspring of the family society began the weakening of their ties to the clan and a tendency to regard their parents' involvement in them as old-fashioned. Finally, in the 1960s, a new cause of decline came when liberalized immigration quotas stimulated the first full-scale Chinese immigration since the nineteenth century (see Chapter 10), bringing to Chinatown large numbers of immigrants from Hong Kong, many of whom were surprised to find clan associations still intact. They saw the traditional institutional structure of Chinatown as further evidence of its social backwardness as compared to the cosmopolitan society of Hong Kong. The presence of these immigrant families and their urgent needs, moreover, placed a new strain on the traditional Chinatown institutions and threw them into crisis.

Several older men who had at one time been deeply involved with their clan associations spoke quite frankly about their decay. Al Chin, an electrician, remembered the associations had maintained their tremendous influence in Chinatown almost through the fifties, as long as the majority of Chinese entering the United States did so on false immigration papers. "For most people, who had a lot of fear about their immigration status, the English secretary of the family association was the only contact they ever had with the law or the city government or anything outside. You can see how much power this gave the associations in the past." In the 1930s and 1940s, he felt, the clan associations had been easily used as bases by officials who took unfair advantage of their power. "Anyone who had a knowledge of English and was appointed the English secretary of his association had the sole right to wheel and deal with the Caucasian public and the Caucasian families. In our own family, there was an instance where one of our men became secretary in the district association and put up some money from its treasury to buy a building for himself. Well, in the course of doing business, he got the hard end of the deal. But since he had been the sole signer of the contract, he just sold the building to a Caucasian and took off for China. By the time it came to light it was too late, so the family association had to foot the bill." Over time, he felt, the associations had become less and less oriented to the real needs of the community, to a point where, in the face of the severe problems accompanying the recent influx of immigrants, they had been unable to respond. Carpenter Jack Wong recalled his disillusionment at the reaction of his own family association when he suggested they hold English classes in its building for recent immigrant members. "Their excuse was that it wasn't their business to provide services like this. The public school had the money for that. Why should they have to pay seventy-five dollars extra a month to clean the room? Let the public school do it." Both men expressed real regret that the clan associations, which once had answered a genuine need in Chinatown, seemed unable to re-mold themselves to the new situation in Chinatown. Jack said, "I feel as though the new immigrants since the 1960s have changed the nature of Chinatown itself. They seem to be more militant and more demanding. They really want something from the elders and when there's no response they fall back onto associations of their own and refuse to have anything to do with the family associations, which is a tragedy." He felt that unless the associations are able to attract the youth and new immigrants they will surely collapse as the old men who depend on them pass away. From another older man who left his association after a long feud with some of its members, we heard complaints that gambling, rigged elections, bribery, and waste of funds had for decades crippled all the clan associations in Chinatown.

Younger Chinatown residents (those below thirty-five), who had had far less direct experience of the clan associations than these older men, tended to be harsher in both their condemnation and their predictions of collapse. A majority expressed indifference and ignorance about the associations, which they had contact with only on the rare occasions when it "meant something" to their parents. Unclear about the nature of the clans even during these periods of contact because of their inability to speak Cantonese, such younger American Chinese tend to speak without differentiation of "family associations" and "tongs," as part of "the establishment" in Chinatown, which they describe as decrepit, corrupt, and given over to gambling. A small nucleus of American-born Chinese and immigrant social workers in this age group made a direct attack on the family associations (and the whole three-tiered structure) in 1965 when Chinatown's elders fought against the establishment of federal anti-poverty programs in Chinatown. Emerging from the bitter struggle with a concrete sense of both the continuing strength and the conservativeness of the family associations, these liberals now see them simply as bases for perpetuating the interests of a narrow group in China-town, incapable of providing the community with any of the services it really needs. "I'm sure I could go up to any-one in the Wong Family Association and I wouldn't be able to get a dime for a cup of coffee," quipped one anti-poverty worker. "There's just no such thing in the wealthy family associations. Their purpose or goals may have been good in the beginning, but they have never been really worked out and they are now dominated by very limited, narrow people. They don't look on it as any kind of instrument for social improvement, it's strictly a banquet deal. Pay your money, pay your dues, go to a couple of banquets, eat your share, and what you do the rest of the year is of no importance. At this point, the associations perpetuate treasuries, not service." Only a very few of these younger liberal leaders, aware of the clan associations' political potential as broadly based grass-roots organizations, envision some role for them in the community's future change.

What, then, is the real force behind the continuing presence of clan associations' existence in Chinatown? Invariably, the most positive statements about the associations and their role in the community came from the men who have been elected to lead them. "To me, the family association is one of the most important things that Chinese culture has contributed to society," a treasurer of the Lee Family Association told us. "Filial respect for the elders within the family breeds respect for the laws of the society as a whole. To me, this is the way to keep law and order." Since generous contributions of time and money are necessary for leadership in the clan association, these officials tend to be successful owners of businesses in Chinatown who, as one told us, "could take time out for meetings and you don't have to ask the boss." As men of considerable influence in the community who had been involved in its institutional life for many years, they spoke knowledgeably and authoritatively about the persistent strength of the associations in Chinatown life. In the most basic sense, they pointed out, the permanence of the clan associations is guaranteed by the fact that most of the land and businesses in the core area of Chinatown are held in the names of different clans. Since Kwangtung custom has long prohibited the sale of collectively owned family land, this in itself will ensure the involvement of the clans in some administrative capacity in the community for years to come. In addition, clan ties still have an important influence on many business relationships in Chinatown. "A lot of Chinese still buy from the same family," one importer said. "The Lees have quite a number of stores and restaurants here, for example, and most other Lees will tend to go to a place they know a Lee owns. This can make a big difference in the business." Nor has the long-practiced custom of hiring one's own relatives entirely disappeared from the community. While the nineteenth century "credit-ticket" system is no longer in use, it is still a common practice for established merchants to pay the passage of needy relatives from Hong Kong, who then reciprocate with a certain period of donated (or low rate) labor. In such cases, the employer-employee bond is strengthened by the clan tie. Family associations, where boss and worker have social contact outside of work, reinforce their sense of loyalty and mutual obligation as "relatives." Most important of all in the eyes of these officials, clan associations are an essential key to leadership in the community. Membership in this basic unit of Chinatown's institutional structure, they told us, is the *sine qua non* for entrance to its higher levels.* Once a member of a

---

* The *sintong* substitute as family associations for the Chungshan, Sam Yup, and Hakka people who continue the nineteenth century tradition of boycotting the Sze Yup–dominated family associations, i.e., Chin, Wong, and Lee. Since all *sintong*, including those for Sze Yup people, were originally set up to send bones of the dead back to native districts in Kwangtung, present-day *sintong* still carry on the responsibility of providing burial services for members. See interviews of Dr. Rolland Lowe and Lambert Choy as examples of people for whom the *sintong* is a family association.

clan association, one is eligible for election to the district association and, after years of service, may reach the pinnacle of power in the Chinese Six Companies.

THOMAS MOON, 63

An insurance agent and instructor in the Chinese lute. He was angry, and eager to give his story: "I don't want you to have a rosy picture of Chinatown." His wife, who sat beside him during most of the interview, was anxious. She feared repercussions within the family association and subsequent loss of business.

Yes, I'm involved with the Moon Family Association,* I've been elected to several offices in this association, and I know what's going on. I know who's honest and who's dishonest, I know who's doing the right thing, who isn't. Now we're supposed to be a nonprofit organization, right? Something like the Lions' Club, or the Rotary Club. We're supposed to do all these good things for our family members and the community, OK? Instead, every year they put out a big banquet, the so-called Chun Yin or Spring Feast, spend about five or six thousand dollars and gobble it up in one day. This isn't only the Moon Association now, this is every association in Chinatown. You might be surprised, I guess, because their dues are very small, but they have the collections from the properties they own, rents, and they have donations, because if you're in business you have to donate a certain amount, and then they get donations from the winners of mahjong and *pai gow* games. Yet every year they waste—I can't calculate how much—but they completely waste many, many valuable dollars.

A lot of us would like to change this, but all these so-called officers, so-called presidents of the association never listen to you. That's one thing I feel strongly against. As a matter of fact, we're having a big squabble in the Moon Association right now over the election. Someone's always fixing the ticket, forcing members to write their names in,

---

* A fictitious name. Thomas Moon belongs to one of the largest associations in Chinatown.

and then they pay them off, bribe them, you know, so they can control. You have big prestige if you're president of the Chin Family Association, or the Wong or the Lee. Now, the year before last, a group of people I was involved with, mostly younger people, was elected to office. Our president was very young, about thirty-five, and very progressive. The former president had cosigned a loan of three thousand dollars in the name of the association, and he hadn't kept up payments. So our new president, the young one, paid and made good that loan out of his own pocket. He felt that was his responsibility, you see. But then these old fogeys didn't like him. He wanted to change things and do things the modern way, and they didn't like it, so they ganged up on him and kicked him out. They called an emergency meeting and summoned all the leaders from all over the United States for a re-election. Then they ousted the new president and told him he couldn't run for office for ten more years.

And not only the Moon Family Association, all the family associations, the Six Companies, any young person who wants to make some changes, they call him a communist right away. He's redcapped right away. They use all kinds of tricks to run him out. You see, in old Chinatown, they didn't respect a scholarly person or an intelligent person, the person with good intentions, a good philosophy, a good heart. Anyone who wants to change something, they're against. I think the reason is, a lot of these people have a little business, they're doing pretty well, they have no ideas about how society might change. They hold on to everything the way it was in China, in Kwangtung. Even though we're in a different society, a different era.

I've observed very closely, as I say, I know what's going on. And one thing I've found out is that even today these people are still set, their minds are set. All the associations and all the different tongs are very, very backward. Now fifty years ago, a hundred years ago, if they had operated this way, I wouldn't blame them. Because the Chinese needed these associations to help each other and to solve different problems. But these days we can't use the same methods. Especially, we can't use all these tricks against each other, against our own members. But the associations

are still used for business purposes. A lot of these old-style
businesses are still involved with the associations, and if
you want to get into that business, you have to join. Another
thing, if you don't have any business, you'll never be nomi-
nated to an office in any of the Chinatown organizations.
Not only that, you have to play ball with each other before
they'll let you up there. You know what I mean, don't you?
Like if there is a big banquet, there's always some deal.
someone's getting something out of it. After all, when there
are fifteen or twenty restaurants in Chinatown, you don't
choose a place because the food is good! You give that guy
your six thousand dollars worth of business because of
some arrangement he's made with you. Well, I don't have
to elaborate on that. But it's going on all the time. I know it,
but I can't say anything about it, because the majority rules.
And all these old ways are handed down from generation
to generation. To me, these associations should get a lot of
the blame for the unprogressive nature of the society here.
Because it is in such a condition, so corrupt, that you can
never change, never improve anything. I hate to say this, as
a Chinese, about my own society. But this condition exists,
these are the facts. I don't want to give you a rosy picture
of Chinatown.

ROLLAND LOWE, M.D.

*A young and influential community leader, he was respon-
sible for bringing the NEMS federal health program into
Chinatown. While he has worked closely with liberal social
workers in the anti-poverty program, he insists that meaningful reform in Chinatown must take place within the
framework of its traditional institutions, which still claim
the strongest grass-roots base in the community.*

The community in my own mind is basically a semi-colonial
type of community. I would say it reflects China as it was
forty years ago. It was carried over and it hasn't moved, it
really hasn't been influenced by the changes that had gone
on in the mainland. First of all, if we take the basic struc-

ture as the family association, there's still a feudalistic
structure there. Because the family association is built on
the concept of family clans. For example, right now in our
own association we have to decide if a gal who marries out
can still belong to the association. The oldtimers say no.
Once she marries out she belongs to that other person, that
other family. She has to resign. Another feeling the oldtimers have is that the association structure should operate
without any real democracy. Whatever the boss says goes.
So if the president of the family association decides something, that's it. They don't even ask for a vote. So in many
ways it's like the feudalistic concept of king. A benevolent
king will ask around, ask everyone's opinion, but a benevolent king still makes up his own mind.

Then, there's a tie-in from the economic standpoint. A lot
of people are still brought over from China because the
brother or an uncle, or someone, paid their passage and then
they're under an obligation to serve them back, at pretty
cheap labor. So in that sense there's a sort of a semi-
serfdom. Now back in China there were no landowners or
industrialists quite large enough to really control a big unit.
But here, when the family and related people are tied
together in business relationships, you can understand the
tightness of the structure. You can see the difficulty of trying
to unionize people, get them to demand better wages, and
so forth, under this sort of system.

Well, I'll tell you a little bit about my own concept of
leadership. I think Chinese, like many other people, are very
wary of leadership. They think there are only two reasons
why someone would get into the leadership game. One is for
power and prestige. The other is for personal financial gain.
That's why you find real estate agents, insurance agents,
active in community affairs. For contacts. And there are the
professional politicians eager to follow the politician's
route, and people know that. I'm a doctor. They know I'm
really busy with my practice in Chinatown. So when I commit my time to some extra service to the community, I think
they respect that, too. I've always felt that people who
wanted to serve the community should be sure to find out
what the community wants, not what they think it wants.

They have to be willing to come down and serve, not just to lead.

More than anything else, my involvement with the family association has illustrated my belief that it *is* possible to work with the establishment. The establishment basically wants our respect. You just have to realize that the establishment simply does not have the know-how. We shouldn't expect them to have it. So we have to show that we're willing to give them our expertise, but that they will get their credit, too, and not be left out of things. We're willing to work for them provided they agree on that general principle. So one of my rules is never to threaten power. All I do is ask if people agree with my ideas or not. If they agree, I will plug in the hard work to realize it. They can get all the credit for it if they want. I will never challenge their positions.

Now, let me show you how this all worked out in my own family association. I went into my family association and sat on the board for five years. I was vice-president of the board for the last two years, and I sat for three years. My concept was that whatever the members wanted, we would do. I would show them that I could perform in my capacity on the board. I would do the best job on whatever they wanted of anyone they had ever had before. Well, first of all, I had to find out what these members really want. I found out that they wanted a cemetery. A decent cemetery. That was what they all first thought about. Second, where did our expertise come in? We got together three or four of the younger members and formed a committee for planning a new cemetery. We had to show that we could raise money, we had to show that we could plan the cemetery, you know, put new roads in it, new parking facilities, a water system. And we even enlarged the vision for it, on the principle that there's no reason why a Chinese cemetery should look lousier than a Caucasian one. Again, we were appealing to pride, you know. The same concept. Why should a Chinese cemetery look dumpier than a Caucasian one? So we all pitched in. Did I talk about anything else for five years? No! But I established the fact, you know, within the family association, that we had the ability to do what they wanted.

Then after being vice-president for three years, they asked
me to be president.

LAMBERT CHOY

I remember very clearly the day of my father's funeral. I
still think of it as the largest funeral I've ever seen. The
mourning was excessive, it felt like my mother was in tears
for a month. They didn't let me sit in the front row. All the
rest of my family sat in the front row. It was an open casket,
which is probably the reason why I detest open casket
funerals today. I sat with an aunt in the fourth row, and
when it came time for everybody to process out, after they
had viewed the body, they wouldn't let me go up to see the
body. We went as far as about twenty feet away from the
casket, and I peered over, trying to see my father. My aunt
said, "Don't look!" and before I knew it they had closed the
casket and were outside.

All through the service I kept a stone face. Everybody else
was in mourning and crying and tears and wailing and what
not but I kept a stone face because I didn't know what was
happening. Then when we got in the limousine I sat in the
back and they had a bump seat. They put the bump seat up
and this I remember because they bumped me with it, and
that's when I started crying. The first person who saw me
said, "Oh, what a good son he is!" And I was only seven, and
the first thing that came to my mind was that it hurt and
how stupid this man was saying I was a good son, and I
didn't know what was happening. But I remember it as the
longest procession I had ever seen of cars going out to the
cemetery. And he was buried in the Chinese cemetery,
which is god-awful.

My mother's not a traditional person, but when she talks
about my father she becomes very traditional. In all other
aspects, you know, she doesn't believe in burning incense or
these kinds of things. But when anything has to do with her
deceased husband, whom she never refers to as her deceased husband, but only as "your deceased father" or
"your past father," she's very scrupulous. We used to go
out to the cemetery annually, or sometimes more than

annually, to burn paper money, paper clothes, and everything else. We used to do that. It used to be fun for us as
kids, and my mother would bring her chair out and watch
us do it, as obedient children. But actually, half the time we
used to almost burn the cemetery down because there was
so much wind and everything would go flying all over the
place (laughs). So we were putting out more small fires than
was worth the effort, and five years ago my mother decided
not to do any more burning. But she still goes through all
the entire ritual once a year, and in addition she goes out
to the cemetery as often as she can. We don't even ask her
now, in fact, because we know whenever we're around on
a Sunday and we're free, that's where she wants to go. So
we go out, I'd say ten or fifteen times in a year, which is
excessive as far as I'm concerned.

The ritual was that when we got there everybody had to
gather around the headstone. There was my mother and the
four of us. We would stand in a semicircle around the headstone, and then my elder brother—no one else—would get
the stuff out of the car. There was a red cloth before the
headstone and only my brother and I were allowed to lay
the stuff down. We would put three teacups out, three wine
cups, three pairs of chopsticks, and three plates. We would
fill the plates with a chicken a piece, *cha shew bau*, and
every other kind of food that you can think of. Then we
would fill the wine cups, light the joss sticks, and put them
in the ground near the headstone. When we were very
young mother used to ask us to bow three times before the
headstone, but as we were growing up I guess she sensed
that we felt a bit ridiculous, because I remember later she
never asked us to do this. So after we had laid everything
out we would all stand back. The sons, my brother and I,
would stand in front of the headstone where everything was
laid. But my two sisters would always stand on the side with
my mother. And we would just stand there. In the younger
days I used to want to wander around, but this was forbidden until all the joss sticks had burned down to the end
of the stick. Then when everything was burned down we'd
gather up the plates. But we left the food. I used to ask her
who it was for, and she would tell me, "For your father."

And she always answered, she never failed, "You know, white people bring flowers for the people to smell, well, we bring food for your father to eat." And we would start breaking up in hysterics, laughing at the cemetery.

And then, just two or three years ago we brought my father's bones up. My family association had announced that they were digging up all the twenty-year-plus graves because they needed the land for something else. So we went out with an uncle and waited for them to open the grave. Well, they opened the grave and the first thing my uncle did was get down on his knees before the headstone and start calling through the opening, *"Ago, nei hai bin dou."* "Brother, are you there?" I was standing next to my mother and I just broke out laughing, I didn't know what was going on. I was twenty-six years old and I got the chewing out again for laughing in the cemetery. My uncle told me, "This is what we have to do. We're moving your father someplace else, now. First we have to wake him up." So that's what he did. Then when they opened the casket my uncle went down and if I hadn't seen it I wouldn't believe it. He laid out the entire skeleton, from head to toe. He literally looked for every bone of the fingers and the toes, I don't think he found them all, and he laid them out and left them there for a couple of hours to dry. Then he went back to put them in a little concrete box, and he wiped every piece of bone before he put it in. The job of closing the concrete box was mine. That was the one thing I got to do (laughs). And I had to carry it to the car. It was a little box, but damn heavy. You had to carry it so that the head was out and not facing toward you. When you put it in the car it had to be facing a certain way, too. And then we drove to the other cemetery.

It was a choice as to whether to put him back into the old Chinese cemetery or move him someplace else. My mother left the choice up to us, but we knew that in her own heart, although she never said it to us, she wanted our father to be put back into the old cemetery simply because it was the Chinese cemetery and they have celebrations every year. But we made the decision to buy land in another cemetery where we thought the upkeep and everything was better. She went along with our decision. But in the beginning, every once in a while when we went out, she'd say, "Not too many Chinese here, are there?" We pacified her by arranging with the caretaker for her to bring incense and do all her rituals there. Some cemeteries don't want you to do that.

And I remember picking out the plot of land my mother allowed us to choose, too, but she kept pushing this plot which was closest to the road. I questioned this and she told me that close to the road there was more accessibility to getting out, if my father ever wanted to. "There's a way to get out," she said. And she told me she thought that when she died, she'd want out, too. She's become very humorous in her old age.

JIM MOON, 19

A student at San Francisco State. Unlike most of his friends at college, he is active in the Moon Family Association.

For one thing, I've found that it's easier to work through the establishment than by just starting from scratch without any base. You know, we gave a Christmas party last year, we advertised it in the Chinese newspapers and the family association footed the bill. They bought all the material, we had movies, skits, fried chicken, ice cream, even a Santa Claus to give everyone a gift, and it was a great thing. About three hundred kids showed up, and these are kids that aren't very well off, most of them were recent immigrants. Now, at the same time Youth for Service and the Berkeley Asian Studies group put a lot of effort into giving Christmas parties. And they really had a hard time going around to stores asking for donations, trying to get funding, looking all over for a place. Then when the parties were finally set up a lot of parents wouldn't let their kids go because they're quite guarded, you know, and the Asian Studies people are considered to be left-wing. Whereas with the family association, you already have a place, you have money to buy the gifts, and the parents know the family association is safe.

The kids hear all this talk about the establishment on campus, even in high school there's generally a negative attitude toward it, and to them the Six Companies, the family associations are "the establishment" in Chinatown. So they just automatically think they're bad. About the only people who will join them are a few recent immigrant kids who are kind of shy and who are used to belonging to one in Hong Kong. It's sad, really, because the associations are all for youth activities, nothing would make them happier. They've been trying to organize them for years. But, for instance, my association just purchased about one thousand dollars worth of equipment for learning the martial arts. They think that's the only thing kids are interested in these days—lion dances, kung fu, Chinese dances. Well, this is good for the immigrant kids, but they can't get most of the American-born to go for that. A dance, a sports league, even something like a peace march or a protest march would have been better. Probably the march, in fact, because social action things are replacing sports and dancing for the American-born Chinese now. Instead, they have one thousand dollars worth of equipment lying around up there.

On the other hand, some of the older people have given up on the kids because they've had some bad experiences with them. About four years ago, I remember, they were going through the usual thing of trying to drum up interest in a youth group. They decided to have some dances. Now, usually in the association everyone's supposed to be related, because they all have the same name, so dating is discouraged. There's a lot of family pressure about that. But I guess they said it was OK to bring dates in to this dance, and they planned to hold the thing upstairs where the altar is. Well, the altar is kind of a sacred place, you know, and in those days there was always a lot of making out in the back during dances, so . . . you can imagine, when the elders walked in and saw the kids doing that in front of the altar, it was a pretty bad scene.

Another problem is that the elders always think the kids should help in the association. But for a lot of these kids, especially the kids in high school, there are all these new federal and city programs which just help them without expecting anything back. So there are the elders, expecting the kids to respect them enough to come to meetings, move chairs, greet people at banquets . . . but the kids figure why should they hang around and work when they can go someplace that's all recreation? They don't look to the association for political advantage or business connections, they're too young for that. So they just go where the entertainment is better.

8. Victory

Every year, over two decades following the victory of Communist forces in China, an advertisement placed in major newspapers by the "highest representative body of Chinese in America," the Chinese Six Companies, has reminded the American public that "twenty-one million overseas Chinese loyally support the Republic of China." In autumn 1971, barely a month before the historic United Nations election which resulted in the admission of the People's Republic of China and the ouster of Taiwan, a staff member at Nationalist China's consulate in San Francisco still assured us that this commitment of American Chinese had not changed. "I believe they are loyal. I can say that definitely," he insisted. He called attention to the limelight position held by the Chinatown community in San Francisco at that time because of its unyielding opposition to integrated school busing. "This just proves how conservative the Chinese people are. The family is still the most important thing to them and their family associations are very strong. Communism will never penetrate." What, we asked, was the precise relation between the Chinatown community and Nationalist China? "We support them," he answered. "We support them as long as they are loyal."

Behind the exchange of "loyalty" for "support" between Chinatown and the Republic of China lies a process several decades long, which culminated with the establishment of direct organizational ties between Chinatown's highest institution and the Nationalist government of China. To those outside of Chinatown, the striking existence of this well-organized political life directed toward China has reinforced a sense of the community's distinctiveness and "separateness" as a unit. Few, however, understand its complex causes and its relationship to the position of Chinese in American society. For it was hardly preference alone, but the pressure of powerful historical forces bringing about a coincidence of need between a desperate Republic of China and the leaders of the community overseas (still essentially powerless in American political life and eager to bolster their position in Chinatown earlier in the twentieth century) which led to the pledging of allegiance between the two. In form, the alliance meant the absorption of men from Chinatown's most powerful indigenous institution, the Six Companies, into the Republic of China's official political party, the Kuomintang, and finally into the Nationalist government itself. In effect, it meant a guarantee of strong support for the increasingly isolated Republic of China on the home ground of its most important ally, the United States, and a heightened prestige for the Six Companies which provided the crucial support for its supremacy in Chinatown for more than twenty years. As an ironic result of the process, however, the very institution first called into being by the devastating isolation of Chinese in America now found itself forced to perpetuate that isolation—by preserving the loyalty of Chinatown as the virtual fiefdom of a foreign government—in order to maintain its own position of control within the community.

The highly active political life which existed in Chinatown at the turn of the nineteenth century continued in full momentum even after the revolution of 1911. Indeed, the founding and publication over its hundred year history of more than thirty-five different newspapers in Chinatown, surely the highest number for any community of comparable size in America, may be directly related to the intensity and diversity of political activity which has thrived in the community. In the main, the focus of this activity has been China. Up until World War II, continued denial of citizenship rights to China-born immigrants reinforced a naturally deep concern for developments in the motherland in a majority of the Chinatown population. Thus, ever since the visit of nineteenth century reformer K'ang Yu-wei, who founded the paper *Mon Hing Yat Bo* (*Chinese World*) in 1891, every major political figure and movement in modern

Chinese history had been able to amass a following and usually to publish a newspaper in Chinatown. Even among the early, American-born offspring of the family society, moreover, a deep interest in China's development tended to be the case. Although American citizenship had been their birthright and many had received college educations, failure to find employment during the Depression in occupations for which they had trained disillusioned these younger American Chinese and led to ambivalence about their position in American life. Many felt they might better contribute their skills to the challenging task of modernizing China and dreamed of going back. "China needs men who aren't above putting on overalls, soiling their hands, and going into the interior to work," wrote journalist Lim P. Lee in the *Chinese Digest,* founded by young American-born Chinese in 1935. "Of course, job opportunities are limited for Chinese in this country. But those who go back must be prepared to endure hard work." Throughout the first four decades of the twentieth century, while there was little improvement in the situation of American Chinese, the fervor for Chinese politics which had characterized Chinatown during the visit of Sun Yat-sen was maintained.

The decades which followed the 1911 revolution, however, proved disappointing for many in Chinatown. Older men who helped finance and arm—and in some cases had even fought in—Sun's revolution had dreamed that the strong and united China which would emerge out of the destruction of the "foreign" Manchu dynasty would save China from the yoke of Western imperialist domination, lead her industrialization, and end years of humiliation and suffering by restoring Chinese civilization to its former grandeur. Such a new China, they believed, would restore their dignity and respect in being Chinese and, furthermore, ensure the safety and protection of overseas Chinese throughout the world. From Chinatown, they had watched the progress of the new republic with eagerness and anticipation.

Instead, Sun's early abdication of the presidency to Yuan Shih-kai, who shortly declared himself emperor, launched the chaotic and inglorious life of the new republic. Yuan's subsequent fall and the failure of the monarchical restoration plunged China into a decade of bitter warlord rivalry. In 1919, the impact of Russia's October Revolution and the blooming of the May 4th Movement ushered in a brief period of intellectual ferment and revival of patriotism in China. The early twenties saw the reorganization of the Kuomintang under Comintern envoy Michael Borodin and the birth of the Chinese Communist Party, and also brought the beginning of an ill-fated first united front between the two. A combination of social revolution with national unification and liberation from imperialist domination was the aim of this first united front. While Communists in the organization were building workers' movements in Shanghai and Canton and a young Mao Tse-tung was giving his support to the controversial peasants' movement in Hunan Province, a highly nationalistic generation of Whampoa military cadets prepared for the northern expedition to quell the northern warlords and unify the country under the leadership of the Kuomintang. But ultimately the two goals proved incompatible within the framework of the Kuomintang, whose primary base of support was China's landowning class. In 1927, as the victorious Kuomintang army moved north, Chiang Kai-shek shattered the uneasy alliance of the united front by calling for a purge of Communists within the organization. On April 12 and 13, his bloody suppression of the workers' movement in Shanghai effectively obliterated the most advanced wing of Communist-led organizations in the cities. Chiang then forged a new alliance which bound China's large landowners to her compradores and bankers and was symbolized by his own marriage to Wellesley educated Mayling Soong, the daughter of one of Shanghai's wealthiest bankers.

The ascendancy of Chiang to power marked the end of the revolutionary phase of the Kuomintang and the beginning of its accommodations to imperialism. To those watching from afar, China at the end of the 1920s seemed even more vulnerable to foreign aggression than it had been at the beginning. Japan, which had occupied the Shantung Peninsula after World War I and delivered the humiliating terms of her Twenty-one Demands, was now rapidly embarking on a policy of military conquest and colonization of China. China's attempts to industrialize continued to be thwarted by the domination of foreign powers in the treaty ports and by her own decaying agricultural economy. As Chiang Kai-shek pursued the "bandit suppression" campaigns in a furious attempt to exterminate his last Communist opponents, famine, drought, flood, rapacious landlords, and bandits continued to devastate the fabric of social life in China's vast countryside.

As the failure of the dream of the republic became more and more apparent, the question of how to strengthen and unify China once again became a burning issue in Chinatown. In the wake of the Kuomintang-Communist split, divergent views crystallized and generated a new period of intense political debate among American Chinese. Factionalism and a fresh proliferation of political parties in Chinatown marked these years with passionate and sometimes bitter contention between the groups. Chinatown's largest political party was still the Kuomintang, sprung from the Tung Meng Hui and including in its nucleus some former activists from Sun's early revolutionary party. Response to Chiang's 1927 suppression of the Communists, however, had split the Kuomintang into rightist, centralist, and leftist factions, the latter following the position of Madame Sun Yat-sen in China and strongly sympathetic to the Communists. By the thirties, each of these factions had set up newspapers in San Francisco, Chicago, and New York, and there were constant polemical exchanges between them. Yet as the Japanese invasion of China continued to mount in the years which followed, criticism of Chiang and the Kuomintang itself for failure to negotiate a second united front with the Communists grew widespread among American Chinese. In 1936, protest against Chiang's policies by students in North China sparked the formation of a similarly critical Chinese Students' Alliance among the American-born and Chinese foreign students on campuses on the West Coast. In Chinatown, a newly formed Constitutional Party attracted many critics of Chiang. In its influential newspaper, the *Chinese World*, this party voiced support for a third-force solution in China. As one Chinatown journalist expressed the mood of 1936, "There is strong sentiment in the country now for the Chinese to have a united front against Japan, but it is doubtful that Chiang, who has fought the Communists for so long, can do this."

The emergence of a final bloc in the community's political arena, however, revealed that the intensity of Chinatown's political rivalry in the thirties had roots beyond mere debate over the China question. This bloc was composed of Marxist worker and student groups. Resentment against merchant domination, manifested in the development of the tongs in early Chinatown society, had welled beneath the surface during the first years of the twentieth century as merchant control of different associations entrenched itself and extended even to the tongs, while laborers lacked any effective organizations of their own. In 1910, Sun Yat-sen's strong following among Chinatown workers, in defiance of the warnings of the Six Companies, was symbolic of the rift between the two classes, but led to no outright clash. After the Kuomintang-Communist split in 1927, however, leftists in Chinatown coalesced to form the Great Revolutionary Alliance of Chinese Workers and Peasants, which opposed the Kuomintang right. Street rallies held by the alliance provoked anger in the merchant-backed conservative factions of the Kuomintang, often ending in physical fighting between hecklers and members of the group until the alliance was eventually forced out of existence.

By the mid-thirties, the example of vigorous Marxist movements in both China and the United States had provided new ideas and leadership around which workers in Chinatown organized. Groundbreaking research by Chinatown historian Him Mark Lai has recently documented the history of this process.* Spearheading the Chinatown movement, according to Lai, was the Chinese Workers' Mutual Aid Association (CWMAA), made up of the large number of Chinatown men who were employed by Alaskan salmon canneries during the winters and tided themselves over during the off-season on whatever work they could find in

---

* See Him Mark Lai's essay on leftist movements in Chinatown, Asian-American Special Issue, *Bulletin of Concerned Asian Scholars*, San Francisco, Fall, 1972.

Chinatown. During the American Depression, unemployment councils set up in San Francisco had attracted these
workers and introduced a small number of them to the
American labor movement. In 1936, a coalition of Chinese,
Japanese, Filipino, and white workers organized to fight the
contract system which was still being used to hire cannery
workers by the season at substandard hourly wages.
Through this campaign they succeeded in unionizing Alaskan cannery workers and won the right to collective bargaining. Following the strike, a group of Chinese workers on a
ship returning to San Francisco made plans to form their
own organization, one which would attempt to draw
Chinatown laborers into the national movement but which
implicitly would focus its attack on the feudalistic working
conditions in Chinatown. Thus the Chinese Workers' Mutual
Aid Association came to be established in September 1937.
Beginning as a gathering place where returned cannery
workers could gather, exchange experiences, and receive
information about employment openings, the association at
its height held lectures on Marxism, the labor movement,
and other topics, weekly meetings to discuss problems of
Chinese workers, and operated a press which printed the
first Chinese-language editions of essays by Mao Tse-tung
ever printed in America. Claiming four to five hundred
members at its height, the CWMAA maintained strong ties
with CIO and AFL unions such as the Cannery Workers'
Union and the International Longshoremen's Workers'
Union, as well as with the American Communist Party. In
the early days of the Sino-Japanese war its members were
the first to set up picket lines against the Greek freighter
Spyros, which was loading scrap iron for Japanese military
manufacture. They were later joined in the picketing by
thousands of members of the community.

The activity of the CWMAA among workers in Chinatown
was accompanied by the development of leftist organizations among students. One of the earliest, the San Francisco
Chinese Student Club, had been formed in response to
the 1927 Shanghai massacre but, like the Great Revolutionary Alliance, was quickly forced out of existence following a raid by San Francisco police, who accused it of

carrying on communist activities. The late thirties saw the formation of numerous youth groups to support the Chinese war effort, several of which coalesced in 1942 to form a clearly non-Kuomintang-dominated organization, the Chinese Youth League (CYL). In its headquarters on Stockton Street just a few doors away from the headquarters of the Kuomintang, the group sponsored drama and choral performances to raise funds for the war effort, sent publications and letters to servicemen, and maintained contact with liberal and progressive groups outside of Chinatown. Although the CYL lost membership after the war was over, in a smaller form and with a changed name (the Chinese-American Democratic Youth League, familiarly called *Min Ching*) it continued to be the focus of intense activity in Chinatown. By the late forties, the *Min Ching* had set up, in its headquarters, the largest Chinese-language library in America, including works of Chinese classical literature and history as well as the early Chinese Communists' works. Student members of the *Min Ching*, finding a major source of inspiration in the social vision of Mao's forces in Yenan, held study groups to discuss Marxism and essays by Mao and to follow political developments in China.

Unpredictably, it was only with the defeat of nationalist forces in China and the Communist victory in the civil war that the Kuomintang achieved ascendancy over all other political groups in Chinatown and achieved its semi-official status within the community. This gradual rise to supremacy began in the midst of the factionalism and debate of the thirties. In 1937, a decision by Chiang Kai-shek to follow Sun Yat-sen's example in actively organizing moral and financial support from overseas Chinese was the first step. To firm up the base of support in overseas communities at this time, envoys from the Kuomintang's Central Executive Committee were sent out to various overseas settlements to reorganize their factionalized Kuomintang parties according to a clear hierarchy of authority which would be directly responsive to Chiang. Hawaiian-born Kalfred Dip Lum, envoy to San Francisco, found Chinatown ripe for this task as he entered in late 1937 when a sense of urgency had swept the entire community in an effort to raise funds and medical supplies for China. Earlier that autumn, $30,000 of war relief had been raised in Chinatown in one week alone. Inspired by the successful forging of a second united front between Chiang and the Chinese Communists in the same year, conservatives, liberals, and even leftist groups like the CWMAA cooperated together in the picketing at the docks, in campaigns for medical supplies, and in parades where a huge republican flag was carried outstretched through the streets of Chinatown to receive coins and bills to send to China.

Lum, however, keeping long-range interests of the Kuomintang in mind, sought to establish a permanent base of the party in San Francisco which would guarantee support even beyond the immediate period of fervor for the cause of "national salvation." This was accomplished through a skillful policy of securing for the Kuomintang the lasting loyalty of key leaders in the community by appointing them to the highest official positions within the newly reorganized party branch. Thus, in January 1938, when the *Chinese Digest* announced that "a new KMT headquarters was established in Chinatown with the establishment of special commissioners appointed by the Central Committee of the KMT in China," it listed among the new commissioners men of the highest influence in Chinatown's indigenous power structure. In particular, Lum appointed as a commissioner a man called Wong Goon Dick, who occupied what by that time had come to be seen as the most influential position on the Six Companies Board of Directors: a combination of the positions of representative of the largest district association (the Ning Yung), the largest family association (the Wong), and the presidency of the powerful Bing Kung Tong. Leadership of the new Kuomintang branch in Chinatown, directly responsible to the Central Executive Committee in China, thereby became virtually synonymous with the leadership of the Chinatown community itself.

In a sense, Lum's action merely formalized a relationship which had existed between Chinatown's Six Companies and the established government of China since the formation of that body at the suggestion of the Chinese consulate in 1880. The strength of the tie had already been displayed in

1910 when the merchant establishment gave its support to the Manchu government despite nearly unanimous backing for Sun Yat-sen among other sectors of the community and in the earlier stages of the Sino-Japanese war when the Nationalist government in Nanking had channeled its requests for war-relief funds through the Six Companies. The creation of official positions for Chinatown leaders in the Kuomintang, however, cemented and greatly strengthened the previous tacit alliance. Titles offered by the Nationalist government as a means of winning support were eagerly accepted by merchant-leaders who sensed it would enhance their legitimacy as leaders of the community (particularly at a time when public opinion in America was highly favorable to Nationalist China). After the retreat of the Nationalist government to Taiwan, even greater need for support on the homeground of its most powerful ally led to intensified efforts to maintain the bond. When Wong Goon Dick died, Wong Yen Doon, the man who succeeded him to the three-fold power-base in the Wong Family Association, the Ning Yung District Association, and the underworld of Chinatown, was given yet a more prestigious position: he was made a member of the Chinese Nationalist government itself, as "National Political Advisor" to Chiang Kai-shek, with a seat in the Taiwan National Assembly. Since the early 1950s Wong Yen Doon, who at eighty is still considered the most influential man in Chinatown, has flown back and forth across the Pacific regularly to attend meetings of the National Assembly. Over the years he has repeatedly organized the community's various demonstrations of support for the Republic of China such as its elaborate welcomes to visiting Taiwanese officials; he and a small group of Kuomintang members engineered the desperate, nationwide campaign of American Chinese in 1972 to protest the admission of the People's Republic to the United Nations. A secondary, but interesting, manifestation of Wong's status has been the Taiwan government's designation to him of exclusive rights to import its popular black mushrooms into the United States, entitling him to modest commission payments from all other distribution outlets in the country.

Yet the Kuomintang could not consolidate its position in Chinatown until another historic event brought new dimensions to the meaning and practice of "loyalty" in Chinatown. In 1949, the unexpected victory of Communist forces in China and a resulting wave of hysteria in the United States focused a new spotlight on American Chinese and brought the familiar convergence of internal and external pressure which has so often been decisive in the history of the community. In 1950, as the United States confronted Chinese Communist soldiers in Korea and Senator Joseph McCarthy began the search for "communist traitors" in the high level of American government, a rising tide of anti-communism reinforced the prestige of the Kuomintang in Chinatown. Kuomintang members could now accuse opposing parties not only of failing the cause of China but of treason to the United States. It was by rallying behind itself this force of American public opinion together with law enforcement agencies such as the Federal Bureau of Investigation and the United States Immigration Office in a thorough suppression of opposition parties that the Kuomintang, supported by and reinforcing the merchant establishment, won its way to two decades of ascendancy in Chinatown.

Tension between the Kuomintang and leftist groups in Chinatown had built up quietly since their appearance, but the support of strong leftist groups outside of Chinatown and general cooperation in the wartime campaigns had prolonged an uneasy coexistence between the two. On October 9, 1949, a joint committee of the CWMAA, the *Min Ching*, and a smaller liberal businessmen's group in Chinatown had sponsored a celebration of the founding of the People's Republic of China in a large Chinatown auditorium known as the CACA hall. Members of the group had prepared speeches, decorated the walls with flowers, and hung a large red flag over the speakers' podium in the front of the room. As the celebration opened, about eight hundred people were in attendance, including a sprinkling of white dockworkers from the ILWU. Suddenly a group of twenty men rushed into the hall, tore the red flag down from its podium, and proceeded to throw the meeting into chaos.

The men, recognized by many in the audience as members of the Hop Sing and Bing Kung tongs (the latter led by Wong Yen Doon) left after ten or fifteen minutes and did no serious violence to anyone attending the meeting. On the next day, however, a black list drawn up in the style of the old tong war days cited the names of ten members of the CWMAA and the *Min Ching* and offered a five thousand dollar reward for the death of anyone on the list. Those who had been named, mainly leaders of the CWMAA, immediately went into hiding.

The years after 1949 brought successive weakening blows to opponents of the Kuomintang in Chinatown. Chinatown felt the first reverberation of America's anti-Communist reaction during the McCarthy period. Subpoenas were issued and various members of the community were investigated by the FBI while a mild revival of anti-Chinese feeling spread on the West Coast. Greater tension was felt in the community with the outbreak of hostilities in Korea. News that American troops were facing Chinese Communist forces in Korea revived all too recent memories of Japanese-American relocation camps during World War II. In 1954, as business in Chinatown restaurants and tourist shops began to drop slightly and Chinese merchants were finding themselves objects of the jibe, "You Chinese are killing our boys in Korea," from Caucasian associates, the Kuomintang began to mobilize the fearful community to make public expressions of anti-Communism. At the suggestion of Pei Chi Liu, who had been sent by the Kuomintang Central Executive Committee to take over the editorship of the *Chinese Nationalist Daily* during World War II, the Chinese Six Companies sponsored the formation of a Chinese Anti-Communist League in all American Chinatowns. Its purpose was "to let the American people know that the Chinese are not communists and to rally all overseas Chinese people against communism and to support the Republic of China." The Anti-Communist League sent letters to American politicians urging them not to recognize the Communist government in China, assuring them of the support of American Chinese for the regime of Chiang, and, as one Chinatown newspaper editor recalls, "succeeded in convincing the

American public that Chinatown was one hundred percent in support of Chiang Kai-shek."

At the same time, the league carried out a systematic purge of Chinatown leftists. Members notified FBI agents of CWMAA or *Min Ching* members who were suspected of being "communist sympathizers," and there began a long period of harassment by FBI officers and the Immigration Office which slowly wore down the members of these groups. Since the use of false immigration papers was still common in Chinatown during the forties and fifties, the threat of deportation by the Immigration Office was constantly used to intimidate leftists or their relatives who had entered with false papers. Laborer members of the CWMAA, many of whom were "paper sons," were particularly susceptible on this point and gradually were forced underground. The Anti-Communist League simultaneously organized boycotts of the newspaper *China Weekly*, which had been backed by the CWMAA, and caused it to dissolve during the first year of the Korean war. Other economic sanctions were applied to members of the leftist groups. In 1958, refusal to renew the lease on the meeting hall where a small number of *Min Ching* members still met signaled the formal defeat of leftist activities in Chinatown. *Min Ching* members went on to careers as professionals or white collar workers usually outside of Chinatown. A very few remain deeply involved in the community as liberal leaders today. The experience of harassment by the FBI and Immigration Office, however, was traumatic and they are reluctant to discuss their former involvement.

With the suppression of their political opposition, the Kuomintang and Six Companies leaders successfully maintained the appearance of almost unanimous loyalty to Chiang Kai-shek and the Republic of China for almost twenty years. The most widely read newspapers in the community were now either supported or directly controlled by the Kuomintang. A well-publicized celebration of the anniversary of the Republic of China became a major event in Chinatown each year, including a commemoration of "compatriots killed by communism" and a ritual burning of the effigy of Mao Tse-tung. To the present day, in all family association and district association buildings, flags of the Republic of China and a large portrait of Chiang Kai-shek are prominently displayed, and the most effective way of discrediting an enemy is to call him a communist.

FRANKLIN WOO, 43
Chemist

We got to know him in the summer of 1970 and did this interview in the library of his house in August. Although he is usually open and expressive about his political opinions in conversations with friends, he was nervous about having these recollections of Min Ching activities taped and seemed to avoid going into his memories in depth.

Of course, during the period of the united front, it was just accepted by people in the study group that the Communists were as legitimate as the Kuomintang. I was actually pro-Kuomintang all the way through the Sino-Japanese war. I guess we were rather isolated in Chinatown then, it would have been impossible to get news directly from the liberated zones anyway, and all we heard was that Chiang Kai-shek was leading the fight against the Japanese, saving China from the invaders, and all that. I remember as kids my father would take us all down to the wharves to protest the sale of scrap iron to Japan because that iron was made into bombs and planes which were used against China. We heard about the rape of Nanking, the bombing of Chungking, we used to watch movies of Chiang and the Nationalist army rallying the nation to fight the Japanese. My father used to tell us how brave and courageous the Chinese had to be to stand up against the Japanese. Of course, he only read the *Chinese Times** and the *Young China Daily*, so we didn't have a very broad picture then. But by 1947 I gradually realized more and more the corruption and ineptness of the Nationalist government. I felt that it was crumbling, certainly China needed

---

* A "moderate" paper founded by the Chinese-American Citizens Alliance (CACA). Since the forties, it has strongly supported Chiang Kai-shek and Nationalist China and become increasingly conservative.

a change. At the time, the Communists were the only ones who could promise that kind of change, that kind of honest government. And China needed an honest government.

I think by 1949 it was clear to most people in Chinatown that Chiang was going to lose the civil war, and I would say that many of us wanted a new government for China by then. You know, there had always been criticism of Chiang in some of the Chinatown papers, papers which I began reading myself by that time, and there was a lot of enthusiasm, actually a lot of knowledge, about Mao's writings among the leftist groups of students and workers at that time. Well, in October 1949, when the People's Republic had just been established, I heard that the Chinese Workers' Mutual Aid Association was going to hold a celebration of the victory as part of its twelfth anniversary program. I heard they had invited some speakers from the League for a Democratic China, the League for Peace and Democracy, and Harlan Roberts' California Labor School Chorus to give the first performance of the Yellow River Cantata in English. I guess it was just a natural expression of the enthusiasm among *Min Ching* members that we all decided to participate. Then a few days before the meeting I began to hear rumors that the tongs were going to do something. There had been tension between the Kuomintang and the leftists for quite a while, but for some reason none of us took these rumors very seriously. We sort of scoffed at them, in fact. "This is a democratic country" (laughs), "Nobody would do something like that." The Chinese Workers' Mutual Aid Association had had strong ties with the Longshoremen's Union (ILWU), and they could have called in plenty of guards if they wanted to, but no one did. That's how lightly we took it.

That night, October 9, the celebration drew a full house. I would say about five hundred people showed up at the CACA hall and we filled the whole place, even the balcony. It was a pretty exciting moment, actually. There were a lot of new faces, including workers from the Longshoremen's Union. But during the second speech we heard a shout from the door, then all of a sudden two lines of men ran through the aisles to the speakers' platform, tore down the red flag, knocked over the vases of flowers, and began throwing some kind of blue dye around the audience. There was some scuffling and I remember one Caucasian guy who tried to protect a poster got beat up pretty badly, he got a broken rib. The men didn't stay long, though, maybe about five minutes, and there were just twenty of them. I guess it was because it came so suddenly, and when everyone was caught up in the excitement of beginning the celebration, that it kind of caught us off guard and we panicked. After about fifteen minutes we pulled ourselves together, somebody began singing the "March of the Volunteers," the Chinese national anthem, and we all joined in. But by that time a lot of people had left because the thing shook them up. The rest of us stayed and continued the program. Jerry Ja finished his speech. Then William Kerner spoke about the founding of a new, democratic China. It wasn't until I heard the Yellow River Cantata that I felt a spirit of celebration again. Then we all went home. I don't remember whether we talked about the disruption when the meeting was over or not.

The next day I guess the Kuomintang expected trouble at the Double Ten parade, because one of my friends told me there were a lot of tong men standing guard on the street. A couple of guys got beaten up because they were thought to be leftists; actually, they weren't. When we heard about the death notice going out, we took that pretty seriously. Of course, I wasn't on the list, I was just getting into the *Min Ching* then, but all the people whose names were there went into hiding. I just stayed home for a while. I don't think the rest of us tried to plan any kind of protest, or at least not to my knowledge. You see, the Kuomintang had had the upper hand in Chinatown since the Second World War. We were only students in the *Min Ching* and besides, we only had about forty active members. The Chinese Workers' Mutual Aid Association, even though they must have had about five hundred members, were nowhere near being strong enough to take on the Six Companies, the family associations, the merchants, and the Bing Kung Tong. They were just much stronger than the left. Then in a few years, with the McCarthy terror, the Chinese army in Korea, and this immigra-

tion business, they had all the cards. You know, a lot of the
people in Min Ching came in on false papers. Obviously,
they played that to the hilt. So in a few years, the left was
just smashed.

The McCarthy terror didn't affect Chinatown as much as it
could have, I guess, but still I was very careful about cir-
cumventing things when I talked. You had to make sure you
didn't sound anti-American. Actually, I think the Korean
war had a greater impact on Chinatown than McCarthyism.
The whole atmosphere here then was fear. If you weren't
careful, you could be thrown into a concentration camp.
That was when the FBI stepped up its activities in Chinatown. The only left-wing paper, the Chinese Weekly, folded
then under the new pressure. The Chinese Workers' Mutual
Aid Association also began to fall apart about that time,
although it didn't disband completely until 1956. A lot of the
men there were hounded by the immigration service and a
couple were deported. The Min Ching kept up its weekly
discussion periods down in our basement on Stockton
Street. We continued our Mandarin classes, dance group,
choir, plays, even though we were all getting more and more
apprehensive. We knew the FBI was keeping a close eye on
us, and we even suspected there was an informer among us.
I guess that's one thing all of us feel bad about now, that we
had to be suspicious of each other. The FBI people began
coming to our homes, going to talk to our relatives, friends,
where we worked. I guess when they got the Immigration
Office working on us, though, we knew the Min Ching was
coming to an end. I remember the immigration people would
stop Min Ching members on the street and demand to see
their papers, just to harass us. Once they discovered somebody had false papers, they would begin proceedings for
deportation. I guess I've never been able to explain that well
to people who haven't experienced it, how painful this immigration harassment can be to Chinese. Say, if a Min Ching
member is discovered to have false papers, his whole family
will be affected because probably they didn't have the
proper papers either. So they'll go from you, to the uncle
who brought you in, his wife, and it goes on and on. Well,
too many of us had illegal entries somewhere along the line.

It wasn't a quick thing or a big decision. People just slowly stopped coming down to the basement. A couple of people every few months. Then we'd lose touch with people who had dropped out, although some of us have still kept up our friendships, I guess my closest friends are the three or four former members I still see. But by 1958 the lease on the basement had run out, the Anti-Communist League had pressured the owner not to renew, and there weren't enough of us left anyway to make it worth keeping. In the end, just a few people were actually deported. But I know former Min Ching members who even today have no permanent residence status because of their Min Ching affiliation. They just live here as stateless people.

PEI CHI LIU, 73

We interviewed him at night after the office of the newspaper Truth Semi-Weekly, *for which he still works, had closed. In a cubicle at the back, Pei Chi Liu sat at a wooden desk in his overcoat, with its frayed cuffs and collar, a small electric heater barely taking the chill off the room. He told us he was writing a 100,000 character history of the Sung dynasty, one of a series of Chinese dynasty histories he has written in the past few years for publication in Taiwan. It will be a pleasure to spend a few hours with us talking about history, he says. After we've been in the cubicle for a while, we recognize the continuous rattle of mahjong chips in the room above our heads.*

Pei Chi Liu is one of the oldest leaders of the Chinatown branch of the Kuomintang Party. He was sent to Chinatown by the Central Executive Committee of the Kuomintang in 1940 to assume an editorial position on the Chinese Nationalist Daily. Photographs show him as a tall young man with wavy hair, wearing earphones as he receives shortwave broadcasts from the wartime Chinese Nationalist capital, Chungking. Another photograph shows him in the Kuomintang headquarters on Stockton Street beneath a large portrait of Dr. Sun Yat-sen. He is sitting with the famous "mayor" of Chinatown, Albert Chow, and community leader Doon Wong. They await the arrival of Madame Chiang

Kai-shek in San Francisco. A decade later, after the defeat of the National government by the Chinese Communists, Pei Chi Liu organized the Chinatown Anti-Communist League with the aid of the influential Doon Wong.

After the civil war began the situation in China got worse year by year. The Communist propaganda affected all the people of China. Even in the United States, the newspapers began to print Communist propaganda. Now I was working for the newspaper, I got all the UP reports. And I know that lots of those American reporters, even when there was a victory, they would report us dead. They helped the Communists, you see. Maybe you don't believe that. When we defended Nanking, for example, there was no news. They just said that Chiang Kai-shek's base was collapsing. That he was not good. That he was falling down. But when the Communists took a small town, even one that was barely on the map, the American correspondents reported that they were winning the war. Just propaganda for the Communists. In fact, my view is that the mainland fell into Communist hands forty percent by the Soviet Union and fifty percent by the United States. Only ten percent by Mao Tse-tung. Because the United States reporters supported the Communists with their propaganda. The FBI even checked me, you know, to find out why I was against the Communists. Of course you know after the forty-nine defeat, the FBI checked all the Chinese Communists. But in 1946 they checked us. You don't believe that? All the other newspapers were against the Chinese government. That was the United States government policy. Until 1944, the United States government supported us. Then Henry Wallace went to China and things got worse year by year, until the Communists took over. Of course the American government didn't directly support the Communists, but they indirectly influenced the Chinese people. Because when Wallace supported a coalition government, people in China began to think the United States government felt favorably toward the Communists. Then they began to feel favorably toward them, too. And so from within, China was lost. Outside people may not know this, but I know the real Chinese, I know this.

All through the Second World War the people in Chinatown were supporting the government in China, they were
sincerely supporting it. The Six Companies organized fundraising, and the Chinese people here sent more than twenty
million dollars to China. Medicine, too. Then when the Communists took over, the people in Chinatown hated this, but
they didn't know what to do. After the takeover, they just
received a letter from the government, but they didn't know
about Communists. What were Communists to them? They
felt there was no hope. Then the Communist propaganda
came, on radio broadcasts, in the newspapers, and it began
to affect people here, too. Our newspaper was still against
the Communists, but after a while our business went down.
People bought the *Chinese World,* got all the news from the
Communists, and they were affected by the propaganda. Our
Young China Daily's business went down. After two years,
the Communists decided no Chinese people could come to
Hong Kong, and they purged all the people. People here
received letters that their relatives had been killed by the
Communists. Then they all knew what communism meant. I
knew that. I told the people at first but they didn't believe me.

There really wasn't much of an organized group that supported the Communists during the civil war. Mainly it was
just individuals. I remember, by October 1949, the Communists had taken over more than ninety percent of China.
Their troops were making inroads to Canton City. The
Chinese Communist supporters here, not many, just about
one or two hundred people, were very happy. On October 9,
they rented the CACA Hall to hold a celebration of Communist victory in China. But some of our people went inside
and beat them, you know, knocked them down.

In the Chinatown newspapers, again, it was most often a
case of indirect support of the Communists. The *Chinese
Pacific Weekly* was very typical for that time. They didn't
say anything directly communist, but inside they helped the
Communists. They printed all the local news. No news about
the Communists. But here and there they'd have one sen-
tence, just a few sentences against the Kuomintang. So they
indirectly supported the Communists. In fact, the man who
was editor of that paper was an old schoolmate of mine.

During the civil war period he came here and asked us for a job. I told him the one condition was not to write anything against the Kuomintang. He said, "Yes, I understand," but then he put out an article which was actually quite damaging to the KMT. And he wrote the news in a way which was good for the Communists. So we have to kick him off. Then he started his own weekly.

Of course, as a member of the Kuomintang committee I was very much concerned about the situation in 1949. But for a while there was nothing much I could do. I just tried to report the news correctly, even when our circulation went down. It wasn't until the Korean War that I had a chance. Before the Korean War I hadn't said much, but after the Chinese Communists crossed the Yalu River, I could see the Communists were coming up. Even the American people began to be afraid. There was a lot of trouble in Chinatown with people looking for communists among us. Some people stopped coming to Chinese restaurants. The Six Companies was searching for a way to show that the Chinese are not all communists. I saw a good chance to organize. Do you know Mr. Doon Wong? He was a member of the Six Companies, a big member. I suggested to him that we should set up an anti-communist league in Chinatown to prove to the American people that we are against communism. He talked to all the other members, and after that it was easy to organize. Each organization in Chinatown sent two representatives to the first meeting. Then Los Angeles and many Chinatowns in the United States set up their own organizations.

The primary aim of the league was to let the American people know that the Chinese are not communists. The other thing was to rally all overseas Chinese people against the Communists and to support the Republic of China.

Mr. Doon Wong helped me. He's in the Kuomintang, and he's been my partner all these thirty years. Since 1940, he has been manager of this newspaper. I was editor-in-chief. He's a very important man in Chinatown, you know. When there are big problems, big things, people always ask Mr. Wong to help. He's the leader of the Chinese people here.

The Chinese people believe in him. His name is very well-known.

You see, one thing is he has a big family, a big district. He's from Toishan. In the Kuomintang he represents Toishan, too. This gives him a lot of influence with the government of China. They believe in him, and they gave him a very high official position in the government—National Political Advisor to Chiang Kai-shek. So he's a member of the National Assembly of Taiwan, representing the Chinese people here. And then, he's a member of so many other groups! He's an elder in the Bing Kung Tong. And three days ago, when there was a convention in Los Angeles, he was elected president of the Wong Family Association. He didn't want to do it, you know. But there were too many candidates, and he was the only one who could beat all of them. They made him president to settle the dispute.

He's something more powerful than even the president of the Six Companies. The president changes every two months, you know, so it's not so important. The permanent influence is on the Board of Directors. They decide everything the president carries out. Mr. Wong is on that. And he represents the Ning Yung District Association, which happens to be the largest district association in the United States. So he has the main power there. He's quite popular and everyone usually agrees with him.

I still think ninety percent of the people here are against the Communists. Of course, in the last few years, the immigrants have changed a lot of things. From 1954 to 1960, you know, there were still strict rules about immigrants. About ten thousand people from Hong Kong came over during that period, but the American consulate checked on every little detail before they let them come. So they were all good people. They supported the American government and the government of China. They were people with good values, too. But in 1962, when Kennedy liberalized the immigration laws, it was much easier to come from Hong Kong. I'm sure a lot of Communists have come. And hippies. They've made a lot of trouble in Chinatown. At one point we even asked the immigration officer to send some of these troublemakers back. But it's too hard under the new law. So now there's trouble again in Chinatown, just since the past few years.

Like these so-called Red Guards. They go around saying they believe in communism. In fact, you'll notice that all of them were born here. They don't have one idea what communism means. The young ones born in China don't join them, you know. Well, at any rate, Mr. Wong took care of them. They aren't in Chinatown now. He just sent some of the other young people down. You know, they went into the office and tore down all those stupid posters of Mao Tse-tung. I guess they broke a few windows. So Red Guards are afraid to come back.

American young people don't understand the Vietnam war. They listen to people like Senator Fulbright, or Mansfield . . . it's all crazy! Everyone knows that if Indochina falls into communist hands, Thailand and Malaysia will fall, too. Then what will happen to the United States market in the Far East? That's a realistic question, you know. Thirty percent of all American trade is in the Far East. If Southeast Asia falls into communist hands, that's the end of the market. The end of the raw materials. Right now, when we get raw materials from Southeast Asia, you can make the goods here and sell them to the Far East again. The United States gets its money back.

GILBERT WOO, 60

Editor of the liberal Chinese Pacific Weekly. *When the paper was first founded in 1946, it was the object of a boycott attempt by the Kuomintang.*

My political outlook? I was in normal school at the time when the Communists and the Kuomintang were together, that was during the northern expedition in 1927. It was a time when there were demonstrations all over Kwangtung Province, but in school we had no political orientation one way or the other. We were taught that Sun Yat-sen's Three Principles were the best thing for China. I studied a little bit of Marxism, but I didn't know much about communism. So, politically speaking, I think the Three Principles trained me to be what we call a liberal here. In the international context you want nationalism, in the political field you want democracy, in the economic field you want some sort of socialism. I came here in 1932 and not very long after a lot of American liberal magazines attracted me. Like the *Nation,* the *New Republic*—I became their fan, you know (laughs). So maybe that was my political education, too. I've never missed one issue of the *New Republic.* So that has been my political thinking and my editorial policy.

The first paper I worked for was the *Chinese Times,* but I had an argument with the boss over an article I wrote and I quit. About a half a year before, the Kuomintang paper, that's the *Chinese Nationalist Daily* on Sacramento Street, had tried to recruit me and I had refused. I didn't like the partisan thing too well, and I didn't agree with their line at that time. But since I needed work, I spoke with the manager there, and he gave me freedom to write the way I wanted, news reporting and my own column, I just didn't handle any of the editorials. That lasted until 1946, when the KMT sent someone in to take the whole paper over. I didn't trust him, and it was clear there would be no future in the paper for me, so I decided to start my own paper, a weekly, with a liberal editorial policy. But since I had criticized the Kuomintang when I was with the *Times,* they were suspicious of my starting the *Chinese Pacific Weekly.* They knew it would be critical of the Chiang government, and they tried everything they could to stop me.

Well, you know, all I had to do was pick up the liberal American magazines. Even the New York *Times,* Mr. Atkinson, at that time, was critical of Chiang. So we just picked up this position. It wasn't based on communism. We just wanted to criticize what the Nationalist government was doing. The corruption and that kind of thing. I had no idea Chiang might be overthrown by the Communists. We just criticized the way we would criticize the president or the White House.

Well, the Kuomintang tried to warn their people not to subscribe to the *Chinese Pacific Weekly.* "Their people," meaning the associations and the tongs that the KMT controls. Especially in some of the small communities in Sacramento and Stockton. You know, one time a dealer there had sold out about fifty copies, and two weeks later he notified us to stop sending the paper. "We don't want to risk any danger for just fifty cents"—they made about three cents a copy—"too small a profit to risk." They were told our paper was pro-Communist. I think that was the most serious thing they did. It's pro-Communist, so don't sell it, don't buy it, don't put ads in. But where the Chinatowns were bigger they didn't have so much control.

There was no physical threat to us. They said things indirectly, they hinted, some of my partners were scared. But I was pretty sure they wouldn't do much. Nothing really happened until 1949, when the Communist army had almost overrun the whole China. We didn't say anything editorially, we just reported this as straight news. The Communist army had occupied this town or that town, or wiped out so many Nationalist divisions, inflation had brought the exchange rate up to one million yuan per dollar, and so forth. All this was news. But to my ex-colleagues it was pro-communist news, because their paper didn't report this (laughs). And when Chiang finally had to flee to Formosa, they blamed us for his overthrow by the Communists! That was when the KMT really tried to move against us, by reporting us to the FBI.

There were always a few communists here in Chinatown. But in 1949 they tried to come out from underground. I think they had a few Caucasian sympathizers, or members maybe, mostly from the International Longshoremen's Union. And in 1949, with the Communist victory, they decided to hold a mass meeting in the CACA hall. Halfway through a bunch of men came in, tore down the red flag, starting beating people up, breaking furniture and windows. The whole meeting was smashed, and there was never another public, pro-communist demonstration until the Red Guards last spring. Anyway, although I hadn't even attended the CACA hall thing, the KMT accused me of being one of the instigators. They reported to the FBI. The FBI checked a lot of people about me, but they didn't talk directly to me for another five or six years. In the meantime, late in 1949, another group began putting out a pro-communist daily. The Kuomintang concentrated their efforts on boycotting them and the *Chinese Pacific Weekly* was put aside (laughs). They didn't care much about us any more. However, when the Korean War broke out, that newspaper folded. Too much pressure on them.

In 1949, I think eighty or ninety percent of the people here at this time felt that there had to be a change in China. You know, it's not uncommon for people here to oppose the established government in China. Like during the Manchu dynasty, there were more anti-Manchu newspapers than pro. K'ang Yu-wei was not exactly anti-Manchu, but his group criticized the Manchu government. The exception was that the Six Companies tended to support the government in power. But before the war they were not supposed to be involved in partisan politics. There were a number of anti-KMT people in the Six Companies. But as the civil war went on the KMT, I think, knew they should cooperate with their supporters here. You know, by giving more titles, empty titles like commissioner and national advisor, to some of the leaders here. Then they would have something to work for. I think from that time on, the Kuomintang has controlled the Six Companies in Chinatown. For instance they always pick somebody in a big family like Wong or Lee, somebody who had a tong affiliation, the more powerful the better. They always pick these people to be Commissioner for Overseas Affairs, national advisor, and all that.

Another thing is the so-called Anti-Communist League. The Kuomintang organized this within the Six Companies so that it would be a "community organization" instead of part of their own apparatus. It was established at a time when many Chinese were nervous about anti-communist feelings in America. But actually the league is affiliated with the anti-communist league in Formosa and carries out the anti-communist policy here. Such as criticizing people who seem to be too much on the left, issuing circulars naming people as communists and telling the community not to associate with them. Again, leadership in the Anti-Communist League always goes to men with influence in the community, heads of family associations and tongs. Like at the CACA smash-up, those, of course, were tong people. I think three tongs got together and sent their people in to do the job. Now this doesn't mean every tong member agreed with the action. But a group of them, either for profit or idealism, participated in the violence.

There is no formal relationship between the tongs, the Anti-Communist League, and the Kuomintang. This is done completely through the leaders. In three of the tongs, the political leanings of the leadership have fluctuated between loyalty to Taiwan and sympathy to the mainland. The Anti-Communist League would not count on them to do anything. But two of the tongs, the Bing Kung and the Hop Sing, have always been sympathetic to the Kuomintang. They depend on these two for action. People say that these two tongs also recruit youth gangs to do work for them.

I suppose people have talked to you about a man called Doon Wong? They'll say he's the strongest man in Chinatown, the man who really runs Chinatown behind the scenes, although he's never mentioned in the white press. Well, he's probably the best example of how all this works. He's very powerful in the Wong Family Association, which is the biggest family association. He was elected their national president last year. He represents the Ning Yung, the biggest district association, on the Board of Directors of the Six Companies. And he's head of the Bing Kung Tong. Now he's the man to whom the Taiwan government has given its highest title, National Political Advisor. He flies back and forth between here and Taiwan several times a year.

But the interesting thing about a leader like Doon Wong is that, as an individual, he's not really very well-to-do. His business has never been that successful. Maybe he's too generous! You know, here's a man with a fourth grade education and yet he holds people, he can control people here in Chinatown. I think he has some old Chinese quality of leadership, he treats people generously. He doesn't hoard money. When they need money, he just goes to those who have it and asks for them. The younger leadership, the ones that are coming up, aren't like that any more. They take care of themselves first and are not as generous as he. Well, I suppose with the Bing Kung Tong supporting him, the Wong Family Association and the Ning Yung District Association, he doesn't really need anything. Since they're three of the most powerful organizations.

And I should add that where political differences are concerned, Mr. Wong is a very different man. All he can feel for people he thinks are communists is hatred. He hates the Red Guard youth. He not only hates them, but he hates people like me, the liberals. You know, he won't show anything outside. When he meets you on the street, he'll say hello to you. But deep in his heart, I know where he belongs.

9. The Establishment

Outside and inside Chinatown, extravagant tales circulate about the leaders of the community. From "feudal moghuls" to nabobs who "control treasuries of millions of dollars" and "own land all over California and the West" descriptions vary, most emphasizing the possession of vast wealth and despotic degree of control within Chinatown. It comes as a surprise, then, to find the leaders of Chinatown's merchant establishment where they really are: in the narrow storefront of the Light Company on Waverly Place, sitting beside the cash register in a Jackson Street restaurant, working after hours in a newly opened pharmacy on Washington Street. They are small businessmen, here and there the owner of a mildly prosperous import-export house, some garment shops, an occasional real estate or insurance agent. The few Chinese millionaires, they explain, have rarely stayed in Chinatown once they've done well. "No, it's the ones like us who stay." Most tell a similar story: years of work beside employees in a local store, adherence to the ethic of hard work and frugality, a little success, the move to the suburbs; finally they were able to send the kids to school, and "get into doing something for the community." Today, a late model car, part ownership in one of Chinatown's luxury restaurants, may give a hint of economic prosperity. But their conservative suits, distrusting brusqueness, and feel for a sharp, fast-talking line persist as hallmarks of the ghettos' self-made men. "Yes, I'll talk to you if you'll tell me why it's worth my time," was a typical start to many of our conversations with Chinatown's leading men.

Since the founding of the district associations by wealthy traders, in the nineteenth century, merchants have dominated the institutional life of Chinatown. The Chinese Six Companies has been the central institution through which they have exercised political leadership, the height of its power and authority coinciding with the peak of the family society in the 1930s, 1940s, and 1950s. An examination of the position of the Six Companies in Chinatown today reveals both inherent limitations in its structure as a governing body, as well as the decline and disruption of the society in which it thrived.

Today, the delicacy and resourcefulness with which the Six Companies' structure was tailored to the historic needs of the Chinatown community is easily overlooked. As it emerged in the 1880s, the Six Companies attempted to extend its jurisdiction over the community through an extraordinarily comprehensive system of organizational ties and thus to achieve a sensitive balance of representation for Chinatown's highly factionalized population. Its concern for this was due to the fact that in its earliest conception, quite to the contrary of what is often supposed, the Six Companies was not envisioned as a highly centralized executive organ but rather as a consultative body with arbitrating power within the community. The name of the early Six Companies reveals this, for it was originally seen simply as a *gungso*, or meeting hall, where leaders of the powerful and often rivalrous district associations in Chinatown could confer on matters which affected the community as a whole. Around 1880, when the high pitch of anti-Chinese agitation created an urgent need for stronger leadership to defend the group, the congress of district associations was reorganized and formally recognized by the Chinese consul-general as the leading body of Chinatown. Even then, however, the emphasis remained on consultation and creating harmony among the many factions which had characterized the original *gungso*.

In its structure as the highest representative body within Chinatown the Six Companies was perhaps the most unique early American Chinese institution, including in its synthesis even some features adapted from American political life. By placing itself as a symmetrical third tier above Chinatown's clan and district associations, the Six Com-

panies based itself solidly within the pre-existing social
structure of early Chinatown. At the same time, it sought to
achieve a stable balance between the competitive clan and
district associations by a system of combined representation according to region and numerical strength in much the
same fashion as the American Congress. To accomplish this,
the Six Companies divided its officers into two groups. The
first group, known as the Board of Presidents, embodied the
principle of equal representation for all the significant re-
gional groups in Chinatown's population. Each of Chinatown's seven largest district associations—the Ning Yung,
Hop Wo, Kong Chow, Young Wo, Sam Yup, Yan Wo, and
Sue Hing—had one member on the Board of Presidents.
Simultaneously, a second group of officers, the Board of
Directors, was composed of varying numbers of representatives from the different district associations according to
their numerical strength or weakness in Chinatown. Thus
the Ning Yung Association, composed of immigrants from
Toishan county, who have from the beginning been an overwhelming majority among American Chinese, had the largest
number of representatives on the Board of Directors,
twenty-seven. The Sue Hing, Young Wo, Kong Chow, and
Hop Wo Associations, also strong in Chinatown, have eight,
five, five, and six directors respectively. The Sam Yup Association, whose wealthy merchants left Chinatown in large
numbers after the rise of anti-Chinese agitation, and the
Yan Wo Association of Hakka people (always a minority in
Chinatown) had respectively three and one. The prepon-
derant strength of the Ning Yung delegation of twenty-
seven in this wing of the Six Companies is clear.

The effort to combine equal representation according to
district with adjustment for the numerical strengths of
different groups in Chinatown was manifested even in the
division of function between the two wings of officers.
Executive power to make decisions and handle the ordinary
business of the Six Companies was vested in the Board of
Presidents, where all districts were represented equally. The
Board of Directors, in which the Ning Yung group predomi-
nates, merely approved or disapproved decisions referred
to them. A further mechanism of checks and balances was

then incorporated into the Board of Presidents. Presumably to prevent monopoly of executive power by any one of the rival districts in the nineteenth century, the office of chief executive on the seven man board was constantly rotated every two months.* However, adjustments were made for the Ning Yung majority: it was stipulated that during the rotation every other term (and therefore half the terms of the year) must be taken by a Ning Yung president, thus requiring two years to complete the cycle. In practice, minority groups in Chinatown have claimed, the ultimate effect of this mechanism has been to shift the balance of power in the Six Companies toward the Ning Yung group. They also point out that, despite the formal "advisory" status of the Ning Yung-dominated Board of Directors, its veto power has proved to be decisive. By the 1930s it had become common for a man who combined presidency of the Wong Family Association (Chinatown's largest) and the Ning Yung District Association to be recognized as the most influential member of the Six Companies.

The internal structure of the Six Companies delineated above has persisted intact to the present day, its eighty year history leaving the current members a heritage of weaknesses and strengths. Today, the primary contribution of membership in the Six Companies to the power of an individual in Chinatown remains the broad constituency over which the Six Companies claims jurisdiction through its ties to the district and family associations. Formally speaking, anyone who is a member of a family association (which elects its representatives to the district association from which they go on to the Six Companies) is "represented" by and recognizes the authority of the Six Companies. Furthermore, as was perhaps inevitable given the small size of the Chinatown community, over the years it has become customary for men who earn positions in the Six Companies to be elected to the presidencies of other organizations in the community outside the framework of the clan and district groups. The leaders of the different tongs, of the

---

* In order to have an even number of six districts per twelve month year, the Yan Wo District Association, because of its very small constituency, is not included in the rotating Board of Presidents.

powerful Garment Contractors' Association, of the Kuomintang, and of Chinatown's Anti-Communist League have
all traditionally been men who held positions on the Six
Companies. Six Companies men are also members of the
Chinese Chamber of Commerce (although recently they
have not been elected to the presidency of this group because most lack fluency in English) and a few are
members of the Chinese-American Citizens Alliance. Two
other extremely influential bases of power for Six Companies men in the community have been the Chinese Central
High School and the Chinese Hospital (founded in 1924).
Given responsibility, in its constitution, for the welfare of
Chinese in areas where they were neglected by the American system, the Six Companies originally raised funds for
and organized the construction of these two institutions,
and Six Companies members today sit on their boards of
directors. Through their positions in all these different
bodies, the fifty-five members of the Board of Directors of
the Six Companies form a virtual interlocking directorate
of the important organizations in Chinatown.

An inherited legacy of the Six Companies which has
continued to be important as the city of San Francisco
develops is control over land and buildings. A look at the
landholding chart for the core area of Chinatown reveals a
maze of small parcels, sixty-five percent of which are held
in the name of clan, district associations, or less frequently,
in the name of the Six Companies. The Six Companies, as
an arbitrating body, does not have legal jurisdiction over
this property collectively owned by the districts and clans.
Nevertheless, since the most influential men in the clan and
district associations are one and the same as the men who
sit on the boards of the Six Companies, the dispensation of
the greater portion of Chinatown's land hinges *de facto* on
the discretion of these fifty-five men. Although at present
traditional sanctions against selling clan-owned land seem
still to be strongly felt by its officers, in recent years the Six
Companies has been consistently courted by both commercial and government agencies keenly interested in the future
development of Chinatown's high-value land. As successful
businessmen who also have private holdings of their own,

Six Companies men form the decisive landholding bloc in Chinatown.

Another strength accruing to a position on the Board of Directors of the Six Companies is an extensive sphere of personal connections. The network of contacts provided by the district and clan associations, not to mention the other organizations in which Six Companies men have prestige, is still the largest in Chinatown. A typical example of the sphere of influence commanded by a Six Companies man is the case of John Ng. Owner of a restaurant and several garment shops, Mr. Ng has over the past twenty years been repeatedly elected president of his own family association, representative to his district association, president of the Six Companies, president of the Suey Sing Tong, president of the Chinatown Garment Contractors' Association, and member of the Chamber of Commerce. Because of the respect they command and the strong personal ties they have developed over the years with the members of these various organizations, such men have a key influence on the action and behavior of people in Chinatown. The success of the Six Companies in implementing community-wide boycotts against its political opponents in the fifties and early sixties is but one example of the considerable influence wielded by these men. (A Six Companies organized boycott of the pro-Peking newspaper *Chinese Voice*, as recently as 1969, limited its advertisement backing so severely that the newspaper operated at a loss until it collapsed in 1972.) Occasional newsletters and bulletins issued within the family associations are influential in molding community opinion. It should also be mentioned that Chinatown's most widely read newspaper, the *Chinese Times*, although officially published by the Chinese-American Citizens Alliance, has since 1950 almost invariably supported the Six Companies' stands on community issues. The broad circulation of this newspaper thus also falls within the sphere of influence of the Six Companies.

Continuing to lend strength to the Six Companies is the fact that, as one former president put it, "the Six Companies can still raise more money than anybody else in town." This is partly because members of the Board of Directors, by

Chinatown precedent, must themselves give large sums to any drive sponsored by the body during their term. They must also participate vigorously in fundraising, even going door to door to ask for contributions. According to the same former president's description: "It's just that one guy knows another, and when he comes around you give him a few bucks to get him away. The Chinese think of it as gaining face. But anyway, that's how you get money." Leaders of almost all older social service groups in Chinatown claim that a letter of endorsement by the Six Companies is a prerequisite for fundraising in Chinatown.

Recognition from the outside, initially granted the Six Companies because of its genuine claim to represent Chinatown, has over the years been a final factor perpetuating the status of the organization within the community. Throughout the first half of the twentieth century, as long as the majority of Chinatown residents still lacked citizenship, the community's tangential involvement in San Francisco politics was carried on almost exclusively through the medium of the Six Companies. On the rare occasions when city policy had to deal directly with Chinatown, city hall officials consulted with the Six Companies; the Six Companies in turn learned to use its power to raise campaign money and to "deliver" the small bloc of Chinatown votes to give it some kind of leverage with influential politicians in the city. The type of influence a Six Companies leader could exert in American politics can be seen at its peak in the figure of Harry Truman's flamboyant friend, Albert Chow. Chow, a long time member of the Board of Directors of the Six Companies, reached his height of prestige in the 1950s, when he became well-known, both in San Francisco and outside, as the "Mayor of Chinatown." (Community legend has it that in a dark moment when Truman feared losing his reelection campaign to Thomas Dewey, Chow, whom he visited every time he went to San Francisco, took him to the Kongchow District Association Temple to burn incense for good luck. Truman later liked to attribute his victory to this act.) Since Chow's day, no Six Companies leader has quite equaled his élan. Nevertheless, the custom of conferring with the Six Companies on relevant decisions

is still continued by city hall. In summer 1971, the appointment of a Six Companies man to be the first American
Chinese member of San Francisco's Board of Education,
despite open community backing for younger liberals, is a
recent example. As long as the Six Companies can point to
incidents of this type as evidence of its continuing "in" at
city hall, it has been able to maintain an image of importance. Intimate ties with the government of the Republic of
China, which carries on most of its political dealings with
Chinatown through the office of the Six Companies, have
also proved an invaluable access to prestige and the appearance of political legitimacy.

Yet the Six Companies has also manifested crippling
weaknesses over its history. The most serious of these is an
inherent structural weakness resulting from the deep cleav-
ages between the leaders of Chinatown's different groups.
A high level of rivalry and factionalism among representatives of different district associations has plagued Six Companies meetings throughout its history. Time and again the
use of checks and balances by different groups has left the
body deadlocked, despite urgent need for action. Rivalry
between the smaller district associations and the Ning Yung
has been particularly bitter, leading to a frequent blocking
of any Ning Yung-initiated action by alliances of the smaller
groups. Even today, enmity between the presidents of the
Ning Yung (also de facto head of the Bing Kung Tong) and
the Young Wo (also de facto head of the Suey Sing Tong)
associations is so deep that the two men refuse to address
each other directly, even after years of meetings on the
same Board of Directors. Six Companies men say that
because of this internal tension every effort must be made
to skirt potentially explosive issues during regular meetings
of the Six Companies; only when there is a crisis situation
are the controversial issues faced. In general, throughout its
whole history, the Six Companies has proved itself capable
of united, decisive action only in the face of powerful
threats from the outside and pressing neccessity—for
example, during its early attempts to fight racist legislation in the late nineteenth century, or its construction of
the Chinese Central High School and the Chinese Hos-

pital. As a merchant-dominated organization, the Six Companies has also consistently acted as a unit to defend merchant interests in Chinatown (as in its support for the Garment Contractors' Association against the International Ladies Garment Workers Union campaign to unionize Chinatown garment workers in 1969). Otherwise, however, the Six Companies has been prey to debilitating factionalism within its own ranks. Two other structural features have added handicaps: First, the fact that its meetings are held in Chinese bars English-speaking American-born Chinese from potential involvement in the Six Companies. Among offspring of the family society, the preference of some American-born businessmen for the Chinese Chamber of Commerce, and later of certain professionals for the Chinese-American Citizens Alliance diluted some of the influence of the Chinese Six Companies. Also, a precedent of not opening meetings to the public has perpetuated ignorance about the Six Companies and isolated it from the community.

Nor has the Six Companies' history of recognition as Chinatown's spokesman to the outside necessarily enhanced its image in the eyes of present-day members of the community. Its origins in the period of most severe anti-Chinese discrimination molded its relation to politicial bodies outside in a pattern of defensiveness, nonaggressiveness, and accommodation from which it still cannot break free. Today, residents of Chinatown claim that the relationship of the Six Companies to city hall has been maintained more by its financial contributions than by any genuine attempt at political participation. "The way I see it, you have to be a citizen if you're going to vote, and up to 1945 nobody could become citizens," one social worker commented. "People never thought of using votes because in those days they just didn't have votes. I would say the lack of political involvement in Chinatown is due to the fact that its leaders have had to sidestep to get around politics by using money and so forth." In the face of harsh and growing criticism from younger American Chinese, today's leaders of the Six Companies—men whose youthful memories stretch back to more difficult days—still cling to the older patterns and continue to be both cynical and timid in dealing with the city government outside. Men from the Six Companies who have recently received a smattering of minority political appointments in San Francisco because they were known to city hall have drawn bitter complaints for their unde-manding stance and tendency to downplay the questions of continuing discrimination against American Chinese. In-variably, however, these men have argued in response that for the small weak American Chinese minority, accommoda-tion is the only possible political style. The psychology and world-view of men in the Six Companies vis-à-vis the soci-ety outside come through clearly in these words of one city hall appointee:

The younger generation, because of their total unawareness of their forefathers' past, view themselves as Americans and exercise their rights like Americans and speak like Ameri-cans. They weren't born in the days when there were gang-up fights against Chinese. Politically speaking, I think Chinese with the old background have always been a bit on the passive side. It's carried on from their forefathers' day that they're not the demanding type because they realize how tenuous their position is. They feel that whatever they want is through the offices of the white politicians. So there is still a tendency of not making their demands too brazen, too open, and too aggressive.

Among the senior members of the Six Companies, lack of confidence and a still vivid memory of the historic experi-ence of defeat have militated against emergence of the vigorous leadership needed by today's community.

An unexpected weakness of the Six Companies today is lack of funds. Despite the status of its members as relatively prosperous merchants in the community and their success in sporadic fundraising campaigns, all this must be seen within the context of the low economic level of Chinatown itself. In real terms the amounts of money in question are very small. We were surprised when a member of the Board of Directors informed us of the net total of the Six Com-panies' annual drives to support the Chinese High School and the Chinese Hospital: each of the community-wide drives annually brings in from ten to fifteen thousand dollars. The only other regular drive of the Six Companies is for Chinatown's contribution to UBAC, San Francisco's Community Chest. This drive nets a maximum of thirty thousand dollars. "People outside don't see the whole picture. They don't know our income is really this low," this director told us. In earlier days, when the number of men returning to China yearly was still high, the Six Companies levied substantial income from exit taxes. Today, with the practice of returning to China ended, this lucrative source of income has disappeared. The remaining source of income for the Six Companies now is its property. Here, however, although the amount of land held in the name of district or family associations is large, plots directly held by the Six Companies are few.

It is a combination of the factors above, against the background of the changing complexion of Chinatown society, that has led to the most serious weakening of the Six Companies power today: a profound erosion of its constituency. Increasing numbers of American-born Chinese under thirty reject its authority. As we have seen in a preceding chapter, only a small portion of immigrants find it necessary to affiliate themselves with a family association and thereby place themselves under the jurisdiction of the Six Companies. Not only have feelings of clan and district loyalty been considerably diluted in these urbanized immigrants, the fact that they lack the immigration fears which haunted earlier generations and have the right to United States citizenship through naturalization means that their degree of dependency on the Six Companies is minimal as compared with immigrants of the past. If anything, the overt identification of the Six Companies with business interests in Chinatown has made them the object of resentment by these immigrants, most of whom eventually take up working-class positions in the community. A bitter feud between the Six Companies, crusading for "law and order" in the community, and Chinatown's street gangs (mainly immigrant youth) in 1969 is evidence of this cleavage. Moreover, no matter how genuinely it may desire to gain the loyalty of the new population, the Six Companies finds itself crippled by its scanty funds. In the face of the massive housing and unemployment problems faced by incoming immigrants, the few thousand dollars of the Six Companies is less than a drop in the bucket. It is for this reason that the establishment of the relatively well-endowed federal anti-poverty program in Chinatown was seen as such a threat by the Six Companies. With the anti-poverty program, moreover, a new core of vigorous and aggressive leaders entered the community. Drawn from the ranks of both Cantonese-speaking immigrants and college-educated American-born Chinese, the social service workers launched a powerful attack on what they considered Chinatown's hopelessly backward and inefficient leadership. Political acumen, fluent English, and a new sense of confidence made it possible for this group to attract even public attention outside Chinatown to its attack, in the process of which the image of the Six Companies as "sole spokesman" of the community has suffered a blow from which it will probably never recover. "When we came into Chinatown, we criticized the Chinese Six Companies, the Chamber of Commerce, all the family and district associations for not being able to do anything for the Chinese community and for suppressing the problems of Chinatown," one liberal leader recalls. "They have been challenged and their effectiveness and credentials have been totally destroyed."

And yet the Six Companies survived with a strange resiliency. It weathered perhaps the most critical blow to its prestige when the federal anti-poverty program was set up in Chinatown in 1965, although the Six Companies had insisted bitterly that it was not needed. After two stormy years of challenge from anti-poverty workers, however, leaders of seven prominent family associations suddenly appeared on the program's board of directors and cleverly bullied control of the EOC program back into the sphere of Chinatown's most powerful fifty-five men. In 1972, the extent of influence of the Six Companies was again stunningly revealed. Having announced its opposition to the busing of school children as early as 1969, the Six Companies began a high-powered campaign against the measure the summer before busing was to begin. Daily editorials in the *Chinese Times* exaggerated the dangers of busing and

supported the views of white, right-wing anti-busing groups
in the city. In district and family associations fundraising
campaigns to support interim "freedom schools" were
begun. When the first day of the autumn 1972 school
semester began, only six children from the Chinatown
community boarded buses. The boycott was kept up with
over ninety percent effectiveness for the entire year. A
month after the beginning of the boycott, signs went up on
the buildings of the Six Companies and all the associations
on Grant Avenue supporting San Francisco's anti-busing
mayor, Joseph Alioto. After two years of keeping the
ornate, but fading, doors of its headquarters on Stockton
Street closed against the rallies of student radicals and the
threats of delinquent youth, in September 1972 the Six
Companies proudly opened them again to announce the
commencement of its Immigrant Development Program (an
employment training program for immigrants), flaunting the
plum of a substantial grant of funds from the United States
Department of Labor to finance the new endeavor.

GERALD WONG, 38
Owner of two pharmacies in Chinatown

In the summer of 1970 it was the policy of the Six Com-
panies, after several years of harsh attack from its enemies
in Chinatown, to refuse all interviews with reporters or
members of the public media. Gerald Wong, however, made
time for an interview late at night after finishing work at the
pharmacy. He explained that he had been the youngest
president ever to serve a term in the Chinese Six Compa-
nies. Alarmed by rising juvenile delinquency in Chinatown,
the elders had recruited him to take the position the previ-
ous spring. Looking back on his term he said he felt he had
made a positive contribution but that what he had been able
to achieve was limited by the datedness and inefficiency
of the Six Companies.

Let me first tell you that I'm no longer in the Six Companies,
I shouldn't be a spokesman. I know I'm one of the most
accessible ones, I try to be of help to anyone, as you notice,

I don't even know you. But the poor beggars on the streets of Hong Kong, they ask me to help them, so that's my nature. But as far as I'm concerned, certainly the Chinese community is going through a lot of changes. If the Chinese Six Companies wants to maintain its leadership, there's certain things, certain areas where they have to move fast and quick. Because they are still operating the same way they were in the early 1900s, but now times are changed so much. In 1900 it took three months to get a boat over from China, and now we go to Hong Kong in twenty hours. In order for any organization to stay abreast it's got to adapt. Any organization that does not have youth going into it is going to die. Otherwise, as I can see it, this organization will be dominated by a few selfish individuals. But no one will be stopping the tide, it's just like the waves of the Yangtze, you know, waves after waves, the ones that will be coming after. The old will not live forever and it will be up to the younger professionals and the businessmen working together to really lead the community into its rightful place. Otherwise it will fall down the drain.

I think it's inherent that the businessmen are well-represented in the leadership of the Six Companies. Because for the Chinese, well, a basic understanding is that if you're not pretty well off you don't go into doing something for somebody else, you don't start trying to get a name, you know. If you're a worker, you cannot spare the time. The boss won't let you go to participate in some of the meetings and functions. So it's usually the ones involved in business that do have some free time to get away. He's his own boss, so he can get in and participate. Most of the men in the Six Companies work their way up through the family associations and the district associations, which takes time. Very few are like myself. When I went in I went straight to the top.

In spring 1969 it was the term that the Ning Yung Association was supposed to send somebody up to be the president of the Six Companies. So they approached me, even though I hadn't any office in the family association. Well, I thought the whole thing over for a week, the pluses and the minuses. There were a lot of negatives, of course. First, it

costs you money. During the last year it cost me about
$10,000. You have to lead all these different fund drives.
You give your heart and your soul and your money.

But one of the overriding reasons was, since the Six Companies has been an organization for over one hundred years,
the Caucasians are more ready to accept it as the organization representing the Chinese in America. All these years
we have been neglected. I felt with my involvement I can
exert pressures outside to get things done for the Chinese
community. Then the second reason was that around that
time the confrontation with youth was building up to the
point where Chinatown was really becoming a jungle. Since
'66–'67 businesses were dropping at the rate of about fifteen
to twenty percent a year. The Chinese Chamber of Commerce called meeting after meeting, but no concerted effort
was made to unite the entire community. I felt the biggest
problem at that time was that there was no communication
between the establishment and the discontented groups. I
wanted to bridge the gap. Lastly, another possibility would
be an honor in the way of a challenge, what I can accomplish for the people.

Now the Six Companies, sometimes you can attack it,
sometimes you have to respect it. Of course it has this group
that's gone through the mill all the way from the family
association, becoming a senile, inactive group, and mostly
a non-English-speaking group that, once you get up there,
it's more or less of an honor for them. So a number of them
they just sit on their laurels, go to meetings once a month,
get introduced at some of the banquets, and they're happy,
without bothering to do any work for the community. But
there was a time when this organization was supposed to
be the highest part of the Chinese establishment, tending to
the safety and welfare of the Chinese in America. And the
difference between this organization and the younger
groups is that the older group, if they go around they always
raise a few dollars for the establishment.

But the problem, like with the EOC, is that these guys
start something and then they don't follow through to over-
see the whole thing. You know the structure of the Six

Companies, the Board of Directors will raise hell if the president does something they don't like, and he only has a two-month term anyway. So unless he's really a daring type, he doesn't move, he can't really carry anything through. So, see, these guys didn't follow through with the EOC so then what happens? The other side begins to infiltrate it and really run the thing the way they want.

During my term, particularly in the youth area, I wanted to deal with the problem of security. Now, supposedly it falls within the domain of the Chinese Chamber of Commerce to protect their business membership so they will enjoy a prosperous Chinatown. But they'd been talking for months without any concrete solution. So again, acting on the basis of protecting the welfare of the Chinese in America, I felt the Six Companies should call a mass meeting, with representatives of about one hundred groups in Chinatown, to discuss the problem of Chinatown security. We really tried to attack the root of the problem, whether it would be better to hire your own guards or to attack the youth problem by really trying to work with youth, communicate with them, and get them back on the right road. We decided to build a youth center. And that was when there was the formation of the "Committee on Chinatown Security," composed of the Chinese Six Companies, the Chamber of Commerce, the tongs, the CACA, and the *Fah* Yuen and *Tung Wah* associations. We tried to raise funds and also got Mayor Alioto to help us. So that was how the Youth Center on Clay Street was built.

So in most cases I feel I was really able to pick up the ball and run with it. I was moving on the garment industry thing, the Cultural Foundation, law and order, jobs and education. A lot of times I surprised them. Like when this cardinal came over from Taiwan, Cardinal Yu Pin, we had the biggest banquet any president ever got together in this community. We had a Double Ten parade, one of the biggest they had ever witnessed, and on October 1 we had this commemoration on Portsmouth Square for our millions of compatriots massacred by Communist China. You know, we burned the effigy of Mao and all that.

W. K. WONG, 62

Businessman, public relations executive, former president of the Chinese Chamber of Commerce, and founder of the Chinese New Year Festival in San Francisco. He says, "All my life I've been a salesman." For many years he was a business advisor to the Chinese Six Companies.

This is how it happened . . . Yes, it was my idea to initiate a public celebration of the Chinese New Year in San Francisco back in 1953. I generated the idea of a public celebration, and the project was a united effort of hundreds of businessmen and citizens who pitched in to make the pioneering fete, today of international fame, a success. Then, as today, this festival resulted from the pooling of the community's manpower, talent and resources, and the cooperation of the public.

One of the reasons that caused me to think about it was, well, you see, Chinese love to gamble at festival time. So I always saw the newspaper headlines "Chinatown Gambling Raid" or "Chinatown Gambling Arrest" in the pre-Chinese New Year Festival days. I always grumbled, "What's the matter with them? There are so many good things about Chinese and our Chinatown. Why do they play up this gambling?" That bothered me. I said, "Why don't they write about the better things? Chinese have an ancient culture with many outstanding contributions to civilization. We have rich traditions, colorful legends, and authentic pageantry. Our art, music, dance, fashions, etc., etc., should be showcased for the public and shared with our American friends." That's one of the reasons, the other is that New Year to us Chinese is the holiday of holidays, a sort of Christmas, Thanksgiving, and Fourth of July rolled into one. It is our most joyous period of the year, a time of conviviality and pleasantries, a period of good omen, of family reunion, renewal of friendship, visiting, feasting, and expression of good will to others. I thought this would be the appropriate time to invite our American friends to share in this happiness and to appreciate and learn things about Chinese. Many celebrants who come to Chinatown for this grand New Year never knew that Chinese New Year was celebrated privately prior to 1953. The introduction of the Chinese New Year Festival in 1953 eliminated that "mystery Chinese" feeling of people outside of the Chinese community.

Did it affect tourist business in Chinatown? Oh, there's no doubt about that! In the shops, in the restaurants, everybody was chum-chum-chum-chum!!! Whenever and wherever people read about the Chinese New Year Festival they always think of San Francisco Chinatown.

Now in 1956, the chamber added the Miss Chinatown contest to the New Year celebration. I requested the committee to permit me to do a story on it, and I worked up that story, released it, and we were on the wire, coast to coast, all over the world. I recalled a story I had heard about *Sam Chung Sze Duck*, the three paramount virtues of Chinese womanhood. I only knew vaguely what it was about when I started. But I talked to a lot of old men, scholars, I looked through some Chinese books. Then I finally wrote it and polished the item down to one paragraph about what the Chinese woman should respect: first your father, then your brother, then your husband. A truly beautiful concept. So I sent to the news media, "Chinatown Elders on Quest for Queen with Ancient Virtues of Chinese Womanhood." Now that made newspapers all over the nation.

Now a lot of younger community leaders today complain about all this discrimination against Chinatown. Well, you wouldn't call me a youngster, I'm over fifty and it all depends on your outlook. You have to take it and don't be so darn serious. I think some kind of discrimination is worldwide. It's natural, you'd find it in China too. I know today and fifteen years ago are two different worlds, two different worlds entirely. The young people are in a different stage of life, they have different problems and reactions. But for my part, I was one of thirteen kids and my parents worked real hard to see that we got fed, period. We lived in two rooms above Grant Avenue. My father died in 1937. But one does not eat butter unless one has had butter before. So if I never had butter it didn't mean a darn thing to me. Whether they allowed us in the Palace Hotel or not in the

old days, it didn't matter because I never even tried to enter
the place. Forget it, who wanted to go there? I didn't have
the time. I had to study. I had work, so therefore I overlooked it. I accepted a lot of this as natural and I think the
activist type of today is too darn serious. Everyone practices
discrimination. I have friends of all races, but I still prefer
to choose my friends, not just anyone. So that's a form of
discrimination. I am one of the persons who has always
worked in Chinatown and never gone outside to work. So
I can't really answer your question. But if you're talking of
today, none of us, meaning the so-called older generation,
feel any obstacle to entering American society, although
down deep, there is that feeling. In 1936, I remember five of
us drove up to Portland, Oregon, for a series of tennis
matches. At nine out of ten restaurants en route, not one of
them was busy, we were refused service. We were clean,
well dressed, good-mannered, not smelly, dirty, or obnox-
ious . . . but we were Oriental. On the return trip, we didn't
lick the social problem but we satisfied our food and drink
requirement by bringing our own. As far as I can see,
today's young people have never really been touched. The
last fourteen, fifteen years is too recent, you have to go
beyond that period. Some of the oldsters really had it tough.

Did you read my story in the *Examiner* Sunday section
on "My Belief for 1970"? Probably the most profound article I have ever written. I am not a profound writer, but all
these ideas are engrained in me. Some people could write
the same article in ten minutes, but not me. I really had to
work at it. Why did I do the story? Because I feel there are
still many misconceptions of Chinatown. So I wrote basically what I think. This is exactly what I would like to see
happen. I would like to see our wonderful traditions maintained, upkept, and used. People say, "What is your hope?"
Yes, this is my wish and hope, because it is my belief and
I am prideful of our community. You see in this paragraph
where I mentioned about the Golden Dragon? This, in one
paragraph, is exactly what Chinatown does for the New
Year. But actually it was written with a bit of needling of
the city officials in mind. I'm talking about what the government, the city fathers, *could* do if they wanted to. Because

I feel in this particular case, we have been prejudiced against. The Columbus Day parade goes right down Columbus Avenue in Italian town. That's no different from the New Year's parade going down our Grant Avenue. But they give you lot of reasons why it shouldn't and I don't think they really made an effort to do it. They say the street is narrow and congested and they're afraid of fire and all that. Yes, it is narrow and congested, but what about New Orleans? That Mardi Gras? They got more people, their streets are just as narrow, yet they have it. Why? Because they made an effort, an honest effort. So this particular paragraph said exactly what we're working for. This is what we want. But I didn't come out and say we're prejudiced against. The facts are there, I just do it politely because this is the only way *I* do it. I know lots of people would read this and say activist action might be better. In the last five years, there are people who make a fuss. But this is not a good nor truthful image of us. If you're politically strong, like the blacks or the Mexicans, you can go up and demand this and that. Chinatown has never really demanded anything because, up to now, there just aren't enough of us with political muscles . . . to be able to demand, one must have something to back one's demand.

I was selected as one of the three cochairmen of the Mayor's San Francisco Chinatown Factfinding Committee. I was criticized for what I stand for. People said, "Who's this man, he writes nothing but good things about Chinatown?" It appears sinful to be pleasant, friendly, and optimistic yet I do not seek to hide my head in the sand. But my outlook is optimistic and I say so.

During the early days of the factfinding work, a young leader of the Leways gang came into my office, at that time, still down on Grant Avenue. He came in and said, "Are you W. K. Wong?" By the tone of his voice and the look on his face, I knew there was trouble. So I let everything go and said, "Yes, why don't you sit down and have a little chat. What's on your mind?" He said, "I understand you're working on the factfinding committee, right? And you're gonna slam us, you're gonna attack us?"

I was amazed. I said, "Gosh, I'm surprised. What makes

you think we're going to do that? We're just getting the facts down on paper to be evaluated and hopefully for the benefit of Chinatown and our city." We spent about an hour together talking. It turned out they had a very unhappy experience with the establishment who rejected their demands and said, "Why should this group of youth come and bother us and make demands on us?" Thinking back, I would say the establishment people could have said, "Why don't you young people send us your suggestion for us to consider?" Anyway, in the conversation we had, I said, "I think you're sick and tired of the older generation telling you they worked hard for their money and you should work just as hard too. But let me tell you this. I have worked hard all my life. I have." And I showed him my hands. He looked surprised. I said, "You see my hands? That means I worked not only with my mind, but also with my hands. I do just as much as my employees." My point is this, because we worked hard we don't want you young people to work like we did. I respect youth and I feel that youth should respect the elders—it's a mutual feeling. "Because," I said, and I looked straight into his eyes, "Where the hell would you be if it weren't for your father? And where do you think your father would be if your grandfather didn't come over here??? That man who came one hundred years ago had a lot of *courage* and *guts!!!*" That's what I said to him, they understand words like that. So he thought it over and said, "Gee, I didn't know you felt like that." I said, "The reason you don't know is because we never communicate. Honestly," I said, "I think we all have faults. I think the older generation should come up and do a little more communicating. But we are so busy with our own little world that we don't do it. This is our fault, it's true. You have to run a business, you work like mad and you barely have time to sleep—that's wrong too."

Of course, there are some problems in Chinatown but I wish to make the following observation. I traveled with some Caucasian friends to the Orient. Americans are inclined to interject their thoughts, feelings, and standards on everybody else in their travels. As Americans with two car garage, twin baths in the house, and steaks every evening,

they want everyone, whatever country they're in, to have
the same standard and level of living. That's just one standard, we operate by a different standard. I'll give you a good
example. When I traveled with my friends to Hong Kong, I
saw this fellow mending pots and pans on the sidewalk. It
was six o'clock, and a little girl, a little boy, and mother
came to the spot. They unpacked a dinner carrier, laid a
sheet of brown paper on the sidewalk, placed chopsticks,
spoon, and dishes of food on the paper and promptly sat
down to eat. I took a look and said, "Oh, boy, good food!"
The family was chatting away and eating with gusto. I took
a closer look at the food, it's clean, it's cooked, and it smells
good. And it is rice, good white rice. Now, the Americans
would want them to have a white tablecloth, linen, silver-
ware, heaping platters of steaks, but this is their way of life.
It's the only way they know and there's nothing wrong with
the way they enjoy it. I looked at their faces, they're happy!
They're together, they're a family and they're having something wholesome to eat. Well, I think Chinatown is like this,
too. I think one member of the factfinding committee made
this remark, when the census came out with those figures,
forty percent of Chinatown below the poverty level or
something like that. "They mistake frugality with poverty,"
you see.

PART **4**

THE EMERGENCE OF
A NEW WORKING CLASS

10. The Rebirth

In the quiet decade of the fifties, that particular confluence of historic factors which had kept Chinatown in existence for a century seemed to dissolve. GIs who returned from the Pacific theater as American citizens found the restrictive covenant on real estate lifted in 1947, making possible for the first time the purchase of land by Chinese anywhere in the city or state. With the post-war boom in the economy, job opportunities multiplied, and college educated sons and daughters of Chinatown's small business families were absorbed in growing numbers into the expanding white collar and professional sector of American society. As these young civil service workers, accountants, engineers, doctors, and businessmen sought modest homes in the suburbs of San Francisco and cities up and down the peninsula, the dense population of Chinatown's core area began to decline. Older people remained: the owners of small groceries and laundry shops, the aging bachelors, a younger group of men who had entered Chinatown as "paper sons" during the forties, spoke no English, and depended for their living on employment in the restaurants, markets, and small factories which served the community. Businesses which catered to the specific needs of the Chinatown community, or to the tourist trade, continued to operate quietly, but there was a sense that Chinatown had outlived its usefulness and, like so many other ethnic communities at that time, was on the wane. Even the physical disintegration of the community was foreseen in the not too distant future. "It is difficult to make recommendations concerning the future of Chinatown," a San Francisco Community Renewal Program report stated in 1965, when extensive redevelopment plans were being carried out in San Francisco. "There is some evidence that this ethnic enclave is breaking up. Many younger Chinese are choosing to live away from Chinatown." All suggestions to construct new housing in Chinatown were rejected. For a decade, life went on within the static structure of the community, physically circumscribed by the same boundaries it had known for a hundred years.

In the mid-sixties, however, on the very eve of its decline, two events set in motion a process which has revitalized Chinatown in answer to a new need. On May 23, 1962, the signing of a Presidential Directive for refugees from mainland China by President John F. Kennedy broke through quota restrictions which since 1943 had held the number of Chinese immigrants to 105 per year. Three years later Lyndon Baines Johnson abolished permanently all laws limiting immigration on the basis of race or nationality, raising to 20,000 per year the quota for each Asian country, the same number set for Europe. For the first time in the history of the United States free immigration leading to the acquisition of citizenship through naturalization was possible for large numbers of Asian people. The two historic acts signaled the start of a new Chinese immigration to California on a scale matched only by the nineteenth century flow preceding exclusion, which has reinvigorated Chinatown as a place of residence, a business center, and a community. A sharp difference in the nature of this immigration from that of the nineteenth century, however, coupled with the changed character of American society into which it has been absorbed, has placed the reborn Chinatown in a new confluence of factors from that which gave birth to the old. While the infusion of two to four thousand new residents per year has swelled the boundaries of Chinatown and reaffirmed its existence as a physical unit, the predominance among these new residents of low income working-class families is rapidly changing the nature of Chinatown society itself and posing a severe challenge to the institutional continuity of the community. The future of Chinatown's century-old organizations, spawned by the bachelor society, adapted to the family society, and now confronting the needs and life style of this emerging working class, hangs in the balance.

Marked differences between the Chinese immigration of

the 1960s and that of 1850–1880 have transformed the position and meaning of Chinatown both in American society and in the lives of American Chinese. Most importantly, the liberalized immigration policy has meant that Chinese immigrants of the 1960s enter the United States as families, not, like the early laborers, as single men. They therefore lack the bond to China which weighed on the shoulders of men who had left their wives and children there, and confront American society as the permanent context for their lives. In addition, almost all immigrants who have entered under the 1965 Act have spent a considerable portion of their lives in Hong Kong. Fleeing the villages during the Sino-Japanese war or the period of revolutionary land reform, they have had to spend years or even decades in Hong Kong awaiting approval of their immigration. Exposure to the cosmopolitan culture of Hong Kong and the experience of working in factories, department stores, and large offices have provided a basic sense of familiarity with the workings of a big city as well as preparation for assuming some role in an urban economy. Finally, as recent Chinese immigrants have begun the process of assimilation, their transition has been further aided by the existence of nationwide movements for minority rights spawned by the black civil rights movement of the early sixties. Active struggles waged by younger, American-born Chinese have already achieved some degree of success in opening areas of employment previously closed to Chinese, thus reducing dependency on the Chinatown economy and the narrow range of occupations defined in the nineteenth century. All these factors guarantee that never again will a community of Chinese in America exist with the degree of isolation that characterized Chinatown in the past.

The high proportion of Chinese immigrants now entering the United States in a professional or technical status has been another striking distinction of the present immigration from the peasant-laborer immigration of the nineteenth century. In 1970, 3,715 Chinese professionals and technicians entered California, as compared with 2,098 service workers. In the American experience of these professional and technical immigrants, Chinatown has proved to be superfluous.

Although those who have received their training and advanced degrees at Chinese institutions generally experience a brief period of downward mobility in their first few years in America, they are usually able to find jobs commensurate with their training. Other members of this group, immigrants from upper-class or professional families on the Chinese mainland who had received training and advanced degrees at American universities, have found the movement to professional positions even more smooth. In California, they have found satisfying positions in universities, laboratories, hospitals, or architectural and engineering firms and have settled in suburban homes and good residential districts. It is generally Chinese from these two groups who are the highly respected scientists, architects, scholars, or financiers well-known to American society today. While they may come to Chinatown from time to time to visit restaurants and buy food, nothing in their situation demands establishing direct ties with the community and they do not identify with it. Of Chinese professionals now living in San Francisco only a small minority of graduate students, recruited as bilingual community workers by the anti-poverty agency, have become involved with Chinatown on a day to day basis. Indeed, as the number of Chinese who work and move freely in all areas of American society increases, Chinatown is slowly losing its significance as the center of American Chinese life.

Yet if Chinatown is no longer an inevitable necessity for all Chinese immigrants, its continuing existence is symbolic of the needs and difficulties of many of them. Despite the obvious improvement in the general situation of American Chinese over the nineteenth century, examination of the immigration of the sixties reveals that the ease of entrance into American society is still strongly affected by the social background of the immigrant. The relatively painless assimilation of recent, upper-class Chinese immigrants, thus, has not been duplicated by an equally large portion (nearly half) of Chinese who enter the United States in the status of service workers, machine operatives, craftsmen, and household workers. And what is the social background of these Chinese? By and large, they are the family members of older

Chinatown laborers, separated for years and even decades by harsh immigration laws. With the liberalization of the immigration laws, they emigrated from Hong Kong, partly to reunite their families and partly in the hope of attaining a measure of economic improvement from increased occupational and educational opportunity in America. A long chain of circumstances, however, has determined that the realization of the dreams of this group will be slower and less certain than those of their professionally trained counterparts. As sons and daughters, or perhaps grandchildren, of Chinese overseas, most immigrants in this group grew up in families which were barely above poor peasant level in Kwangtung. Most began work when they were teenagers, as did their fathers, and never received more than a high school education. During the Japanese occupation, World War II, or the Chinese civil war, they fled to Hong Kong with little or no savings, and found employment in sweater, jewelry, or plastics factories, and occasionally as white collar workers. In some cases, money sent in remittances from America allowed the family (because of a favorable exchange rate) a living standard which was somewhat higher than average in Hong Kong. But when the move to America at last came, all family possessions were sold and the savings of both father and children exhausted to cover transportation expenses. As they entered San Francisco—with no financial resources, with experience in manual labor but no professional skills, and with no ability to speak English—the welcome extended to this group of immigrants bore little resemblance to that experienced by the other half. The tight job market brought on by the economic recession of the late 1960s and residual discriminatory practices among many small trade, construction, and craft unions critically affected the nonprofessionally trained. Sensing insuperable language difficulties, many eventually rely on fathers or relatives (whose knowledge of English is often only slightly better) to find them jobs. Inevitably they are then thrown back, for both employment and living side by side with the last of the bachelors in aging or months of their arrival to America, they find themselves living side by side with the last of the bachelors in aging tenement houses in the old core area, and working next to

the "paper sons" who came before the Second World
War in the restaurants, markets, and small factories of
Chinatown.

For such immigrants who find themselves forced back to
Chinatown, the realization that they have entered a status
in American society even lower than the one they had in
Hong Kong comes as a blow. Perceiving English as the only
way out of the vicious cycle of low-paying Chinatown jobs
in which they have been trapped, they may enroll in night
adult education courses or try to enter recently established,
federally funded, English programs for Chinese. But the fact
that they are already mature adults, lack academic training,
must spend as much as sixty hours a week at their jobs, and
study in small apartments where it is difficult to concen-
trate makes thorough mastery of English an unrealistic
hope for most of them. All but a few eventually abandon
the effort, and at that point the patterns and conditions of
life which still prevail in Chinatown today—long hours of
work, low pay, substandard living conditions and little
expectation of change—slowly begin to make their lives
bear greater and greater similarity to those of their fathers.
Social workers who have watched the progress of the earlier
immigrant families say that within a few years severe problems have arisen. Often they appear first in the adolescent
children, who find themselves having little contact with
their hard-working parents, encountering tremendous difficulties of adjustment in school, eventually dropping out and
taking to the Chinatown streets. Within four or five years,
when all the efforts of the parents to find better jobs and
housing have failed, cases of divorce and even suicide may
bring about the eventual disintegration of the family.

The continuous absorption of these new immigrants into
skilled and unskilled manual positions (whether in Chinatown or outside) has transformed the nature of Chinatown's
working class which previously had been made up almost
exclusively of single men. Since the late 1960s this new
working class made up of the families of recent immigrants
plus those of middle-aged "paper sons," enabled by the new
laws to bring in their wives, constitutes the majority of the
population of Chinatown. In accordance with its life style

and needs, it has changed the community to such a degree that those who knew it in the "quiet fifties" say they no longer recognize Chinatown today. Not only have the resurging density of population, the outcropping of scores of tiny stores piping Hong Kong popular music into the street, and a constant flux of faces in and out of Chinatown remolded the physical face of the community, the contours of its social structure itself are being subjected to intense pressure.

On a most fundamental level, the disruption of China-town's social fabric grows out of the qualitative difference in the life style of its new working class from that of the former small business family. In contrast to the close integration of business and family life which prevailed in Chinatown's small stores, alienation of work from family life characterizes its new working class. The severe limitation in employment opportunities for non-English-speaking immigrants, forcing both parents to take low-paying, long-hour jobs which require their absence from the home for the greater part of the day, has led to a tragic disintegration, among Chinatown's new working class, of the close and stable family life which had often in the past been seen as the basis of Chinatown's relative stability as a low-income ghetto. An explosion of juvenile delinquency which has rocked Chinatown since the sixties is the most conspicuous symptom of this. Covered sensationally by the San Francisco press, it has caught the attention of the public at large, giving rise to a sense of confusion and apprehension about the future of what had for so long been regarded as a "model ethnic community."

Simultaneous to dramatic changes in Chinatown family life has been a flaring up of age old problems in the ghetto, now exacerbated under the pressure of unprecedented numbers of incoming residents. Basic demands for employment, housing, health, and education, which had formerly been met, in however makeshift a fashion, through Chinatown's institutions and tradition of collective responsibility, are now straining the community's resources to the breaking point. Unemployment, always high in American minority communities, was estimated at thirteen percent for Chinatown in 1971, without taking into account the underemployment or parttime employment of hundreds of its population. Housing in the core area of Chinatown was in the most acute state of crisis of any ethnic ghetto in San Francisco. With the second highest population density rate in the nation, seventy-seven percent of the housing in this area is substandard by city codes. Communal kitchens and communal bathrooms are still a way of life in the old tenement houses, where immigrant families often find themselves forced to crowd three or four people into barren 9' by 12' rooms built fifty years ago for single laborers. In the area of health care, as well, a crisis situation had developed by the late sixties. The old Chinese Hospital, built singlehandedly by the Chinese community during its period of severe isolation, offered sixty beds to a population which had swelled to over forty thousand. In 1969, despite the fact that Chinatown had the highest suicide rate in the nation, there were only two Chinese-speaking psychiatrists in the city of San Francisco and an estimated twenty hours of direct psychiatric service available per week to the entire non-English-speaking, low-income population of the community. For the first time in their history, the institutions of Chinatown face a crisis the dimensions of which they lack even the physical resources to solve.

A final impact of the immigration which cannot be overlooked lies in a spiritual dimension. Despite the disruptions they have caused and the new sense of crisis in Chinatown life, the immigrants have infused a new energy and hope to a community long overshadowed by its history of defeat. In the majority of immigrant working families, this hope is expressed by a tenacious commitment to struggle on in the face of all the obstacles they are currently encountering. No matter how difficult their situation here, most say it represents an improvement over their hardships in China and later in Hong Kong. Since they have not yet encountered such a devastating force of discrimination in America as that which bore down on their fathers and the older men in Chinatown, they refuse to despair completely of someday overcoming their present difficulties. In their children who, at the very least, will receive in America the benefits of an education which they themselves could never obtain, they find hope and consolation. The small group of immigrant professionals who have committed themselves to the Chinatown community have also contributed a new force for change. The addition of their strength to younger groups of American Chinese who are emerging as leaders of Chinatown will be a strong determinant of the new character of the community. Like the working-class immigrants, they have not had to grapple with a culture of defeat and their response to the American context has been bold and aggressive. Their education in the cosmopolitan society of Hong Kong has endowed them with valuable professional competence, fluency in English and Cantonese, and a sense of ease and familiarity in both Chinese and Western cultures. As children of refugees from mainland China, they witnessed the revolutionary transformation and emergence of modern China from universities in Hong Kong or America, and caught from it a sense of confidence, élan, and social vision. They have brought both a new self-confidence and a new perspective to the American Chinese situation as they have joined in the vigorous struggle of younger American-born Chinese for full equality and participation in American society.

SUM CHEUNG, 40
Night janitor in the financial district

His wife was not expecting us. It's just past dinnertime and one man in pants and an undershirt stands in the communal kitchen of the tenement house on Stockton Street watching us knock on the door.

She stands in her slippers on the only space of open floor in the room. We figure the room cannot be more than ten feet across, ten or maybe only eight feet deep. Yet Mrs. Cheung and four kids are in it when we come in. Beside her, a handmade bed fills almost half the room—we wonder how many people sleep in it at one time. From the other wall, a square card table juts into the center of the room toward the bed, the three older kids are doing homework at it. Yim, who's twelve, sets aside her books to talk to us. Jimmy, wearing a plastic construction worker's hat, flips through the pages of his book while he follows the conversation. The whole time we are in the room, Kwok does not look up. Methodically, his eyes move back and forth from an open, blue and white textbook to his notebook on the table. He's writing longhand, answering questions about the text. A medal of the Immaculate Mother hangs down from his neck on a chain, sways over the notebooks.

We had spoken to her husband four months ago at the Chinese Newcomers' Center. At the time, he had been unemployed, and worried about finding a job during the recession. He had been working as a janitor most of the four years he had been here, he told us, but this spring the building he worked in was torn down and he was laid off. He had been looking for a job for two months already with no luck. He was worried, he said, because his unemployment insurance was only fifty-three dollars a week. He was the only breadwinner in a family of eight, and with fifty-three dollars a week he had barely enough to pay the rent. He told us his family lived in two small rooms in a tenement on Stockton, each cost fifty-five dollars a month. They had been on the waiting list for the public housing project at Ping Yuen for four years, but there were never any vacancies. Yes, he knew they might be able to find a larger, cheaper place outside of Chinatown, but they couldn't live too far away because of the language barrier. For instance, if something happened, if there was a fire or some emergency, he wouldn't even know how to call the neighbors for help. Besides, he liked to live near Chinatown because his father lived there. He and the kids usually walked down to see him every weekend.

We tell Mrs. Cheung we came to see how the family had been over the summer. Yim says, "My father is working again." He's got a job as a night janitor. "Oh, good. Then do you think you may be moving soon?" Mrs. Cheung says they have asked at Ping Yuen five times but they are always told nothing is open. They can't move anyplace else. "So you're kind of settled here for a while." Yim and her mother nod. Yim says they are very busy now. School opened and

*Jimmy's teacher isn't very good, he has to do a lot of study-
ing at home. In fact, even this summer, all of them spent
most of their time at home, studying. We notice a shelf of
books that has been built over the head of the bed. Those
are her father's books, Yim says; the kids keep their books
in the bookbags underneath the table.*

*We ask Mrs. Cheung about the hours of her husband's
new job. She says he leaves the house around five at night
and gets home after two. So he sleeps while the children are
in school? "Not exactly." She says he doesn't sleep much,
actually, he likes to walk around. We try to settle on a convenient time to come and see him. On Friday, is eleven in
the morning good? "Well, sometimes he gets up late." "One
o'clock?" She doesn't know. "Three?" He always walks out
to get the newspaper at three. She asks us if we can wait till
Saturday. Yes, Saturday at one. We leave a note behind and
say good-by.*

I didn't leave Kwangtung until 1950. I was running a small
salted fish factory, we made and sold salted fish, but when
the Communists came into Kwangtung they took over all the
salted fish companies. I had to figure out another way to
make a living so I left China. In Hong Kong, the company I
worked for was pretty big. It had six buildings, each one
was four stories high. It was a wholesale agency for fabrics:
nylon and other kinds of cloth. Actually, in Hong Kong I had
an easier life than here because my job wasn't too hard. I
just had to answer phone calls and write down orders from
customers.

But I didn't like Hong Kong. It was too difficult for the
children to go to school. There were so many children trying to get into good schools and even when my salary was
fairly good, I couldn't afford to pay the tuition. Now when I
was young, my mother wouldn't let me go to school. I had
to work because I was the oldest son. So one thing I resolved was to let my children have an education. That's why
I decided to come here, for my children. I realized that if I
came here I would have to work hard, but I don't care too
much, because I came here for the sake of my children and
their future.

Actually, it was my father who suggested that I come over here. My father has been here for over forty years. He applied for my immigration in 1960 and we got the papers in 1967. I don't know why it took so long, but maybe he had to wait to become a citizen here before he could get the papers. Anyway, he asked me in 1960 if I wanted to come. I told him my income and my life in Hong Kong were pretty good, I would come only for my children's sake. He told me to come. He said the life here was more stable. There was a better chance for the children to go to school. He said, "One thing about coming to America, if you're not lazy and you're willing to work hard, you don't have to worry about hunger. It's not like the mainland where people were faced with starvation, famines, and so forth." So I decided to come. I wanted my children to go to better schools. And as a son, I came so that my family could look after my father. Before I came, you know, I had never seen him. If I didn't come, we would never have the chance to see each other. Of course, when I arrived, I didn't know a word of English. Not even ABC.

When I was in Hong Kong, my father didn't have to send much money to us. In the mainland, he remitted about three or four times a year. Not too much. Maybe one hundred dollars each time. Sometimes, when business was bad at the salted fish factory, he sent more. No, he never told us he was having a hard time here. Sometimes just a little. But I think he thought if he told us life was hard, we would feel we would have to come and help him. He didn't want us to worry at all. So he just gave some advice to us and sent us money. Nothing else. No, he didn't talk about discrimination in America. When I got here I found out he had different kinds of jobs in the past, such as a dishwasher, a bartender, and so forth. He was just an unskilled laborer, you know, because people in the past didn't know much English. When I got here he told me that because of the language barrier he couldn't go too far to work. He said he never went out of Chinatown.

I think my father had a more difficult time than I. Now, there are a few organizations to help us, with people who speak our own language. Whenever we have problems, we can go to them and ask for help. There wasn't any such thing in my father's time. His language barrier must have been more serious than the one we have now. So now, even though life is hard for me, I hope when my children grow up and learn some English they can find better jobs.

I don't know how others might feel, but I think housing is the number one problem for me. We can't live too far away from here, but there's no room for us in the housing project, even though we've been waiting four years. You know, even in Hong Kong our situation wasn't so bad because we had a whole apartment, with a kitchen and a bathroom in it. Here, there are quite a few families in a building that has only four kitchens and four bathrooms. We have to cook turn by turn. There are as many as fifty families sharing the facilities.

Get on each other's nerves? Not the adults. But the children sometimes do. In such a crowded place, they have to use the same table for dinner and then they all have to do their homework there, too. So they fight sometimes. There's so little space. To tell you the truth, I don't like to get home from work early. I feel sick when I get back.

But otherwise I don't have any problems getting along with my children. I love my children very much. I see a lot of the other young immigrants getting into trouble in Chinatown. They say there's a generation gap or something like that between the old and the young. But not for my children. I think they know, if I don't love them I wouldn't have come here for their sake. I could work in Hong Kong, just sitting there answering phone calls. Also, all my children except my daughter are too young to join those youth gangs. I try to tell her to stay away from them. She uses her spare time to study piano. The boys, who are between eleven and twelve, go down to the Salvation Army building to play. I don't let them go anyplace without my permission. Sometimes they play in the park at Portsmouth Square or they go visit their grandfather. Of course, I always encourage them to study. I tell them if you're not studying, try to read something. I help them make a schedule for the time when they study and the time when they play. After they go to public school during the day, they go to Chinese language school. I don't think they have time to mix with the bad youth.

I myself am not involved in any Chinatown associations or activities. Because I have to work at night and usually when I get up in the morning, it's nine or ten o'clock, and it's late already. I try to study a little bit in the afternoon. I take a walk sometimes, but the thing I prefer to do is read. I have quite a few books at the front and rear of my bed. Since I don't know much English, I try to buy books of English novels or stories with Chinese translations on the opposite page. The kind they make in Hong Kong. If I don't understand something, I ask my children about it. But I don't have time for any other activities.

No, I don't worry much. I don't demand too much from my children. As long as I can bring them up so they can make a living, I have done my duty. They're free to do whatever they like for a job when they grow up. And the situation of the world, well, that's not my worry because I'm just an ordinary man, I can't do much about the world situation anyway. At my age, I have been through the Japanese aggression in China, the Second World War, and then the Communists. I've suffered from starvation and cold and all those hardships, I don't think anything could be harder than that. If I worry, it's only about practical things. Maybe I worry about losing my job.

MRS. WONG, 35
Housewife

She, her husband, and ten children recently moved into one of the older Ping Yuen buildings on Pacific Street. She has just finished sewing curtains for the windows of the apartment out of odd pieces of unmatched fabric. She's slight, a little bit full around the waist, and wears her hair in a ponytail. She's girlishly shy, but friendly. While she talks, the kids make a terrific racket in the house. They fight with each other, run in and out of the bedrooms slamming the doors, and into the bathrooms. They're fireballs, with an encyclopedic vocabulary of four-letter English words.

Her father brought her out of Hong Kong in 1960. Like
Sum Cheung's father, he had been in California forty years,
as a restaurant worker. He returned to his village only twice.
When Mrs. Wong, her mother, sisters, and husband first
came to the United States, they worked as onion pickers in
Fresno. Later, in San Francisco, her husband worked as a
dishwasher in a Chinatown restaurant for eighty dollars a
week. When Mrs. Wong became ill and social workers at
Self-Help discovered the family could barely afford to keep
eating, they assisted her husband in finding another job and
enrolling in an English training program. He now makes
about six hundred dollars a month.

We always talked about coming to America, thinking that
to come to America, to the Gold Hill, was great. Who would
know, when we arrived, it would be like this? The main
problem was not to be able to speak. There were no Chinese
in Fresno, everyone was Mexican. So how could we speak
to them? Also the climate. In the winter, the children were
cold. It snowed there and they didn't have enough clothes
to wear. But here life is better. Look at the situation, it
stands to reason. Here, you have to work for your food, too,
but life is better here, better food, and the main point is
better climate. Enjoyment of life is more. Don't you agree?
How can the city be like the farm?

Oh, I am satisfied now. The main thing is the apartment.
Without the low-income housing, no matter how much
money you make, you can't save. If you have a place to live,
then the main thing is food. If you have a lot of money, you
eat more. If not, you eat less. Chinese are used to being
frugal, they can get by on anything. Not like the Americans,
so choosey. Of course, when we depend only on my husband, it is tight. We get by with what we can, but now the
kids go to junior high school we have to pay carfares and
things, I have to spend less.

To tell you the truth, prices are rising. In the morning, I
give the kids bread, two pieces per person, and a glass of
milk. That's two loaves of bread and two quarts of milk. A
pound of beef now is over a dollar. If I buy one pound of
beef, it lasts exactly one meal. Maybe with a smaller family,

you have leftovers. But with us, it just barely goes around. Vegetables, salted fish, and rice, that's what we usually eat. And even the cheap rice we buy now has gone up. Seven dollars if they deliver, $6.75 if you pick it up yourself. At fifty pounds a bag, we use up three bags a month. Oil is over two dollars a can, we use up one can a week. So you can see how fast the few hundred dollars go. A lot of people give clothes to us, so at least I can let the children wear old clothes till they get older.

Savings? We have nothing. About three hundred dollars for the children's education. Really, we have no money to save. When I do have twenty or thirty dollars left, I give it to my oldest boy. He goes to junior high and he puts it away, he won't spend it.

I don't have many friends. When we get together, we talk about the kids. When we shop, we talk about trivia. If you want me to talk about serious things, I don't know how. Everyone else works, and I don't. The other women usually sew, maybe they go to the movies or the Chinese opera, but I stay home all day. I don't go to movies or anywhere. Who would take care of the kids? I have to cook two meals, wash the clothes, then the day is gone. (She sighs.) To tell the truth, the children are so small, it will be a long time before it's my turn to go out. When will it ever be my turn?

No, I have no particular hope. Nothing I want for myself. Look, we have a house to live in, rice to eat, I'm satisfied. My only hope is to eat, to live, the children can study till they are ready for work, then go out and work. No matter where you bring your children up, it's the same. If the family upbringing is good, they won't go into the bad road.

LILLIAN SING, 30

She's a Shanghai Chinese. Her family left China in 1949 and settled in Hong Kong. She studied social work at Columbia University, married a prominent young American Chinese ophthalmologist, and became involved in community work as a social worker in the Chinese Newcomers' Service in Chinatown. She has a young daughter to whom she speaks Shanghainese, and plans to become actively involved in the campaign to initiate bilingual education in public schools. She told us that she feels sending children to private Chinese language schools makes them feel unnatural about learning Chinese.

I think when they first get here the immigrants have a lot of strength. They have a great deal of ego strength when they come because they have not been discouraged by too much discrimination in Hong Kong. They are used to thinking that if they try hard enough they'll make it, whereas it's a different problem once they get here because they meet a force that is beyond their control. You know, before they come they have this feeling that the United States has great opportunity for everyone, all you have to do is work. But when they get here they find that many things are limited. There's the language problem, limitation of jobs, and then even though they want to try very hard, they just can't make it. A lot of them don't speak English, which is a major setback. I think most immigrants make the final decision because of their children. They come here because education in Hong Kong is so expensive, there's very little possibility of a child going on to college after high school. And you have to pay a very large fee even for elementary education. They know that here, if a child wants it, he can have a college education free. So a lot of them know that if they come, they won't be very successful themselves, but their children might pull through. When you talk to a lot of people who feel very strongly about this, it's one point you pick up.

But then if you look ahead, think of the burden that's going to be placed on these children! If the parents are unhappy, children always know this. If the parents keep saying I'm doing this for you, and the child doesn't come through, that's going to be terrible. Yet with the job situation the way it is, and so many wives who have to work, it's very difficult to have the kind of family atmosphere that supports a child in school. In Hong Kong the education system is very rigid, children bring homework back and the mother is always there to supervise the child's activities, while over here with the mother gone and the father gone, the child is really left very much to himself. And if he gets discouraged at school, which a lot of immigrant children do, he's left with no one to help him and very often he just takes to the streets. So in Chinatown the family unity that is supposed to be so strong in Chinese culture often disintegrates.

In the past two years, the employment problem for immigrants has become much more severe. Just this summer a Baskin-Robbins opened downstairs from us. They planned to employ just three or four young men, but do you know over nine hundred people signed up for these jobs? Nine hundred people in one week's time! We see a lot of people come in who were plumbers in Hong Kong, or carpenters or welders, they know that to get good wages for this type of work you have to belong to a union, but somehow even finding the initial chance to get into a union is very hard.

I think some people, when they first find this out, may want to go back. The others more or less stay on because they feel that this is better than Hong Kong in the end; as I told you, they feel that even if they don't do well themselves, the children can go to school, they have a chance. But I often wonder how realistic this is when I look at the educational system here. Most of the immigrant children come without much English. If they're very young, they might have time to pick English up as they go along, and they'll be able to compete with the other children and get to college. But if you come with no English at fifteen or sixteen, how much can you learn in those few years? No matter what their educational background has been, many of them are already discouraged in that period. So they drop out, or even if they stick to it and want to go on to college, they can't really compete.

I wasn't surprised by these conditions when I first came here, but it made me feel angry and it made me want to get involved. It turns out I really enjoy working with the immigrants because they have so much potential. I think in a lot of ways the future of Chinese in this country depends on the immigrants because they have not been as suppressed as some of the older Chinese-Americans, they still have the will to fight in order to improve. I think at one time someone described real poverty to me as a condition where people lack aspiration, when they no longer have the will to fight. That's when people are really downtrodden. But the immigrants, even though they are poverty-ridden, have housing problems, employment problems, still have the spirit to do something. I think it's mainly because they haven't been discriminated against so much.

CHART 1. DISTRICT ASSOCIATIO

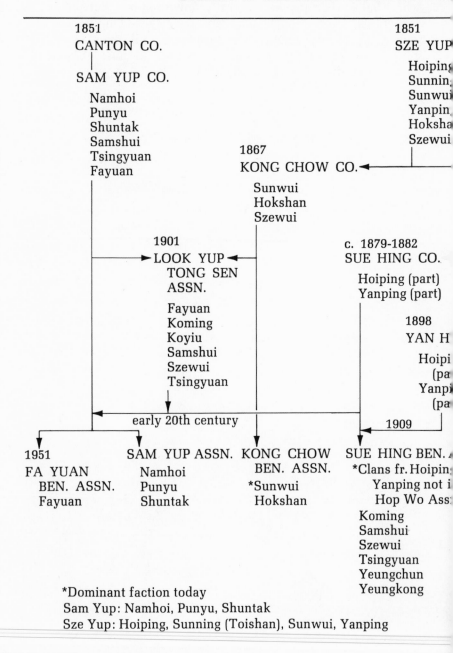

1851
CANTON CO.

SAM YUP CO.

Namhoi
Punyu
Shuntak
Samshui
Tsingyuan
Fayuan

1851
SZE YUP

Hoiping
Sunning
Sunwui
Yanping
Hoksha
Szewui

1867
KONG CHOW CO.

Sunwui
Hokshan
Szewui

1901
LOOK YUP
TONG SEN
ASSN.

Fayuan
Koming
Koyiu
Samshui
Szewui
Tsingyuan

c. 1879-1882
SUE HING CO.

Hoiping (part)
Yanping (part)

1898
YAN H

Hoipi
(pa
Yanpi
(pa

early 20th century

1909

1951
FA YUAN
BEN. ASSN.
Fayuan

SAM YUP ASSN.
Namhoi
Punyu
Shuntak

KONG CHOW
BEN. ASSN.
*Sunwui
Hokshan

SUE HING BEN.
*Clans fr. Hoipin
Yanping not i
Hop Wo Ass

Koming
Samshui
Szewui
Tsingyuan
Yeungchun
Yeungkong

*Dominant faction today
Sam Yup: Namhoi, Punyu, Shuntak
Sze Yup: Hoiping, Sunning (Toishan), Sunwui, Yanping

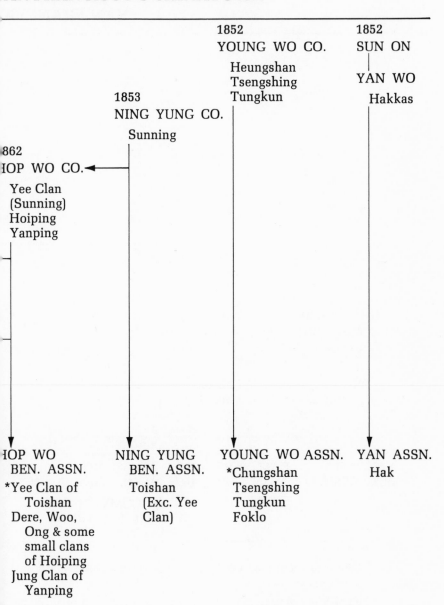

1852
YOUNG WO CO.

Heungshan
Tsengshing
Tungkun

1852
SUN ON

YAN WO

Hakkas

1853
NING YUNG CO.

Sunning

862
IOP WO CO.

Yee Clan
(Sunning)
Hoiping
Yanping

IOP WO
BEN. ASSN.

*Yee Clan of
    Toishan
Dere, Woo,
    Ong & some
    small clans
    of Hoiping
Jung Clan of
    Yanping

NING YUNG
BEN. ASSN.

Toishan
(Exc. Yee
Clan)

YOUNG WO ASSN.

*Chungshan
Tsengshing
Tungkun
Foklo

YAN ASSN.
Hak

Compiled by Him Mark Lai, 1971.

CHART 2. RELATIONS BETW
SAN FRANCISC

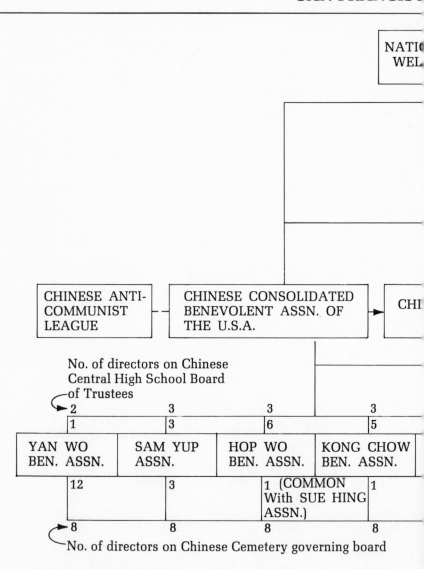

NATI(
WEL.

CHINESE ANTI-COMMUNIST LEAGUE

CHINESE CONSOLIDATED BENEVOLENT ASSN. OF THE U.S.A.

CHI

No. of directors on Chinese Central High School Board of Trustees

	YAN WO BEN. ASSN.	SAM YUP ASSN.	HOP WO BEN. ASSN.	KONG CHOW BEN. ASSN.
	2	3	3	3
	1	3	6	5
	12	3	1 (COMMON With SUE HING ASSN.)	1
	8	8	8	8

No. of directors on Chinese Cemetery governing board

Note: The president of each association is automatically a director on the Chinese School and Chinese Cemetery boards.

Compiled by Him Mark Lai, 1971.

IESE
NCIL

CHINESE CONSOLIDATED
BENEVOLENT ASSOCIATION
in other states

CHINESE HOSPITAL

KUOMINTANG
CHINESE CONSTITUTIONAL PARTY
CHINESE YMCA
CHINESE FREE MASONS
CHINESE CHRISTIAN PARTY
CHINESE CHAMBER OF COMMERCE
C.A.C.A.

RAL
OOL

Number of directors on the
Board of Directors of the
Chinese Consolidated
Benevolent Association,
◄U.S.A. (Chinese Six
    Companies)

	13	3		
	27	5		
	NING YUNG BEN. ASSN.	YOUNG WO BEN. ASSN.	FA YUAN BEN. ASSN.	

Number of directors
representing each
◄District Association

OMMON
HOP WO
I.)

| | 1 | 12 | 1 | |

| | 8 | | CHINESE CEMETERY |

NING YUNG
CEMETERY

CHART 3. ORGANIZATIONAL STRUCTU

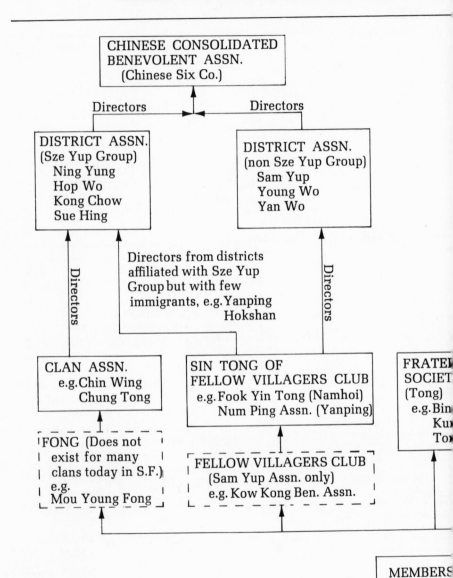

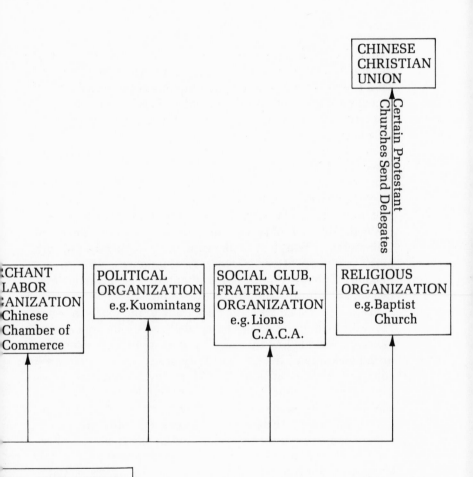

CHINESE
CHRISTIAN
UNION

Certain Protestant
Churches Send Delegates

RCHANT
LABOR
GANIZATION
Chinese
Chamber of
Commerce

POLITICAL
ORGANIZATION
e.g. Kuomintang

SOCIAL CLUB,
FRATERNAL
ORGANIZATION
e.g. Lions
C.A.C.A.

RELIGIOUS
ORGANIZATION
e.g. Baptist
Church

IESE COMMUNITY

Compiled by Him Mark Lai, 1971.

11. Why Chinese Restaurants Are Cheaper

"Good-by, and enjoy your Chinese lunch." At the end of several hours of discussion of Chinatown's housing and land problems, a director of San Francisco's Redevelopment Agency ushered us into the elevator. Several days later, at the city's Convention and Visitors' Bureau, we learned that on a survey which inquired of tourists, "Which three places in San Francisco did you enjoy the most?" Chinatown had rated third in the city and "restaurants" was checked by the majority of respondents as its primary attraction. "Nearly everyone in the city goes down to Chinatown now and then for a cheap meal out," one San Franciscan explained. He had observed that even tips were lower in Chinatown. "You just look around. Downtown, for any meal, you'll tip fifteen percent. In Chinatown, you tip ten percent. Nobody thinks twice about it. The meal is low-priced, so naturally the tip is lower, too."

While there is an unwitting accuracy to the tourist's sense that all of Chinatown may be symbolized by its good, inexpensive food, his low tip reveals a critical misunderstanding of the meaning of the symbol. Why are Chinese restaurants cheaper? Not because overhead is low. Land values in Chinatown, in prime position next to San Francisco's financial district, have soared in the last five years and rent for a Jackson Street restaurant is higher than for any other area of the city except Market Street or the famous Fisherman's Wharf. Nor are wholesale food prices lower for Chinese restaurateurs. The owner of the Jackson Cafe, crowded every evening with Caucasian and Chinese customers, claims that the same half pound of double E beef which wholesales for about one dollar a pound, and which he offers in a $2.25 dinner, costs a customer approximately

$3.75 or $4.00 downtown. Chinese restaurants are not cheaper because the labor force has been cut either. Quick service, another prominent feature in their reputation, usually results from a labor force two or three times larger than that which would be employed in a downtown restaurant of the same size. It is difficult, however, for a visitor in the crowded Jackson Cafe to see behind the yellow, swinging doors at the back for long enough to count the number of people working at the stoves, the sink, the busy tables in the kitchen. Nor is he apt to know the common Chinatown rule of thumb: that if his waiter is a younger man he is a recent immigrant from Hong Kong, living singly or with a family in a small room in one of the older tenement houses; that if he is an older man he has worked in the restaurant for over twenty years, and now lives with a family of two to five children in Chinatown's low-income federal housing project, the Ping Yuen apartments. He does not know that both waiters work ten hours a day, six days a week, for wages that average from $350 to an occasional high of $700 a month. Why are Chinese restaurants cheaper? The tourist does not know this, and he leaves a lower tip.

The importance of restaurants, brought home to a visitor in Chinatown by their numbers and conspicuousness, is understood by its residents in terms of necessity. Ask anyone in Chinatown and the proliferation of restaurants as well as their low prices are related to a labor crisis. In 1972, restaurants continue to provide the only source of employment for thousands of Chinese residents of San Francisco. The following statements, written by students in the Chinatown Vocational Innovations Program in 1971, describe characteristic experiences of Hong Kong immigrants searching for employment in San Francisco.

A. I am looking forward to my future, although I am now a dishwasher. This is really not what I want to do, but my family needs my support. I remember I first applied for a job as X-ray technician in Mary Help hospital. It was in September 1966, four months after I got to this country . . . I asked my friend to go with me because I wanted him to be my translator. The manager of the X-ray department asked me some questions about X-ray knowledge because he wanted to see how much I had known. All the questions which he asked, I answered, they were about ninety percent correct. But the manager didn't accept me to work in the hospital because I couldn't answer them in English. The manager said, "I believe your X-ray knowledge is good enough to work as an X-ray technician, but you can't speak English well. I suggest you go to school, when your English gets better, you may apply again."

The problem for me, as I said before, is that I have to support my family. Because of my family I have to work hard every day. I don't have enough time to study and when I am studying I have too many worries about my family....

(A former X-ray technician)

B. In March 1970 I arrived in San Francisco on an immigrant visa. Now I am working as a busboy at the Fairmont Hotel. In Hong Kong, my profession was in the field of building construction. After I arrived in the United States, however, I found I could not go back to my profession, for I possess neither a knowledge of the English language nor the educational background and working experience necessary in this country. Under the circumstances, then, I can only work for restaurants. I feel extremely painful about the situation.

C. The experience I had in looking for a job for the last two years made me feel bad and disappointed, because I didn't know where to go to find a job suitable to my background. All the jobs I tried to apply for had no openings. Some employers said I was not educated in America and some gave me the answer that I was not an American citizen. Some said I did not have American experience. At least, no one said I was too old. I am a Chinese with a background in chemistry and I do not like to be considered inferior. But I do not grumble about the inconvenience, or not getting a fair deal, because I know a lot of my deficiencies.

It is obvious that it is a mistake that most Chinese in America, or Chinese immigrants, whether they were educated or not, will do nothing but labor jobs when they come to this country. Limited to restaurants, groceries, and laundry shops. I don't want to be this way.

D. When I think about the next generation and the security of my whole family, I feel I have to stand the worst situation and face the difficulties boldly, to act like a man struggling from being drowned.

I got a job as a busboy so I could solve problems of board and lodge. Simultaneously, I can make use of the daytime to look for a better job which will be closer to what I earned in Hong Kong.

I sent out letters like falling leaves to different companies which advertised in the newspapers. Most of the replies said that either their position was not suited to my background and experience, or that my résumé was not applicable to the requirement of the job.

I also received letters stating that I could not get a job because I am not a citizen, even though I had passed a series of tests. I applied to a job as a sheet metal factory foreman immediately after obtaining my citizenship. I passed my written test but I failed my interview because the nature of the work was different from my field. . . . I am now working repairing and servicing stoves. I help to solve problems in commercial cooking equipment, I meet different kinds of people. At any rate, in this job I have the opportunity to use my common sense, wrenches, and screwdriver.

（A former mechanical engineer）

A lawyer and member of the Chinese-Americans Citizens Alliance explained that the entry of several thousand immigrants into Chinatown since 1965 and their severe difficulties in finding employment elsewhere in the city make the Chinatown labor market "like a self-filling barrel. . . . When you have approximately forty thousand people living in a twenty-seven-block area with a large segment of them non-

English-speaking, you create what is known as the employers' market. Those people whose job opportunities are
little or nil outside of Chinatown, and who have to depend
for making their living on employment inside Chinatown,
drive wages down. Because job opportunities aren't available outside of Chinatown, they all have to find work inside
of Chinatown, so this gives the employers the right to pick
and choose. This drags the wage scale down. But the average employee is faced with a choice of either taking it or
going on welfare." The seventy-two-year-old owner of the
Jackson Cafe told us prices are also kept low because the
restaurants serve people who live in Chinatown and have
low incomes, often lacking cooking facilities in their own
apartments. "There's too many restaurants, too much competition here. The Chinese have nothing to do. What can you
do? You run a restaurant here, or you work long hours and
you get low pay. But if you go outside you won't find anything. And if you raise the prices here, how about the
customers? Are they going to eat or not? If the prices are
too high, the Chinese can't stand it. You know, the local
people, not everybody's income is good."

S. L. Wong, the director of a small English language
school in Chinatown, explained the difficulty of recent immigrants. Unable to find employment in their previous field of
work, they are thrown back into the Chinatown job market
which for years has been flooded by older American
Chinese who encountered similar problems in finding employment in the United States.

Jobs are so scarce now that demand is little in Chinatown.
I heard of a case where a job was available in Chinatown
making *cha shew bau,* Chinese lunch pastries. One fellow
applied and was told the job required six days of work
every week, ten hours a day, for $310 a month. He said,
"I have one other possibility for work. May I wait until I
go for that interview and then let you know?" When he
went back two days later, he found someone else applying
for the same job at $280 a month. In another two or three
days, the job finally went to someone who was willing to
take $250 a month. Most immigrants coming into Chinatown
with a language barrier cannot go outside this confined area
into the mainstream of American industry.

SHEN LEE

A middle-aged man in Hong Kong-cut trousers and a light
sports coat. He was standing outside the Chinese Center
Employment Agency reading the notices on the window.
Inside the office, he told us through an interpreter that he
has been trying to get a job in an American restaurant, but
he could not because of his English problem. He says he
doesn't get along well with the older workers in Chinatown.

I owned a plastic factory in Hong Kong but after the riots in
1967 my business was not good, and I decided to come to
America. My feeling was like this. On the one hand, I was
reluctant to come because the place would be new and
strange to me. But on the other hand I had already sent my
children to school here, because the cost of education in
Hong Kong is so high, and my wife was with them. I wanted
to join my family, so I decided to sell all my business
properties.

Two or three months before I came here I learned that all
my sons had found jobs on the weekends and could cover
their expenses. While I was winding up my factory in Hong
Kong I decided to take lessons to learn to be a cook. But
when I got here I found there were no jobs for myself. Of
course, to be what they call a "China cook" is not hard. You
can work in a place run by Chinese. But if you want to
work for Americans, you have to speak good English. I
know so little English there's nothing I can do. I have been
without a job for almost one month now. Before that, all I
could get was substitute jobs.

Yes, I had been hoping to work for Americans. According
to my feelings and also those of my friends, who are mostly
recent immigrants, the old overseas Chinese seem to reject
us. If you are working in the kitchen of a restaurant and
you're new, you have to ask some of the old overseas
Chinese where things are placed. Usually they won't tell you.
One friend who went to work in a Chinese restaurant was
hired as a busboy. Since he was new, he wanted to work
fast, so he finished all his work. He asked the others in the
kitchen what to do next. They told him, "Don't do anything.
Just stand there." So he left the kitchen after one day. When

you go to work in a kitchen, if you don't have much capability the old ones will look down on you. But if you work better than they do they're afraid the boss will get to like you instead of them, or maybe even fire them. So there is this resentment in fighting for jobs.

That's why, for myself, I prefer working for Americans. I tried to learn English at first. But after a while I had to work, so I stopped my classes. Now I've forgotten some of what I learned. So, of course, the language is the problem for me. If you don't know the language, how can you even know what American culture is? I feel just like a blind man here. The older overseas Chinese don't know that much English either. I don't think they know what culture or science is in the United States because they're confined to the Chinatown area. In Hong Kong, where you know how to read and write the language, everything is easier. For example, just by reading the newspaper, you can understand events all over the world. In America, no matter what the events are, I am quite blind and ignorant of them.

DANNY LOWE, 21

We met him standing beside the door of the Tung Sen Association on a Sunday afternoon. It was a warm day and Danny, his coarse hair carefully combed, wearing a lavender shirt and a heavy metal ID bracelet, was ushering people up the stairs to the family association banquet. He didn't know us, but he invited us in to the banquet, kept running up the stairs to fill our plates with food. He told us this was the only time in the year that he came to his uncle's family association, but he didn't have much social life and it was fun meeting people at a big party. At the end of the hectic afternoon, we made a date to meet the next day, and walk around Chinatown together.

The next day in Fong Fong Danny was quiet. Same shirt, ID bracelet, he sat in the booth and wouldn't let us pay for his root beer. He kept apologizing for mistakes he made speaking English. Then we walked around for a while; we were surprised at all the older men Danny greeted on the street. He told us he got to know these men working in the

Chinatown markets. It was Labor Day, late afternoon. Danny decided we should go to Portsmouth Square and sit on a bench there while he told us about his experience coming into San Francisco and finding a job in Chinatown. He talked for a long time and we were all cold when the conversation was over.

When we first got to know Danny, he was hopeful about learning English and beginning work someplace outside of Chinatown. During the period while we were writing the book, however, this hope never materialized. We met Danny often sweeping the sidewalk in front of the fish stores in his stained white smock. Beneath the smock, he was always dressed as when we first met him, pastel shirt, ID bracelet on his wrist. He says hello, tells us he is still learning English, trying to get out of Chinatown someday.

Everything is beautiful. I mean in Hong Kong they think in here is the best place in the world. Even if they got no people in here, no matter what they have to do, they just try to get here. So when I got here I thought everything's alright, everything's beautiful, everything's nice, you know. When I stay here, then everything's different, see. I mean the jobs. First year I had to be a fishman, work in the fish market here. I was thinking I can get a better job or something, I mean I'm not interested in that job, but I had no way, so I had to do it.

First day's alright. When the United States government told me they can let me in I was so happy, you know. But when I looked for a job then I knew I got a problem in here. The language is different. At home I didn't know that every kind of job in here is terrible for us, see. Dishwasher, janitor, cook goes to us, right? Before I was a painter in Hong Kong, but I can't do it here. I got no license, no education. If I want to join a union, I have to take a long time. So I take that kind of job because I need some money to spend. I want a living, so it's dishwasher, janitor, or cook. I have no way to think about it. I have to take it. And if I don't want to take it, somebody else is going to. So that's how we view it, see? That everything is hopeless. When we've been here then we know it.

I had to ask everyplace before I found a job. My uncle, he doesn't speak English at all, he's been a dishwasher for more than thirty years, so he could only take me to the stores in Chinatown. It took about two months. One guy working in the fish market quit, my uncle's friend told him, so I got the job.

I started seven A.M. and our shop opened at seven-thirty. I got up thirty minutes before I got there, and I didn't eat breakfast, because they gave us three meals a day. So at seven the fishmen come and we put the fish in the freezer. Then we take some of the fish from the freezer to put on the table, put a sign on it and wait for the people to come in and buy it. After nine o'clock we have breakfast, one by one, for fifteen minutes. At one o'clock we have lunch and that should be fifteen minutes, too. We start to work again and at six o'clock we have dinner. Then we close the doors and we have to clean up all the walls because the waste is dirty, right, and the walls really smell. So we get off work seven or seven-thirty.

But it's not the same every day. It depends on whether the day is busy or not. A couple of years ago they opened on the holidays, too. The holidays were very busy and we had to spend more time, but they didn't pay us for overtime, because they pay by the month. Then, sometimes guys take summer vacation, right? The boss doesn't call someone in to help us, so we have to do his job, too. Those are also very busy times. When it's the next guy's turn, we do the same thing again.

Twenty guys work in the shop. Yes, we have many departments. They sell fish, barbecue, they have a chicken department, too. But you can't stay in one department. Now when I first went to get the job, the boss just put me in the fish department, right? If he had put me in the barbecue department, it would have seemed very busy and I would have thought it was very hard work, but that day the fish department was quiet. So he said, "You work there." But then a few days later he put me in a very busy department. Of course, I had no idea of saying no or something to the boss. So I just had to say OK.

In the beginning I earned $280 a month. After that the

boss said he would see how much expense I got, but I mean, in Chinatown the expense doesn't matter. No matter what, he'll never pay more than $400. I knew many guys who worked for him more than twenty years, and they still get $400. Even though they work more than ten hours a day. But if they don't like it, the boss will tell them, "OK, you gotta go. I don't need you, because I got so many people waiting for the job." When you hear that how do you feel? I mean, you're still a very good worker, you're busy all the time. When the boss says something like that to you it hurts your feelings.

The boss just pretends he's a king, see. He doesn't even have to live in Chinatown. He lives in another place. All the bosses these days live in the Richmond district, out in the Avenues, Diamond Hill. Because they speak very good English, they know everything and they know what's going on, see. Not like us. They do know the law, too, but they don't do things by the law. They know people make much more outside Chinatown, but they don't want to pay like a union pays. All the rich men in Chinatown, that's what they do.

And what can we do? Say all the workers talk together. We know everything, we know the boss is fooling us, but we got no way to do. You know you don't want to stay in that place, but how can you earn a living? How can you get some money to spend? I mean to pay for your rent. And some men are like me, they owe money to a relative who helped them come over. For a couple of years they just have to pay that back. Well, I paid that now anyway, so I don't want to stay on this kind of job.

I got no idea what I want to do next. The thing is, I got no experience in America. Before I did know how to paint and I was thinking I really would like to get that kind of job. I talked to many people, and one friend who works with a painting company took me to his boss. That boss asked me, "Do you know how to paint?" I said, "Yes, I do. I painted in Hong Kong." But he didn't believe me, so he said, "Well, OK, when your experience is good, I will pay you four dollars an hour. But at the beginning anybody who joins us has to train for a while." So that means he wouldn't pay four dollars an hour. Training pay is just two dollars an hour. He didn't care about my experience at all. So it's just fooling people, see. Everywhere is the same. The only way to do it is to get some money and open your own business. You become a boss and then you got more power, you can do everything that you want. The only thing you can do is just get money and try to be a boss.

The union's good, yeah. If I had a chance to, I would join one, but I don't know how. Unions have something, control over the boss. Not like in Chinatown. In Chinatown they got no union, and if you want to say something to the boss, the boss won't listen to you. I'm too small, see, and he's too big. If I had a union, I could talk to the union first, then the union would talk to the boss, that's much easier.

Still I never was around with white people, see, so I don't know that much about working outside. When I first got here, I couldn't go outside of Chinatown because my language is different. I didn't understand what the people said so I was scared. I've been in this country for six years just being around with Chinese. I work in Chinatown, I go to Chinese movies, and I'm a Chinese, right? I do lots of gambling, too. But maybe after this I will work outside or join an American union.

For me, the only thing is that I don't want to bother people and I don't want the people to bother me. I just want to go to work, you know, finish work and go home.

12. The Garment Shops

Awareness of the garment shops in Chinatown is constant, like the sensation of people in the street. Along Stockton and Powell, in all the alleys, up and down Commercial Street, the wooden buildings with drab curtains drawn over their front windows, a black NO SOLICITING sign on the door, appear every several buildings, sometimes in rows of three or four. No other signs identify the buildings, as if every effort had been made to blur and obscure their façades, yet the plain wood and curtained windows are conspicuous, doors open and close, the creaking of wheels and pedals flows into the street, the crack makes visible crowded space, rows of machines, piles of colored fabric. At all hours, there are women going to or coming from the garment shops on the streets. They walk with small children and drop them off at school. They carry paper shopping bags filled with a sweater, a skirt, an apron to be worn at work, maybe sewing finished the night before at home. On Saturdays, and even late at night, the work goes on in the shops. If you walk by, the narrow space of glass above the curtains will be lighted, and the creaking noise, whenever a door happens to open, is steady. "I think a lot of this is unknown to people outside, that jobs are so scarce in Chinatown here." Emily Young described her mother's working hours in the shop. "A working day might start anywhere from six or seven in the morning and not end until late at night. You know, when you pass the streets at night, the doors are shut and it looks like the shop is closed, but then you can hear the machines going inside, which means that people are still working." We learned that seam-stresses compose the largest labor force employed by any single industry in Chinatown. They produce close to half of the total volume of apparel manufactured in San Francisco each year.

THE JENNIE LEW CASE

At seven-thirty at night we climb up to the apartment in the Ping Yuen Housing Project where Jennie Lew lives with her husband and six children. Jennie opens the door a crack behind the lock-chain and asks who's there before she lets us in. She's short, with very fair skin, bright red lipstick. The hall behind the door leads toward the bedrooms, one for Mr. Lew, one for Jennie and three kids; the three other kids sleep together in the room just behind the living room. Jennie takes us into the living room. It's yellow and looks bare, a single cord from the plastic clock stretching down the wall. All the furniture in the room has been lined up against the walls to leave an empty space in the center. Jennie sits down beside a table dominated by a large framed photograph of her husband's family, twelve members in it, taken when he was nineteen years old in Canton. A vase of plastic flowers—chrysanthemums, roses, plum blossoms—and a coffee can filled with sticks of incense stand in front of the photograph. On the other side of the room is another row of more tables, beginning with a small one close to the floor where Jennie says her youngest son does homework. The older daughters take turns at two card tables when they study.

Jennie talks to us with her oldest daughter, a thin and nervous girl of twenty, and two boys in the room. She says she began working in the garment factories about fifteen years ago, when Donna got old enough to keep an eye on the younger ones. Of course, she worked off and on, she says. She'd stop for four or five months whenever a new child was born, and her health hasn't been too good, so she had to take time out for that. In all, she worked in three different garment factories until she stopped. She had worked in the last place, on Powell Street, for seven years, making men's shirts, women's blouses, and overcoats. She followed pretty much the same schedule every day while she was working. She'd get up at seven and make breakfast for her husband and the kids. She'd walk the older ones to school, go to the factory at nine, and work for two hours until eleven. At eleven, she'd pick the kids up from school, make lunch for them at home, walk them back to school, and be at work again at one. At five, she would take another hour off to cook supper for everybody. At six or six-thirty she'd go back to work again, sew until ten, then come home to bed. On Saturday she would put in about five hours, and take home something to sew on Sunday. She was paid by piece-rate, not by the hour, earning between $4.50 to $8 per dozen depending on the complexity of the pattern.

We ask Jennie what the shop was like and she says we should go up and take a look for ourselves. Not on weekends, because they keep the door locked then, but we might try going down on a week day and asking to go inside. She says there were about thirty machines in the shop. It was noisy because there were so many people running motors, but the main thing is that it was messy: an old building, no one painted or dusted the walls. She laughs and says, yes, it's true, on Sundays he keeps the door locked because people are working in there. Jennie says she didn't expect to do work like this when she was a girl. In fact, she never liked sewing. "But that's the only thing we know how to do when we get here. It's the only kind of job we can get." Donna says Jennie is impatient and she used to scream at them sometimes when she got fed up with sewing. She'd make them feel guilty by saying she wouldn't have to do work like this if it weren't for them. Even now, sometimes she gets really emotional and she says she wishes she had been a nun, and never gotten married at all. "After a while, we just turn off on it when she starts yelling like that. You get the feeling she couldn't control anything about her life, and it makes you feel awful. I mean, she could control some things." Donna says Jennie goes in and out of religions all the time, too. She was a Buddhist for a while, then a Catholic, now she's a Buddhist again. She points to a place on the windowsill where a plastic Saint Joseph statue stands next to a somewhat larger Buddha figure.

Jennie does not have much to say about the other women

in the shop. Toward the end, when she was having trouble, she had called around and asked some of the other women to come to court with her and testify against the boss. Not one person volunteered to appear. They were all afraid of losing their jobs. "They want the money more than anything else." Jennie says she understands that, because she knows how hard it is to find work, but she says she still feels bitter about it, there's no one in the shop she goes to visit now.

The problem started the first year she was working on Powell Street. Jennie had always been paid by piece-rate, but in the years since she had begun at Powell Street, the effort to unionize the Chinatown shops had intensified. Chinatown wage levels had been exposed and become the center of a bitter, city-wide controversy. In 1963, when she began working for him, Kim Wah Lee informed her that a prerequisite for maintaining her position as a worker at his shop would be that she, like the other workers, fill out a bi-weekly time card certifying that her wages came up to the standard for the state minimum wage of $1.65 per hour. He instructed the women in the following procedure: as before, their wages would be piece-rate, calculated according to the number of pieces completed, not the number of hours worked. They would, as before, hand in a slip for every dozen garments completed. But at the end of every two week period, Kim Wah Lee would give them a separate time card to take home and fill out, showing, as federal law requires, not the number of pieces completed, but the number of hours worked. With each time card, he would enclose a brief note of instruction stating precisely the number of hours to be filled in on the time card. The number was, of course, not calculated on the basis of a record of actual hours worked, but by dividing the actual amount the woman had earned by the state minimum wage. If she worked eighty hours and earned fifty dollars in two weeks, she was instructed to fill out the time card to show a total of no more than 30 hours, at which rate her pay for the two-week period would appear to fulfill the minimum wage of $1.65 per hour. Jennie said for a while she didn't understand why she was being asked to do this. After a few months, her husband noticed her working out figures on the card every two weeks. He began to blow up whenever she brought the time card home. Jennie's husband, a delivery man, is not in a union either, but she says he was furious. He would ask her what kind of business she thought she was working for, "You're not supposed to fill in your own time card!" He urged her to quit and look for another job. But she was convinced she couldn't find work outside of the garment industry and she needed money. She and most of the other women were aware they were being cheated. "That was obvious, but what could we do? Most of us can't speak English. Even if a few of us wanted to start something, like file a petition, we couldn't get support from the others. People are hesitant about starting anything, because they can lose their positions so easily. So no one wants to stir things up, you know."

Jennie went on working at Powell for five years, despite the conflict with her husband and the fact that her wages were often lower than one dollar an hour. Why did she keep going, for all those years, earning so little? "How did I feel?" Jennie repeats the question as if it was one she had never thought about. Donna blushes. "I'm afraid she's very materialistic." She apologizes. "Basically, she always just thought that, well, earn enough money and you eat well. Eating well was the most important thing. She thinks that's the only way to spend your money, you know. Eating the right things, sleeping well, not buying more clothes than you need." Something else comes to Donna's mind. "Of course one thing she always liked was going to Reno." Jennie grins, not the slightest bit embarrassed. She says we probably know about the special bus that goes up from Chinatown on Saturday night. You pay $13.75 and get $8.75 back; 2 tickets for Keeno, a $2 cocktail, and a $2 meal. Donna says Jennie never took much money, maybe $25 once a month. Usually she breaks even or comes back with a little more. Lately she's been trying to get Donna to go, too. "Nothing wrong with taking a chance on earning some extra money," she tells her.

In the summer of 1968, Jennie began going to the North

Beach health clinic complaining of dizzy spells, headaches, backaches, and general fatigue. Her health deteriorated through the fall and winter, and in the following spring the doctor advised her to stop work for an indefinite period of time. Because she was anxious about losing the supplementary income for the family, Jennie hesitated for several months. Donna repeats that Jennie is too emotional, too easily upset, and this undermined her health more. In late June, Jennie developed mononucleosis and was hospitalized for three weeks. She took sick leave from work for another month. In August, when she decided to apply for unemployment insurance, she was told that she needed a letter from her employer, stating the reason for her inability to continue work. Jennie took the form to the shop. Her boss refused to sign it and told her her sickness was all in her head. Jennie says she exploded. "There's no other way to explain what happened. I was just fed up. Before I even thought about what I was saying, I told him if he didn't fill out that card for me, I would sue him for all the hours he'd never paid me in four years. He just said, 'Go right ahead,' and told me to leave the shop." Jennie went home and collected the receipts of the paychecks she had received in the year period before she had to leave work. In the period between August 19, 1967, and June 22, 1968, she earned $969.00.

It was difficult to get Jennie to explain the steps which led her to become the first garment worker in Chinatown history who successfully won a court battle against her employer in 1971. She says it was not her husband's pressure which led to the decision, it was just the rage that built up in herself. She was fed up. She went to the Economic Opportunity Office on Stockton Street where she had learned to come for food stamps, and someone on the staff advised her to discuss her case with the ILGWU (International Ladies Garment Workers Union) office on Howard Street. The union urged Jennie to prosecute the case, and referred her to the Chinatown-North Beach Neighborhood Legal Assistance Office. For two years, Jennie and Jack Seidman, a young lawyer in the office, put together the evidence on the case. Jennie was able to produce several time cards, with the usual bi-weekly instructions on them; these became critical evidence in the case. Neither her lawyer nor Jennie were able to obtain the agreement of any other women in the shop to testify in court. Jennie's two youngest children, however, were able to provide evidence of overtime work by giving the hours of the day and the times of the week when their mother was away from home.

Jack stressed that he felt legal blame for Jennie's experience did not rest only on the proprietor of her shop. "Legally, this Chinese contractor is not even considered an independent business. In this case, he was merely an extension of the manufacturing company downtown. In the strictest sense, it is the company, as the prime contractor, which is the employer of the seamstresses and responsible for the substandard pay." He says he approached the downtown firm about the case, but they were so anxious to keep it out of court and out of the public eye that they offered to settle all expenses themselves. Since he felt the success of a court case might be one of the biggest breakthroughs possible for workers in the Chinatown industry, he and Jennie went on to court. After seven months they won a settlement. Jennie received $2,100 in back pay for the five year period, plus a $1,650 punitive fee which was imposed on her employer.

In the spring of 1970, when she was well enough to look for work again, Jennie found a new job. She is now a maid in a large hotel on Geary Street, outside Chinatown. Jennie says it's hard work, she has to get up even earlier now, at six o'clock, to be down there on time. But her work hours are a regular forty hour week. The pay is $2.25 an hour, and she has a paid two-week vacation and sick leave. Jennie says she would never work in the garment factory again.

A POLITICAL ECONOMY

There was no area of Chinatown society about which it was harder to get information than the garment industry. At the start, we found rumor, secrecy, and conflicting reports at every turn. We arrived during a period of uneasy truce after the fierce campaign by the ILGWU to unionize Chinatown's seamstresses or zone the garment industry out of Chinatown completely.* By the summer of 1970, Chinatown factory owners and the Six Companies had fought this campaign to a halt and held to less than one-third the number of unionized shops in Chinatown. From news accounts and pamphlets published during the struggle emerged a picture which seemed hard to believe: unnaturally cruel factory owners were shown driving enslaved workers beyond the limits of normal physical endurance. The words "sweatshop" and "exploitation" appeared again and again. We read that there were women in the Chinatown shops who worked for forty or fifty cents an hour, seventy-two hours a week. We read of immigrant women, their husbands dishwashers who earned $250 a month, keeping small children with them in the airless shops during long hours of work. We read that the owners of the shops would not let seamstresses leave their machines for lunch breaks, that they falsified time cards to avoid prosecution for their workers' illegal hours and pay, that they held back wages for periods of up to eight months while workers, afraid of losing their jobs, could do nothing. If the women took time away from the shops for sickness, bosses fired them. If they refused to work seven days a week, bosses fired them. A pamphlet published by the union during the campaign presented the testimony of a seamstress who said she had worked for one hundred hours sewing 118 blouses and 28 dresses for forty-one dollars. The pamphlet described factories in low-ceilinged cellars crowded with machines, poor light, unsanitary toilets, and constant violations of regulations. The headlines amazed us by their similarity to the rhetoric of the nineteenth century Workingmen's Party: HONG KONG COOLIE LABOR POURING INTO THE CITY; SERFDOM FOR IMMIGRANTS; WIDESPREAD TB; one article headed CHINATOWN CLEAN-UP ORDERED BY THE CITY described the ghetto as infested with rats. When we tried to enter garment shops, talk to people, and actually corroborate these reports,

---

* Manager Cornelius Wall of the ILGWU proposed an amendment of the city zoning ordinances which would declare Chinatown a strictly residential area and "that all garment shops and factories shall close and cease," an act which would have caused severe economic depression in the community and put thousands of families on the welfare rolls.

we met angry rebuffs. On the first afternoon, twelve out of fifteen shops demanded that we leave as soon as we stepped through the door.

In fact, the symptoms of the sweatshop did not strike us dramatically in these early moments of exposure. We found that the garment shops were usually in older buildings which had once been ground-floor stores or warehouses; they contained fewer than thirty machines. Dust and age were conspicuous, bare pipes and fuse boxes protruded on unpainted walls. There had been obvious attempts to economize. The machines were heavy black Singer models which looked about twenty years old. Sometimes, the lights built into the tops of the machines had been broken and worn metal desk lamps stood on the tables, just behind the machines, to substitute. In place of waste baskets, cardboard cartons stood in front of the machines for scraps. There were makeshift cooking facilities in the backs of the shops; rusty gas burners, perhaps a refrigerator, a dingy sink. But in all the shops there were also signs that recent improvements had been made. Large fluorescent lights extended over the working areas, many of the old machines were attached to trim, new formica tables, in several of the shops popular music from Hong Kong was piped in on a small PA system. The women were usually carrying on relaxed conversations when we entered and we were surprised at the sudden current of tension which ran through the room. Women at tables refused to talk to us, kept their heads bent over their machines, and directed us with fingers to a foreman or boss who curtly requested us to leave. A few times the women themselves drove us out of the factory with angry shouts from behind their machines. Several days later friends told us that, as strangers, we had probably been taken as union organizers. This accounted for the speed and anger with which we were asked to leave the shops.

Our confusion increased, however, when contacts within the community broadened and we had our first opportunity to talk with people directly involved with the garment industry. From seamstresses, from factory owners (technically "sub-contractors," almost like foremen for the shops, who negotiate with apparel manufacturers for pre-cut garments

sewn together in Chinatown), from union officials, and from
the large manufacturing firms downtown, we received
sharply conflicting statements. Workers told us they wished
they could earn higher wages in unionized factories downtown, but they could not speak English. Because of their
small children, they depended on the unstructured hours of
the Chinatown shops. Some claimed that their bosses would
fire any worker who tried to organize support for the union
in Chinatown and that the names of such workers were put
on a black list so it would be impossible for them to find
work in any other Chinatown shops. Factory owners, however, insisted that their seamstresses earned as much as they
could in a unionized factory outside. They claimed that
Chinatown seamstresses had been intimidated and terrified
by union organizers and that most of them feared the
union's discriminatory policy against Chinese. The ILGWU
officials, in turn, rejected the factory owners' stories as
falsifications. They held that union policy sought to improve
the situation of all garment workers, regardless of race, and
condemned Chinatown bosses for creating an atmosphere of
fear in which their workers were kept ignorant of the actual
benefits offered by the unions. Nevertheless, they told us,
the main obstacle to unionization did not come from the
Chinatown bosses but from the powerful "prime contractors," the apparel firms which threatened to cut off business
from any shop which unionized. When, finally, we approached a few of these firms which wholesale fifteen million dollars' worth of goods produced in Chinatown garment
shops every year, we were brushed off with a sharp comment that the union was fomenting trouble in Chinatown.
Spokesmen assured us they were sure all Chinatown seamstresses were earning standard or better wages for their
work.

It was only after several conversations with representatives of the four elements involved in the struggle over the
Chinatown garment industry that we began to decipher the
pattern in what we heard: areas of contradiction in the interpretations advanced by the different groups could be cor-
related exactly to the conflicts of interest between them. In
every case, secrecy, or reluctance to give precise informa-

tion, marked the point of vital concern. Thus seamstresses, although we found they would discuss their wages and complaints uninhibitedly in their homes, generally refused to speak with us at all when they were actually in the shops. A wrong comment might cost them their jobs. Shop owners, on the other hand, consistently evaded questions about their own incomes and about the wages they paid their employees. They held back hard figures with the excuse that "how much you earn depends on the season," "every year business is different," and that, "when you pay by the piece-rate, some workers are fast, others are slow, it's impossible to calculate an average wage." We encountered similar areas of reluctance in the union officials. By ignoring requests to arrange interviews in unionized Chinatown shops, officials who emphasized the benefits they offered to workers lent substance to the observation of many social workers in Chinatown that the union was more interested in adding to its income from the dues of Chinatown seamstresses than in materially improving the conditions of their work. Later, workers told us that wages were about the same in union and nonunion shops, the only benefit for seventy dollars a year dues was the health insurance. The highest degree of secrecy, however, was maintained by the prestigious manufacturing companies, which either refused to submit to an interview about their Chinatown contracts or granted us only a terse conversation by phone.

In the end, our most liberal supply of information came from conversations with seamstresses and shop owners in Chinatown. From the repeated observation that the statements of workers and owners contradicted each other on certain issues, while they reinforced each other on others, we learned to differentiate the two conflicts which were inherent in the Chinatown garment industry. On the first, immediate level within Chinatown, we discovered potential conflict between seamstresses and those who hired them. We learned that a steady influx of new immigrants, willing to accept extremely low pay, and the large number of non-English-speaking women seeking work, placed the owners of garment shops in a powerful position within Chinatown. They could virtually dictate the terms of employment to those who came in search of work, assured that these women had no other alternatives. They could name low wages and lay off anyone who was dissatisfied, while the seamstresses, in a situation of built-in job insecurity, lacked any leverage against them. Allegations of withheld pay were verified by several sources in the community and most dramatically by an independent investigation which had been carried out by the San Francisco Human Rights Commission during the union campaign. The commission's employment representative discovered twenty seamstresses at the Hoi Ming factory on Kearny Street who had worked unpaid for periods of up to six months because they feared they would be fired if they demanded wages. Jennie Lew told us that not a single worker in her shop was willing to testify in court about the falsification of their time cards for the same reason. In a broader context, however, seamstresses and shop owners shared a sense of solidarity and unity in their relation to more powerful forces outside. The small, workshop settings of the shops encouraged the development of personal and often warm ties between employer and worker, despite the unequal terms of the relationship. In many cases, owners expressed a paternalistic feeling of responsibility for their employees which was matched by a sense of obligation and loyalty in the workers. Members of both groups described a loose and unstructured atmosphere in the Chinatown shops which differed from the tight discipline of the assembly line factory. Women sewed complete garments, chose how many hours a week they wanted to work, and came in and out of the shops as they wished. Their isolation in the small workshops where they sewed side by side with their bosses made it far more natural to identify with the shop and its owner than with representatives of a distant association of workers outside. The sense of unity was even more strong vis-à-vis manufacturers who contracted to the shops. Seamstresses and shop owners alike pointed out that the real source of low wages and unsteady income in the Chinatown shops lay in contracts negotiated with the downtown firms. They both complained that these contracts were unreliable, that there were long stretches of little or no work during off seasons, or during periods when the contractor, hearing about a lower bid from another shop, took his work elsewhere. If a shop owner insisted on higher rates, the manufacturer could cut off contracts completely. They pointed to the frequency with which Chinatown shops changed hands or closed their doors and went out of business. They held that there was a conspiracy of consent among all downtown firms to keep the piece-rate as low as possible. Seamstresses and owners both endorsed the union claim that unionized shops are systematically boycotted by these firms. In the course of the recent ILGWU campaign, a third of Chinatown's shops had buckled under public pressure and agreed to an arrangement which made them "company unions." To maintain formal union membership, these shops pay dues in a lump sum taken from the seamstresses' wages. The piece-rate, however, remains exactly the same as it had been before in order to maintain the critical volume of business from downtown firms. To these people who viewed the Chinatown garment industry from inside, the union appeared simply as a sporadic threat, while two inherent conflicts perpetuated constant tension. Within Chinatown, a secondary conflict of interest created tension between low-paid, insecure seamstresses and the relatively powerful owners of shops. In the primary, determining conflict, however, seamstresses and owners stood together as one unit pitted against the strength of the large downtown firms. There lay the source of the much condemned exploitation passed on by the sub-contractor factory owners to the shoulders of the seamstresses in Chinatown.

Familiarity with the Chinatown situation thus revealed perfectly understandable reasons for what had at first seemed inexplicable and unnatural in the garment industry. The different aspects of irregularity in the shops were impossible to miss. They had been put up with little capital in makeshift accommodations. The buildings were run-down and sometimes lacked heat. The working hours were irregular, wages were irregular, the women hired were often lacking in standard qualifications and unable for various reasons to put in a standard work week. But they were also women for whom the "regular" economy had no place and who depended on the Chinatown garment industry for survival.

Most of them were the wives of Chinatown's waiters, dish-washers, store-workers, and janitors, men whose low wages made the employment of father and mother alike the pre-requisite for raising a family. Since, as wives of Chinatown's workingmen, they had not been permitted to enter the United States until the World War II period or the mid-sixties, most came as mature women with no knowledge of English. Domestic work and sewing had been the only sources of employment open to them. Rapidly burdened with children, they had been further prevented from taking jobs which required them to leave the immediate Chinatown area for any extended period of time during the day. It was for these women that Chinatown's numerous garment fac-tories, where work was done by the piece-rate at open hours, provided a critical source of income with which to raise families. With marriage and their arrival to America, they found themselves wedded as well to the small facto-ries, extension workshops of downtown firms, through which their own needs were channeled and fed into the persistent demand of San Francisco's garment industry for efficient and inexpensive labor.

Ten Ponts of Information on the Chinatown Garment Workers

(Taken from an independent investigation conducted by the San Francisco Human Rights Commission, during the ILGWU campaign in 1969.)

1. *Income:* Sixty-eight percent of the women interviewed during this investigation earned *below* $2,900 annually for the equivalent of a forty-hour week or longer. Only four percent of the workers earned higher than $4,000 annually.

2. *Family situation:* Seventy-one percent of the women had husbands who were service workers or had retired. (The majority of such "retired" husbands are older Chinatown laborers who, after 1965, brought wives fifteen or twenty years younger than themselves into the country and had children by them. We noticed a number of these older men caring for their children during the daylight hours while their wives were at work.) Only two percent of the women identified their husbands as "merchants." Thus for the major-ity of women working in the Chinatown garment shops, the

income from their work represents an equal, or even higher, proportion of their family's income than the wages earned by their husbands. Even with both parents working, many of these families fall into the forty-one percent of Chinatown's population which is below poverty level by federal standards.

3. *Working hours:* All of the women interviewed said they worked six days a week. Only fifteen percent worked less than eight hours a day. While the others may take very brief breaks to drop off or pick up children at school, they put in eight hours and often longer at work. Forty percent of the women interviewed worked from 9 AM to 7 PM with a twenty minute lunch break. Twenty-seven percent worked from 9 AM to 5 PM with a lunch break. Eighteen percent worked from nine in the morning until ten at night with a lunch break and an average break of one hour to fix the evening meal for their families.

4. *Overtime pay:* None of the workers received pay for overtime work.

5. *Vacations:* None of the workers reported receiving vacation or sick leave pay.

6. *Medical insurance:* Eighty-eight percent of the workers were not covered by any medical or health plan.

7. *Feeling about being a garment worker:* When asked if they would like to work outside of Chinatown if that was possible, sixty-two percent of the women answered "yes." Fourteen percent were undecided. Twenty-four percent preferred to stay.

8. *Educational background:* Eighty-six percent of the women interviewed had under six years of formal education.

9. *English ability:* Seventy percent said they had "very limited" facility with English.

10. *Why they are garment workers:* When asked what was the strongest reason for becoming a garment worker, forty-eight percent of the women answered, "This is the only type of work I can do."

A few positive results of union pressure were revealed when a checkup survey was conducted by the commission in the spring of 1970. The most striking change was in the provision of health insurance to workers, which is now found in nearly three-fourths of Chinatown shops as opposed to twelve percent in 1969. There was an increase of twelve percent in the number of workers who earned over $4,000 a year. The high percentage of women who earn less than $2,900 as garment workers, however, remained as nearly half (forty-four percent) of the labor force. In autumn 1971, a compliance officer in the San Francisco Wages and Hours Enforcement Division of the United States Department of Labor gave us his personal estimate that seventy percent of Chinatown shops still pay below the state minimum wage of $1.65 an hour. He felt the average worker did more than eight hours of work daily, making up for time she had to take out during the day by sewing at home at night. Since the union campaign, he has noticed a very slight increase in the number of seamstresses who attempt to report that they are being underpaid. Most of these attempts take the form of anonymous phone calls. The two main complaints are (1) that employers who claim they are paying an hourly wage are actually paying by piece-rate and (2) that no pay is received for overtime work, even in "company union" shops.

*   *   *

THE SHOP OWNERS' SIDE

In the Chinese Garment Contractors' Association we found our first receptive source of information in Chinatown. While workers were timid and often reluctant to discuss their jobs, the members of this group, active and articulate factory owners who had been mobilized by the union attack to the defense of the Chinatown industry, were self-confident and eager to publicize their positions. Many had already spent months negotiating with city and union officials to forestall the zone-out of the garment industry from Chinatown. Edna Fong, an attractive and energetic woman in her mid-forties, had sent letters to all the Chinatown subcontractors during the campaign urging them to fight off the union by "getting good light and good heating, cleaning up your places and keeping them that way." Chuck Lai, a slight, older man known among his friends as a good speech maker, had served as president of the Six Companies, his family association, and his tong. Although he was strongly anti-union, Chuck converted his factory to a "company union" during the attack. Dick Lim was a recent arrival from Hong Kong, and there were several older women owners. Together they composed an aggressive, shrewd, and dynamic element among Chinatown shop owners. In interviews which were rich in twists and turns, all emphasized the lack of job opportunities for Chinese women and what they saw as the spiteful and discriminatory policies of the union. They spoke idealistically and paternalistically of the role of the garment shops in the lives of their employees.

Edna Fong gave primary emphasis to the importance of garment shops to Chinatown mothers:

Some of the ladies have many children. I myself have five, you know. Now you know Chinese women, they care more about their children than their own lives. How can they go downtown when they have to worry about their children all day? Sometimes in a day they run out two times to walk their children back and forth to public school, and then they have to take them to Chinese school, too. I know some women, if they have quite a few children, make as many as six trips a day. When the Chinese school is over they all go home together for dinner. Now downtown nobody will hire a woman like that, who wants to go out of the factory so many times a day. But these women have to help their husbands support the family. They don't fit the union scale, but here we can help them earn something.

Edna also spoke of the value of letting older women work in the Chinatown shops. Although many of them put in just two or three hours a day, the work and contact with other people helps them to overcome feelings of depression and futility as they grow older. She described a recent case:

I've been teaching this woman about fifty years old who just came over from Hong Kong. Her husband died and then her daughter brought her over here. Since her daughter ran a grocery store she told her mother, "Now, mother, we have all the money we need. You don't have to work any more. You just stay home and relax." But after a few months she noticed her mother was beginning to lose a lot of weight. Then she got sick. She told them she had dreams of her husband every night. Even though her daughter gave her everything she needed, she said, she felt very lonely. "I can't speak English and I don't have any friends. Sometimes I just feel like I'm in a prison here." So the daughter brought the old woman to my place and asked me to just let her try anything. I tried to think what would be best. I told her mother, "OK. Now you just sew straight seams." I taught her how to do that and now she works very fast. Very fast! Of course, sometimes I don't have that many straight seams to do, only one or two hours of work a day. But she's very happy and she's gained at least ten pounds.

Chuck Lai, an active member of his own family association, stressed that the qualities of loyalty and collective responsibility, especially between family members and relatives, were still central in Chinatown where incoming immigrants faced tremendous difficulties in finding work. He claimed that a feeling of mutual responsibility underlay the employment of women in Chinatown garment shops:

Suppose there is a thirty-year-old woman, an immigrant who just came from Hong Kong. Her husband sent for her and she can't speak English. Now suppose her husband makes a little money, but not enough for the family, so she goes out and looks for a job. She finds it's no good, she can't get a job anywhere. She begins to feel very worried. Then her husband comes to me. OK, now downtown they would put a woman like that through a test for one or two weeks before they hire her. If she doesn't suit the job, she's out of luck. But in Chinatown we don't operate like that. In Chinatown, we have a feeling that friendship is worth more than money. If you ask me for something, and I won't do a favor for you, I feel ashamed. Especially if this man is my relative and I don't do my part, I feel ashamed. He'll walk all over town and tell my other cousins, "Gee, Chuck didn't help me. What kind of cousin is he?" Maybe if I hire this woman, I can't afford to pay her two dollars an hour, but the old policy is that we have to help each other, no matter how hard it is.

Another woman contractor spoke of the strong sense of loyalty she felt to the women in her shop, most of whom she had known for over twenty years. She told us that ten years ago, when she made a major decision to shift the factory's line of work from men's overalls to ladies' sportswear, she did so only after obtaining the consent of each of her em-

ployees. Edna Fong described the relation between Chinatown owners and their workers as that of sisters.

I treat them just like my sisters. We're very together. I think
in most Chinatown shops they are very together. Maybe some
contractors are bossy, I don't know. The world is so big,
right? But mostly they are very friendly. They sew right
alongside the girls and they are very close. My children help
me a lot in the factory, you know. They like to play together
with my workers' children and sometimes I hear them saying,
"Oh, your Mommy's working with my Mommy," and we all
feel very close together. That's why I don't think the union
can ever win over the girls in Chinatown. We are more like
a family, not like a boss and worker, you know. If I hear one
of them has a husband who needs work and I hear of a job,
I tell them. I help them to find a very good job for their husband. Or, say we have an order that is very rushed. I don't
boss anybody. We plan ahead of time to take care of all the
children. One lady says, "Okay, my older daughter is off
today. Some of you can bring your children to my house and
she'll take care of them and we can all rush the garments
out." Whenever there's a rush order we all help each other
out like that and then we can get the order out very fast.

Edna told us that the women in her shop got along so well
with each other that they even spent time together after
they got off work. A few months earlier several women from
the shop had gone out very early in the morning to wait in
line and buy all the seamstresses in the factory tickets to a
special performance of Chinese opera. Every one of the contractors scoffed at the idea that huge, unionized factories
could reproduce the intimate and humanistic atmosphere of
the Chinatown shops.

But perhaps unconsciously, the contractors' glowing picture of the Chinatown shops also revealed a keen awareness
of their own position of power in the community vis-à-vis
the large numbers of women who needed employment. We
were surprised to hear this expressed quite bluntly by
Chuck Lai when he became caught up in an argument justi-
fying the technically illegal practice of hiring overage
women in the Chinatown shops:

Now if you beg me to hire you, that's on your own conscience. In this industry, you have to be a fast hand. If you're

old, your hand can't move fast. You are not a qualified
worker. If you go downtown anyplace at all, they won't hire
you at this age. Unfortunately, we have a lot of old ladies
like this in Chinatown. What can you do about it? The unions
say they should go on welfare. But they feel ashamed. They
want to work for themselves. But can you get anyone downtown to hire them? Not a single one. Just because I give
them work, then, I don't have to pull an extra dollar out of
my pocket for them every hour, right?

Not long after she had finished her story about the old lady
who sewed straight seams, Edna Fong revealed a similar in-
tuitive understanding of the Chinatown labor market when
she elaborated on her dreams for the future of the community's garment industry:

The best thing is to have our own union here in Chinatown.
Then we could have a very big factory. You know, the city
only lets us have twenty-five machines in our factories in
Chinatown, and that's not fair. That's not enough to do
section work. We need a very big factory and then we can
hire more and more people from Hong Kong, because most
of them don't speak English. We can even give the older
people work, because they just do one part, you know, like
straight seams, day and night. In Hong Kong and Taiwan
they have corporations like that. If all the contractors here
could get together, maybe we could get work from the government or some place like that.

Contractors, moreover, consistently sidestepped direct questions about the wages earned by the women in their shops.
Many adroitly avoided answering the question by simply
stating the state minimum wage. "How much per hour does
your average worker make?" we asked Edna Fong. "It has
to be $1.65," said she.

Invariably, however, members of the Chinese Garment
Contractors' Association were unperturbed by any slips
which might shed light on their own motivations, and included in their discussions a scathing condemnation of the
viciousness and corruption of the union. They firmly held
that workers in Chinatown had nothing but fear and mistrust
of the unions and absolutely no desire to join. They claimed
that the methods of the union campaign were unquestion-

able proof that it was interested only in adding the dues of Chinatown workers to its coffers. If this could not be obtained, its next goal was to destroy the tiny Chinatown shops which eat up close to half of the city's garment contracts and compete with the union's own factories. Richard Lim, an aggressive young garment contractor who established his business in San Francisco only four years ago when he came from Hong Kong, told us, "The unions have seen too many industries leave San Francisco in the last few years. They lose so many members every year that they're desperate to get control, and the dues, of the people here." Contractors ridiculed the suggestion that union organizers could rival their understanding of the needs of Chinatown women. "What about the English problem?" Richard asked. "If they zone the shops out of here and force all the workers to unionize, what about the English problem? Downtown factories don't want to hire a worker and then have to explain and explain. It's too slow. But if we work together in our shops here, we get the same work done." Edna claimed the unions had no concern whatever for the hundreds of women who would be permanently out of work if there were unionization:

Now when I was negotiating with the union, I asked them, "If we join the union, can you guarantee that everyone here has work, even the slow girls? Even the mothers who have to keep taking breaks to care for their children?" Whenever I ask them something like that, they just skip the question. They say, "A worker has to meet the union requirements for speed and skill." I say, "What about the old women over fifty in our shops?" and they skip the question. They just say, "They can go on welfare." So I say, "OK. Then you're not really thinking about our problems. All you want is our money."

Contractors gave vivid descriptions of threatening tactics used by union organizers in the Chinatown shops. Richard Lim claimed that the union had hired young people who charged into the shops as if they were fighting a war, telling the women to sign, sign, sign. "The women can't understand what they're saying. They have no idea what's going on. This really frightened them." However, one contractor who had related a dramatic story of being beaten in the shop by a group of union organizers was embarrassed when we later asked to release the story in the book and asked that the interview be withdrawn.

THE WORKERS' SIDE

It was not until one year later, usually after we had become friends with a relative or a family member, that we were able to have frank and relaxed discussions with garment workers in their homes. We found the most striking characteristic of the women we met was one which had been suggested by the difficulty we had approaching them: their isolation. From Mrs. Yu, the fifty-year-old resident of a Washington Street hotel who went down to the factory whenever she needed money, sewed buttonholes for fifty cents an hour, and never would have dreamed of being ungrateful for it, to Mrs. Chan, wife of a dishwasher, mother of four children, and recent immigrant from Hong Kong, the lives of the women we talked with were characterized by an almost complete lack of contact with society outside Chinatown. The impact of the language barrier in continually obscuring the views and opinions of garment workers themselves was brought home to us by the fact that eleven out of twelve of these women spoke no English. "I think my mom would have welcomed a union if she could have understood the organizers when they came in," Emily Young told us when we visited her family in Ping Yuen. "But if you don't know the language you never know what's going on. And the employer is usually the one who interprets for them because the employer, simply by the fact that he has to negotiate downtown, is usually someone who knows a fair amount of English." Only one seamstress spoke to us in fairly confident English about the pros and cons of unionization. A capable woman who had been born in Chinatown, drove her own car, and after twenty years of work in a garment factory had invested in buildings in Oakland, she told us the obvious, that she was an exception among women in the shops. Since her husband ran a successful business in Chinatown, work as seamstress had never been a necessity for her. She spoke some English, there had been other alternatives open to her, but she chose the garment shops because they were nearby and convenient. She wanted to earn pocket money and gain a certain sense of independence in her own life. (In the Human Rights Commission survey, less than twenty-five percent of the interviewees fit into the same category as this woman, as workers whose "spouses' occupations" were such that there was no real need for supplemental income.) The rest of the women had husbands who were restaurant and grocery workers, janitors, or retired laborers. Most were women who had originally come from small Sze Yup villages, had little formal education, and spoke no English. Four were illiterate. Since coming to America their lives had been circumscribed by Chinatown's male-dominated society and had centered on obligations to their husbands, their children, and relatives to whom they still sent remittances in Hong Kong. They saw the garment shops as an unquestioned part of their daily lives, and had little sense that there were other possibilities. If anything, a feeling of gratitude and loyalty to those who had provided them with work was, as the factory owners themselves had predicted, prevalent. It was the rare worker, usually one who no longer depended on the Chinatown shops for a living, who perceived any danger in this. "I think those women in the shops never had a chance to speak for themselves," Jenny Lew's husband told us. "They were always too scared to say what they thought."

Among the seamstresses we spoke with, it was the minority, those who were no longer connected with the Chinatown shops, in any way, who expressed a sense of dissatisfaction uninhibitedly. Jennie Lew, of course, spoke openly, and Emily Young's mother, whose health during her life as a garment worker had been so undermined that she was now unable to work, felt a bitterness which Emily communicated vividly as her mother sat beside her on the living room couch.

My mom sometimes says it's really amazing how the Chinese exploit themselves. The ones who are lucky enough to own a sewing factory or something, just go on and make more and more money for themselves, and the Chinese workers

can't do much. If they complain, well, the boss can always
kick them out. They don't even have to do it directly, they
can do it indirectly, like by making the worker do her sewing
all over, and by complaining about every single stitch. My
mom used to work at a sewing factory. Now her health is
failing so she can't work at all. But she always says that,
well, some of the bosses are good, but a lot of Chinese
bosses have favoritism. They play of lot of favorites, and if
they like you, even if your work's not perfect they won't
make you do it over. They'll just say, "Fine, fine. Why don't
you take another batch and do it while you're home on your
free time?" Which is supposed to be illegal, of course. At any
rate, whenever you're out of favor in a garment factory, the
boss will always tell you your stitching has to be done over.
Which really hurts, because even if they say they're paying
by the hour, most factories pay by the piece.

When my mom was in good health she used to be able to
sew pretty quickly and turn in batch after batch. But after
a while people talk about you and there's too much jealousy.
People who get ahead are looked down on after a while.
My mom has worked in about five or six factories and she's
come across some good bosses, too. But a lot of times, no
matter how hard the employer tries to be fair, the other employees will try to hurt you. They tell the boss this and that,
fill the boss's ear. When the employee they don't like steps
out to make her dinner, everybody starts talking. "Oh, we
can't stand her, she sews too fast," or "What a relief, she's
gone for a while," things like that. So after a while you get
fed up, go to another factory, and make new friends there.
Then if you work too fast, you run into the same thing. I
know some people say the factories have a family spirit and
all that, and maybe it's true. As long as you don't sew too
fast! If you're chummy and talk to everyone and sew about
one stitch an hour, maybe you'll do okay.

The attitudes of a woman regularly employed in the
Chinatown shops were perhaps most typically expressed by
Mrs. Mark. At the age of sixty, and after thirty-five years as
a garment worker, she lives with her husband and her
daughter's family of five in a two-story house on Powell
Street. Mrs. Mark is a very thin woman with white hair, and
while she speaks she looks at us through thick glasses. She
answers questions in very brief sentences. She began sewing
overalls as soon as she got here, when she was twenty-five.

"I was so surprised when I got here, people were just working all the time. I asked my boss, 'Why does everybody work so hard in America?' He just laughed." In a few years, she became a mother, and began raising her family in a tenement building on Grant Avenue. She used to go down to the shop at six in the morning in those days, she remembers one of the children helping to carry work she finished the night before. Yes, sewing at home was already illegal then, that's why they had to take it down so early in the morning, so no one would see. But how could she have worked in the shop all day? The children were too young. At the same time, the family needed money. Her husband couldn't earn enough sewing overalls, just a few dollars a day, and they had to keep sending remittances to a sick uncle in Canton. If they wanted to have the children properly dressed, or get a refrigerator some day, she had to work. She says she was very grateful to the owner of the factory for giving her things to sew even when she couldn't do them in the shop.

Mrs. Mark has been working in her present shop for the last ten years. "Oh, I'm still a fast enough hand to get a good income from sewing," she says. We ask her how much. "It comes out to about a dollar an hour most days." But she tells us her husband had a stroke six weeks ago; since then, she hasn't been able to work at all. We ask her if she could have gotten higher pay if she joined a union. "Only a little bit higher." She says she doesn't have strong feelings about the union, she prefers not to talk about it. "He can't pay wages like union wages because then the manufacturer would take the business away and we would have no work at all. It's very hard for a Chinese shop to get business, you know." How does she feel about her boss? She feels he's quite fair. All the women in the shop have worked there for a long time and feel friendly with him. He's loyal to his old workers. "When my husband got sick, he told me not to worry. My machine will be there waiting for me whenever I want to go back."

Younger immigrant women, who now compose one-third to one-half of the labor force in Chinatown factories, expressed attitudes which were basically similar to those of older workers like Mrs. Mark. Tenacity and ambition for the future of their families was a marked trait in many of these women, tempered by a realization of the limitations of their situation as non-English-speaking immigrants. Mei Wong, a mother of five living in a poorly lit three-bedroom apartment on Grant Avenue which she rents from her cousin at $125 a month, described the difficulties both she and her husband experienced when they first began looking for work in 1969. The only job her husband could find which did not require English was that of cook in Daly City, a suburb of San Francisco. To supplement his income of five hundred dollars a month, she too took a job which did not require English: sewing. After working in a downtown shop for a month, Mei returned to Chinatown, which she found more comfortable because she could speak Chinese. The flexible hours permitted her to care for her children.

When I first got here I worked downtown for one month in a Koret factory. I prefer to work for Koret because the wages are higher, but I have too many children to look after. Koret has shorter hours and better pay. $2.40 an hour. In Chinatown, $2.00 an hour is the best. But also, I got sick after I worked in Koret for one month. There is more tension in Koret and if you slow down you get fired. In Chinatown you can do as you like. I work whenever I have free time, about seven or eight hours a day.

Mei told us that she works six days a week and earns about $300 a month. With her husband's income of $500 a month, they have just about enough to cover expenses: rent, $125 a month, $400 a month for food and other living expenses, $125 a month remittance to her parents in Hong Kong, and $100 a month for unexpected expenses. She says her biggest worry is that someone in the family will get sick or have an accident, "then all the savings and work will be gone."

Like Mrs. Mark, Mei Wong emphasizes the friendly atmosphere in her shop. She feels her boss is a good person. The women in the shop had close relations with her because many of them are her relatives or friends:

She is a good boss and I like her. She came to America when she was very young and she worked very hard, so now she owns her own factory. She and her husband work right along with us. Of course, I don't know how all the others feel, because only a few of them are immigrants like myself. The older ones have been here a long time and they speak Sze Yup together. But most of them are relatives or very good friends with her. We all get along very well and help each other in the shop.

CHINATOWN AND DOWNTOWN

The repeated failure of our efforts to obtain interviews on the Chinatown question with manufacturing firms downtown revealed their conscious policy to keep the situation as much as possible out of the public eye. Outside observers in the Federal Wages and Hours Enforcement Division, the union, and the city's Human Rights Commission corroborated that this had been a consistent practice. The commission's employment representative, who discovered the case of twenty unpaid seamstresses at the Hoi Ming factory, told us that the shop's contracting firm had privately settled the claims of all the women in the shop against the owner in order to ward off the publicity that would have been aroused by a suit. The Hoi Ming factory itself had been forced to close its doors soon after. We were told that this technique of private settlement was a standard practice of prime contracting firms, although in public they declared they had no responsibility for conditions in Chinatown shops and were completely independent from them. Assured of maintaining power over the Chinatown subcontractors by their silent threat of taking contracts away, manufacturers tolerated vicious attacks on the Chinatown sub-contractors which were believed by an ignorant public. The attacks helped to blow up and distort the secondary conflict within Chinatown, while distracting attention from the primary conflict in which the downtown firms themselves played the determining role. The Chinatown subcontractors who depended on the firms for business thus became their scapegoats as well, taking on themselves the blame for all the injustice and malpractice of the Chinatown garment industry.

The factors which perpetuate the existence of Chinatown as a low-income ghetto within contemporary San Francisco emerge nowhere more clearly than in the garment industry.

Whatever the problems which arose out of their relationship in Chinatown, the statements of both owners and workers reinforced each other in a single theme: that the garment industry was essential to survival. While women like Mrs. Mark or Mei Wong tended to sense this in personal terms, owners spoke of the garment industry in terms of the welfare of the community as a whole. Edna Fong, for example, described how she convinced the Six Companies to back the contractors in their fight against the union:

I went to the Board of Directors and told them, "You know, if everyone doesn't come out and help us, you won't have any of this industry left." They said they didn't understand what I meant and they asked me to explain the whole situation. I said, "The union wants to zone the garment industry out of here." But they still didn't respond. Then I told them, "OK. Try to imagine what it would be like if two-thirds of the women here had no work. Do you think Chinatown will have business like it has now? Do you think the grocery stores would have business? The restaurants? Nobody would have money and they'll have to go on welfare. Then how will you gentlemen feel about that? You must at least have a wife or a cousin or somebody in the factory." Then they said, "Oh, yes, this is very important!"

Through the garment industry, which employs the single largest working force in Chinatown, both workers and owners recognized that a critical source of Chinatown's economic subsistence lay outside, in the firms which gave contracts to individual shops. In this sense, all felt themselves as a part of a larger unit, the Chinese community, which was dependent on forces outside for its existence. These were the factors which ultimately determined conditions within. This awareness was repeatedly revealed in the statements of workers such as Mrs. Mark, who admitted that she received low pay but excused her boss of responsibility for this. "It's very hard for a Chinese shop to get business, you know." Emily Young saw the garment industry as integrally tied to the perpetuation of Chinatown.

"You can understand a lot about this place from the garment industry," she said after our interview with her mother. "People don't live here because they want to. It's the ones in a rut who live here. They come over, they don't speak English, the man gets a job in a restaurant and the woman in a garment factory down here. In a few years, they think they'll learn English, save some money, and move out. Everyone talks about that. But you look at someone like my mother, most of the women in Ping Yuen, they've lived in Chinatown ten or twenty years. They earn just enough to keep going, they've hardly saved at all. They don't get exposed to English at work, they're too tired to study at night. The job they got to tide them over ends up as a lifetime occupation. It's like a vicious cycle. If they didn't have the garment industry, or those restaurant jobs, a lot of people in Chinatown wouldn't make it. But as long as they have those jobs, they'll never get out of here."

For their part, owners spoke of the constant difficulty of getting fair and steady contracts. They told us that almost all apparel companies which do business in Chinatown do so as secondary contractors. The regular, primary contracts of the firms are to factories downtown; only surplus orders and excess work in busy seasons is sent to Chinatown, where it is contracted at lower rates. They mentioned long, idle periods when there was not enough work to open shop. All expressed anxiety that their contracting firms might move away, particularly to the Southwest where Mexican labor was cheap. They told us that in the last campaign, even the union had finally admitted that it was the prime contractors, not the sub-contractors, who were the real obstacle. Richard Lim, who had kept clippings during the union struggle, showed us the article recording the ILGWU's decision to drop the zone-out effort. The ILGWU "acknowledged the economic hardship of the sub-contractors" and felt it was necessary to "join forces with them to fight against the prime contractors who suppress sub-contractors with low wages." Dick, and most owners, estimate that the total yearly value of business done by all the Chinatown shops was six million dollars. "That's why I've been fighting this thing so hard. We depend on that money." He pointed out that the survey done in 1969 estimated that the wholesale value of these goods was eighteen million dollars, three times what the manufacturers pay for them when they get them from the Chinatown shops. "And then the price probably goes up, say, another one hundred percent when they go out to the American consumer. But we depend on that six million dollars." Both owners and workers in the garment industry rationalized the depressed level of their income hierarchy as the price for economic survival.

Despite their powerful position vis-à-vis workers within the community, we found that shop owners who rise above middle class by nationwide criteria are exceptions. Kim Wah Lee, when he was being prosecuted for doctoring Jennie Lew's time cards, produced an income tax statement of $20,000 for the year 1967–1968. He was an owner of several shops. We were unsuccessful in getting exact figures from other employers and even from the city tax records, which classify the garment shops as extensions of their contracting firms, rather than independent businesses. But two owners we spoke with lived in modest homes in middle income residential districts outside Chinatown, the others lived in spacious apartments in Chinatown and the extended areas. Perhaps the most striking fact was that all but one of these owners had formerly worked either as garment workers or manual laborers themselves. During our last visit with him, Chuck Lai spoke personally of the process by which he had become a garment contractor, a process which seemed to symbolize the continuing tenuousness of the existence of the Chinatown garment shops in America's economy.

I worked as a waiter for five years and then as a clerk in a grocery store. I decided to start the business with my wife and some friends in 1952. At that time I didn't have very much capital. But we could get secondhand machines downtown and we didn't even have to make a down payment on them. We got them for one hundred dollars apiece, they were so old, and we didn't have to give a darn thing in down payment. You could begin paying for them whenever you started to make money on the shop. I think in all I put down about five hundred dollars to start the shop, and my partners put in about the same. The first year we didn't make any money. In fact, we lost money because we had to pay the rent. My two partners couldn't afford to keep going, so I took over the whole thing. But I still didn't earn much, because it was so hard to get work, the manufacturers didn't supply us with much, you know, and I just had to go downtown from door to door asking who needed a contractor.

When one of them said yes, he'd cite me a price per dozen . . . and I had to figure out in my head how much I can give to the workers and how much percentage I make. You've got to do that, or you'll lose out! About eighteen years ago, the percent was very little, maybe twenty-five percent. Even now, in Chinatown, we can't have mass production, you see. We don't have big shops. Now there's a law that requires Chinatown shops to have under twenty-five machines, but even before the limit we had small shops because we didn't have much capital. We couldn't afford a bigger place and there wasn't much space in Chinatown. Also, even if you had a bigger place, you're hardly going to get enough work to keep it going. For instance, if you have a hundred workers, where are you going to get enough work to supply them? So we are not mass production. We are just family style.

Unfortunately, all my generation doesn't have very much education. We depend on this work to make enough money to get along. Even now, I have to work as many hours as my workers. If I just sat there and didn't do anything I wouldn't last. So I sew, I make buttonholes, I do pinking and over-stitching. If I didn't do some sewing myself, I wouldn't even make the volume to cover my overhead. I even sweep up the place myself to save money on a janitor.

It's different downtown. They have fifty or eighty machines and they make a lot by doing a big volume. They can give hours to the worker every day, but we don't have work the whole year round. Maybe eight or ten months out of the year is average. So you don't get rich. But I try to do the best for Chinatown because we depend on this money. If you keep that six million dollars here, well, Chinatown may be old, but we have our schools and our stores. We can't buy steak and all that, but we can buy our fish and pork, our oranges and lemons. But if you cut this money out of Chinatown, I won't even be able to buy a lemon! Each individual and each family is going to be hurt so much we have to think of a way to protect them. That's why so far the union hasn't been able to do any damage. But if we don't get together to protect our own interest, one of these days it's going to be pretty bad for Chinatown. Maybe if we can keep getting this income, then the younger generation can get a good education and can do better than working in the sewing shop.

13. Ping Yuen: *The Projects*

Constructed between 1951 and 1961 as the first public housing made available to the Chinese community, the three Ping
Yuen project complexes sprawl over two blocks of Chinatown, their upper stories rising conspicuously above the
older tenements. In contrast to the other buildings, the
projects are still thought of as "new" in Chinatown, although in the earliest constructed complexes chipped window casements, fading walls, and the caking earth of the
courtyards already reveal the passage of twenty years of
wear. Still, the four hundred housing units at Ping Yuen are
the most sought after in the community. Their low rent,
adjusted to income, and proximity to the center of Chinatown make them ideal for non-English-speaking workers
who earn their living there. Since demand for the apartments so much exceeds supply, older immigrant families,
often those of "paper sons" who brought in wives in the
fifties, tend to predominate in Ping Yuen. More recent immigrants, settling temporarily in the crowded tenements, may
remain on waiting lists as many as five years before they are
able to move in. Despite distinctions in their length of stay
in America (although these are often made much of among
themselves), however, the occupational status of those who
live in Ping Yuen is uniform. Almost without exception male
heads of families fall into one of four employment categories: janitor, waiter, store clerk, or cook. An outstanding
characteristic of Ping Yuen among housing projects in the
city is that invariably the wives of these men work, too.
Usually they are employed in sewing factories in Chinatown. Since the salaries of the men are low, even with the
additional earnings of their wives, the total family income
will remain within the official limits set for federal housing.

(Maximum income limits for tenants at Ping Yuen run from $4,000 a year for a single person to $7,300 for a family of eight.) Because these occupations and income brackets correspond to those which are average for the community, families at Ping Yuen may be seen as typical of working families in Chinatown today.

In the absence of both parents from home during the greater part of each working day, family life in the projects manifests a striking departure from that centered around the small businesses which predominated in Chinatown in the past. As soon as the first child is old enough to take care of itself (or younger brothers or sisters), mothers take on full-time employment which, though it may allow for several brief trips home during working hours, nevertheless from then on separates them from their families during the major part of their daily activity. While their parents are gone, children go to school, but also spend many free hours in late afternoons, on weekends, and in the summer, amusing themselves with children from other project families who gather on the playground areas in front of the buildings. In contrast with children growing up in family shops, therefore, the lives of these children are relatively unstructured and unsupervised by parents, lack a sense of participation in family effort, and rapidly begin to center around peer group relations and the activities which they share with "the other kids." Fatigue of the two parents when they return from work, and the fact that they themselves have shared no common activity during the day and may have little to talk about, further weakens the attraction of the nuclear family unit. "We all come home and have dinner at night," one older Ping Yuen adolescent described. "But no one would think of talking about what they did that day. My mother washes the dishes and then, she's tired, so she goes right to bed. It's like a bunch of strangers sitting at the same table." On Sundays, even if parents are lucky enough to have holidays on the same day, family projects or outings are rare. After six days of work at ten-hour jobs, adults prefer to spend the day resting; lack of a car and limited funds usually preclude the possibility of going far out of Chinatown anyway. A similar inertia tends to curtail social life outside the family. Casual visits are exchanged with friends who live nearby, but there is little time to participate in the activities of family associations and clubs, and workers tend to regard them apathetically. "The Six Companies? My parents don't even talk about that," Sharon Yu told us. "Although they do sort of know about people in the Six Companies as big shots—'this big shot did this, this big shot did that'—they don't really relate to it personally." Children describe their parents as being "passive" and pessimistic about what can be accomplished through participation in community organizations. "My father goes to the family association banquet once a year, but he'd never express an opinion there because he'd figure what's the use," said one teenage boy. This lack of active social life, combined with a scarcity of adult friends and a tendency for apartment-dwelling families not to have older relatives living with them, all reinforce a sense of starkness and isolation in the nuclear family life.

Increasing barriers to communication in the family as children grow older is another common theme in project life. Unlike the small stores where the habitual presence of parents speaking and giving directions kept children constantly in contact with Chinese, ability to speak the language weakens more quickly in project children once they enter school and simultaneously find that their mothers are at home for fewer and fewer hours of the day. The growing language barrier, combined with the fact that shared interests among members of the family are already rare, minimizes family conversation. Not infrequently, children speak of their parents as being taciturn and withdrawn at home. "I haven't talked to my father intimately for a long time," an eighteen-year-old City College student told us. "He's kind of aloof at home and we try not to talk to him unless we have to. He'll watch TV or listen to the ballgame at night, or sometimes he'll just sit in his room doing nothing for hours. But he won't have much to do with us." Mutual awareness of an inevitably widening cultural gap and disparity of values also discourages communication. Although the practice of sending children to Chinese school persists in the majority of project parents, it is only in exceptional cases that attendance lasts beyond three or four years. In the meantime, observation of Chinese holidays or rituals in the home often becomes haphazard, with parents making little effort to explain the meaning of what they do to their children. Eventually, some parents even abandon the effort to enforce discipline at home. "You'll hear my father say, 'Well, just don't disgrace yourself' or 'Just don't forget that you're Chinese,' but that's about all. Neither of my parents have ever been able to control the young children and by now they're resigned to it," the same City College student observed. "Sometimes my father will get upset and try to force something. But usually he just keeps his distance and tells them what they do is their own affair." When children reach adolescence, a sharpened sense of the barrenness and functionality of communication at home often emerges in the form of intolerant criticism. Home is described as "boring" and "hard to take" because "there's never anything interesting going on." Teenagers, too, then become increasingly withdrawn at home. Chances to visit at a girlfriend's house may be eagerly sought by high school girls. Less studious adolescent boys spend more and more of their time "just hanging out" on Jackson Street, in coffee houses and smokeshops in Chinatown, with clubs or gangs of other friends. It is in part these gangs (although Chinese-speaking gangs of very recent immigrants have played the dominant role) which have been responsible for the recent wave of juvenile crime in Chinatown.

For the overwhelming majority of project children, however, school and intense efforts to achieve academic success rapidly fill the void left by family life. Indeed, whatever the qualitative differences in their lives, working families in Chinatown today maintain the same great emphasis on education which characterized the small business families. As in the family society, parents explicitly or unconsciously rationalize their own difficulties and hard work in terms of the future of their children and tend to communicate this to them. The observation that it is only with a college degree that children will be able to avoid the type of low-income, low-status jobs which they themselves have is made habitually. "My father feels a lot of bitterness about his own life.

He feels he was never fully educated, and this is why he was never able to get a good job," a high school senior said. "He keeps telling us, 'There's a time and place for everything.' He was born in the wrong time, and the wrong place —because there was no such thing as free school in China— so he never got an education. He's always saying the time and place are right for us now." As their own frustration with the stark and work-dominated life at home mounts, children identify with and internalize their parents' driving concern for education as "the only way out." For some, devotion to studies plays a dual role by also providing a means of shutting out the family, a counterpart to the peer group activities of those less academically inclined. "He played a lot and we never thought he was very serious when he was younger," a college boy half jokingly described his high school brother. "He changed in the first summer of junior high. Now, we'll ask him to go out or go to a movie, but he won't do anything. He doesn't seem to have any friends and he's always working in his room. Really, for the last three or four years the only thing I've known about my little brother is that he gets good grades." Although such diligence clearly represents an extreme, it is something close to it which accounts for the college entrance of nearly ninety percent of the Ping Yuen children—the sons and daughters of waiters and cooks and seamstresses—a statistic which has given the project a special reputation among low-income housing in the city. "In most projects you find a lot of people hanging around at home," one Housing Authority employee visiting Ping Yuen commented. "Here, as soon as they finish high school they have to get out. If they can't get into college, which is rare, they'll get a job. But nobody just loafs around or drops out."

SHARON YU, 20

An outstanding record in high school won her several awards and a scholarship to the university where she is now preparing for law school. She recalls her childhood in Ping Yuen simply and matter-of-factly.

Well, my memory as far as the earliest years of my life goes isn't a very good memory, but I'll say whatever I remember. Before we moved into the Ping Yuen projects we lived in a house on Sacramento Street, I don't remember it too well. The Sacramento house had something like a public bath, where the people on the floor would use the same bathtub, and the facilities were very communal. So when the Ping Yuen projects were completed and my family found out they were accepted to move in, we were all really relieved.

So I grew up in the projects. One thing nice about it was that there were a lot of children my age, and you could play with them and talk with them, there was a huge yard where you could play on the swing and the slide, so it was like a small playground for us. I think it was a good place to grow up in, with a lot of people around you. Of course with a lot of Chinese families, and in the project you can see this, too, both parents work almost all day and a lot of times the kids are on their own. So when we had this playground to go to, you had some recreational outlet instead of just having to go out on the streets or stay at home and mess around with the stove.

I remember during the summer my brothers, I have three brothers and two sisters, every day during the summer we would go to the library early in the morning, to the Chinatown branch, and check out six books. That was the maximum you could check out at one time. We had these library cards—it was before there were machines to stamp on the date—and the librarian would have to record by hand when the book was due and use a rubber stamp, then when you used up a whole card you would get a new one. So we used to have a little race, and every day we would check out six books at the beginning of the day, read all day, and finish them by evening so the next day we could all go back to the library together. The aim was to outdo each other and see who could get through the most cards the fastest. But we'd always end up about the same because we all had the same limit of six books a day.

So I grew up in the projects and I went to school. Although I don't remember exactly what I learned in kindergarten or first grade, all of a sudden around fourth grade I got very interested in what I could learn on my own, rather than what was required of me in the classroom. I don't know, it seems like it was just so sudden that I realized everything you did in the classroom wasn't all there was to learn. So, all through the fifth and sixth grade I kept up this interest, I always liked to read books, you know, and I used to go to the library every day. I remember reading a lot of animal books, Freddie books like Freddie the Detective, a lot of fairy tales and folk tales. I think we checked out a few Chinese books but that was not too much because they didn't have too many there.

Most of the time I was in grammar school we were living on the fifth floor, and my father had been working as a waiter in a restaurant in Chinatown. At one point the owner of this restaurant lost his lease or something and my father had to look for a new job . . . well, that was kind of hard. Mother kept on working in the sewing factory, while he looked, and for a year or so he had to work quite far away, but then he found a job in the financial district, which was closer to Chinatown, and since then he's been there.

I think a lot of what kept my parents going at the time, and what they used to tell us, was, well, if you work hard you'll always get what you need. You have to put in the amount of effort required, you know, work hard and don't play too much. In fact, I think my mother overemphasized the need to work and to study. She used to point me out as an example and tell the rest of the family to look at me, which I really hated, because it's no way to bring up a family, comparing your kids to each other. It just creates a lot of conflicts.

But, you see, the Chinese are very competitive. They like to outdo each other, even in education. I know this was true especially in Chinese school. In the Chinese Central High School, for instance, a lot of the people in our class were very good in Chinese. Particularly the ones who came from Hong Kong; technically they were far ahead of us American-born, and there was always this latent feud between us. And whenever an American-born did better than a Chinese-born boy, you better watch out (laughs). In fact, one of the American-born girls in the class used to hang around with me a lot and have me do some of her homework for her. Of course, I would just do it, without thinking anything about it, but one day suddenly I found she didn't want to have anything to do with me any more. I couldn't figure out why until someone told me, "Well, that's because you did better than her." We had just gotten our report cards, you see, and everyone in the class had gotten a rank. It seemed as though I had ended up higher than her and after that she just didn't talk to me again.

I think it's that same kind of competitiveness that made my mother emphasize work so much and always push us to do well. When I think about it now, I wish she had taught us to spread ourselves in different areas more. Spend some time on books, some time with friends, having a good time— to be well-rounded.

Of course, we did play a lot of sports with kids in the playground. And when we were small my mom used to teach us Chinese dances and songs. I remember there was one melody she used to hum a lot when we were young. It's funny but I was listening to the radio this summer and I heard something and I thought, "Wow, this sounds familiar! I wonder where I've heard it." It was Dvorak's "New World" Symphony, that's the one she used to hum.

She used to hum that and quite a few tunes and teach them to us when we were very small. But then after we'd gone through about third grade or so she didn't spend that much time with us any more; because she herself spent most of her time at work as soon as we were old enough to be on our own. And gradually we'd forget the songs because we were trying to become Westernized and catch on to the language. You know, I didn't know any English when I started school. I had to learn it on my own. And then, since it had sort of created a problem, my not being able to communicate with the teachers and all that, I thought it would be kind of beneficial to the rest of my family to pick up English, so we all began speaking English to each other at home. And we never sang her Chinese tunes after that. So the other day, after a long, long while I heard the "New World" and it sounded so familiar I thought, "What is it?" I even asked my mom, I didn't know. But for her, with all the orchestration and everything, she couldn't pick it out either. She didn't know what it was. Then I started humming the melody and she said, "Oh yes, I used to hum that, you know, to you people when I was taking care of you when you were small." And I said, "Oh yeah, I remember that now."

JAMES SHEN, 18

A student at City College. His mother has recently been pressuring him to enter the business administration course. When he saw his interview, he said, "Yep, this is the down to earth story."

I was really a bad kid, I guess not in the sense of being bad like it is now, but just mischievous. Which was typical for a project kid, it was more or less the same with my brothers also. We would play with my uncle's family, they had eight kids, and we would roam around the whole projects, playing hide and seek, chasing cats, and things like that. I was really clumsy at that time, and I was always falling off fences, breaking a lot of things, once I set fire to the sofa. My mother had this dusting thing, this Chinese dusting brush, and she would always use that to whip you on the hands and legs, and she hit me quite often because I was so mischievous. She was working in the sewing factory and I recall, one time when she was trying to go to English school, she started using a rope to keep us out of trouble. And she was pretty smart, too, because she used to put us in one room, tie up the door and tie it to the door of another room so we couldn't get out. She just locked us up in that room and then she went to school.

After I was about ten I didn't play around the projects any more. My father started working at Annabelle's Candy Company, and he joined the union, and ever since then, you know, he got pretty good pay. I mean, he was making five to six thousand dollars which at that time was quite a bit. So they kicked us out of the project because he was making too much money. We moved about a mile away, onto Union Street, and then we didn't live right inside Chinatown any more.

In elementary school I was always the mischievous type at school, too. I was always hanging around with the boys. At that time they didn't really have hoods, but I was one of the roughest guys in the school. I beat up on kids once in a while and all that. I never did well in elementary school, and in seventh grade I had a C average, I recall. But in eighth grade that was the big difference. I don't know why, but all of a sudden I got all Bs and one or two Cs. I guess I was developing, I was getting older, a little more mature. I was getting into less fights, I went to the library, I was studying more. I think in the low nine I got all As and only one C in English.

Maybe it was because I started to feel like I had a goal then. My grades went from C to B and then I got some As. Wow, I'd never seen As before until the ninth grade. So then I got more or less on an ego trip. I had my athletic block, my service block, my music block. I got pretty involved in the choir. So I was playing the game. I was trying to succeed in life. I think that was a turning point, ninth grade, and my parents saw that also, they wanted me to succeed too, so they were really pushing me at that time.

They would tell me to study, they gave me a little more freedom, they would let me go to the library, and they really pushed me to do well. In the high nine I graduated with straight As. Then I had to go to high school. I chose Galileo because that was just the school in the community. But because I was on that ego trip my parents wanted me to go to Lowell, see. I guess at that time Galileo had a name of starting to be a bad school. That was about 1964, the first time when any kind of juvenile delinquency happened in Chinatown. My mother didn't want me to go to that school because she heard rumors it was bad. She didn't want me to be a typical bad guy, because I never hung around with them any more, see, I had changed. She wanted me to continue on with my goodness. So, in a sense, she forced me to go to Lowell.

Lowell was basically a completely whitewashed school. Well, there are a lot of reasons I regret going to Lowell. It was always an ego trip. At my junior high school, Marina, they were basically Chinese there. But this is the first time where the majority of people were white. At Marina I still hung around with my Chinese friends. I didn't know any whites at that time except maybe a few athletes. But this was the first time I ever encountered people that talk really well, you know. They talked, wow, gee, they talked so well! I didn't believe it, they had so many brains up there. And I said, I didn't think I could compete with these people. Then I sort of lost my ego trip. I still had a B average, but I didn't compete like before. In math I still got As because it was just natural thinking, logic. I guess I could reason, it was something in which I didn't have to compete. But English, well, at Marina if you were lacking in it, they didn't care, so I didn't put any special effort into English. But at Lowell, this was the only class I was ever in where there were only three Chinese students. All the rest were white. I think this was the first D I got in my life. I knew I couldn't compete with them, so I just gave up.

At that time I also took music and I was really getting involved in it. I started that in junior high school and I developed it in high school. There I was still kind of on an ego trip and I tried out for the all city choir. And I made it three times in a row.

I was accepted and I sang bass. That was for three semesters and when I was a middle junior I was also in the school choir. Then all of a sudden a very basic turning point at that time also happened. In one of the practices, we were practicing and I made a mistake, I guess I sang out when I shouldn't have, and the instructor, he yelled something at me. He called me a name at that time. He told me to sit down, he didn't want me to practice any more. Naturally I listened to what he said. Then when I was walking down he called me inferior. At that time, you know, I didn't really know what he meant by inferior. Because I just thought it was low-down. I didn't really know the meaning of it until maybe another half-year afterwards. Now I wish I had done something at that time. I might have really jumped on him. But I guess I wasn't that mean of a guy then, I just felt bad. I was lonely because when he called me inferior all the rest of the choir just looked and I walked out and they were looking at me. And it was the first time anybody called me inferior, especially a white guy. I was wondering why did he use the word inferior? Since that happened, especially for a year following that, this stayed on my mind.

I don't know. Until that point, I felt little bits of racism but I hadn't really ever developed any strong consciousness of racism. At that time I did feel kind of inferior, but not that much, I also felt kind of assimilated, that I was one of them. But when he yelled that at me then I thought maybe I'm not one of them, maybe I am different, because why did he use the word inferior? If it was a white guy, would he have used another word? But why in my case did he use the word inferior? And I really thought about it, and sometimes it got to me in dreams, you know, I'd dream, well, I'd go back and I'd get some cherry bombs and throw them at him, or something like that. But I've talked to people since then, and they say I don't need to worry about him. He's just one of those really strict assholes.

Well, I dropped out of choir, and then after that I didn't participate in any kind of activities at all. I did join a chess club, but that was more or less on my own and I didn't go very often. I was still trying to assimilate, because I had to associate with white people. But my friends at that time were Chinese. Whenever I came back to my own area, Chinatown, or whenever I had to do anything, I would associate with Chinese only. I felt more at home than with whites. Another time that really freaked me out was the first time I ever went to a white person's home. I didn't really like this guy, he was in the choir, also. He invited me, but I think he was just trying to show off that he invited me to his white home. And he showed me his stereo system. Never before had I really got close to a white person, been to his home. I saw a lot of luxuries at that time. A color TV, wall to wall carpeting, things like that. We didn't have a color TV or a washing machine, we didn't really have a neat house, I would say. That gave me the impression that the stereotype white, most whites, were like that.

Well, another thing that happened was that my grandmother came over just about this time, when I was in high school. She could only speak Chinese, and I didn't speak

Chinese at all. She slept in our living room and her style of life was completely different. She was very poor in Hong Kong, so she would eat anything and she would never waste, she would save anything. She would find things and save them. She was very tight. My father was kind of a tight individual, that was how he saved, but my grandmother was entirely different, from a different culture. My parents had been, not really assimilated, but they followed some of the American patterns, whereas my grandmother was still very low-cultured. She didn't believe in doctors, so every time she felt sick she had to go see a herbalist.

She wouldn't wear nylons, her nylons were just those very brownish type, and she wouldn't wear a dress, just those black pants and an old coat. She was always complaining of being sick, but we wouldn't send her to the herbalist because we didn't feel they were effective. And she would always be eating her cockroaches, you know, she had a kind of grasshopper that she brought over and she would cook it and eat it as medicine. And we really hated it, because my parents didn't like that, because they were too different now. And I didn't like it but she kept on cooking it and burning the pots. My parents couldn't get along with her and I couldn't get along with her. It was bad enough between my parents and us, but now it was three constant clashes. There were arguments all the time, but she was our grandmother, and what could we do, you know. We gave her a bed in the living room, but she complained that she didn't like that bed because in Hong Kong she never had a bed. She lived in a room the size of a restroom, and all she had was a plateburner and a wooden bed. So she demanded to have a wooden bed and finally to satisfy her we just bought a piece of plywood and put it there and she was satisfied. Because the style of life she had in Hong Kong was very poor, she used to scrounge, and she could live on anything, she would pick up anything. When she ate bones, she would chew them to death. She wouldn't waste them, she would chew them and then spit them out. Get all the flavor out of one bone. I guess that may be the way in Hong Kong, but here it's not so. And sometimes when we brought her to banquets she didn't have very good manners, her eating style was the same way. Eating fast and making noise when she eats because she's never been conditioned to this kind of eating before.

So she was really different, a lot of people wanted to see her because she just came over, but after she lived with us for about four months we just couldn't take it any more. We used to play around with her, we tickled her feet when she was sleeping and made her laugh and things like that, because we couldn't get along with her. Like I was kind of ashamed of her at that time because I didn't have any Chinese culture anyway, that was in high school. I was still on an assimilation basis, still on an ego trip trying to be white. And since I was a math major I couldn't understand why she was so different, why she did that. Finally we got in so many arguments that my parents sent her to an apartment in Chinatown, a one room place with a hot plate and her bed and that's it. We pay for her rent, I think, we pay for her electricity, just to get her away, but come to think of it we shouldn't have done that. My mother still despises her quite a bit, she always yells at her, tells her to follow the American tradition, to change. That's because my mother's still trying to learn English and make money and all that. Maybe that is why she's never been able to keep any relatives in the house.

JUNE CHAN, 16
She will enter college on advanced placement this fall.

I don't associate very well with people my own age. It sort of hurts, you know, because like I'm going to Cal Tech and nobody's ever heard of a person that's gone to Cal Tech. I guess I'm an introvert. I'm a worker and I like to keep to myself. Most of the time I like to watch things instead of getting into them.

For instance in the summer I think the main thing I do all day is sew and play the guitar. I've been sewing for a long time, at least six years, although it's not to earn money like my mother. I sew too slowly for that. It's only a hobby, you know. And also I'm very meticulous. I think most Chinese are, sort of. I have very good workmanship and I spend a lot of time on my clothes. When they come out they're pretty perfect.

I think I resemble my father more than my mother. Because she is extroverted, she has lots of friends and they're always coming over to the house and bringing her stuff. But nobody visits my father and nobody hardly ever talks to him. He just likes to keep to himself and watch. After he came here, he worked in a laundry for about twenty years ironing shirts and stuff like that. He worked really hard to get some money and then he went back to China for a wife. He picked up my mother but I don't think he really liked her at the time. I mean, they get along but they don't really like each other, if you know what I mean. I mean, they have four kids, so, well, they must get along but they aren't in love or anything. They fight off and on. But I don't mind. It's just one of those things.

He's not easy to talk to. Because, like if I talk to him in English, he doesn't speak that well. And when I speak to him in Chinese he speaks so well he's always correcting me. I just can't stand it after a couple of minutes. The littlest things! Like one time I was talking to him about Lake Tahoe. I didn't know how to say "lake," so I just said *hoi,* which is sea. Any body of water is *hoi* to me so I said, "I'm going up to this *hoi* in the mountains." You know. "You don't know that? Are you stupid?" Then he explains to me the word for lake, the word for river, the word for stream (laughs). I mean he is just so fussy. He knows a lot of English, too, but he'll never use it because his pronunciation is pretty bad.

I talk to my mother entirely in Chinese. And well, she's the kind of person I would like to be more of. Because, like, I am what my father is pretty much. And she's very, she's always thinking about the other person, really friendly and generous. And once again hardworking. Things in the house, and repairs, you know, she'll always do herself. Like that couch right in front of us is an old couch she bought and covered all by herself. But she does relax a little bit more now. When she first came out here she went, well, I think you can say that for all Chinese when you first come out here you go through hell. When we first got here, they couldn't speak the language. And, you know like trying to get something to eat, they just didn't know how to buy it, so they went hungry. We didn't have any clothes, really, and my father kept saving all the money so we could get enough to buy a house. Two weeks after we got there my sister went out and worked as a busboy. She was fifteen but she had to start working then. It was in Bakersfield. You know, Bakersfield is 110° in the summer and it snows in the winter. When we got the house my father still had to save money so he wouldn't let us turn on the gas and we just froze! And then in the summer he wouldn't let us turn on the cooler. I think we turned on the cooler for about two hours a day. Anyway, my mother had to go out and work in the fields. She picked fruit and washed *bok choy*. My father worked as a herbalist. When we still couldn't make money, we moved to San Francisco. So it's a good thing she's strong willed. She's stronger than I am.

But I think one thing that you might be interested to know is that now my mother thinks that all this trouble in Chinatown is developing because of the immigrants, the new ones. She's an old immigrant, you know, so she's better. All the trouble is from the new immigrants who don't have any morals. She thinks they're all communists, all of those things.

Of course, I don't think so. But you can't help, like I said, there's always this prejudice against immigrants. Even among the immigrants themselves. The newer you are, the worse it is.

Actually, I don't know that many immigrants. They were usually put in immigrant classes, you know, Americanization classes. And they'd always hang around their own group, and we'd always hang around our own group. And we'd never really talk to each other. It was just as if they were black and we were white or something, and maybe even worse because you couldn't speak the same language. Couldn't talk to each other. You can always tell if it's a Chinabug, you know, because they wear funny colored socks or funny looking shoes. Or dresses that don't fit or are too long or have holes in them, or they have holes in their socks. So that's how they are, and we just never, never talked to each other. We looked down on them. It was just the natural thing to do. You know how cliques form, don't you? I think it was just natural that we did it. Many people were teased, too. I remember this girl, I don't think she was even in Americanization. Her parents were sort of poor and she couldn't get good clothes. Then one day somebody saw her pick her nose. So we called her "snot," and she was stuck with that for the rest of her term. It's the kind of thing that can't be remedied very well unless you have money.

When I was in grammar school, we were poor like that too, but it sort of helped to speak English well. It sort of helped to be smart. The fact that I was smart overcame the fact that I was poor I guess. But I don't know, I always analyze myself. I think I spend too much time doing that. Just wondering why I act the way I do. Things like that. Never get an answer. I guess I take things too seriously.

Lately there's been a lot of talk about the "gangs." People say the kids are angry about how society treats them but I don't agree with that. See, I just can't stand myself when I get too emotional about things. I feel sometimes it's better to forget about certain things and not, you know, think about them all the time. At times I think about the things they talk about, all this racism and this and that, this and that. Sometimes I do. And I think, yeah, that's right. But I think they're a little too extreme. You just have to wait. I don't mean sit on your hands, but you can't go around beating everybody on the head.

Anyway, they aren't my type of people, I don't have much to do with them. My people are more or less kids whose parents are hardworking and they come from China, but they have intelligent children who can speak English pretty well. We didn't have any problems with spare time or anything. We always had something to do. Read or something.

I don't know what I want to do. There's all kinds of people in me, and sometimes they say different things. Like right now Upward Bound is beating on my head. "You're supposed to go back to your community and help do this and that." You know, that makes me feel guilty. So I tell everybody "Well, I'm going to come back and do something." But then after a while I get tired of thinking about the community all the time. And I say I'm just going to move away from everybody.

I'm going to miss this place a lot when I leave it. Because I remember I went down to Cal Tech just for one day, one complete day just to take a look. I came back and I looked at everything, and I looked at it like I'd been away for years, years, you know. Like I looked at the view outside our window, and I said, "There's Coit Tower," as if I had never known that was Coit Tower before.

14. Angry Young Men

JOE LOUIE, 19

It is thought that there are only three hundred to four hundred boys in the Chinatown gangs, and yet between 1964 and 1969 arrests and citations of Chinese youth in San Francisco skyrocketed six hundred percent from 85 to 514. People in the community claim it is the same kids who get arrested again and again, "A few rotten apples. They won't stay in school, they won't get a job, and now they're picking on their own." Social workers say the kids get involved in the gangs out of frustration. Most of them are new immigrants. For years, they lived without responsibility on their father's remittances in Hong Kong. Now they're here, disappointed, they fight with the old men, they're humiliated in school because their English is poor, they can't stand the menial jobs they know are waiting for them. "They're like a bunch of wild stallions and you just can't break them in."

We met Joe Louie in front of Sai Yon. He says street gangs are nothing new. He started his own gang, the Raiders, back in the early sixties and there have been a lot of other gangs since then: the Drifters, the Bugs, the Country Club Boys, the Brothers Ten, the Project Boys 895, the 880s, then the Wah Ching,* the Junior Wah Ching, the Baby Wah Ching, the Yao Lei. He noticed, however, that a lot of the American-born gangs have broken up now. The immigrant kids have taken over the streets. "It used to be that the American-born would beat up on the immigrants. Now it's just the opposite." Joe worked with the gangs as a street worker last year. He says he quit and now he's just drifting again.

I was born in Canton. We came over in 1950. My father came over first under a false name. When he came over

---

*Wah Ching, literally "immigrant youth."

he didn't have enough money to bring all of us. He sent back some money to my mom and me to come over and we left my older brother behind. I was living right in the center of Chinatown, on Jackson and Grant, and at that time I was pretty young and then, you know, Chinatown was pretty quiet, didn't have any hassles at all, no gang activities. And so I grew up with some friends, we went to school together and when I reached about junior high school, then I started, you know, to see the gangs. These older people, they start hanging around together, then they get restless and they go out and cause trouble because they got nothing to do, they have no money. So at that time I was new to here, I don't know what to think. Then later on as I grew older in my junior high school years I start to see why they are like that cause I turned that way, too. I start getting older and then I got sort of like into a gang.

They were the ones that had all the excitement. They were the ones that are always doing something. Other people, like they're home reading. I couldn't dig on that. I like to go out and, you know, have some fun, so I think maybe I should start a gang myself, so I did. It was called the Raiders. This is in the last year of junior high school and I started out with a few people, then people start coming in and when it reached a climax there was about fifty people in our club. We hang around the projects and in the beginning stage we were just doing like playing softball, bike-riding, and harmless things. As we grew older we started to change, we started going out and we don't have no money because we all come from poor families.

My father was a cook and my mom, she worked in a garment shop. So we start going out and first there was shoplifting. That's the first thing we do that really got us in trouble. And then we start going down Chinatown, raid all the stores and stuff like that, that's where we got our name. Then after that we start going into fighting. We fight with people that come in, foreigners that come from elsewhere. We never fight among Chinese, but like tourists, and actually some of them are just visitors that come around, not adult tourists but kids about fourteen or fifteen, close to our age. So that's where we get our experience in street fighting. It was pretty exciting then because after a fight we used to clobber the guy and we can talk about it, celebrate. Cause at that time we were the one that, you know, went out and cause all this trouble. But sometimes they would come down and try to start trouble, too. Like they would come around in a car and say, "Fucking Chinks!" or "God-damn Chinaman." And they would come back another time and then when we would say, "What? Can't you come out and fight?" They just go rrrrrrm, rrrrrrm with the motor and take off. So you know, it sort of gets to your mind, chickenshit people, and then you start to hate white people. Just one incident like that and you think all of them are like that. So we kept that on for a while and then we went into deeper, like strongarm robbery, burglary, and auto theft, and like me, I used to get away with it but I caused a lot of damage. The only reason why I got caught was I got finked on by my own buddies cause the pressure was on them. They got caught, they weren't slick enough to get away and the police just put pressure on and got information from them.

So they arrested me, and at that time I say, "Well, I'll go along and I don't want to cause any more damage because there'll be so much more charge against me." So like what happened was the judge committed me to six months in a camp. It was mostly bloods up there but then I get along with them because I can communicate with them, and we were having a good time, really tight, you know, and we help each other out. They kind of respect me because at that time I was a student of the martial arts. And I had a few fights with them and they can see that I do know something, they can't beat me, and word gets spread, so in a way they're kind of afraid of me. But then I don't come on and bully people, see, so they respect me. They would like to be friends, so I say that's cool, I don't care what race they are. If the person is cool to me, I'll be cool with them. So I got along quite well in camp, and I learned quite a few things up there, too. When I got out after five and a half months, I never got arrested after that.

I have more understanding when I got out and I started changing quite a bit. At first I was working on the martial arts, I dedicate my whole life to it for a while, but then I know I can't just keep taking it and no way of income. So I decided to take up some kind of job. I like to work with kids so I came down here. Then they knew me from all the shit I went through. And I'd been helping the kids, like when there was a fight I would try to break it up, and if they don't want to cool it I just jump right in and fight myself. And when I got started working as a street worker, I just try to talk to them, just try to help them and get their minds away from stealing and stuff like that. Because I grew up in this area and I went through what they're going through, I understand the situation. Like I wouldn't consider what they're doing really wrong, you know, and I try to help them through my own experience.

But you have to be pretty slick, like there are ways where you tell them something wrong and then they counter with something right, and naturally they win. And if they win that helps them get on the right track. Like you might make a mistake deliberately, "You guys need money. Why don't you just go out and find some old man out in the street and kick his ass and take it?" And sometimes they would say, you know, "No, man, that's not the right way of doing it. What I need is a job, you know." Stuff like that. Because anyway they know what is right, they can feel it in themselves. It's just that they got influenced into doing this stuff by their friends. Like they bullshit together and a guy says, "Let's do this, that's cool," and even though they don't really want to do it they commit themselves to do it.

I became a leader at first because I was the only one that could fight best. And secondly I'm smart, I make decisions that's more sound, so they follow. Mainly these kids respect power, they respect a guy that can fight, because that's the way they grew up, you know, just fighting. So when a guy comes along who can fight, they think, "Well, maybe we can get to know him and he can help out." So I think that's the first thing they look for in a guy, how bad he is. And secondly would be how smart he is. Because if his mind's shot, he won't be able to fight anyway. So that's what the kids respect right now, because they've been faced with all this violence, and they participate in it a lot, so any dude that comes along that can prove he'll do something for them, they would respect. I guess that's how I earn my respect in the beginning, and now they respect me in a different way because I never mention fighting that much or show off what I can do, they respect me now more as a friend.

I guess the main problem for the street kids would be money. They have their own problems, too, different for every kid, minor problems. I think just about every one of them has money problems. They just don't get enough income to go out and have fun, which is what they want, and they don't really want to work too hard for it. They feel that way, you know, working is not too cool. Cause they feel that since America supposed to be one of the richest countries, it is the richest country, the people should be living pretty good. And not have all these bums out in the street and all these guys starving. They start to think, "Wow, what kind of establishment do we have?" They're rich, they got their money, they're keeping it to themselves. They're just shining on the people." And it kind of get to their mind and that's why they're always fighting the rich people. Like the rich people, they come around like they own the goddamn street, you know. Like sometime they drive around in a Cadillac Belvedere and if you stop to pick up somebody all of a sudden they'll be there pumping, howling, honking their ass off, you know. And if you tell them to cool it a minute, they start talking back. Now these kids, man, like they tend to get uptight about that kind of stuff. They just come out and tear up that car, you know, with the person in it. Not just a white guy, anyone. Like usually kids like to have things their own way, they like to be free. But here they're really restricted, they can't do much, and they worry about that. There's lots of problems on their minds and pretty soon they have to let it out, so they go out and kick some ass.

Even though I still feel angry now, I know how to subdue it and I feel I have to maintain it, keep it cool within myself and not put it onto others, because I learned how to do it. My training in the martial arts, *kung fu,* kind of ease all the tension. You know, since I was a little kid I was watching the *kung fu* movies in Chinatown. And I look at it and I see the people, the masters, they got class, the way they handle situations so cool, so I got to learn it myself. At first I studied in books, and then when I was twelve I feel it's the real situation that counts so I went out and study in the streets. Then it start developing my mind further and further, I start to have a better concept of mind, and I also got my body coordinated. Like I feel great now, I can control my body any way I want. And I feel this kind of training will be really good if there's someone who's qualified to teach it to the kids. I mean the right way, not just to go out and kick ass but on the self-defense basis first. Like you never attack a guy first, you have to wait for the attack to come to you.

Right now, of course, there's not as many attacks on whites as before. The tension is mainly between the Chinese groups. Like they all want to be at the top. Most of the trouble with the whites was two or three years ago, when I first started working. We were breaking up a lot of fights then. Like I'll tell you one incident two years ago when they have this street fair in Chinatown during Chinese New Year's. A group of youths had a hassle with some white youths and they came up and asked us to help. We were actually street workers then, we were trying to keep it cool because we were taking care of the street fair, keep the hassle away from the fair, so me and Allen went over there to break it up. So we cooled it and then we said to the white guys, "You better split, you know. Because if you don't you're going to get your ass kicked." And the whites said, "No, we're going to stay here and call the police on those guys." And I said, "Man, if you do that, you'll be dead before that police ever gets here." And the whites said, "No, we're going to stay." So I said, "Well, if you don't split right now I'm going to kick your ass myself." The main guy still said no, so I didn't bullshit around with him. I kicked his ass, knocked him down, he got blood all over my shoes, too. But, you know, if he's gonna be that way, he needs a lesson. I already told him what's gonna happen so if he stick around he might as well face the consequences. Then the next time he wants to come around he'll think twice about it, because he's going to get his ass kicked. Well, you know, sometimes we did things that way, because if we didn't do it, this gang would have, and he'd be in worse shape. He might even be killed. But to a certain extent I would hold back when I fight, not hit the guy really hard, you know, just hurt him enough to show him we ain't gonna get pushed around. And if we really didn't do nothing, well, these other cats got knives and everything and he'd probably get killed, too, cause there's so many of them. So there's a lot of different situations. You have to learn to cope with each one then and there.

Well, in Chinatown the establishment is controlling the people and these kids feel they should be the ones controlling the establishment. They want to take control themselves, they want, like "power to the people," you know. They feel the people is the one that count and not the establishment. The establishment is just sitting back in a chair and smoking a cigar, and reading a newspaper, doing nothing. They're having all the money come in, but the people get barely enough to survive, because the parents work hard for it. They're not getting enough where they can really say, "Life is cool," you know. They think life is fucked up because they can't do this, they can't do that.

I feel the same way because when I was a kid money was hard to come by. I had to steal to get it. Whether it is from my parent or from another source, I still had to steal for it. If it's a penny, or a nickel or a dime, I had to steal just to get candy because at that age it's easier to steal the money, you know, than the merchandise. So when I was about six years old I was stealing already because if I want something the only way is through money. So the first thing I think of is getting that money, and if I know where it is, even in my own house, I just take it.

CLIFFORD FONG, 17
Galileo High School student

He hangs out with the guys at the Country Club Billiard Parlor at Washington and Van Ness, at Mike's Pool Hall, or in the office of the Chinatown-North Beach Youth Council, an

*anti-poverty agency. He's soft-spoken, and walks with a cool
saunter. Like the other street kids, he wears a black jacket
and dark trousers. He says the Chinese have been docile
too long. "We should stand up and fight back like the blacks."*

Well, the last couple of years Chinatown has gotten a lot of
publicity and right now they're beginning to feel the pressure from our community. A lot of it is necessary, threats
and things like that, because if there's no threats or riots or
anything the federal government isn't going to help you at
all. You know, like a lot of us don't agree on violence and
all that, but when people do it, it helps us. Like when the
blacks start a riot it helps Chinatown because they get
more money to go to the anti-poverty program. That's how
the whole thing started. When they had the Watts riot, they
came out with the anti-poverty program. A lot of it has to
do with how the government works. When you scream you
get them worried, when you shoot a couple of pigs on the
block, you know, then they start worrying. It's too bad, but
that's how those politicians think. Because up in Washington, D.C., our community to them is on a piece of paper.
That's how they look at it.

One of the biggest problems we used to have, you know,
was that the white man didn't recognize us as having any
problems at all. Because, like we have some of the best
restaurants in the city here, we have fancy shops, we have
bus tours going through here, you know. There's no bus
tours going through Harlem or Watts. Because the people,
even the outside white people, know what's happening down
there, what they read and what they see on TV has a lot
to do with it. But what they read and what they see on TV
about Chinatown, you know, it's a clean place where everybody's happy, and there's no trouble. And that means a lot
of people are getting screwed up down here and don't
receive no help. So that was, you know, one of the biggest
jobs. Just to let the outside people know what's happening.

Like the tourists, tourists in Chinatown are important for
all the money, but it's just that the money don't benefit all
the people. It benefits the businesses, see. You know, if
you're rich, you're very rich, if you're poor, it just keeps on

going like that. I think the tourists come in to use, to take
advantage of the way Chinatown is set up. You know, it's
cheaper than other places and even the so-called white
hippies can afford to come down. Like they made this, I
don't know, one of the hippie papers made this pamphlet
"How to Live in San Francisco" and they list a lot of Chinatown restaurants, the cheapest place you can go for a good
meal. So a lot of tourists just come down and they expect
the Chinese to wait on them, serve them hand and foot.
They expect all the Chinese to be what they see in the
magazines and the cartoons, you know. Practically wearing
a queue and everything.

It used to be humble, docile, you know, hardworking,
industrious, you know, little man that never starts any
trouble. The white man looks upon the Chinese as very
humble, a short little guy with buck tooth, glasses, round
thick glasses or something like that. Isn't masculine at all
as far as the guys are concerned. And they all like to work
hard, never start no trouble. And I guess in San Francisco
things are a little bit more liberal, but maybe in the Midwest
or the South there are some people that never saw a Chinese
in their whole life. Or some kids that only saw Chinese on
TV where we acted as butlers, waiters, houseboys. Even
in the movies that were made on the Chinese, or the Japanese war movies, like there's the white American sergeant
six feet tall, you know, John Wayne type, and then the little
Japanese soldiers so small that ten of them couldn't take on
John Wayne even though they all got guns. And that's all
the white man sees. Well, like I said, last year we begin
speaking up a little bit more and maybe in San Francisco at
least maybe white people are awakening a little bit.

As far as a lot of the youth is concerned, when the tourists come down they expect us to act like our stereotype,
especially the youth. Cause we're supposed to be well-
behaved and everything. And then when they see all the
so-called juvenile delinquents standing on Jackson Street,
you know, they're shocked. Because a lot of tourists think
they can come down and take advantage of our humbleness
and stupidity in being docile, never defending ourselves, and
especially like the guys being unmasculine and everything,

and they think they can get away with pushing the Chinese around and they'll never fight back. That's why a lot of these tourists come down here and when they get wise or something then the street kids get in trouble with them. You know, they're real resentful of any white man who would take advantage of them. So that's why a lot of white men get their ass kicked when they come down. Cause the street kid has it in his mind, "Fucking white man going to try and take advantage of me, white man thinks he can take advantage of Chinese." So even the smallest remark, the smallest thing is an excuse for the Chinese to kick the white man's ass.

Because I think like the main thing is the economic exploitation of all the people, you know. Especially when it comes to Chinese because again that stereotype of we're supposed to work hard and keep our mouths shut and it doesn't matter what you get paid. A lot of white business-men take advantage of this. Richer Chinese take advantage of poor Chinese. Even if a guy owns a restaurant making thousands of dollars, he'll still pay that dishwasher fifty cents an hour. Which goes back to the old thing they say in China, the plain greed of the businessman. Why not if you can get away with it? Why pay the guy a dollar if he takes fifty cents? So that's why a lot of people are suffering in Chinatown and a lot of people are getting rich, too.

Well, you know, whenever I talk about white as exploit-ing and all that I don't mean the white race, I mean white America. That's a pretty big difference to me. And you know it's not a lot of white people doing the exploiting and everything, but as far as I'm concerned all white people are to blame because all white people are ignorant of the things that are going on. And if you're ignorant you don't care what's happening. There are a lot of poor whites that are getting ripped off, too, in this country, that's true. But this is a pretty rich country, so in the end a lot of it has to do with our race. A poor white will get work easier than a poor black or an immigrant just because of the color of the skin. Like, you can even see in the way the police treat minorities. Like when they make a raid on the Black Pan-thers and when they search and make them strip all the way down, you know, pants and everything. So they're naked and

that how's they treat the Panthers when they're in on sus-
picion of something. But they don't do that to white people.

The Black Panthers I think, you know, I agree with some
of their points, but they advertise too much. They hang up
posters of revolutionaries like Mao, and yell "Off the Pig"
so the FBI got them all tagged down. That's why Huey
Newton and Eldridge had to run away. So I think if they're
fighting, if they're going to go on violence alone they're
going to lose. But a lot of their fighting is probably propaganda. Cause they know they're going to get killed, but they
do it anyway, so that it'll shock the people. Like I said
before it takes violence to move our society. So they have
to sacrifice their lives to it. I respect them for that. That's
why so many black people get what they do. There's so
many getting killed and the government's getting scared.
They don't want any more people getting killed, including
police officers.

Yeah, I think a lot of what's going on back in China. I
think communism is good for that country, China. Because
when they had kings and all that, or when the Nationalists
were running the country, the majority of the people were
suffering. I think Mao's government is helping out the people more and that's good. But that doesn't necessarily mean
that communism will work here. It's a different thing altogether, people think differently, live differently. So it's good
for China, but you can't say it's good for the United States.
Then there's still Chiang Kai-shek saying he's going to
invade China with those one hundred thousand old men.
But I don't know too much about it. I've only been to Hong
Kong. I think if it is possible to get in there, I would like
to see more of mainland China. So I hope, during my lifetime, I will go back just to see the place. I think I will be
handicapped because I don't speak Chinese that well. But
I still will like to go back just to see how life is.

JAMES LIU, 19
Student at City College

*The son of two professionals, he was raised in Chinatown
and still lives there. His parents are white collar workers.*

We didn't observe too many Chinese customs. I think just
things like on birthdays, eating noodles for long life. I
remember one time just recently, we went to an Italian
restaurant on my mother's birthday. We forgot to order
noodles and she was really sulking and then afterwards she
said, "Oh, you want me to die." Maybe she was in a bad
mood, her period or something, but she got really mad
because we forgot to order noodles or eat spaghetti or
something. I think both my mother's parents died of cancer.
So my mother's afraid of dying that kind of death. I guess
it's the most horrible thing she can think of. My father
doesn't want to die, either, well, my father doesn't really
mind dying, I don't think, it's just that he doesn't think he
accomplished too much. I think he'd like to be remembered.
I guess my mother fears death because of the pain that is
involved. As far as pain and all, I don't think my father
fears dying so much as dying without doing anything, which
is different. Of course, I might die in Vietnam or something
if I don't watch out. I'm not too careful about my draft or
anything. Inside I make fun of my father, feel contempt
because he doesn't like to talk about dying, whereas I don't
really care about it. I'm not too respectful about dying. I
think if I die, so what?

What would I like to accomplish? Oh, get prestige,
money, and beauty in that order. Prestige is more powerful
than money, prestige means getting peers and people around
you to respect you and recognize you. And then money, so
you can fool around, be decadent, like you could stay up
all night with a girl, drink wine, and glut yourself. You could
have money to go to a good health bar or gym afterwards
and get all rejuvenated again, and do it over and over again.
Get really messed up, then get well again, and get messed
up, and then get well again, have your face lifted and stuff
like that. Have beautiful wigs, custom tailored clothes, the
best pictures, and the most snotty artistic people, and just
float into their arms. The most beautiful bitches, you know,
be surrounded by all the latest styles, lots of junk, be rich
enough so that sometimes you live in a Japanese teahouse,
and then another time you live in some junky gilded Victorian palace, and then sort of like the Playboy Club . . .

no, I think it should be more higher class than that. Be a
dilettante in every field, in every artistic and intellectual
field, so that people figure you know something. But you
really don't. But anyway you're always invited to sym-
posiums all over the world, see lots of good-looking, rich,
stupid people, and then commission stainless steel and diamond jewelry to give to your one night stand, or something.
And then meet all the businessmen and industrialists in
Singapore, fool around with their wives, and fool around
with their maids, you know, and stuff. Have lots of maids
and have beautiful Oriental ones that could be fucked,
too, and then they'll enjoy it from you, maybe. Take your
maid and houseboy on vacations to Hong Kong, Tokyo,
and stay, fly back to San Francisco and then go to Egypt,
go to Afghanistan, buy lots of purses and set up a little
boutique for your girlfriend to run with stuff from Afghanistan and Persia and stuff. Have all your girlfriends decked
out in brass and tin and rubies and corals from India, and
then go to South America and be a handsome Chinese with
your eyes all slanted up, no flesh on you, just sort of bony-
looking, wear a white suit and white shirt, white tie, and
sort of bronze-color skin. You'll have a suntan because
you're rich and can have a suntan, then go to Brazil, then
meet Chinese girls whose families are from Shanghai or
someplace and they're growing up luxuriously in Brazil,
their father is a retired banker, these are kind of Chinese
playgirl types who always read *Vogue* and all kinds of magazines and dress real nicely. Go to nightclubs with palm
and white colored furniture, then fool around with these
South American guys with really dark tans, white laced
shirts, and tight tan-colored pants and shoes from Italy,
hang around with them, have lots of girlfriends and all
that. Then go to Hong Kong, get to know all these Chinese movie stars and starlets who are just trying to get into
Cathay Films or something, and help them. Then make a
movie yourself, with all these pretty people, and then I
guess you should give some money to different charities.
Like . . . maybe if my father dies of cancer, then have a
party for the cancer foundation, and then have your artist
friends spray Chinatown gold, paint it all gold like a free

palace, then unpaint it, get it all unpainted so that people don't get mad. Then I guess be a dictator actually and, oh, that's my vision.

I don't know why I said it, but I do have those ideas. Am I ambitious? I don't know, I think I just have a big ego or something like that. I'm kind of ashamed of it. I don't want to think those things, because think about the people that aren't in a position to think about such hedonistic things . . . Just knowing it's a possibility kind of depresses me, actually. I mean, I haven't done much actually because I've lived here all my life, so I feel kind of stupid. I'm always admiring young people who have done so much stuff, been in all sorts of places and stuff, that's what I'm most jealous of. But I guess it's my own fault, because if there's a will there's a way obviously. I just don't have the will, no will power, so that's why I haven't done anything. I should have been out of my house by the time I was fourteen or fifteen, been all over the world by now but I'm nowhere.

I'm nineteen. Yeah, but I haven't done anything. Just a bunch of talk, that's all. Even my father has actually done something, he's experienced a lot of things, me, I haven't done anything. That's why I'm mad at myself, yet people are always saying I should stay in the community, blah, blah, blah. Actually I don't care about the community, to tell you the truth. I hate to say that, but, you know, I just don't have any human sentiment, I don't care whether people are stuffed one hundred people into a two-room apartment or something like that, I don't care whether people have no meat to eat, or their parents work for twenty-four hours. I mean, you know, it sounds cruel, but I guess I really don't care because it's not my situation. I think God will punish me by killing me fast, you know, in a stupid place like a supermarket or something, so I won't have time to work. And then people will say, "Oh, that kid got what he deserved, because he's not concerned about all the other people, and he got it fast, no use for him." Too bad, you know, because I think a lot of people think I'm sincere and that I have a lot of skills and could help my community. Well, I don't know. I don't give a goddamn about my community, actually.

PART 5

RADICALS AND THE NEW VISION

15. Returning to the Community

With a sense that the understanding of the past offers a key to the direction of the future, an intense effort to analyze and evaluate the meaning of the American Chinese experience has gained momentum in Chinatown in recent years. In the late sixties, the crisis brought on by the emergence of the immigrant working class was accompanied by a sudden awakening of interest in Chinatown on California university campuses. Social problems brought to public attention by the anti-poverty programs became subjects of concern to second and third generation students who had already witnessed the dramatic rise of black radicalism and the birth of ethnic consciousness among other racial minorities. The long and bitter Third World Strike at San Francisco State College in 1968 was a pivotal event for American Chinese students in the Bay Area. Those who participated emerged with a new awareness of continuing discrimination against racial minorities in America which gave rise to militant anger and a renewed sense of identification with their ethnic community. The tumult at San Francisco State was followed by the Third World Strike at the University of California, Berkeley, in 1969, and the subsequent rapid growth of an Asian-American student movement on campuses throughout California. At the university, the Asian-American movement focused on continued participation in anti-war efforts and the establishment of Asian-American ethnic studies programs. At the same time, motivated by a deepened sense of responsibility to their own ethnic community, increasing numbers of students returned to participate in concrete projects there. For many, the experience of living and working in these communities for the first time demanded a searching effort to come to terms with their ethnic heritage and its significance. Among young intellectuals two interpretations of the American Chinese experience are currently emerging from these efforts: one which stresses the historic political and economic oppression of American Chinese; another which perceives the more critical area of oppression as cultural and psychological.

Political radicals view both the historic and contemporary experience of Chinese in America within a Marxist framework which identifies American Chinese as a non-white ethnic group which has been and continues to be exploited as cheap labor by the American capitalist system. They feel that as victims of racism and economic exploitation, American Chinese share a similar experience with blacks and other minority groups in the United States as well as third world people in Asia, Africa, and Latin America. They see themselves as standing in solidarity with these people and the international workers' movement in a broadly based political struggle against a common oppressor which they have identified as American imperialism. They stress, however, the necessity to integrate their Marxist world view with the concrete situation of the Chinatown community and have endeavored to do this in various ways. Thus, the first issue which brought wide-scale participation of radical students in the community was the fight to save San Francisco's famous International Hotel, which for decades had provided low-income housing for elderly residents of the community. After the success of this campaign, having secured in the hotel building a base for their activities, the groups have persistently focused on bread-and-butter issues in Chinatown: such as low-cost housing, public health, the crisis of the garment industry, and bilingual education for American Chinese children. Through political struggles directed to the economic needs of the people, as well as their newspapers and educational programs, they hope to introduce ideas of resistance and struggle into Chinatown which will heighten its political consciousness and reawaken its latent class struggle in the form of a dynamic workers' movement.

The new political groups share the Marxist orientation and international spirit of the old Chinatown left and see themselves as carrying on its tradition. Unlike the *Min Ching*, however, which took its inspiration directly from political movements in China, and was oriented rather more to the area of Chinese politics than American, the radical groups in Chinatown today stress their roots in the American New Left and insist that their activities must be integrated with the broader movement for the radical transformation of American society. While they feel admiration for the Chinese revolution and have been inspired by its example, unlike the Chinatown Kuomintang, they reject the idea of direct ties to a foreign government, and are directed towards maximum participation in American political life.

At the present time, however, radical students in their headquarters on Kearny Street still stand symbolically on the borders of Chinatown, their future role in the community undefined. As long as liberal leaders of Chinatown maintain bases in the government social service agencies, the attraction of radical programs may be weak. At the same time, in the six years since its introduction, certain limitations of the anti-poverty program have become clear to many people in Chinatown. The effectiveness of the government agencies has been curtailed by their dependency on government funding, which is uncertain from year to year, and which is being cut back. Budgets of various agencies also reveal that the highest proportion of anti-poverty funding is spent annually on the salaries of a small number of social workers, leaving little for the actual programs; many of these salaried workers have by this time begun to appear as a "new establishment" in Chinatown, secure in their positions and jealous of the status quo. While the anti-poverty programs have been able to offer minimal services such as medical assistance, different types of welfare funding, and some English language training programs in Chinatown, they have been helpless to resolve the basic economic contradictions which lie at the root of its continued isolation as a subordinate community. Problems of low income, unemployment, underemployment, poor housing, and juvenile delinquency in Chinatown all have, in fact, increased in severity since the anti-poverty agency was introduced. At best, the government agencies can provide residents of Chinatown with temporary "bandaid services" to alleviate these long-term needs; at worst they divert attention from the critical problems of the community with a labyrinth of bureaucratic paperwork. Because the agencies have extended the arms of the government deep into Chinatown, in the future they may play a dual function as organs of social control or even political repression. Radical students, on the other hand, who are dependent neither on government funding nor the approval of merchant leaders in Chinatown, have a freedom of expression and movement lacked by the agency liberals which allow them to exercise daring and innovative leadership. Their training as intellectuals makes them likely vehicles for the introduction of new ideas into the community, while skepticism about the viability of temporary reforms within the framework of basically contradictory economic relations has kept them at the cutting edge of social change in the community. The steady growth and proliferation of the projects undertaken by these groups in the past three years has demonstrated considerable commitment to long-term work in the community.

In the view of a second current of thinking in the Asian-American movement, however, political activitists have over-emphasized the importance of economic subordination of American Chinese. While they recognize the position of Chinatown as a low-income ghetto within American society, they point out that Chinatown itself has now become largely a way-station for newly arrived immigrants, while increasing numbers of American Chinese are joining the professional and white collar middle class. The real oppression which continues to be experienced by these American Chinese, they hold, is not so much economic as psychological and cultural. Extensive research into developing images of American Chinese, from their first appearance in nineteenth century journalism and fiction through later movies, plays, music, and popular literature, forms the basis for the theory developed by these Asian-American intellectuals, which holds that both blatantly and subtly racist images of Chinese (from Charlie Chan or Dashiell Hammett's Lillian Shan to the bucktoothed Confucius on Hallmark greeting cards) are still so visible in American culture that the majority of

American Chinese cannot but be influenced by them. Since the acceptance and internalization of the images is unconcious, however, few realize the ways in which they are affected. Writer Frank Chin, whose essays, plays, and novels develop the above ideas in depth, points to the existence of a split self-image in most American Chinese as the primary manifestation of this oppression. One's good qualities are identified as American, according to Chin, and one's bad or "backward" aspects as Chinese, while the experience of being constantly identified as Chinese by those outside leads to accumulating feelings of self-contempt. These feelings are in turn projected onto others of one's own race, leading many Chinese, particularly after the move from Chinatown to the suburbs, to deny their past and reject the validity of much of their experience. The most persistent element of the stereotype developed for Chinese, moreover (as distinct from other ethnic minorities), has been identified by Chin as the image of foreignness, personified in the familiar comic character of the strangely dressed, pidgin-speaking "Chinaman." Such images have defined Chinese in the popular imagination as perpetual aliens in American society, choosing to live apart from the mainstream of its activity and barred from even the most elementary communication with other Americans by inability to speak English. The tragic result has been the almost total absence of American Chinese participation in the national cultural life, despite the long history of Chinese settlements in the West and their deep involvement in American history. "People like to point to examples of the Chinese success story. So and so is a successful engineer, so and so is a successful biologist or mathematician," Chin says. "This is supposed to mean we're assimliated. But are we? Can you name me one great Chinese-American poet, playwright, or actor? I bet you can't name one."

Inspired by a vision which seems not so much an alternative to that of the political radicals but complementary to it, "cultural radicals" in the Asian-American movement see a new exploration of their ethnic tradition and its deep roots in American soil as essential to the restoration of integrity and dignity to American Chinese life. It was this idea which lay behind the founding of the Combined Asian Research Project (CARP), in 1969, which holds that the emancipation of Asians will never be complete without the recognition of a unique Asian-American sensibility in terms of which they may express fully their real experience. Dedicated to the achievement of this goal, CARP members in the last three years have worked intensely to discover and foster the development of authentic Asian-American art. The group has searched exhaustively for unpublished manuscripts and fragments of early literary works by Asians in America and has sought out older, little-known writers from both the Chinese and Japanese ethnic groups, reproduced their works, and put them in contact with younger writers. Aware that much of the richness of the American Chinese culture is as yet unrecorded and exists only in its oral tradition, some members of CARP have also traveled extensively to Chinese settlements up and down the West Coast seeking those with a deep experience of the past and recording their memories. By bringing together young artists of both Japanese and Chinese ethnic heritage for cooperative work and to encourage the creation of plays, fiction, and poetry, the CARP group has in its short lifetime already sparked a burst of creativity among Asian-American writers on the West Coast, which has borne fruit in the production of several pioneer anthologies of Asian-American writing.

CHINATOWN COOPERATIVE GARMENT FACTORY

The factory has been set up in one corner of the big basement of the International Hotel. There are seven machines separated by a plasterboard divider from the rest of the basement area. The divider is decorated with photographs and posters: landscape scenes from the People's Republic of China, a picture of two Vietnamese women sewing in a makeshift factory in the jungle, sculptures from the Rent Collection Courtyard. In the front of the factory, a blackboard has been nailed to a heavy, green table, REFERENDUM, RECALL, INITIATIVE, AUDITORIUM, the words for the day's English lesson, are chalked onto the board.

Three women who will be taking citizenship tests soon drill each other with questions in English while they sew.

Although it was originally envisioned as a self-reliant factory which would maintain independence from the downtown contract system and distribute through its own outlets, extremely limited capital, lack of business experience, and the small size of the shop made it impossible to break into the highly competitive apparel market in San Francisco. Within a few weeks, the shop ran out of capital. In order to provide wages for the two seamstresses who had joined the cooperative, it found itself bidding for contracts from downtown manufacturers along with all the other Chinatown garment shops. Gradually, members were able to negotiate enough contracts to establish the shop and bring in four other seamstresses. However, the piece-rate for garments sewn under these contracts has consistently been so low that the cooperative has had to rely heavily on subsidies from fund raising activities in order to pay their two-dollar-an-hour minimum wage. Even though in a cooperative shop they have been able to eliminate the exploitative relationship between owner and workers, they told us, downtown manufacturers have kept the piece-rate so low that seamstresses in the cooperative have still been unable to earn standard wages simply on the basis of work done in the shop. This, and the unsteadiness of their contracts, has shown them why Chinatown garment shops close down so frequently and why wages are so low.

It was emphasized that the primary aim of the Chinatown Cooperative Garment Factory is educational, both for its members and for Chinatown seamstresses who come down to observe the shop and ask how it is doing. They feel the shop is arousing a high degree of interest as knowledge of its presence spreads among seamstresses, but women from the Chinatown shops are also skeptical of its chances for success. They feel if the shop succeeds, it will not be difficult to popularize the model within the community, but they too have become increasingly conscious of the difficulties of maintaining a cooperative shop in the context of a highly competitive capitalist system. Although they had initially conceived of the cooperative as an alternative to unionization in Chinatown, they told us, their confrontation with the harsh economic realities of the garment industry is now bringing them to reconsider the possibility of forming an independent Chinatown union affiliated with the ILGWU. They feel that such a union might provide Chinatown seamstresses with a first instrument for collective bargaining with the downtown manufacturers.

The garment cooperative had not started regular operations during our first summer in Chinatown. We visited it in the summer of 1971, when it was one year old. At the time, spirit in the cooperative garment factory seemed high and positive despite uncertainty about the future. This was the first shop in which the seamstresses spoke to us spontaneously without asking permission to do so. They told us they donated extra work time willingly to the shop because they were enthusiastic about making the project a success. The cooperative was the only garment shop in Chinatown which made all its books and financial records open to us.

FRANK NISHIMOTO, 24

Japanese-American graduate student in nuclear physics at Berkeley
He joined the Asian-American student movement in 1969 and helped to organize the Chinatown Cooperative Garment Factory.

We did a lot of homework and the facts we found were rather depressing. I guess we kind of knew all along that they were going to be depressing. We were doing a study of the situation for our course on the community, and we got hold of some of the books that told us exactly how much money the ladies in certain garment shops were making. Then, a lot of us had friends and relatives who had worked as garment workers and they would tell us what actually went on, how many hours they worked, the way they were blackmailed into keeping silent, the fear that they had. I think in the last thirty years there have only been a small number who actually tried to go on strike, or actually tried to call attention to their plight, and they've been blackballed, they have to work in the south of Market now. They can't work in Chinatown. So there's a tremendous amount of intimidation for these ladies. They know that if there's any hint that they're organizing, they'll be labeled communists, they'll be fired, put on a blacklist, and sent into the streets. But we managed to find out quite a lot about the workers' situation.

Then we tried to approach the unions and see exactly what they were about. The ILGWU was very happy to see us because they had wanted to organize in Chinatown for a long time and were having trouble with the language barrier. But we came out of the whole thing feeling that they wanted to use us essentially. Naturally, when you ask them whether they can help the Chinatown workers, they'll show you the list of union benefits. But when we checked into some of the Chinatown shops that have been "unionized," we found that in most of them it makes very little difference. Workers still get substandard wages or the bare minimum, they're still afraid to speak out about it. In fact, the union manager admitted to us that the union couldn't ensure a minimum wage in Chinatown, because employers in union shops will just doctor the time cards. In a way, union workers may end up being worse off, since they're paying an extra $5.60 a month for dues. Then we checked the ILGWU records for the rate of increase in workers' salaries it had achieved. We found it had one of the lowest rates in the country. So we became kind of pessimistic. It seemed the main thing the ILGWU would achieve was to get more dues money for itself. Of course, the Teamsters had also been agitating in Chinatown at the same time. But from what everyone has seen of the way they operate, their use of strongarm tactics like intimidation, blackmailing, it's been very hard for them to win any trust from the Chinatown workers.

I guess you're already beginning to see why we came out with such a depressing picture. On the one hand, you have an inacceptable working situation in the garment shops. Yet the traditional alternative, the union, is either impossible to organize in the first place, or can only be organized at the price of its remaining ineffective. The employers have all the strength, and there seems to be no way around this with the situation in Chinatown the way it is. You know, in an economy like ours, it's expected that the laws of capitalism will function in such a way that the supply and demand curves intersect and reach a stable equilibrium. But Chinatown is completely out of balance. There are too many women who need work, too many immigrants who will work for almost anything, and keep their mouths shut about almost anything in order to hold on to their jobs. The result is that the individual worker doesn't have a leg to stand on versus the boss. As far as the owner of the garment shop is concerned, any worker is dispensable.

Well, that was how we saw the situation in 1969. Since we've gotten into the belly of the beast (laughs), I think there's just one thing I can add to the analysis. It was probably inevitable that in the beginning we saw the problem very much within the Chinatown context. We tended to focus on the worker-employer polarity, to place the blame with the employers, for exploiting the workers right and left, cashing in on the competition for jobs by keeping wages low. But one thing we began to realize as soon as we were running our own place is that owners of garment shops don't really make that much. The bidding prices of manufacturers have consistently been so low, the number of garment shops in Chinatown so high, that, in fact, the competition between owners themselves is cut-throat. Most of them live with a very real fear that competition can wipe them out at any moment. That's why this thing we went to yesterday, where they auctioned off machines from a folded-up shop, is a common occurrence in Chinatown. You know, if you take the clothes I'm wearing, they probably cost two dollars to make. When I bought them I paid twenty dollars. Now judging from the way our bidding has gone, I'd say the owner of the place that made them got about two dollars for them. Who got the eighty percent margin? Obviously, the department store that sold it to me, which will then use the money for its advertising, its overhead, its labor, and its profit.

So if you want to get to the very bottom of the garment

shop problem, one thing I've learned from our experience is that you have to take it beyond a Chinatown-only context. It's true that Chinatown bosses are taking advantage of workers and this can't go on. But in the end even these bosses are only middlemen. It would be ludicrous to talk as if the whole thing was set up just for them. It's the large department stores which deal in clothes that are skimming the cream off what's going on in Chinatown now. They're the ones who really want to see that it continues.

BECKY LEE, 22, AND DAVID LOUIE, 20

Becky graduated from Berkeley last year and is now a full-time worker in the factory. Becky says the shop would prefer to deal with a steady contractor. For the past year, one contractor has been fairly steady, but his prices have gotten progressively lower. He doesn't come to the shop any more, just sends a delivery boy down with the material and instructions, so they can't negotiate. If they want to ask for a higher price, they have to call him up or go down to see him. Now, during the Christmas season, a day's delay might cost him a contract with a retailer, so he may be anxious to have the shop take work even at a slightly higher bid. Even so, if they push too hard, he will simply withdraw his job and look for another shop. By the middle of the week, business will fall off again, and the Chinatown contractors will have to go back to calling the manufacturers for work. Becky says during the normal season, the contractor pays them two dollars per dress for most of his lots. He wholesales these dresses for fifteen dollars apiece to stores like I. Magnin and Macy's, where they go for thirty dollars apiece.

I guess the best way to begin is to tell you the few possibilities we had when we began. Everyone had heard something about the situation in Chinatown with the garment factories. The study group did about six months of research, not only reading, but going around and talking to people like Cornelius Wall, the president of the ILGWU, and a lot of the sweatshop managers. Most of the people in the group had relatives—mothers, aunts, or grandmothers—who were working or had worked in a garment factory. So from them and our own observations we had a realistic idea of how bad the conditions in the shops are. After we put all the information together, there were three possibilities that seemed to spring up for dealing with the situation. One was to join the ILGWU and try to recruit more Chinese workers to the union. Another possibility was to form an all Chinese union which wouldn't be part of either the ILGWU or the Teamsters, the two existing unions for garment workers. The last possibility we saw was to develop a new alternative to the present garment shop: a cooperative which would do away with the contradiction between worker and boss altogether. A factory like this could educate workers about their rights and offer them administrative skills. They would also have an opportunity to learn English. But mainly it would be a place where the people who performed the basic labor also controlled their work, made their own decisions, and acted on these decisions themselves.

We thought we'd go into making our own products right away. Actually, we had a really minimal amount of capital. We got a place to work, with machines, and those of us who knew how to sew taught those who didn't. We put some interview ads in the paper, but since we didn't have much money, we hired just two professional seamstresses in the first month. One had already worked in San Francisco, and one had just come from Hong Kong. Then we had a small crisis, because we ran out of money (laughs) very quickly. But that was when this whole thing about seeing what you've been reading in books began. We needed work so badly we were just constantly phoning manufacturers, making appointments, going out to bid with them. And that was a completely new world for us, seeing firsthand how the economy of this country really works. Of course, it seemed like swallowing our pride at that time to look for contract work, because we'd just assumed we'd start out self-reliant and it would be smooth all the way. But we realized that was the only way to bring work in, and we were concerned about providing work for the new women. Actually, a lot of the time when we got back the workers would mumble a little, they'd point out we'd taken an especially difficult dress or something and that the price wasn't very good. But in the end we were glad we'd gotten right into contract bidding because, after all, this is what most of the Chinatown garment shops go through.

Then we really had to struggle until the older women began taking things into their own hands. The main problem that we've had in the co-op was this, getting across the feeling that it belonged to the workers. I guess when you're used to being told what to do, always being an employee, it's kind of hard to believe it when a bunch of young people just tells you, "Well, you're the boss, you control things." People don't seem to know exactly what's going on. I think, in the first couple of months, they still had the feeling of coming someplace for eight hours or so and then going home and that's it. It was still just a job to them, and whenever we'd say something, they'd always tell us it was good. So slowly we started asking, "Well, what do you think?" about this and that. And as it became clearer how obviously incompetent we were (laughs), they started offering suggestions.

The first breakthrough didn't come for a couple of months. We were getting really low prices, you know, and we'd all complain together while we were working, but then when the designer or the manufacturer would come around, no one would say very much about it. At one point we were dealing with a manufacturer who was really cheap. It was a time when we had no work at all, but we had gotten some new workers and we were trying to supply them with something, just to keep going. So this cheap guy had come around five or six times to drop off orders and tell us to have them done by a certain time. Now the students were handling all the negotiating then, because we were the ones who spoke English. But by that time we'd been having shop meetings for a few months and the older women had really gotten involved a lot with the management, they were worrying about finances and whether we could keep the co-op going at all. Well, one day, after finishing one of this guy's orders, they felt they'd just about had it. He came in to pick the things up that same afternoon. And before any of us had even realized what was happening, all the ladies were standing around him and yelling in Chinese. And with what little English they had picked up in the classes here, they were yelling at him in English, too, telling him that the price was ridiculously cheap and that they just couldn't afford to do anything like that again. The guy was stunned, you know, he couldn't figure out what was going on. Here were these women telling him how much work had to go into these dresses, that he should pay them a higher price for them, how much he charged for them on the market, and how much he was making off their work. Suddenly this English word came up, "You're stin-gee, stin-gee" or something, the woman could barely pronounce it. But finally it dawned on the manufacturer that she was telling him he was stingy (laughs)! And he began to say, "Well, I don't know, I don't know," and finally he raised the price. And since then we've always been able to get him to raise the prices for certain orders, because the older workers have been speaking out and they don't feel the least bit self-conscious about it. When a guy comes in they just tell him, "Well, you're cheating us, that's all."

David: A lot of people who find out about us are enthusiastic about the co-op as a social or political experiment, but one thing most of them wonder about is whether it's actually efficient. Does it improve production? I think most of us have found that discussing everything out, letting everybody have their say, facilitates things. Because when people become aware of all the different aspects of keeping the shop going, they can understand just why they're doing what they're doing. They can get more into it. If you're just doing something that's meaningless to you, that you think is terribly stupid, you won't work as well.

Becky: For one thing, everybody shares the headaches of finances. That's kind of painful at times, but people feel more responsible about it. When something belongs to you, you want to work harder on it, you feel proud of your work and you want to do it. Say we have a special order here, one that has to be done pretty fast and there are a lot of pieces. If it was a regular job, where you just had to work a certain number of hours everyday, you'd just want to go home

when your time was up and forget about it. But here, all
the workers decide if we should work the extra hours and
finish it. Is it worth it to us or not? And a lot of the time
women decide to stay and finish, even though they may
want to get back and cook dinner or something. One thing
they're really concerned about is giving the co-op a good
name among the garment factories. They're always thinking
about that.

Another advantage is that in many other garment factories the workers do things by the dress. One by one.
There's intense competition because some people go faster
than others, so they'll make more each day. It's each individual working for herself. Here we just work together to
finish the work as efficiently as possible. Whoever is fastest
at sleeves will put in the sleeves, and so on. In this sense
it's more like assembly line production, which I think has
been proven to be faster. Also, in other shops, there are
always favorites, certain groups of women will get together
and the manager will give more work to them, things like
that. But I think all of us feel the main concern in our work
here is to have a cooperative spirit prevail over everything.
When we analyze whether something's going wrong, our
basic line is to judge whether it's working for or against the
existence of a cooperative spirit. In other words, we're trying
to make the factory work as well as possible, but it's not so
much the factory itself that's the most important thing to
sustain. The factory could cease to exist as long as the
workers keep the ideas of collectivism. I guess that's because before most of us even went into this we'd come to
feel that adopting a collectivist spirit was the only way our
people would survive. So that's what we've aimed for in the
co-op. We've tried to have all the workers experience a
collectivist way of relating to each other, experience exercising power together over their lives so it can never be
taken away from them again.
Frank: By organizing a co-op, we haven't been able to eliminate exploitation by the white manufacturer, but at least
we've eliminated a certain amount of exploitation because
we've eliminated the middleman. And at least we've been
able to politicize a certain number of workers, and to show

them that it is possible, by organizing, to effect a certain amount of change in their lives. A lot of workers stop in here, you know, to visit their friends and talk to us, and they all think having a shop that belongs to the workers is a good idea. But most of them wouldn't have believed it was feasible in a society like this.

That's why we've essentially tried to mold the shop in a very socialistic kind of way. The workers control a lot of the decision-making, the wages, the policy decisions, collectively.

MRS. CHOW, 37

She was one of the first workers. She saw a notice about the garment shop on the bulletin board of the Asian Community Center. Her previous experience was in a downtown unionized garment factory.

I didn't understand what a co-op was at first. I thought the students were very good and really wanted to help the people in Chinatown. But I didn't think they understood the garment industry very well.

I wasn't the first worker here. I came by here one day to watch them making clothes and I asked if I could have work. The students talked about what the co-op was. They said it was for the people and that all Asians should work together to help each other.

It depends on the people in the co-op whether it works or not. We do the work, so the co-op belongs to all the people who work in it. We talk about how to improve our work. When we have meetings we speak our minds out.

I talk to my friends about the co-op and they said, "If it works, let me know." Then they will come here, too. They hadn't thought about a co-op before.

MRS. LEE, 36

She is studying for her citizenship test. Before her interview, a student is coaching her. What are the three branches of the government? How many senators are there in the United States Senate? Who is our senator?

It's very hard to work in America because many of us Chinese can't speak English. And when we go to adult school to learn, what we learn isn't always too much use. But here we are learning English together and we learn things and words we can use in our work and in dealing with the manufacturers.

I like it here much better but I got paid more at other places. Most of us could get more money working in other places but who could stand the bosses over you all the time? And we do a lot of things together. We go on picnics and see places outside of San Francisco.

Do I have any complaints? Well, when any of us do we should bring them up at our meetings and realize that when we criticize someone it's because of her work quality and not take the criticism personally—you know, how it will affect the co-op's work quality.

I WOR KUEN

The group named itself *I Wor Kuen* after the proto-revolutionary "Society of Righteousness and Harmony," composed of peasants and small craftsmen who rose in the Boxer Rebellion (1900) in an unsuccessful attempt to expel the imperialist forces of Britain, the United States, Japan, Germany, France, and Italy from China. Taking its early political style from the Black Panther Party, the *I Wor Kuen* first addressed itself to organizing youth gangs in New York Chinatown in 1969. After a year's work, however, difficulties in building a serious political movement from unstable lumpen elements led the group to shift its focus to exploring the possibility of awakening a workers' movement in Chinatown. In the fall of 1970 New York *I Wor Kuen* members who had come to Stanford University for graduate work entered San Francisco Chinatown and reorganized the offshoot of the Leway Youth gang, the Red Guard Party, thus establishing the national *I Wor Kuen* organization. In its basement headquarters under the International Hotel, the young radical group is continuing its own internal education and has begun an effort to introduce Marxism-Leninism and Mao Tse-tung thought to Chinatown workers.

I Wor Kuen activities include a small nursery school for working mothers, Mandarin and English classes, worker-student discussion groups, a choir, and the showing of films from the People's Republic of China which, since the beginning of the United States-China rapprochement, have attracted large audiences of families in addition to the bachelor standbys of Kearny Street movies. They are also planning a "barefoot doctor" program to provide basic health education in Chinatown. *I Wor Kuen* defines itself as a "pre-party," organized around principles of democratic centralism. Its programs stress self-reliance and a spirit of internationalism.

CARMEN CHOW, 24

Graduate student from Taiwan at Stanford University. She is married to an American Chinese and is known as a fiery orator and ardent feminist.

If you look back historically, you'll find that in the thirties, during the height of the American left, twenty-two out of the twenty-three newspapers published by the American Communist Party were in foreign languages. One thing I think this points out is the strong internationalist nature of the American working class. America in a way is a land of immigrants. Working people came from all over the world, from many national backgrounds, to work and build America. Therefore many American workers have a strong sense of their own national or ethnic heritage. This is true not only for the Chinese but true also for Italian-Americans and so on. Although for Chinese especially and for third world people to some extent, this sense of national identity distinct from that of the United States is stronger. I don't think this necessarily isolates them from other Americans —both third world Americans and whites—for instance, if we look at what Chairman Mao said about Norman Bethune, he felt that this was a spirit of internationalism we could all learn from. Norman Bethune was a member of the Canadian Communist Party who went to China, and fought and died in the Chinese revolution. That was a very courageous internationalist act.

When we try to do radical political organizing in China-town we face a very complicated question, how do we iden-tify ourselves and our position in American society? Often we find ourselves swinging between different extremes, both incorrect. There's the extreme of saying, "Well, we're all Chinese and we're an extension of eight hundred million Chinese people on the mainland." That would be wrong. The other extreme would be to say, "Well, we're Americans who are no different from white people, brown people, black people, who are part of the American revolution because they are within the boundaries of this state." That would also be incorrect. You see, neither of these positions take into account the concrete realities of the United States and the majority of Chinese who live here. We can't avoid the fact that, within the working class, an overwhelming major-ity of newly arrived Chinese people still see themselves as Chinese. Also, a lot of Chinese-Americans have a special feeling toward China which is quite natural, one they wouldn't have for another country which wasn't a direct part of their cultural and racial heritage. So there is that tie, our history and our families are very closely linked to main-land China or Taiwan; Chinatown itself has always been strongly influenced by events in China and Taiwan. So this is a question which involves our families, our relatives, everything, and to see our development outside of this con-text would be very metaphysical, because we do have these concrete, historic ties.

Secondly, there are many different third world people in this country who will all play an important role in the American revolution, but we have to take into account the differences in these national minorities and in the type of oppression they have experienced here. You see, imperialism oppresses nations of people but ultimately the national question is a class question. The history of how Asian peo-ple were brought to this country and their oppression here is very different from the way in which people from Africa or Latin America or Europe came to this country. For one thing, black people have been here for three hundred years, while Asian people have only been here for one hundred years—we're comparatively recent. Many of us are immigrants. So within the Chinese minority there will obviously be a stronger tie to the homeland than within many others. These are just realities of the American revolution, and we have to become very creative, instead of simply being dogmatic, to deal with this. We have to see that the defeat of United States imperialism will be very different from the defeat of the Indonesian bourgeois class, or the Chinese bourgeois class. It's a qualitatively different kind of struggle, because I think a classical national revolution now, one in which the people of a single nation rise up and overthrow their rulers as they did in Russia and to some extent in China, won't be repeated in America. By its essence, an American revolution now has to be more internationalistic in character, because the United States is the single most oppressive force in the world today, so traditional concepts of what an American revolution might be will not apply. The American revolution will be radically different.

I think it's only when we use the word "patriotic" without understanding the reality of that word that there's a problem. The other week our discussion focused on the question: "What would you do if China were attacked by the United States?" Some of the people in the group immediately said, "Of course, we'd go and fight for China." But then one of the men said, "Wait a minute. It would depend on who was fighting for China and who was fighting for the United States. If the United States was socialist and China was Chiang Kai-shek, we should help the United States defeat China." And everyone recognized this as the correct answer. You know, the Chinese government itself recognizes big-power chauvinism and teaches that to be patriotic doesn't mean to have blind allegiance to a nation. Patriotism is love of a country because you have emotional, cultural, and historical roots in it. But there are classes in every nation. If your interest is that of your class it can't be narrowly nationalistic. So people here have a deep feeling for China, yes, but we realize that the essence of the Chinese revolution is its internationalistic character. We recognize that China has made great advances to the international revolution and this is what we must study.

I think our emphasis on discussion groups and education has grown out of our previous experiences working in the Chinese community in New York. We've come to feel that in a lot of serve-the-people programs there's a tendency toward becoming utopian and divorced from the reality of the society one lives in. We feel this is a crucial weakness in many of the programs. For example, we can open a health clinic here, but we're limited in what we can do in terms of money, facilities, and equipment. We can't pretend to become a miniature hospital that eventually is going to replace the capitalist hospital. That's not the way in which you're going to build a revolution. And this is why we've begun to place less emphasis on service programs and more emphasis on organizing people within the institutions they're at, to fight against these institutions—such as a large city hospital —and make them more responsive to the needs of the people. We feel that inherent in the class struggle is the fact that you can't say, "Well, I withdraw from bourgeois society . . . we will form a socialist utopia here.

One of the directions of the organization is to reach out to Asian workers in factories and plants outside of Chinatown. Most people in Chinatown work in service industries where the entire shop is completely Chinese. But we're trying now to branch out to factories and industries outside of Chinatown to organize Chinese, Japanese, and Filipino workers in factories where they're in the minority. We see that as a very important step in which we're going to become more and more linked with the future of the majority of the working class in America. We're inside Chinatown right now, but we want to reach out to factories and plants where there is no distinct Asian community. In efforts like this we think we will have a concrete basis of unity with black groups like the Black Workers' Congress, Chicano groups like Los Siete, or Puerto Rican groups like the Young Lords, and work with them on a joint basis to organize third world workers in plants.

We believe in self-determination and local autonomy in

the sense that we have the right to maintain our cultural and linguistic heritage. We have the right to observe our own national customs like Chinese New Year and so forth. But essentially we see our future as linked to the future of the third world people in this country. This is why we consider our attempts to move out of the Chinese community and begin to relate to work places which have a lot of black and Chicano and Asian workers as a very significant step for us. One of the reasons we instituted the adult education program is to try generally to break down the isolation of Chinatown from the rest of the world. People here should read more from the American press, learn to understand the media and so forth, because it will help them to reach out of the community.

Another thing we feel very strongly about is women's liberation. You find, for example, in our adult education program it's all men. Most of the men have wives but they don't bring their wives down. Sometimes it's almost by coincidence that we reach the women and their husbands happen to come down, too. We feel within the organization, too, we must be very strong against male chauvinism, every facet of male chauvinism, and we feel that organizing women is one of the most important things in the revolution. We've been pretty successful in organizing around specific things. First, their concern about their children. That in itself is part of a male chauvinist society, but we're trying to relate to women around the question of what this society is doing to our children. How can we as women come together to bring our children up in a better way? How can we as young mothers with small children help each other so we can each have free time to do other things? How can we help each other to fight against male chauvinism? A lot of working women here are beaten up by their husbands. We have to deal with that. But we also want to teach women English and driving skills, and to get more freedom of movement. Most women in Chinatown are limited to about as far as they can walk with three kids (laughs), which really puts limits on what they can do! We feel a lot of the women are very reluctant to talk when there are a lot of men around. So we have meetings of women only, where they can talk a lot. Another thing we're trying to do is break down competition among women.

FRANK CHIN, 32
Novelist, playwright, and essayist

He has been writing fiction since he was nineteen. He represents the fifth generation of his family in California. At the
age of twenty-five, seeking the roots of his own history in
the West, he became the first American Chinese brakeman
to work on the Southern Pacific Railroad. For several years
he made TV documentaries in Seattle and later returned to
Chinatown to work with younger American Chinese writers.
Frank Chin feels his most important mission is to legitimize
the American Chinese sensibility as a distinct sub-culture
which is recognized in its own terms, not as a "blending of
East and West." He is dissatisfied with the commonly used
term, "Chinese-American," which connotes a split personal-
ity, half Chinese and half American. "Call me a Chinaman."

He says, "You're always taught to expect Chinese assimilation into America. Well, the Chinese really haven't assimilated. People who assimilate take on the tools of that
culture and manufacture, make things of their own with it.
I think that's what assimilation means. But the Chinese
haven't done that. There aren't Chinese-American writers,
there is no Chinese-American literature that's recognized or
Chinese-American language, actors, playwrights, anything
in the popular and fine arts. I think it was a teacher in my
Chinese school who first made that apparent to me. And his
words stuck, you know, and seemed to be proven by my
experience, that the Chinese haven't accomplished anything
here." When he was about twelve, Frank remembers how
the old Chinese school teacher who whacked them on the
knuckles with a wooden ruler died one day. A younger man
was introduced to the class, a Chinese graduate student who
had recently come to the United States. "There was this tall
skinny guy, about five-seven or five-eight, in a blue suit that
he wore with all the grace of a banana wearing a paper sack.
He's standing there at a loose parade rest in the center of

the room, his adam's apple is prominent, his hair is close to
his head, and he has these skinny glasses. And the principal
told us, 'Wong shian shian is dead, this is your new teacher,
Ma shian shian.' For the next few days we didn't know how
to take it. Then one day he came in with an Oakland Tribune.
He said, 'I was walking by the store on the way to school.'
—it was this store on the corner run by a Filipino fellow
and we always used to go there and buy cornnuts, or we
would run down to the Golden Dragon and buy cha shew bau
or something and bring them back to school. And he said,
'I was walking by the store and I saw this headline and it
said JOE. And I thought what "Joe" do they mean, Joe
Stalin? Is he still alive? So I bought the newspaper and I
walked in, opened it up, and it said JOE DI MAGGIO MAR-
RIES MARILYN MONROE.' And he said, 'This is American
journalism!!!' and he was off, you know, on the state of
American journalism, the news—there we were, the oldest
of us was twelve, no, the oldest was Flo Wong, she was
fifteen—and he was ranting and raving about journalism,
then he zoomed into Chinese history, ancient and recent,
and the next thing we knew we're talking Dien Bien Phu
and the United States flying ammunition in planes marked
Red Cross. And I didn't know what to think about this shit,
but it was a lot more fun than learning Chinese. So I started
going to the library, taking out books, Snow's Red Star Over
China, Fraser's Nation Betrayed, and things like that, and
reading up on this stuff so I could come in and throw it at
him, because I would never do my Chinese lesson. I would
come in and say, 'I heard Borodin turned Sun Yat-sen into
a communist.' And boom, this would be enough to send him
off, where did you hear that? And he'd run it all up and
down. But there was one thing that he always said that
really shook everybody up, it was like a theme of his, and
it was that the Chinese-Americans, the Chinese in America,
weren't worth shit. He said that they all capitulated to white
supremacy, that they were morally bankrupt, and that their
language betrayed that. He said, 'Why do you want to be
called Chinese-Americans? Because you don't want to be
called Chinamen, because that's what they called your
grandfathers and your great-grandfathers who were the

miners.' He said, 'What did they do to be bad guys? They mined gold, they dug out the tunnels, they carved the way for the railroad, what's so bad about that? The only thing that was bad was that the white man looked on them with contempt and called them Chinamen. And all we can remember is that they looked on them with contempt, you know. And we think it's all our fault, but it isn't, it's the white man's fault that Chinaman is a bad word. And you should never forget that, you should call yourselves Chinamen, not Chinese-Americans.' "

I went to Cal for a while and then I went to Iowa. I was there on a fellowship and all I was required to do was write some stuff, turn it in, and go in for a conference. That's all I did. The sessions would go, well, "This is a fine story, but we've all read Joyce Cary," you know. "This theme is already pretty hackneyed," and so on. I didn't want to go in there to cut people's stuff up, compare it, and try to decide who and where it came from. If the influence was really obvious there was something wrong, but most of these people had some skill, and well, there was just nothing in that for me. So I just did my thing. Most of the stuff I got was the point of view trip. "You haven't used enough of the local color of Chinatown." I would say, "But it isn't local color. I don't want to talk about neon lights and chop suey and funny music." R. V. Cassill was one of my teachers. He told me, "You know, you're writing about the Chinese in a way that I don't think American people would be interested in." Because they were just like people, right? My people. I mean they're common to me. "But don't you think you should make them interesting to the audience?" And this kind of stunned me, you know, because I thought I was just writing. But now I was being told in a backhanded way that I had a point of view and my point of view wasn't white.

I was even then kind of a loner and I was feeling bad about not having a girl myself. Terrible time trying to find one. The Chinese thing kept coming up and the chicks that turned on to me were exotic freaks. And I didn't want to be checked out, see if I had underarm hair or a tail, you know. In Iowa no one—the only Chinese there were foreign-

born, most of them students. Everyone there treated me like
a foreigner including the Chinese students, because I was a
foreigner to them, and that got very depressing. The only
place I could get a job was in the Chinese restaurant in this
town. Getting a place to live, well, this professor befriended
me, found me a room, and took me over to see the landlady.
The landlady came out and I was smoking. The guy said,
"You better put your cigarette out, she might not approve."
I'd just started the cigarette so I bent over, pinched it out,
and I was putting it back in my pocket, kind of hunched
over, and I look up, this lady is bowing to me. I look at the
professor, he kind of shrugs, so I bow, and he bows, and
she says, "Is this him?" "Yes, this is Frank Chin and this is
Mrs. So and So." I say, "How do you do, Mrs. So and So."
She says, "Oh, he speaks English!" "Yes, I do, Mrs. So and
So." She says, "What's his name?" "My name is Frank,
ma'am." "Oh, well that's only your American name." And
I had to admit that's probably all it was, you know. "Yeah,
it's only my American name." And I'm getting really tired
of this. Then she says, "You speak very fluent English!"
"Thank you, ma'am." "Oh, what part of China are you
from?"

"I'm from San Francisco, ma'am." Rather than put her
down and say, "You dumb bitch, I'm not from China." But
she goes on, "How long have you been in this country?"
You know, that was her mental set: all Chinese are foreigners, therefore San Francisco is in China. I said, "Well,
I've been here twenty years or so." And she said, "You
should speak good English, then!" And I said, "Yes, I should,
shouldn't I?"

She took me to one end of the room. "Do you like this
rug?" "No, I don't like this rug." "That rug okay?" "Yeah,
that rug's okay." She said, "Are you going to do any cooking?" I said, "Yeah, I've been known to do a little cooking
so I can eat every now and again." She said, "Alright, I'll
bring you some things. I know, Chinese like to make a mess
when they cook, don't they?" I said no, I didn't know that.
She said, "Oh, yes, I've been to the Philippines and I know
that when Chinese cook they like to have a big mess. I'll
just bring you some cloth to wipe off the stove each time

you cook." I said, "OK. You bring me the cloth and I'll wipe the stove with it. Gladly, gladly." She says, "Well, here we call it 'rags.' " "Oh, 'rags.' Cu-lean-ing rrrrags." "Excuse me. Cu-lean-ing rrrrags." I'm looking at her and she's staring me in the face, mouthing the words "cleaning rags" and I realize I'm being given a lesson in English.

Well, that was Iowa. After a while I had to get out of that Chinese restaurant so I got another job in a restaurant where they called me "The Indian." Farmers would come in who had been in World War II and they'd get drunk and begin to reminisce about the war. They'd see me, feel guilty about bombing my parents in Tokyo or something. I'd tell them my parents never were in Tokyo, they were alive and well. Then they'd think I was making fun of them. After I was beaten up three or four times I quit the job. But it was getting to me. It was getting to the point where I just wouldn't come out of the house at all unless I had a letter from home, something from home reassuring me that this wasn't all there was. I was twenty-one, this went on for six months or so, I was more and more depressed. I was sleeping twenty hours a day and really getting down. One day everything bad happened. I got up and all the strings on my guitar broke. I went and got it repegged, got new strings for it, the strings were too short. Went back, changed the strings, and the peg broke. So I got a new peg, came back and put the guitar away. I was just trembling. I couldn't do anything. I couldn't pick up anything without breaking it or dropping it and I went to sit at the typewriter and I looked at this letter I had been writing to my friends at Berkeley. You know, at the time I could write a hilarious letter. I read it, and it was the saddest, most terrifying thing I had ever read in my life. I said, "That's me? I thought that was funny? What a sick mind I have!" You know, I sat down on the chair to try to correct it and the chair broke. So I'm typing on my ass, my hand up on the typewriter, and I had to get out. I just had to get out. I told myself, "It's the room. I've been in this room too damned long." And I go out of the room and the only place I can think to go is the Chinese restaurant. Only place in all of Iowa, in a one thousand mile radius, it's the only place I have.

I went there and I sat down. Someone said, "What's wrong, Frank?" I said, "Nothing, nothing. Just need some coffee." I had some coffee and I sat in front of my coffee and I said, "I have to get myself together. I have to get myself together." But the Chinese restaurant just wasn't doing it for me. This is where the Chinese students from China are, you know, and they laugh at me because my Chinese is so bad, and I feel kind of awful because they feed me and I haven't done much for them. So I just sat there when a friend from high school whom I had completely forgotten was at the university walked into the restaurant with a white guy. I saw him and I just couldn't control myself. I was trembling and I really began to get scared myself. The guy looked at me and I said, "Man, I got to talk to you." So we went downstairs, through the bean sprouts, the potatoes, and I ran down, "This is a stinking hell hole of a place and I can't take it, I'm going nuts."

Well, another part of this story is that one more guy from high school had been at Iowa, Emmett Ong, he was in the pharmacy school here. And he had been in a lot worse shape than me. Emmett had been all alone for two and a half years. The one way he had more help than I was because Emmett knew *kung fu*. Emmett's counsins or uncles had been Sun Yat-sen's body guards and they regarded themselves as the most dangerous men in the world. After Sun Yat-sen died they split up but Emmett had learned from one of them some stuff. And he used to come over to my place when we were in Iowa, he'd sit in my dreary room, he'd go through these violent fantasies with me. He said, "You know, these guys . . ." and he'd talk about these roving bands of high school kids or ex-marines in Iowa that would beat up anyone they thought was queer or anything, you know. Now when they threatened, I would just go into my usual thing of talking my way out of it, but Emmett was something else. Emmett couldn't talk. In a tense situation, or under any kind of fire, any kind of pressure, he couldn't talk. But afterwards he'd just come and spill his guts to me and say, "I just had to keep walking because if I *really* wanted to, I could have wiped these guys out." And I used to say, "Here, take this book and go read it." You know, any kind of sappy book, but he would read it in one night. Come back and want to talk about it. Emmett wanted to talk about anything, even a comic book. You know, he'd come over, and after telling me how many guys he didn't kill on the way over, he'd be talking to me about what a great book it was. The guy was so lonely that when I'd go take a bath, he'd sit outside talking to me through the bathroom door. Because there was no kind of Chinese-American that he could relate to there. He had no friends, and he had no ability to make them. He hated the place, he hated being looked at as a foreigner. Never encountered people who believed in the stereotype before. And before my first semester was over, one day he came over and said, "Frank, I can't take it, I'm going home." And I was glad to see him go because the guy was really getting kind of freaky. But then I guess I entered his phase of the thing because I'd walk by these people thinking, "Oh, boy, you're not dead. I didn't kill you, you son of a bitch."

But the thing taught me something, you know. That I was Chinese-American, whatever that meant. That I was not an individual, not just a human being. Just a human being in this culture, in this society, is a white man, he can disappear. I couldn't disappear, no matter how enlightened I was, no matter how straight my English was. Someone, just because they saw my skin color, would detect an accent. Someone would always correct me. And well, then I began to look at my writing, what I'd been writing about in my letters and everything was just to this point. The Chinese-American, well, schizophrenia. That I'd been playing a kind of ping pong game, you know. Now I'm Chinese, now I'm American. But up against real Chinese in this isolated setting I saw that I had nothing in common with them. That they didn't understand me, and I didn't understand them. We both used chopsticks, okay, that's recognizable. But that's mechanics, not culture. On a personal gut level that doesn't make us brothers.

So if you're Chinese-American, this is where you come back to. This is your home, your spiritual home, whether you know it or not. But one thing, if you write, period, you're exploiting Chinatown. It's very complex. Writing and art to the Chinese-American is white. I get this when I go out and say, "More Chinese-Americans should write. We should tell them who we are, we should express our sensibility in our own terms instead of letting guys like Tom Wolfe come in and write about us." You know, we should be speaking for ourselves. "Aren't you asking us to ape the whites when you say that?" I'm asked this by Chinese suburbanites who've been college educated. They look on the writing as white, as if there's no such thing as writing and individuality in Chinese culture itself. This is how sick we've become. And the either-or thing. The either-or thing is right in that scientific name we go by, "Chinese," hyphen, "American." At San Francisco State, just as an experiment in a few classes, without giving them my bias and my own trip, I asked the students if they could divide themselves into what they thought were their American and Chinese qualities. Fold a piece of paper in half, the right half would be American, the left half Chinese. Everything that was interesting, adventurous, original, creative, fun, sexy, daring, artistic, was American. Everything old-fashioned, inhibiting, restraining, dull, repressive, uncreative, stultifying was Chinese. That isn't so, you know, these are gross oversimplifications. The whole Christian tradition is as repressive as anything you can dig up out of Chinese culture. If you can say this of Chinese culture, you can say the same thing of Western culture, too. But these kids believe it, and it's what they've been because the title "Chinese-American," the cliché "blending East and West," encourages you to say, "Well, what are my Chinese parts? What are my American parts?" And what you break down, you break down according to the lines of the stereotype. It's something conditioned into you that you don't even realize. It's self-contempt. The Chinese are dumb, the Chinese are inhibited. The Chinese are restrained.

No American-born Chinese-American writer has ever published and become even slightly known and still lives in Chinatown. They don't identify with it any more, they see Chinatown as backward. In fact, the Chinese-Americans who have written come from a generation which strongly believed in the stereotypes as being real. They looked on writing as the proof that they were not of the stereotype, that they were assimilated, nearing white. They bought their way into second-class white status by humiliating their whole race and people and history and fucking up the future. This is exactly what white culture has demanded. Because all the publishers have ever shown an interest in, as far as Chinese-American writing goes, is something like *Flower Drum Song*. So when I write something different, the white publishing world raises its hands in the air and says, "See, one of your own people wrote this book. It must be true. What are you doing?" Or they want to correct my grammar or something. They say that my style is difficult. Well, it should be. It's a new language. It's Chinese-American. I'm not writing white. I'm very consciously trying to write Chinese-American. Most recently, I've been "discovered" by Ishmael Reed in *19 Necromancers from Now,* I'm the only nonblack in the anthology. His point of view is very similar to mine on the kind of white supremacy expressed in everything today. Writing is white, the standards of art and culture are white, and this tyranny of culture by the whites has been an oppressive force on nonwhite arts. He was talking about black art, black writing, but it's true of Chinese-American writing, especially true of Chinese-American writing. I would say that white racism has had no greater success than with Chinese-Americans because, with mass popularization of the stereotype through education, in the mass media, on all levels of writing from the level of Joseph Conrad and Jack London down to Pearl Buck, over six generations, it has managed to produce a Chinese-American character that is without an ego, that has no self-respect, that has internalized almost fatal suicidal doses of self-contempt. A race that has remained silent, has remained completely out of the stream of culture. Not the main stream, not even a side stream, but out of the stream altogether. The only Chinese that appear in American culture are as a kind of debris: playing Number One Son in Charlie Chan movies while Charlie Chan, who is the teacher, is played by a white man. A white man teaches us how to be Chinese. The blacks complain about being emasculated. The genius of white racism in regard to the Chinese is that they never granted them balls in the first place. They convinced them that it's so. That it was a virtue to be passive, to keep your place. So many of us pat ourselves on the back, "Look, look! Look what we're not doing!" We're not doing this, we're not doing that, we're really great. We've made it. Well, we haven't.

If I had had to write something like that in order to sell, I would have said it of the goddamned Chinese as if I weren't one. And that would have linked me up with that first generation of Chinese-American writers, buying my way out of bondage by the rejection of my race. Well, I can't do that any more because I see that if I were to do that it's a price I have to continue to pay, and I'm not willing to do that. In my writing the ills, you know, everything that's terrible about Chinatown, I love them because they were mine. I know they have to be corrected because I lived them. I feel that I have a certain authority to say that they're no good, but in my terms they're no good. I say they're no good, but at the same time I kind of cherish the memory of these things. It breaks my heart that my grandmother lived in this country her whole life, she was born here, and she couldn't speak a word of English. You know, I was in her house when she died. It was a terrible experience and her old friends, some of them are still alive, I remember I was able to talk to them somehow. They couldn't speak English at all. And it breaks my heart that I can't even go up to them now and have the confidence to say in Chinese, "Remember me?" And somehow my Chinese name is even foreign to me. But no white American can claim that misery, that's mine. That's what I write about, that makes my experience unique and that somehow makes me fine and defines my commonality with a lot of Chinese-Americans. And I'm not going to cast that aside to praise chop suey.

What I value most I guess is what I'm doing, trying to legitimize the Chinese-American sensibility. Call it my accident in time and space and that all the talent, everything I have is good only for this. Nothing else is any good until I get this done or started. And if I can't legitimize it, or if Chinese-American sensibility isn't legitimized, then my writing is no good.

Yeah, I guess I'm very Victorian in that I have a sense of
sin and I indulge it and enjoy it. But I have a sense of guilt,
too. I think it's a sense of guilt that causes me to hesitate in
coming down hard on anyone in Chinatown. That somehow
I am an outsider now, I don't belong here, even though this
is my home. I'm not trapped here. So I feel guilty about, you
know, telling people that they're full of self-contempt. What
am I doing to them? I'm knocking everything out from under
them, I'm tearing their guts open and offering nothing in
return. I can't ask them all to become writers. I can ask them
all to speak up and blow their minds, but they're not all
equipped to do that. This generation is responsible, it has to
legitimize the sensibility. At the same time, there's the pain
of realizing that white racism has historically and presently
manifested itself in terms of their self-contempt and humiliation, that a lot of the emotional, moral, and cultural im-
peratives operating within them now are euphemisms for
self-contempt and humiliation. It's too much to ask them to
bear and yet they have to, you know. This is what I'm kicking a few of them in the ass to do. But should I do that? I
feel that I should to some, but at the same time I hesitate.

I don't know if Victor grew up in Chinatown or not. But
it was pumped into my head day and night in Chinese
school that the Chinese were a certain way and if I didn't
act a certain way I would be hurting all Chinese in the
world. Some of that still remains, and part of my insistence
on being an individual, a loner, is just an escape from that,
you know. From feeling I'm responsible to everybody else.
At the same time I'm busting my ass to break back into
Chinatown that I broke out of, so I can break other people
out again.

Not that I can pretend that self-contempt isn't a problem
for me. It manifests itself in me in that I consider myself a
failure. Deep down I really don't think anything's going to
come of this. I think I'll end up like a certain relative of
mine, looked on as a bum by my family, selling newspapers
on the corner of Grant and Washington. Like, you know, the
only choice I see for me is, well, am I going to be a bum in
Chinatown or outside of Chinatown? In my family, and
among Chinese, the question of just physical survival is

almost of paramount importance. How do you live? By their
terms I'll never grow up, I'll never make a lot of money.
I know I'd feel a lot worse if I took some crummy job and
gave up my writing, because I've tried that, and it just did
not work. At the same time this is my sense of guilt, that I
do feel bad when my family looks on me as a failure, that
I disgust them. That as far as they're concerned I'm some
sort of weirdo charity case. And even if I succeed, I will
have failed them.

I identify with my father. My father tried, in his own way
he tried as hard as I am to make it in his terms in this country. Yeah, I think he failed and I think he thinks he's failed.
But in his eyes I'm irresponsible. I'm fooling around and I'm
an insult to him. He was president of the Six Companies,
I've insulted him there. There was one time I came down
from Seattle, you know, I was dressed just like this but he
loves me, I'm his son, and he took me out to get some clams.
He knows I love clams. And we were at *Sun Tōi Sam Yuen*
on Jackson Street and a bunch of his buddies were there.
We were in a booth, and I had long, long hair then. They
recognized him but they didn't see me. So they came over,
shook hands with him, said a few words. But when they saw
me they wouldn't acknowledge me, didn't even ask who I
was. Before, when I was a little neater they would say something, or shake my hand. But they didn't acknowledge me,
and I saw my father die. And there's nothing I can do for
the guy. I felt terrible for him, I was breaking his heart. I
guess for him it was a very noble moment, do or die maintaining himself as my father even though it meant insult.
So they came by, and the wives came by one at a time and
there I was with my pile of clams.

We live in different worlds. And when my world comes in
contact with his we just destroy each other. I look at the
way he tunes the television set, it's all wrong. The people
look like they're dead. They come on looking dingy, gray,
the color of roquefort cheese. But that's the way he sees the
world. And he lives in Chinatown, so it's in Chinatown, his
world. And he can't see that it's partly my world, too. So,
you know, I'll never have his respect. And I could win a
Nobel fucking prize, you know, and prove that my writing's

been worthwhile and he'll say, "You dress like a bum." And then I see that I've broken the guy's heart. So I feel bad about that.

INTERNATIONAL HOTEL COLLECTIVE

For fifty years, the ambling two-story brick building that is the International Hotel has stood on Kearny Street.

Most of the people who live here are retired Filipino laborers who live on social security and welfare checks. A sprinkling of Chinese oldtimers, a few unemployed seamen, a few immigrant families, a few whites living on unemployment checks, and an unemployed black make up the balance of the hotel's 160 tenants. Over eighty percent of the tenants are permanent residents. Some have lived here for over ten years. To these men the hotel is a home which supports a way of life they have grown accustomed to and which they have come to depend upon. Downstairs are the Mabuhay Restaurant and the Mandalay Club, across the street are inexpensive restaurants, poolhalls, bars, the Bella Union Theater, Portsmouth Square, and Chinatown. Rooms at the International Hotel are among the cheapest in the city, but at forty dollars a month, they are all these men can afford. Those who cannot afford even this are asked to pay thirty dollars a month. The hotel is a part of both Chinatown and the small Filipino community which clings to its last block along both sides of Kearny Street, between Washington and Jackson. It stands as the last remaining structure which separates the growing financial district from Chinatown.

In 1968 before the arrival of the first group of students, plans had been set into motion by the owner of the hotel, Walter J. Shorenstein, chairman and principal stockholder of Milton Meyer, Inc., to demolish the International Hotel and construct in its place a parking lot to service the nearby financial center. A mass eviction notice issued by Shorenstein, community and student protest, a mysterious fire in which three tenants died and which has been suspected to be the work of an arsonist, the city's condemnation of the hotel, and ignored coroner's and jurors' reports which concluded after preliminary investigation of the hotel fire: "We, the jury, further find that the extent of investigation for possible crime as a contributing cause for the fire has not been adequate. Further inquiry is warranted," make up the series of events which defined the early fight for the hotel. With the entry of the Berkeley student work teams in 1969 the struggle to save the International Hotel was given new strength and direction. Marches and demonstrations were held in front of city hall and Milton Meyer, Inc., causing considerable embarrassment to Shorenstein. Pressured by adverse public opinion created by the campaign to save the hotel, in July 1969, Shorenstein agreed to lease the hotel for two years with a third year option to a community group, the United Filipino Association (UFA). But the terms of the lease stipulated that rent would be raised from the previous $13,000 a year to $40,000. In addition, the UFA would have to pay $25,000 annual property tax, and $15,000 fire and liability insurance. Although Milton Meyer, Inc., received $40,000 insurance coverage for the damage caused by the fire, the cost for repairing the hotel was left to the UFA.*

The work of rehabilitating the broken-down hotel to meet the city codes was led by Berkeley students who organized themselves into the International Hotel Collective. Reflecting the broad representativeness of the Asian contingent of the Third World Strike, the new collective was made up of students from Filipino, Japanese, Korean, and Chinese ethnic backgrounds, including two Filipino workers, and a white roof repairer. The collective quickly assumed overall responsibility for leading the fight to save the hotel. Special committees were established to take charge of research, public relations, fundraising, repairs, entertainment, and maintenance. Volunteers from among the tenants, community service organizations, local churches, high schools, colleges, and universities were organized to help in the work of repairing, cleaning, and rebuilding the hotel. Donations of paint, used furniture, and building material were solicited from local businessmen. A beautification program was begun in the hotel, the corridors were painted white with blue and gold trimmings, all of the 160 rooms were painted

---

* Figures from "fact sheet" published by the International Hotel.

and remodeled, potted plants and flower vases were placed throughout the hotel, and new bulletin boards were put up in the major gathering places displaying photographs of the People's Republic of China, North Korea, North Vietnam, and the Philippines. A recreation room furnished with a television set, pool table, and reading tables was opened. Nurses from the University of California Medical Center established a makeshift health clinic to provide basic health care to the tenants, many of whom had symptoms of tuberculosis, alcoholism, glaucoma, and other ailments. A small dental clinic was even set up to attend to some of the chronic dental problems of the tenants.

But in July 1971, the Hotel Collective told us they were running on a serious deficit. The high rent, property tax, and fire and liability insurance could not be paid if the hotel was to be maintained as low-cost housing. The hotel was on a deficit of sixteen hundred dollars a month. They told us that the present lease of the hotel would run out in July 1972, despite all the work that had gone into bringing it up to code. Members of the collective are now mobilizing city-wide support for the final struggle to save the hotel. At the very least, they will demand that the land on which it stands be used for new, low-cost housing for the elderly in the two Asian communities.

BILL LEE, 20
Berkeley architecture student

Bill has a quiet manner and is constantly at work. He told us he grew up in a laundry, but did not understand the significance of his parents' lives and his childhood experience until he became involved in the Asian-American student movement, joined its discussion groups, and began radical work in the community.

I guess the first year of the Asian-American movement was a time of realizing the meaning of certain conditions that had been going on, things I knew all my life just because I

live around here. The sewing factories, my parents working
really long hours in the laundry, I knew about all that, but
I never thought of it as a problem. Just kind of saw it as part
of life. I guess the Third World Strike was the first thing
that made politics close to me, because they were talking
about nonwhite people. That got a little closer to me. I
started going to a course that was taught out of one of the
basements down here and in this class, they kept bringing
things I knew about out as problems. Then, when I first
came to the hotel the amazing thing was that all this work
was already started. I saw all these people working. They
were painting the walls and there were maybe fifteen kids
in the hall scraping things down, and really working with
their hands, throwing a lot of time in. And that seemed to
me to be one step past knowing what the problems are. You
know, when you're finding out about things, and you put the
picture together, you just keep asking what can you do,
what can you do? And if you keep doing that all that happens is you get depressed or something. Nothing changes.
It was also that when you work you can see physically
something that you did. And being tired at the end of the
day is a really different experience from sitting in a room
asking what can you do?

When I first came I really didn't have any idea what kind
of life people were leading in the hotel. I would see the tenants just walking around the halls looking at us. It wasn't
until later on, when I started talking to a few more people,
that I got a sense of what it was like. There's a man here
who stays in a bar till two or three in the morning and by
seven he's out in the streets again, or sitting in Portsmouth
Square, just to get away from that room. A lot of the men
here have no one. They're really isolated and they're really
poor. There doesn't seem to be any thought about the future
in the old men, just kind of day to day to day. And the
younger guys here, they've been in America six months or a
year and still don't find work. Whenever I look at it, it just
seems like it's no kind of life. Of course, people do have a
good time. They go downstairs to the poolroom and enjoy
themselves. They enjoy each other's company while they
cook in the kitchen, even though they're not eating too well.

But it makes you want to really attack whatever is causing this situation, where people have to live so badly. So it makes you want to work.

I think before, when I was going to school, I always had the feeling that I didn't really understand what was happening to me. I guess it's something that happens pretty easily in an educational system that just tries to train you for a profession. I could never quite figure out why I did certain things, what would happen to me after I got out of school, what to think about beyond getting a job. But working here I think I've gotten a better picture of what my life is because I can see it in relation to something real, something that's going on, and that's put my education into a new perspective. It's as if things started to fit together more tightly because of some of my experiences here.

I guess the "new perspective" is that I've taken all these things which were part of my life and realized that somebody was responsible for them. For instance, I can take my own family and the things they've gone through. My father had a laundry down in the south Market district in a kind of slum tenement area, and redevelopment kicked us out when I was about ten. Then we moved up to Chinatown. Well, I was always aware of how my parents were living, and what was going on around Chinatown. I knew my mother and father worked until late at night six days a week, that we didn't really have much, and how they tried to save. But I didn't understand this in a general way. I didn't see it as part of what had happened to other Chinese, or to blacks and chicanos. You know, I didn't make all the connections: that the first Chinese who came to this country in the 1850s were used for cheap labor, got the shit kicked out of them every so often, and now, still, my parents are working long hours and making pretty little, other people's folks are, other nonwhite people are, too. But now I can see that all this fits into a picture. I can see that certain people forced these people into this lot, certain things forced choices on them, and I know who does it now. I guess especially knowing that somebody does that, and having an idea who that is, seems really important to me, because it's like a focus.

Who's doing it to whom? The Chinese came into a situa-

tion that was set up to work people, and to have them throw
in their sweat and everything and it would throw them back
just a little. Now to me, that's what a capitalist system is all
about. So it's the capitalist system that's doing it to my family, and to other poor people, and it's the people who benefit
from the capitalist system who are doing it to them. Then,
if you want to be more specific, I can look at the actual situation I live in. I can look at Alioto, with his plans for "developing" San Francisco, by which he means developing it into
a better capitalist center. But at the same time his redevelopment agency wiped out my parents' first laundry, and now
they're putting the squeeze on this hotel. And there's another person, for example, the man who owns this building
and is about to take it away from the people who live here.

For himself, he's just trying to make a good thing, I guess,
trying to increase his benefits from the system. But from the
perspective of the people that live here, that have lived here
for maybe twenty years, he's taking a home away. You
know, I'm sure to him there doesn't seem to be much difference between a crowded little room that just happens to be
in Manilatown or Chinatown, and the room most of these
men will probably find when they're moved out—someplace
down in the tenderloin where there's a narcotics murder
every few days. He just knows he could be making a lot
more money from this building, this space, if it were something more than a hotel for single men. He could turn it into
an office branch for some business, a parking lot so all the
business people working in the financial district can park
their cars here, or he could make it into a big hotel, so businessmen from other cities can fly in, live here, and fly out
again. He'll do this for his own benefit, and yet he can keep
himself in a position where he'll never have to consider the
people that live here. For instance, by being a racist, so he
can think these people are unimportant, because they're not
white. Or by being separated from them physically, so he
doesn't have to listen to them when they cry out. He can go
off on his business and not care.

Even though this is Manilatown, Chinatown is across the
street, so it's essentially Chinatown. It's not like a special-
ized enemy in Chinatown, and another one over in the Fill-

more or something. It's all the same system. This block means a lot to Chinatown because it's a kind of buffer between Chinatown and the financial district. To stop the enemy here means that it will have a harder time attaining Chinatown.

I guess I use the word enemy in different ways. Of course, the enemy is the system, but then again, the enemy is really something within people, too—people's self-interest, their distance, and their racism. Because it's their self-interest that drives them to do these things, within a system that gives them the right to do it, and it's their racism that allows them to hurt particular people with a free conscience. I could say it's a lot more things too. It's the way the government is set up so that it's not responsive to all the people, but just to those who have acquired the power to express their self-interest.

We get discouraged about this sometimes. When we look at Vietnam or something, see the mass of things that are going wrong and the tiny part that we do, it can be really discouraging because you always feel you want to attack the whole thing. And in the long run things are kind of depressing for us, you know, because the lease ends this June, or if it doesn't end in June it ends next July, so we worry a lot about whether the building will be lost. But the way I try to deal with that is by keeping my focus very concrete. A lot of us know there has to be change in this country and that change is going to be very deep, a whole system has to be thrown off. But at the same time we have to think about how much time we need, how big the enemy is, and that the whole people has to be there, not just a group of leaders, because otherwise the leadership would go up there and nobody would support it and then they would fall. The whole people has to be there, and in the meantime they need certain things. You can't just stand on a campus talking through a microphone while people in the cities are still living with rats. You know, you can't let them live with the rats while you're off distributing your leaflets. So I guess until we reach that stage where all the people are together the steps that we take will be pretty small. But we have to take them or else we'll never get there.

I've decided the action I can do right now is to attack the system through this hotel. Maybe it's not even attacking the system as much as resisting it. The system works on us, you know, but if we can keep it from working on us, we're resisting it. We can resist it by not letting real estate men throw people out of their homes. By not letting redevelopment take over Japantown, as it did. By not letting California cut off welfare. And while we do all this, we can educate people, show them that there are reasons for what happens to them, that there are reasons for their being poor.

This year, I'm helping to teach a course on the community. I guess I'm trying to give other people the same experience I had and get them to realize what Asian communities are like, what people go through, get them into working for the people. I guess if people respond to that, that's resisting the system, too. Because what the system would do is have all the kids who grew up here, and made it to college, take up jobs and run away. That's what the system would have us do, because it needs trained people. So it robs the community of all its children, and resisting the system is bringing the children back.

In the end, what the struggle means to me personally is that it's a way of fighting for my own people's dignity, taking a stand and fighting for ourselves. I guess it's mostly that. It means I don't want to be separated from something that is really part of my people and my past. You know, because just by forgetting your past you can separate yourself from it.

APPENDIXES

Appendix 1

PROFILES OF SOCIAL CLASSES IN CHINATOWN:

Old bachelors: They are the elderly men in Chinatown who entered California at the start of the century. Most had fathers, uncles, or grandfathers whose lives as laborers in America preceded their own. The Chinese Exclusion Acts, first passed in 1882, however, forbade not only the further immigration of Chinese laborers, but also the entrance of wives and children of those laborers already in California. These sons and nephews of the early Chinese laborers in California, desperate to leave their villages for jobs in America, bought false immigration papers which claimed they were sons of merchants or American-born Chinese who were exempt from exclusion. Thus they were called "paper sons." After spending their adult lives employed in Chinatown's small businesses, or up and down the West Coast as seasonal laborers, they are now retired and living out their last days in small tenement rooms in Chinatown.

Immigrant workers: They are janitors, delivery-men, gas-station attendants, or cooks, waiters, busboys, grocery and market workers, and dishwashers in Chinatown. For work outside of Chinatown wages are higher, but the general income range of immigrant workers is from $3,500 to $7,000 a year. Men with restaurant jobs work a ten hour day, six days a week; their wives say they wash, eat dinner, read the newspaper, and fall asleep as soon as they get home. Since they have large families, most of the wives also find jobs to make ends meet. Women work in the garment factories in Chinatown, making pastries, *dim sum,* in tea houses, or as maids and kitchen helpers outside of Chinatown. They earn between $1,500 and $3,600 a year. Many immigrant families hope, after their first few years in San Francisco, to have enough capital to open small restaurants or other businesses of their own. Mom-and-pop restaurants set up by such families in old diners, lunchrooms, and cafes, can be found all over San Francisco.

Housing is crowded in Chinatown and the buildings are old, but without English, immigrants hesitate to look elsewhere. They move into the new extended area of Chinatown or into the old tenements built for the bachelors. In the extended areas rent for a one bedroom apartment with kitchen, living room, and bathroom is between $150 and $180 a month. Large families with four to ten children may live in these apartments, in which case all the rooms double as living and sleeping quarters. Older children sleep together in one room, while the parents sleep with the younger children in another. Inside Chinatown, in the tenements and hotels, the rooms are much smaller, usually about five by ten. Families with many children rent two adjacent rooms, paying $60 to $80 a month for each one. Unlike the larger apartments in the extended areas, these tenement rooms lack private facilities for cooking and toilets. Often fifty families on a single floor share two large communal kitchens and bathrooms. The rooms have makeshift furniture and a few secondhand pieces given to the family by relatives. Shelves are made out of wooden crates and cabinets from cardboard cartons, a handmade bed may sleep up to three people. The family's small dining table becomes the desk on which children study after dinner. Electric lighting in the tenement buildings is poor and there is usually no heat. The rooms do not have telephones, TVs, refrigerators, or other standard American household appliances. There may be a plastic radio, an electric wall clock, and hot plates. There are few visible playthings for the children. Immigrant families who live in the Chinatown tenement houses say housing is their worst problem. Many have been waiting four or five years to get into the Ping Yuen federal housing project.

Immigrants who live in Chinatown are sponsored by relatives, usually a father or uncle who has lived in the United States for many years. They spend the first few months in America living with their relatives, but friction often develops during the tense period while they look for jobs, and they try to move out as soon as possible. Crowded living quarters, large families, continued job insecurity, and adjustment problems resulting from inability to speak English create persistent tensions in the home which affect both parents and children. Although many immigrants attend English language classes regularly during their first year in America, fatigue from long hours of work and the discomforts of studying in their crowded homes hamper these efforts and many give up. Immigrants feel uncomfortable with American-born Chinese who they feel reject them. They do not participate in the established social institutions of Chinatown because they feel these institutions are indifferent to their problems and controlled by the older American Chinese merchant-businessmen. They deeply resent these American Chinese proprietors of the restaurants, sewing factories, and other establishments they work in, who they feel are taking unfair advantage of their difficult situation. Thus, social life is restricted to their families, friends, and immediate relatives. They visit each other's homes, chat, play an occasional game of mahjong, but they can seldom afford to eat in restaurants or go to the Chinese movie theaters.

Most Chinese come primarily to assure the education of their children and to escape the burdensome educational fees in Hong Kong. They feel that free higher education in the San Francisco City College promises upward mobility for their children, even though they themselves cannot anticipate significant improvements in status over their positions in Hong Kong. Unless it is through the jobs, they have almost no contact with Caucasian American society. Still, they feel life is better here than in Hong Kong. Politically they are apathetic, inactive, or uncommited. Since many are refugees, they often have an indifferent attitude towards the People's Republic of China. Their concerns are focused around establishing themselves and their families in America.

American Chinese workers: They have the same jobs as the immigrants, but while they may be more secure and steady, they have had very little raise in pay over the years. The men came to San Francisco illegally as "paper sons" when they were still in their teens. They brought wives in only after the relaxation of immigration laws following World War II. Their wives, who often share the same language incapacity as the new immigrants, work beside them in the sewing factories. Since both parents in these older families work, they do not qualify for welfare or the benefits of new social welfare programs primarily designed for immigrants. Inflation and low wages, however, cause constant financial anxiety.

Many American Chinese workers live in the Ping Yuen public housing projects. Their apartments are usually furnished with unmatching pieces of furniture, an inexpensive formica table, old couches, and wooden chairs. They give an impression of sparse cleanliness and tea, oranges, homemade sweets are always on hand for guests. Sewing machines occupy a prominent position in the living room. They are used to finish extra work from the shop and to sew clothes for the family. Since many of the men were middle-aged when they married, they have smaller families than the newly arrived immigrants. There are a few more games and toys for the children here than in the immigrant apartments, usually there is at least one bicycle in a family. People who live in Ping Yuen have private cooking and bath facilities. They have old television sets and some own used automobiles.

The men and children in these families speak English, though the men apologize for not speaking better. They say that when they first came to America as young men, they went to work immediately and did not have time to learn English as well as they would have liked. They urge their children to take advantage of the new opportunities open to Chinese. While they themselves work long hours, they encourage their children to be self-reliant, to play with other children in front of the projects, go to the library to study. Some of the children, however, complain that their family life is cold because their parents are tired and dispirited when they get back from work. The children go on to some form of higher education, usually City College or San Francisco State College, though a few get scholarships and go on to University of California, Berkeley, or private institutions like the University of Southern California.

The men belong to few organizations. Some belong to labor unions but the majority do not. They have a few friends at work and for many, the only social event of the year is their family association banquet, which they attend perfunctorily. Otherwise, they are inactive in the family and district associations. There is an impression they are even more isolated within their own work and family life than the new immigrants. They do not get along with the immigrants, whom they blame for all the recent trouble in Chinatown, but they seem to feel threatened by the younger and more confident Chinese new arrivals. They see themselves as outside the process of American political life. They, too, tend to be apathetic, and pessimistic about the possibility of implementing change by their own participation in politics.

Small shopkeepers: They are the proprietors of small souvenir shops, bakeries, laundries, mom-and-pop restaurants, groceries, and dry goods stores. With their families they do all the work in the business. They do not own the buildings in which they operate the stores, which often are used as their own living quarters. Most came to America as "paper sons" and, through their work as laborers or store clerks, saved a small amount of capital with which they opened their businesses. Work hours are long, sometimes even longer than those of the working class, but there is a sense of greater security and stability. The shopkeepers make just enough to support their large families and accumulate a small savings for their children's education. Some can make small investments. At present, laundries are on the decline because of competition from newer coin operated laundromats; small groceries have had a hard time competing with self-service supermarkets. The other businesses have been adversely affected by recession, rising taxes in the city, inflation, and a recent fifteen to twenty percent drop in the tourist trade. They blame the exploding juvenile delinquency of the immigrant youth for bad publicity which has frightened tourists away from Chinatown. They remember the good old days when Chinatown was safe and they could keep their stores open until late at night.

Merchant-businessmen: They are owners of restaurants, import-export businesses, one or several garment factories, real estate, travel, and insurance agencies; they are bank managers, manufacturers of soy sauce, bean curd, noodles, and other Chinese food products. They differ from the small shop owners in that they hire workers, and often own the buildings where they work. They have the highest income level in the community, ranging from twenty-five to forty thousand dollars a year, and occasionally higher. Some are men who graduated from universities with advanced degrees in different professions such as engineering, pharmacy, and natural sciences in the 1930s but were unable to find employment in these fields due to discrimination against Chinese. Most started their own businesses, a few inherited businesses from their fathers. They concentrated their efforts into building up these businesses and accumulating savings. With success, they invested their money into new business ventures which they entered jointly with other businessmen from the community. They have invested in luxury restaurants, apartment units, real estate, and more recently in the stock market. Their wives often help out in the family business or have white collar positions in downtown Caucasian business firms.

The homes of merchant-businessmen are usually located outside of Chinatown on Telegraph Hill, Russian Hill, Bernal Heights, or in the exclusive Sea Cliff and Diamond Heights districts. However, they are unpretentious houses because priority is given to business investments rather than to conspicuous display of wealth. They may display a few valuable Chinese art objects and several expensive pieces of furniture, but most furnishing and household accessories reflect earlier days when the family was not so well-to-do. The men do not believe in ostentatious dressing, and wear conservative suits which may be bought wholesale from a friend with a clothing business. They do feel it is important to have expensive and good looking cars. Cadillacs and late model Fords are favorites. Their wives show more concern about matters of dress. They send their·measurements to tailors in Hong Kong who make the silk *cheong sam* they wear for social occasions. As they grow older they pride themselves on possessing several carefully selected pieces of diamond, pearl, or jade jewelry. The families travel frequently to Hong Kong and Taiwan, and have visited Europe several times. They recall taking tours through Asia with groups of Caucasian Americans. But the merchant-businessmen and their wives never appear in the social pages of the San Francisco *Chronicle*. Social life takes place in Chinatown, especially at banquets in restaurants like the Four Seas, Kuo Wah, and the Empress of China, in which they own shares with other friends. They like to play mahjong and *pai gow* together; a few play tennis and golf. The wives enjoy working in the social auxiliaries of Chinatown, sponsoring fashion shows, teas, brushpainting exhibits, and the Chinese New Year festivities. Their children attend Berkeley or private colleges in California like Mills and Stanford. They become lawyers, doctors, dentists, and scientists. The less academically inclined children go into the family business.

The merchant-businessmen are the leaders of Chinatown. They sit on the board of directors of every association in Chinatown's establishment. They are active in the Chinese Six Companies, the family and district associations, the Chinese Chamber of Commerce, and form a virtual interlocking directorate of leadership within the community. They are politically conservative, many are members of the Chinese Republican Club. They are the men whom city hall appoints to sit on "blue ribbon" committees set up to deal with problems of Chinatown. They draw into their circle a small group of more conservative professional men who lend them expertise. They complain that they have little real influence in city politics. For several years a small group of these businessmen has attempted to win approval from the Board of Supervisors to build highrise buildings in Chinatown, but they have not succeeded. They say they are treated as second class citizens, but they emphasize that Chinese "have never advanced themselves by the violent

tactics of the larger minorities." Although for years many
have loyally supported Chaing Kai-shek's Republic of China
in Taiwan, they are now having second thoughts as they
contemplate profitable trade with the People's Republic of
China. Privately they express pride in the progress made in
mainland China and would like to visit it as soon as possible.

Professionals: They are lawyers, doctors, dentists, nurses,
teachers, social workers, and clergymen. Most are under
fifty years old. They are offspring of the family society centered around small shops, although some came as advanced
students from Hong Kong or Taiwan and received their
professional degrees in American universities. They work
in Chinatown, and live in the Sunset and Richmond districts
of the city. Their incomes range from twelve thousand to
thirty thousand dollars a year. A high proportion of wives
of professionals also take jobs as teachers, secretaries, key-
punch operators, and nurses when their children reach
school age. They say the family needs this extra income
to cover such expenses as orthodontia and private schooling
for the children.

They own split-level or modern homes which cost thirty
to forty thousand dollars. The homes are decorated in coordinated color schemes, and have wall-to-wall carpeting,
modernistic furniture, electrical equipment ranging from
expensive stereo sets to numerous kitchen appliances and
gadgets. Art work done by their children in classes and
clubs is displayed all over the house. The houses have
dens and studies with bookshelves and racks well stocked
with Western classics, popular American fiction and non-
fiction, Chinese art books, a set of encyclopedias, magazines like *Newsweek, Atlantic Monthly, Life,* and various
professional magazines. They have two cars, a station
wagon for the family, and a small sedan which the husband
drives into Chinatown to work. Insofar as the men have
practices centered in Chinatown, they participate at least
nominally in establishment organizations such as their
family and district associations, but they shun the Six
Companies as being backward and unprogressive. Their
wives are even less socially involved in Chinatown. While

they go in once a week to do grocery shopping for Chinese vegetables and cooking staples, they don't see Chinatown as an important source of social contact. Their energies are absorbed in PTA activities at their children's schools, Girl Scout troops, in social service groups in their neighborhoods. They do, however, place value on sending their children to newly established suburban Chinese schools. The women say once their Caucasian neighbors know that they are professional families, "they treat us differently," but they still feel most at ease with other Chinese suburban families. With these families they enjoy occasional outings to bowl, ski, or camp. Their children are often straight A students in integrated schools. The teenage children participate in student body government, chess and bridge clubs, drama clubs, extracurricular sports, and enjoy parties and folk rock with friends of different races. Their closest friends may be American Chinese. High school and college age children have been involved in the anti-war movement and feel a new concern for Asian-American ethnic identity, but, like their mothers, they go to Chinatown only occasionally and few see it as an important part of their social world. They feel ill at ease there because they cannot speak Chinese and often feel guilty when they come into contact with immigrants, bachelors, and the older first generation working-class families. However a growing number have become involved in community-based projects as part of the Asian-American student movement.

Older professionals belong to the more conservative Chinese-American Citizens Alliance and service organizations like the Optimist Club and the Square and Circle Club. Younger professionals, who think of themselves as progressive politically, may join the liberal Chinese American Democratic Club or a newer, more militant Chinatown civil rights group, the Chinese for Affirmative Action. In the last five years, these younger professionals, especially social workers and clergymen, brought federal anti-poverty programs into Chinatown, fighting the vigorous opposition of the the Chinese Six Companies. As a group they favor improved relations between the United States and the People's Republic of China, and express enthusiasm for the accomplishments of the Chinese revolution. However, they are apprehensive about the appearance of radical Asian-American student movements and militancy among immigrant youth gangs in Chinatown. From time to time one finds a letter in Chinatown's bilingual *East West* newspaper from a suburban wife who deplores the "bad image" these groups are "creating for Chinese-Americans." They urge the immigrant youth to appreciate their opportunities in America and use them to the best advantage. On the basis of their own success, middle-aged professionals do not see discrimination as a serious problem for American Chinese.

White collar workers: They work and live outside of the core area of Chinatown. A small group commutes each morning to Chinatown where they work as clerks and secretaries in banks, insurance offices, real estate agencies, social welfare offices, and government agencies. Though they earn less than the professionals, their life style is quite similar.

Appendix 2

SOME IMPORTANT IMMIGRATION LAWS

Burlingame Treaty of 1868: Ths bill recognized the "inalienable" right of man to free migration and emigration from one country to another "for the purpose of curiosity, of trade, or as permanent residents." It further established the principle of reciprocity in privileges, immunities, and exemptions between citizens of China and the United States living or traveling in each other's country.

Chinese Exclusion Act of May 8, 1882: This act suspended the immigration of Chinese laborers, both skilled and unskilled, for ten years. Teachers, students, merchants, and travelers were, however, exempted from exclusion. It formally prohibited the naturalization of Chinese in the United States. The act was extended an additional ten years by the Geary Act of May 5, 1892. On April 27, 1904, the exclusion of Chinese laborers from the United States was extended indefinitely.

Scott Act of October 1, 1888: This act prohibited the return of any Chinese laborers who had departed from the United States. At the time it was passed, over 20,000 Chinese laborers had temporarily left the United States for China with reentry certificates. The reentry permits were declared void.

Immigration Act of 1924: Under the terms of this act no Chinese women were allowed to enter the United States for the purpose of permanent residence. Previous to the passing of this act, wives of Chinese merchants and American-born Chinese were allowed to enter the country, although wives of Chinese laborers were barred.

Repeal of the Chinese Exclusion Acts in 1943: On December 13, 1943, Franklin D. Roosevelt signed this act which repealed the acts related to the exclusion and deportation of Chinese aliens. This act granted for the first time naturalization rights to Chinese aliens. It set an immigration quota of 105 per year for people of Chinese race (defined as any person with as much as one-half Chinese blood, regardless of country of origin).

War Brides Act of December 28, 1945: This act facilitated the entry of wives of men in the American armed forces to the United States. Approximately 6,000 Chinese women entered the United States under this act.

Displaced Persons Act of 1948: Under this act 3,465 Chinese students, visitors, and seamen were granted permanent resident status as "displaced persons."

Refugee Relief Act of 1953: Allowed the entry of 2,777 refugees of the Chinese revolution, the majority of whom were Chinese. It further granted a total of 2,000 visas to Chinese whose passports had been endorsed by the Chinese Nationalist Government for entry to the United States.

Act of September 11, 1957: With this act "paper sons" who obtained entry visas by fraud and misrepresentation could not be deported if a spouse, parent, or child was a citizen of the United States or a permanent resident alien.

Presidential Directive of May 25, 1962: This directive signed by President John F. Kennedy permitted Hong Kong refugees to enter the United States immediately as "parolees." By June 30, 1966, 15,111 Chinese refugees were admitted. By the end of fiscal 1966, 9,126 of them were given permanent resident status.

The Act of October 3, 1965: This historic act was signed by President Lyndon B. Johnson at the foot of the Statue of Liberty. It abolished the national origin quota system on July 1, 1968. Each independent country outside of the Western Hemisphere has a quota of up to 20,000 per year. Further, the quota is accounted to the alien's country of birth, not nationality or race. Persons born in Hong Kong, however, are charged to Great Britain's quota. The entry of these people is not to exceed one percent of the total visas issued to Great Britain in one year.

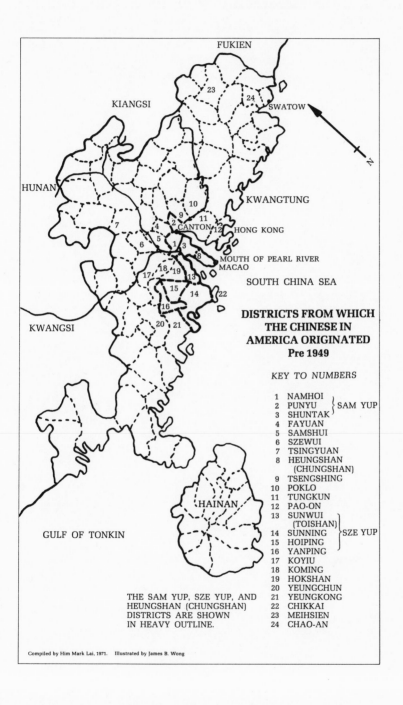

FUKIEN

KIANGSI

23

24 SWATOW

KWANGTUNG

HUNAN

10

9 11

7 4 2 CANTON 12 HONG KONG

5

6 1 3

8 MOUTH OF PEARL RIVER

18 19 13 MACAO

17 SOUTH CHINA SEA

15 14 22

16

DISTRICTS FROM WHICH
THE CHINESE IN
AMERICA ORIGINATED
Pre 1949

KWANGSI 20 21

N

KEY TO NUMBERS

1 NAMHOI
2 PUNYU } SAM YUP
3 SHUNTAK
4 FAYUAN
5 SAMSHUI
6 SZEWUI
7 TSINGYUAN
8 HEUNGSHAN
(CHUNGSHAN)
9 TSENGSHING
10 POKLO
11 TUNGKUN
12 PAO-ON
13 SUNWUI
(TOISHAN)
14 SUNNING } SZE YUP
15 HOIPING
16 YANPING
17 KOYIU
18 KOMING
19 HOKSHAN
20 YEUNGCHUN
21 YEUNGKONG
22 CHIKKAI
23 MEIHSIEN
24 CHAO-AN

HAINAN

GULF OF TONKIN

THE SAM YUP, SZE YUP, AND
HEUNGSHAN (CHUNGSHAN)
DISTRICTS ARE SHOWN
IN HEAVY OUTLINE.

Compiled by Him Mark Lai, 1971.   Illustrated by James B. Wong